SELF-MADE

"Self-made" success is now an American badge of honor that rewards individualist ambitions while it hammers against community obligations. Yet, four centuries ago, our foundational stories actually disparaged ambitious upstarts as dangerous and selfish threats to a healthy society. In Pamela Walker Laird's fascinating history of why and how storytellers forged this American myth, she reveals how the goals for self-improvement evolved from serving the community to supporting individualist dreams of wealth and esteem. Simplistic stories of self-made success and failure emerged that disregarded people's advantages and disadvantages and fostered inequality. Fortunately, *Self-Made* also recovers long-standing, alternative traditions of self-improvement to serve the common good. These challenges to the myth have offered inspiration, often coming, surprisingly, from Americans associated with self-made success, such as Benjamin Franklin, Frederick Douglass, and Horatio Alger. Here are real stories that show that no one lives – no one succeeds or fails – in a vacuum.

Pamela Walker Laird is Professor Emerita of History at the University of Colorado Denver. Her publications include *Pull: Networking and Success Since Benjamin Franklin*, which won the Hagley Prize; and *Advertising Progress: American Business and the Rise of Consumer Marketing*.

PAMELA WALKER LAIRD

Self-Made

The Stories That Forged an American Myth

CAMBRIDGE
UNIVERSITY PRESS

Shaftesbury Road, Cambridge CB2 8EA, United Kingdom

One Liberty Plaza, 20th Floor, New York, NY 10006, USA

477 Williamstown Road, Port Melbourne, VIC 3207, Australia

314–321, 3rd Floor, Plot 3, Splendor Forum, Jasola District Centre, New Delhi – 110025, India

103 Penang Road, #05–06/07, Visioncrest Commercial, Singapore 238467

Cambridge University Press is part of Cambridge University Press & Assessment, a department of the University of Cambridge.

We share the University's mission to contribute to society through the pursuit of education, learning and research at the highest international levels of excellence.

www.cambridge.org
Information on this title: www.cambridge.org/9781108833899

DOI: 10.1017/9781108983136

© Pamela Walker Laird 2025

This publication is in copyright. Subject to statutory exception and to the provisions of relevant collective licensing agreements, no reproduction of any part may take place without the written permission of Cambridge University Press & Assessment.

When citing this work, please include a reference to the DOI 10.1017/9781108983136

First published 2025

Printed in the United Kingdom by CPI Group Ltd, Croydon CR0 4YY

A catalogue record for this publication is available from the British Library

A Cataloging-in-Publication data record for this book is available from the Library of Congress

ISBN 978-1-108-83389-9 Hardback

Cambridge University Press & Assessment has no responsibility for the persistence or accuracy of URLs for external or third-party internet websites referred to in this publication and does not guarantee that any content on such websites is, or will remain, accurate or appropriate.

For Frank
Again & Always

Mr. Bluff: Whatever I have accomplished, I owe it to myself.
Mr. Wise: How delightful it must be to feel so clear of debt.

> Column filler in the *Los Angeles Times*
> March 29, 1925
> Reprinted from the *Kansas City Star*

Contents

List of Figures	*page* viii
Preface	xi
A Word about Words	xiii
Introduction: Challenging the Myth of Self-Made Success	1
1 A New World of Ambition and Judgment	10
2 Self-Improvement for the Common Good in the Eighteenth Century	34
3 Work and Merit in a New Republic	57
4 The Politics of Self-Making in a Self-Made Nation	81
5 Forging Origins in Antebellum Stories	103
6 Character and Money in Mid-Century	128
7 Gilded Age Heroes	153
8 Competing Stories of Self-Help Before 1936	181
9 Stories Against the New Deal	206
10 Targeting the Common Good, 1950–2000	228
11 The Myth's Twenty-First-Century Victories	251
Acknowledgments	276
Notes	279
Index	336

Figures

0.1 Painting of Oliver Cromwell by Robert Walker, circa 1649. National Portrait Gallery in London / Photo by Robert Alexander via Getty Images. *page* 2
0.2 Photograph of Kylie Jenner by Kevin Mazur / BMA2015. Kevin Mazur / WireImage via Getty Images. 3
1.1 Portrait of Captain John Smith, 1616. Library of Congress: Pictures Item 2021653041. 13
1.2 Page of Robert Keayne's sermon notes, circa 1640. "Robert Keayne Sermon Notes, 1627–1646," vol. 3, p. 73; MS. N-1518. Courtesy of Massachusetts Historical Society. 22
2.1 Title page of Cotton Mather's 1693 treatise on "the TRYALS of Several UUitches." Photo by Library of Congress / Corbis / VCG via Getty Images. 40
2.2 Portrait of Benjamin Franklin by Edward Fisher in 1763. Courtesy of National Portrait Gallery, Smithsonian Institution NPG.70.66. 46
2.3 Print of George Whitefield preaching, 1754. Photo by Universal History Archive via Getty Images. 54
3.1 *Bettering House or House of Employment*, watercolor by David J. Kennedy, 1828. David J. Kennedy watercolors (collection #V61). Courtesy of Historical Society of Pennsylvania. 66
3.2 Drawing of George Washington in 1797 at Mount Vernon by Nathaniel Currier, 1852. MPI / Stringer Archive Photos via Getty Images. 71
3.3 Benjamin West's painting of *Benjamin Franklin Drawing Electricity from the Sky*, circa 1816. Courtesy of Philadelphia Museum of Art: Gift of Mr. and Mrs. Wharton Sinkler, 1958, 1958-132-1. 77
4.1 Engraved, autographed portrait of David Crockett. Library of Congress: Popular Graphic Arts, Item 2003666771; no date. 92
4.2 Commemorative print of Andrew Jackson by Nathaniel Currier, 1845. HUM Images / Universal Images Group via Getty Images. 95

LIST OF FIGURES

5.1 Lithograph of the Broadway Tabernacle in New York City, 1856. Photo by Sepia Times / Universal Images Group via Getty Images. 107

5.2 Painting of Eliza Jumel and family by Alcide Ercole, 1854. *Jumel Family Portrait*, Oil on canvas, 97 x 68 inches, MJM 1980.429.1. Courtesy of Collection of the Morris-Jumel Mansion. Photograph by Bruce Katz. 115

5.3 Sheet music cover of *A Song for the Man: A Henry Clay Ballad*, 1844. Sheridan Libraries / Levy /Gado via Getty Images. 124

6.1 Print from T. S. Arthur, *Ten Nights in a Bar-Room*, 1854. Courtesy of Cornell University Library. 138

6.2 Print of "The Symbolical Head, Illustrating all the Phrenological Developments of the Human Head," by Fowler and Strachan. Library of Congress Prints and Photographs: Item 90713998, 1842. 140

6.3 Studio photograph of Phineas T. Barnum, 1875. Hutton Archive / Stringer / Archive Photos via Getty Images. 145

7.1 Photograph of Mellon Bank, Pittsburgh, PA, circa 1871. Courtesy of Carnegie Library of Pittsburgh. 154

7.2 *Breaking Home Ties*, painting by Thomas Hovenden, 1890. Courtesy of Philadelphia Museum of Art: Gift of Ellen Harrison McMichael in memory of C. Emory McMichael, 1942-60-1. 162

7.3 Studio photograph of Henry Clay Frick as a young man, circa 1870. Courtesy of West Overton Village & Museum Archives, PA. 167

8.1 Frederick Douglass speaking at Tuskegee Institute, AL, 1892. "Hon. Fred. Douglass on platform in [the] Pavilion," Booker T. Washington Collection, Library of Congress: Item 98500648. 185

8.2 "The First Troops in Homestead," wood engraving after drawing by Thure de Thulstrup, 1892. Library of Congress / Corbis Historical / VCG via Getty Images. 189

8.3 Photograph of students posed outside dormitory, Carlisle Indian School, PA, 1899. Photo by Choate / Library of Congress / Corbis Historical / VCG via Getty Images. 192

9.1 Photograph of window display of Horatio Alger books on thrift at the Franklin Society for Building and Saving, 1948. Photo by © Ken O'Brien Collection / CORBIS / Corbis via Getty Images. 211

9.2 Photograph of statue of Norman Vincent Peale taken in 2017 outside of the Marble Collegiate Church, New York City. Photo by Bill Tompkins / Michael Ochs Archives via Getty Images. 225

10.1 Horatio Alger, Jr., commemorative stamp and first day of issue envelope issued by the US Postal Service in 1982. In author's possession; gift of Terri Lonier. 241

LIST OF FIGURES

10.2 President Ronald Reagan at his ranch signing the 1981 Economic Recovery Tax Act. Bettmann via Getty Images. 246

11.1 Photograph of George W. Bush interviewed by Oprah Winfrey, 2000. Photo by TANNEN MAURY / AFP via Getty Images. 254

11.2 Fred Trump and Donald J. Trump at the 1985 Horatio Alger Awards gala. Photo by Ron Galella / Ron Galella Collection via Getty Images. 258

Preface

The US presidential elections of 2016, 2020, and 2024 put into stark relief two increasingly divergent approaches to what people and communities owe each other. That's because the four candidates – Donald J. Trump, on the one hand, and Hillary Rodham Clinton, Joe Biden, and Kamala Harris on the other – represent those two approaches, along with the hopes and fears that their stories evoke.

Self-Made: The Stories That Forged an American Myth offers a four-century perspective on those two approaches and their centrality to American history. It recovers narratives told within eternal competitions for the cultural authority that, in turn, supports political authority. We can look through these narrative lenses to see how people made sense of their world and their places in it, how they judged themselves and others, and how they built alliances. As in electoral campaigns, storytellers continuously try to frame the ways we value individuals and communities and the ambitions that they hold.

In the spotlight of 2024, we see in Trump someone who inherited vast wealth in both financial and social capital, but who came to national prominence with claims of self-made success. As a youth, he attended Norman Vincent Peale's church of positive thinking and individualist prosperity. The stories he heard there reinforced those he learned from other advocates of self-seeking, namely that criticism inhibits self-confidence and that concerns about community can only impede success.

In contrast, each of his presidential opponents *did* rise to national prominence from modest roots, yet none claimed to be self-made. All grew up in settings that prioritized self-improvement to serve a common good; all spent their entire professional lives in public service. Their ambitions did not exclude material goals, by any means, but they all developed what Harris calls "our sense of responsibility." Clinton's Methodist upbringing taught a social gospel that fosters individuals' work within communities on behalf of others. Biden came from a labor union family and built a strong record as a progressive, inclusive president. During Harris's campaign, we learned of her mother's admonition not to imagine that we "just fell out of a coconut tree," detached from our communities. Harris

PREFACE

has repeatedly reinforced the insight that "none of us just live in a silo. Everything is in context" ("Remarks by Vice President Harris at Swearing-In Ceremony of Commissioners for the White House Initiative on Advancing Educational Equity, Excellence, and Economic Opportunity for Hispanics," whitehouse.gov, May 10, 2023).

In other words, no one is self-made.

Political analysts and historians will be digging into the 2024 election for a very long time. Toward that effort, I offer this backstory about storytellers with widely diverse beliefs about what people and communities owe each other. Over the centuries of Euro-American experiences, parables of self-making initially called for self-improvement to serve faith and community (both defined narrowly, to be sure). But as opportunities for worldly gain proliferated, another genre of storytelling spun off that promoted individualism and advanced the myth of self-made success. Nonetheless, other storylines continue to interpret "self-help" with an emphasis on self-improvement to *help*. All of these diverse, everchanging, and entangled strands of storytelling about our ambitions and values remind us that ideas about self-making have always been contested. The history of those contests can refocus our sense of what we owe each other as well as ourselves.

A Word about Words

Words and phrases, meanings and uses have changed, often profoundly, over the four centuries of stories that this book offers. The surprising creation and evolution of the phrase "self-made" inspired the work, but it wasn't the only change.

Other words and their uses may be unfamiliar to us now, and at times modernizing them can make them more accessible. For example, the phrase "woman suffrage" sounds odd to us even though it was standard fare when activists rallied for women's right to vote.

Modernizing words and phrases cannot and should not, however, eliminate what we can now find disturbing. Thus, regarding gender, most of the named actors in this story were male, and often whole categories of actors were almost entirely, if not entirely, male. Therefore, when it aligns with that historical reality, I have used masculine nouns, pronouns, and adjectives rather than give false impressions of diversity.

Regarding other identity words, I have followed the advice within the *Journal of the Early Republic*'s forum "What's in a Name" regarding historians' obligations "to consider what we take for granted in our writing, from audiences to contexts to words and language" (*Journal of the Early Republic*, 43, no. 1 (Spring 2023): 149). The storytellers who forged the myth of self-made success represented only a minority of Americans, but I have tried to respect all of the historical actors who were part of this history.

All quotations are identical to what I found in my sources, some of which had already altered original spelling or punctuation. Exceptions follow protocols for adjusting capitalization at the beginning and punctuation at the end of quotes to fit into my sentences. I have also revised the antique tall "s" into the modern "s": "increaſe" into "increase." All emphases, such as italics, are in the original quotations unless I have indicated otherwise. There may also be unavoidable inconsistencies with original period texts to which I did not have access.

Introduction

Challenging the Myth of Self-Made Success

Oliver Cromwell was a stern, Puritan dictator from the seventeenth century, and Kylie Jenner is a twenty-first-century pop culture princess and lipstick mogul. They could not be more different, yet they have in common that they've been tagged with the provocative and powerful label "self-made." Their stories bookend the history of how that identity, once considered a mark of sin, was forged into a destructive accolade.

To begin at the end, *Forbes* magazine announced in early 2019 that 21-year-old Kylie Jenner was the "youngest-ever self-made billionaire." Even before Jenner's coronation, the magazine had featured her on its August 2018 cover for an issue on "America's Women Billionaires." A considerable uproar followed, not about whether or not the "self-made" label was a compliment – everyone agreed on that point – but about whether or not Jenner, who grew up in a high-profile family of celebrities, deserved it. How could the daughter of Olympic champion Bruce (now Caitlyn) Jenner and celebrity queen Kris Kardashian be self-made? For more than two decades, Kris Kardashian had brilliantly cultivated the family's fortunes and celebrity, and Kylie Jenner grew up on reality television, as millions watched and fantasized about *Keeping Up With the Kardashians*. As the youngest member of a family of glamorous celebrities and entrepreneurs, she has a mind-boggling public profile and vast connections. Building on what she calls her "platform," she has cleverly exploited her star status on social media, posting countless selfies for almost 200 million social media followers, beguiling money from them as an "influencer." "Welcome to the era of extreme fame leverage," read the 2018 cover. A *Forbes* defender even referred to her as the "first selfie-made billionaire"![1]

The popular culture controversy over Jenner's trophy underscored values that have developed and evolved along with America's capitalist culture, including the modern belief that being self-made is both possible and a positive attribute, as well as the now-common assumption that making a lot of money is enough to qualify someone as self-made. There are other routes, such as political or moral leadership, but nothing now does the trick as crisply as does piling up a lot of money. But this was not always so. For instance, the hero of the popular

Figure 0.1 Oliver Cromwell's armies conquered England, Ireland, and Scotland, forming the Commonwealth, which he ruled from 1653 to 1658. He always strenuously rejected accusations that he had risen from humble origins, and he intended this portrait by Robert Walker, circa 1649, to show that he was a gentleman and fit to lead. Identifying himself as what we now call "self-made" would have been blasphemous and foolhardy, risking both his soul and the social capital on which his success relied. (National Portrait Gallery in London / Photo by Robert Alexander via Getty Images)

1843 novel *Allen Lucas: The Self-Made Man* applied his hard-won education to serve his family and small-town community. In contrast, his ambitious schoolmate became a powerful and wealthy politician, only to suffer a lonely decline. Likewise, Harriet Beecher Stowe's 1872 *Lives and Deeds of Our Self-Made Men* praises "some of the leading public men of our times" for the "frugality, strict temperance, self-reliance and indomitable industry" that made them models for "the

INTRODUCTION

Figure 0.2 In contrast to Oliver Cromwell, almost four centuries later Kylie Jenner embraced the identity of self-made billionaire, with which *Forbes* crowned her in 2019. She declared that she "worked hard" and, thereby, had earned her fortune on her own, despite her enormous advantages. This 2015 photo in Las Vegas, Nevada, shows her in action as a "selfie-made billionaire." (Kevin Mazur / BMA2015 / WireImage via Getty Images)

young men of America." Not one of the nineteen men she portrayed was known for his wealth.[2]

"I work really hard," Kylie Jenner firmly responded to her critics to justify her acclaim. She recognized that work is a fundamental criterion for claiming to be self-made, whether for celebrities or anyone else. But, what *is* "work"? Is money the measure of how hard someone works? When Jenner was interviewed about her new stature in 2019, she described her marketing efforts this way: "I popped up at a few stores, I did my usual social media – I did what I usually do, and it just worked."[3] Does it make sense to equate the well-remunerated work that celebrities do posing with their fans for selfies, facing stage lights, or sitting through hours of make-up sessions with cleaning other people's houses, slaughtering cattle, or extracting coal from the earth? Or, in the realm of non-physical labor, how should we compare financiers' machinations with data-enterers' monotonies? A long list of comparisons like this presents a challenge for those who explain self-made success by heralding someone's "work ethic," but who don't take into account the range of workers' opportunities, conditions, and rewards.

Turning now to the beginning of this story four centuries earlier, Oliver Cromwell, in stark contrast to Jenner, believed that he had nothing to gain and everything to lose – including his soul – if he or his contemporaries judged his remarkable successes to be self-made, that is, to be of his own making. And yet, unlike Jenner, he did indeed rise out of the modest ranks of England's rural gentry in the seventeenth century with astounding rapidity in political and military circles. He led revolutionary armies that never lost a battle on their way to defeating and beheading King Charles I and forming the short-lived Commonwealth of England, Scotland, and Ireland. Cromwell then ruled with the misleadingly benign title of Lord Protector of the Commonwealth from December 1653 until he died in 1658. Rather than take credit for his extraordinary rise to power, however, Cromwell vehemently rejected his foes' accusations of worldly ambition and accepted no credit for his feats. In a one-and-a-half-hour speech to Parliament in 1654, he made his case repeatedly: "I called not myself to this place; of that, God is witness." Instead, the "Lord's providence ... will give occasion for the ordering of things for the best interest of the people."[4]

Cromwell and his contemporaries in both Old and New England assumed that the individual ambition that underlies worldly gain is selfish and dangerous. At the time, there was no favorable phrase for "self-made success," and words linked to "self" typically carried negative, even sinful, associations, such as "self-seeking," "self-ambition," and "self-pride." In that light, a "conscientious" Protestant minister condemned those who beheaded Charles I, including Cromwell, as "the supreme, self-made authority."[5] Still close to medieval traditions, the English typically avowed that success on one's own was impossible. Worse, attempting it disrupted communities as well as God's order. Supernatural and social forces determined successes and failures.

To proclaim himself publicly as self-made and to feel personal pride in his achievements, Cromwell would have had to defy those powerful forces and the proper balance of individual ambition and community obligations. He shared the prevailing deep faith in providential authority, according to which God governs all human actions and their outcomes. A brother-in-law marveled after an important victory that God "alone is the Lord of Hosts; ... it is himselfe that hath raised you up amongst men, and hath called you to high imployments."[6] This highest of praises recognized godliness and service, not personal achievement. Such providentialism also protected Cromwell and his allies against the sinfulness of regicide, they believed, although their foes sensed more profane forces at play. Whether for good or evil, genuine fears of damnation and worldly censure prevented the assertion of self-agency – the belief that human beings can determine their own fates – even if they could not prevent ambition itself.

INTRODUCTION

A self-made label also would have unwisely spurned the earthly social networks on which all political actors have always relied. Cromwell's family had once been prominent and still had valuable political connections that he nurtured alongside his Puritan networks; both had propelled the civil revolution that created his opportunities. Moreover, both publicly and privately, he boasted of his loyalty to those networks and of his status within them rather than independence from them. He, therefore, insisted, early in his 1654 Parliamentary speech, "I was by birth a gentleman, living neither in any considerable height, nor yet in obscurity."[7] He had to avoid the political and social costs of portraying his rise as from too low a rank to command respect. In short, there was more danger than glory in a grand and self-made rise to power.

This comparison of beliefs about self-agency challenges claims that the meanings of "self-made success" are eternal verities. To understand how we got from attitudes of the seventeenth century to those of the twentieth, we will look across these four centuries at how the myth of self-made success was entangled with many different beliefs and actions, all within changing contexts. Daniel T. Rodgers explained that the joint evolution of the work ethic and its economic context "took shape together as values and practice fused and collided, quarreled with and reinforced one another, in an inextricably tangled relationship." Because the strands in the history of every important idea are tangled, simple stories inevitably mislead.[8] Yet, simplicity and directness maximize stories' persuasiveness. More effective than complex narratives, myths are simple tales that can align individuals' identities with collective identities, individuals' ambitions with group ambitions, and individuals' values with group values.[9] Truly, one of the reasons for the impact of the modern myth of self-made success is that it became a frame for overly simple stories that filter out the intricacies of people's real lives.

Those simple stories also filter out most people. They focus on a narrow foreground – a particular "hero" or heroic type. Everyone else is either an enemy to be conquered or an underling to be slighted, even when their work makes all heroes' triumphs possible. Of course, all of the people working in the background have their own stories, but they rarely reach or appeal to dominant groups. This book recovers some of those narratives to challenge the myth of self-made success and to highlight alternatives to the dominant stories. These can help us reimagine the dynamics between individuals and communities beyond the judgmental terms of self-made success, according to which successful individuals owe nothing and everyone else deserves nothing.

To challenge the myth of self-made success, this book looks to its long history and to the people who conjured its simplistic stories. This meant tracking four centuries of storytelling about the idea of self-agency from its days as a sin against God and community through its evolution into a dominant narrative, one driven by ambitions of many sorts. Because the people who could most successfully compete for cultural authority in the mainstream have belonged to its dominant groups, they are the book's protagonists. Therefore, this is *mostly* a history of how people who dominated the mainstream – especially elite White Protestant males – created, shaped, and exploited ideas about self-making to advocate for themselves and their allies. Although marginalized groups have contested dominant ideologies, this book's purpose is to expose what's behind the myth and the storytellers who built it. Those historical actors are not the whole nation, but their myths have swayed it powerfully.[10]

Simple, persuasive mythology to the contrary, self-made success is impossible. We live and act in a profoundly interconnected world, and our professional lives, like so much else, depend on social capital and our access to many other types of resources, as well as how diligently we work.[11] Given that reality, how did ideas about self-making evolve into a myth that people can and should succeed on their own? Like all evolutionary processes, this one has been competitive, and the prize is cultural authority, which frames what we accept as realistic and ethical. In turn, cultural authority confers the trust and social esteem on which political authority and power depend. Through this evolution, notions about self-making became a shared framework to explain what people experience and how they judge themselves and others. Like any ideology, the myth's rise has depended on its usefulness to persuade and motivate, which has never hinged on its alignment with reality.[12]

Myths have histories, and the myth of self-made success has a surprising and hotly contested one that runs through the nation's history. The concept has attracted a wide range of meanings and uses along the way, which we will watch evolve over the centuries rather than try to pin to a single definition. Those changes call into question today's taken-for-granted uses of the concept, which have had, and continue to have, very real consequences for how we think about who deserves respect, what obligations we owe to our communities, and what ambitions we should encourage.

The concept of "self-made" has been elastic, but, whether positive or negative, its uses always judge. Throughout the nineteenth century, the phrase "self-made" often continued to carry negative meanings. It was common, for example, to see temperance advocates refer to "self-made maniacs" whose alcoholism destroyed themselves and others. A cluster of diatribes in the political arena condemned the "pure, the select, the self-made, bloated patriots."[13] And, of course, until recent decades, "nouveau riche" was not praise but a reference to people with "new" money who had yet to learn appropriate social graces. That sense is long gone as tycoons now pridefully brandish their casual attire and sometimes crude behavior.

By the middle of the nineteenth century references to "self-made" were increasingly positive, but often not what we'd expect today. A newspaper placed an 1843 tribute to "a *self-made man* in every sense of the word" in a way that would seem odd today. It praised the "self-made" Reverend John A. MacMannen for "the remarkable strength of mind and the integrity which have borne him triumphantly through so many privations and difficulties" – standard fare for an esteemed preacher. Directly below that article, however, a single sentence read "The death of John Jacob Astor, for several years past regarded as the wealthiest man in the United States, is announced in the New York papers."[14] The contrast of Astor's scant notice with abundant praise for the now-obscure reverend is startling today. Astor conformed to our current understandings of "self-made": he rose to riches out of obscure origins, yet did not then qualify as "self-made" while the reverend did.

Moreover, when the title of self-made success in a positive sense first moved away from religious and community leaders, electoral politics incentivized applying it to men with political ambitions. When early nineteenth-century fables of self-making began to describe political figures, they increasingly made use of motifs such as the "solitary oak" and "noble eagle." Describing a hero as a loner tells a simple story because it hides from view the forest of people who make that heroism possible: the wives, servants, free and enslaved laborers, displaced peoples, and the impoverished. Andrew Jackson, for example, was often described with those two phrases, as in "the noble eagle perches in silence on the remotest mountain peak."[15] Such narratives make invisible the people in heroes' armies and households, as well as those among their political and financial supporters. Other people often appear as the objects of heroism: as rescued, conquered, or controlled. Nothing but a hero's raw abilities and grim determination affect his success in such over-simplified but powerful renderings. Only the drama of headwinds that challenge heroes, not the advantages of tailwinds, appear in laudatory stories of self-making that are grossly inadequate to explain lives' outcomes.[16] In other words, it's human nature to take credit for our successes and to blame bad luck for our failures, while, conversely, blaming others for their failures and luck for their successes.

Storytellers have forged the myth of self-made success in two senses, both constructing and counterfeiting identities and measures of worth in order to advance their own and others' ambitions. We will follow as the concept of self-making evolved into the myth through the stories of people, many famous but not all. Familiar names include Benjamin Franklin, Andrew Carnegie, and Horatio Alger, Jr. Franklin starred in the early transition, as he did in so many stories of America's founding. However, his role was not the tale of self-aggrandizement attributed to him after he could no longer speak for himself. He never considered himself "self-made." His grandson William Temple Franklin rewrote his memoirs in 1818 into the form we remember now, doing an injustice to Benjamin's intentions, but pushing the notion of self-making into ambition's service. Late in that century, Carnegie needed no publicist to claim for himself the rights and privileges of the self-made, the "fittest," which he did in his 1889 essay "Wealth." Although Alger wrote more than one hundred stories to encourage children and adults to take responsibility for their lives, he also emphasized their responsibilities to their communities. He never advocated for self-making, but opponents of the New Deal reshaped his legacy in the 1930s as if he had. Advocates for an individualist ethos have recruited historical figures – Franklin and Alger foremost among them – contradicting what those iconic Americans in fact said and did.

Although no single ideal of ambition and success has ever fully triumphed, over centuries a simple, elegant, and powerful storyline emerged that increasingly attributed agency to individuals and minimized their debts and responsibilities to their communities. Along the way, it has also served those who want to minimize collective obligations to others who lack adequate "merit" by their lights. Two centuries ago, this storyline began to acquire its own symbolic phrases – "bootstraps," "rags-to-riches," "rugged individualism," and so on. It has since acquired support from powerful people and institutions who champion simple, one-dimensional stories dominated by a notion of individualistic, self-made success that legitimates and, thereby, exacerbates inequalities. Those stories also denigrate people whose conditions constrain their potential, adding especially to the burdens of women and people of color. In fact, their ambitions are sometimes still maligned as dangerous threats to fantasies about a proper social order. In modern individualist tales a claimant to self-made success owes no one. Charitable generosity is appreciated, but not obligatory. Conversely, a culture that exalts self-made success also condemns failure as entirely self-made. "Losers" are readily dismissed as unworthy, compounding their frustrations and despair.

Challenging the myth of self-made success does not in the least dispute that we adults must take responsibility for our own actions. We can, also, rightly take pleasure and pride in our accomplishments, especially those hard-won. Yet, we are all "mutually-made," to apply Judith McGaw's insightful phrase. Honest life stories, therefore, present a balance of individual effort and support to explain their paths.[17] Challenging the myth only requires that we not succumb to the arrogant belief that we achieve alone and, therefore, owe no one. Likewise, challenging the myth reminds us to appreciate our tailwinds and others' headwinds – our advantages and others' disadvantages.

The powerful myth of self-made success has had enormous costs, and, in our own moment, the tragedies confront us daily. Its false assumptions and real harms have, therefore, received considerable attention of late.[18] This book adds to those critiques by tracking the myth's historical origins and contingencies to reveal that there is nothing intuitive, inherent, stable, or natural about the idea, nothing that

INTRODUCTION

sits at the American core. Nor are the harms that its use legitimates inevitable. As inequality grows, we would do well to recall the best elements of America's more complex, socially oriented narratives, the neglected stories of mutual self-improvement, connection, and community obligations. The history that follows can help us avoid being blinded by the brilliant simplicity and power of bootstraps, the terrible elegance of a myth that pretends that we live –that we succeed or fail – in a vacuum.

1

A New World of Ambition and Judgment

For centuries, medieval tradition had exalted poverty, communal obligations, and otherworldly goals, but in the seventeenth century new perspectives and challenges from the Renaissance and Reformation inspired worldly ambitions among Europeans – and sometimes rewarded them. A flood of new opportunities, such as commercialization and explorers' adventures, and new pressures, such as mounting poverty and vagrancy in England, threatened communities and traditions and together inspired economic and cultural innovation. In this context, English adventurers in the early seventeenth century who sought their fortunes in Virginia often foreshadowed individualism. Their failures to recognize mutual dependencies and obligations were famously catastrophic. In contrast, many migrants seeking to prosper in New England held traditional duties dear, especially duties to God and community, even as they carved out paths into the unknown.

To understand the emerging ways of thinking about self-made fates among the early English colonists to North America, we can focus on the lives, worries, and circumstances of Captain John Smith (1580–1631), an explorer and extraordinary promoter of himself and New World colonization, and Robert Keayne (1595–1656), a prosperous merchant in Boston's first decades. Neither shunned worldly ambitions as they helped to build England's earliest North American colonies, and each aggressively sought material success and esteem through incessant work. In the language of their day, they were both adventurers, which meant that they took risks in pursuit of gain. Today, we remember Smith as an adventurer of the swashbuckling sort, most famous because the Algonquian princess Pocahontas rescued him from her father's ire in Virginia. Keayne was an adventurer in a now obsolete sense of that word – he took investment risks, such as financing New England colonies. Like Smith, he advocated for advancing England by building colonies of hardworking families, prosperous farmers, fishermen, artisans, and merchants.

Smith and Keayne illustrate the concerns and goals of two prominent, well-informed, but very different men among the earliest English travelers to North America. They participated in an early stage of shaping the criteria by which

A NEW WORLD OF AMBITION AND JUDGMENT

Americans through the centuries would judge successes and failures. They also talked and wrote incessantly about fostering communities and working for their betterment. At the same time, and like their peers, they guarded the boundaries of inclusion in those communities, defining narrowly who could belong, who merited respect, and whose exploitation and destruction could be justified.

Over several centuries before the seventeenth, European cultures had moved away from medieval traditions through the disquieting eras known as the Renaissance and Reformation. The rise of deliberate self-fashioning during those centuries initiated an evolution of notions about self-agency that slowly laid the foundations for the myth of self-made success. John Smith and Robert Keayne, like their ambitious contemporaries in the waning years of the Renaissance, invested heavily in self-fashioning, in shaping themselves into idealized personas to be respected within their cultural milieus. Self-fashioning required deliberate and often rigorous effort, to be sure, but it was not achievable alone, independent of celestial and earthly forces that set the standards and facilitated – or blocked – one's aims.[1] Well aware of their roots and forces outside themselves, self-fashioners then did not – could not – see themselves as self-made.

In these transitional times, an upstart who tried to change ranks risked getting exposed as a fraud trying to live within a false identity.[2] People in their rightful places did not have to work so hard to fit their station, and anyone who ventured into unfamiliar identities became a target for attacks. In that context, neither Smith nor Keayne described his origins as humble, any more than did Oliver Cromwell. There was no prestige, no esteem, in being labeled an "upstart" in these germinal years of the concept of self-agency, when social mobility was possible but not celebrated, and self-making was sinful, not applauded. Popular fiction acerbically targeted climbers, consistent with prevailing attitudes. In 1592, *A Quip for an Upstart Courtier* amusingly lampooned "Velvetbreeches," an arrogant and ambitious merchant eager for social mobility. Even though *Quip*'s very popular author Robert Greene took a secular approach to his writing and didn't present ambition as a threat to men's souls, his portrayal of the stylish upstart was distinctly unfavorable.[3] Kings could reward those who served them well with new titles and lands, but not for some time yet could someone exercise obvious personal ambition without risking slurs.[4] Smith's and Keayne's narratives and self-fashioning illustrate this prohibition, as well as the emergent notion that toil and work were becoming a basis for social worth and status.

Their experiences and writings make it clear that Smith and Keayne saw themselves as agents responsible for their own lives, but at the same time not isolated from God's providence or their own social contexts.[5] Both rose from modest roots to pursue their ambitions and, in centuries since, have been called self-made men. Despite their accomplishments, however, neither claimed to have succeeded alone, and neither could have imagined doing so. This chapter will consider why this was so and also trace gradually emerging precursors to the myth of self-making. Although notions of self-making and individual agency have since become fundamental to the lore of America's origins, in those initial stages, it was both blasphemous and socially fatal for even the most obviously ambitious men, like Smith and Keayne, to forget their heavenly and earthly debts. Their complicated lives reveal many of the tensions and frustrations that troubled men of faith in a time of profound and disconcerting opportunities and transitions. This makes Smith and Keayne compelling guides to the very first stages of the myth of self-made success.[6]

CAPTAIN JOHN SMITH – PROPHET FOR A NEW WORLD

Captain John Smith was a swashbuckling soldier and explorer. He was also a prolific author, promoter, and a dedicated advocate for what he saw as England's interests abroad. Brilliant, determined, and lucky, he adventured widely and lived to tell the tales. Moreover, his tales were widely read for their exciting narratives, beguiling observations and maps of exotic lands, and their convincing advice for conquest of those places. His bravado and military triumphs in those distant lands won him a coat of arms and the right to be called a gentleman. Smith's writings also promoted and detailed how the English could successfully colonize the New World without a hint of concern for the disastrous costs to indigenous peoples. By example and through his writings and conversations with influential investors, aristocrats, and colonizers, Captain Smith stamped his mark on the New World, including the region that he named New England. Nonetheless, this Renaissance man – although filled with self-agency, self-aggrandizement, and self-fashioning – knew his success was not his alone. Even so, he never hesitated to judge others for how they fashioned their lives. In doing so, he contributed to the cultural authority of work as a bulwark against the evils of idleness, thereby helping to lay the foundation for the myth of self-made men and its power to judge.

Smith was born in Lincolnshire in 1580 to a prosperous yeoman family, well connected but not gentry. Early on he benefited from patronage, as he always would, initially from the support of a local gentleman who recognized the boy's potential and sent him to grammar school. At fifteen, he was apprenticed to a seaport merchant, but, despite his future admiration for merchants as key to England's prosperity, he soon left to seek glory fighting with Dutch Protestants against Catholic Spanish control. "Lamenting and repenting to have seene so many Christians slaughter one another," he wandered around a bit, then struck out for Hungary to fight Turkish Ottoman armies. Smith's contributions were notable enough to gain recognition with promotions and honors, but the

Figure 1.1 Captain John Smith saw himself as a dashing hero, just as this 1616 portrait depicts him. He also saw himself as a hard worker who despised aristocrats as lazy and glorified the virtues of the shared work that colonizing required. (Library of Congress: Pictures Item 2021653041)

Habsburg armies lost anyway, and he was captured then enslaved in the Ottoman Empire. After his escape, he next roved to Russia, around more of Europe, and then through North Africa. By the time he returned to London at twenty-six, his credentials as a soldier and explorer made him a welcome ally for the Virginia Company of London as it planned an expedition to North America. Thanks to his experiences and connections, Smith was the only non-aristocrat appointed to leadership.[7]

When English "Nobilitie, Gentrie and Marchants," as well as potential migrants, first looked to the New World, England was a minor actor in European affairs, envious of the riches in gold and silver that Spain and Portugal had reaped since the early sixteenth century. In 1606, when John Smith joined the effort, the Virginia Company of London aimed to establish a permanent English North American colony although previous English failures had discouraged many investors, political supporters, and possible migrants. They targeted the huge territory Sir Walter Raleigh had named Virginia in honor of Elizabeth I, the Virgin Queen, and in 1607, the Company's three ships landed in the Chesapeake Bay on what they renamed the James River to honor James I. Planning to copy Spanish and Portuguese conquistadors and imagining quick "present profits," in Smith's words, from gold and silver instead of an "honest gain" from "commodities" that required time and preparation, the Virginia Company sent "many Refiners, Gold-smiths, Jewellers, Lapidaries, Stone-cutters, Tabacco-pipe-makers, Imbroderers, Perfumers, Silkemen."[8] For the rest of his life, Smith would complain loudly that an overabundance of elite "Gallants" served the colony poorly, as they "could doe nothing but complain, curse, and despaire, when they saw our miseries, . . . yet must I provide as well for them as for my selfe." Better that "the Tradesmen in London" had instead sent "one hundred good labourers . . . than a thousand such Gallants." Smith also lamented that too many of those sent as labourers were "roarers" and "loyterers" who ate more than they produced, and who "would rather starve than worke."[9]

Many, many mistakes in London and Jamestown, exacerbated by unexpectedly harsh conditions, resulted in staggering suffering and death tolls from starvation, illness, and Native resistance. Eventually, the colony at Jamestown and environs survived, but at horrendous costs in misery and lives, both Native and European. Smith watched men starve and die for two and a half years, until his gentlemen superiors themselves died and he could move into a position of authority from which he could compel his compatriots to work. Smith claimed that during those next nine months only seven or eight men died, in contrast to the huge numbers before then. Survivors built houses and a church, dug a well, and planted corn.[10] Then, either by accident or assault, Smith suffered a serious gunpowder burn and was forced to return to England for treatment. In promoting colonization – and himself – thereafter, he suggested that "toile" was a measure of merit and "idlenesse" was a sign of shortcomings. The budding, ambitious English middling sorts like Smith, who were already keen on working toward prosperity within the era's opportunities, found his analyses appealing.[11] Promotional storytelling in Smith's last two decades on behalf of that measure of merit brought him into the history of the myth of self-made success. An aggressive, self-motivated achiever and wide-reaching promoter, he framed Jamestown's disasters as a result of the ills that befall a group whose members don't pull themselves together and build what they need.[12]

Captain Smith had left behind the medieval distrust of self-interest and dread of commercial enterprises and entanglements, accepting instead civic humanism's approval of personal gain as long as it built something and benefited the commonweal. He wholeheartedly approved of New England's colonists, unlike Jamestown's, and their desire to prosper through work rather than fortune hunting because, he claimed, they "heere by their labour may live exceeding well."[13] He also accepted commercial ambitions and successes as the means to a powerful and prosperous England in both the Old and New Worlds. In describing New England's opportunities, he declared in 1616, "I am not so simple, to thinke, that ever any other motive than wealth will ever erect there a Commonweale; or draw companie from their ease and humours at home, to stay in New England to effect my purposes." He lauded New England's opportunities for the man who had "small meanes" and, instead, "only his merit to advance his fortune." In 1631, the last of his many books advised and encouraged "the Unexperienced Planters of New England, or Any Where" not to hesitate about prospering. He even declared anyone "double mad" who left "his friends, meanes, and freedom in England" for North America only "to be worse there than here." With the right balance of "freedome" and "correction," moreover, "doubtlesse God will bless you, and quickly triple and multiply your numbers, the which to my utmost I will doe my best indevour." For himself, "although I never got shilling but cost mee a pound, yet I would thinke my selfe happy could I see their prosperities" for "I have throwne my selfe with my mite into the Treasury of my Countries good."[14]

John Smith's struggle to achieve moral balance between the common good and ambition paralleled that of his Calvinist contemporaries because, like them, he had to avoid a blasphemous assertion of sole credit for his achievements despite his deep desire for recognition and esteem. In that balancing act, he utilized his talent for self-fashioning, regaling others in print and conversation to persuade and garner support. In 1623, promoting his forthcoming compendium, *The Generall Historie of Virginia, the Somer Iles, and New England...*, he compared his own writing to Julius Caesar's histories. Despite his and others' high opinion of his "atchievments" in rising from yeoman stock to heroic heights as a soldier, explorer, colonizer, promoter, and author, he did not see himself as self-made. Such a claim would have been foolhardy. Beyond the eternal dangers of blasphemy, it would have destroyed his chances of winning over, or at least not offending, the aristocratic sources of patronage crucial to a man of modest origins and immodest dreams. Therefore, Smith did not boast about his social mobility any more than did Oliver Cromwell. Smith's 1630 third-person autobiography describes his family lineage as favorably as possible in terms of rank and explains that he was left an estate of "competent meanes." Understandably proud of his achievements and rise in stature, he could admit to no self-made glory in mobility. Neither his aristocratic patrons nor his belief system would tolerate his taking credit for more than honor and effort. In his last months he wrote: "Seeing honour is our lives ambition, and our ambition after death." He urged his compatriots to "further them that would and doe their utmost and best endevour."[15]

ROBERT KEAYNE – PURITAN MERCHANT

Although modern stereotypes typically portray Puritans as austere, they were not at all averse to wealth and comforts.[16] Seventeenth-century Puritans sought affluence, but their ambitions caught them in a bind that leading minister John Cotton described in the 1620s as "diligence in worldly business, and yet deadness to the world."[17] They intended to prosper, but ambition was supposed to glorify God and aid community, whereas ambition energized by selfishness remained a sin.[18] An uneasy balance to keep, to be sure, as the melancholy fate of the affluent Boston merchant and devout Puritan Robert Keayne shows. Born in 1595 to a butcher's family outside of London, at ten he began an eight-year apprenticeship in the Cornhill district, a London center of commerce and finance. He did very well for himself, was admitted into an elite guild at twenty, and, with the help of an advantageous marriage, he gained recognition as a "gentleman" by 1623. Along the way, he experienced a powerful conversion to Calvinism and read religious tracts intently. To support Puritans in their New World, he invested in Plymouth Colony in the 1620s and, later, in the Massachusetts Bay Company the year before moving himself and his family to Boston in 1635. "Our dear and reverend teacher, Mr. Cotton" was one of the attractions for Keayne after Cotton was forced to leave England or face prison for preaching outside of the Church of England.[19]

Like Captain John Smith, Robert Keayne was an adventurer who took risks in pursuit of gain, but he did so as a merchant. He prospered in New England, just as he had in Old England. He built a large and prominently placed house in Boston, complete with a library and silver plate tableware. He dressed expensively, with jewelry, a watch, a gold cap, and silver lace, and enslaved three Africans to take care of his household. He also filled volumes with notes of sermons, and John Winthrop, the first governor of Massachusetts and an exacting judge, acknowledged Keayne's piety by saying that he had "come over for conscience' sake, and for the advancement of the Gospel here." Within a year of arriving in Boston, he and his wife qualified for full church membership – another measure of regard. As in London, he was active in civic affairs, took on public offices, and received honors as a leading citizen.[20] Then, in 1653, the same year that Oliver Cromwell became Lord Protector of Britain, Keayne spent five months writing "THE LAST WILL AND TESTAMENT of me, Robert Keayne all of it written with my owne hands ..." In the 1950s, historian Bernard Bailyn fittingly baptized this document of more than 50,000 words as "The Apologia of Robert Keayne."[21] The long, haunting essay tells of his life, business activities, and trials for aggressive business practices. Its laments illustrate the fraught dynamic between Puritanism and the lure of profit by disclosing what an ambitious, successful, and devout Puritan thought about his climb and his obligations.

Keayne's "apologia" not only distributed his substantial properties with precision but also expressed his struggle to justify his successful life as a Puritan merchant. What were his sins? According to John Winthrop, the problem was not that Keayne made profits, but that he took advantage of his community in doing so. He sold "as dear as he can, and buy[s] as cheap as he can" and followed other "false principles" of doing business.[22] The Massachusetts General Court found him guilty of overcharging purchasers, but by the time of his writing, he had paid his fines, Winthrop and others had reconsidered his convictions, and no one had come forward "in so many years" with "pretenses" of "debts and unjust frauds." He considered that he had earned his dignity and freedom from reproach.[23]

Keayne was caught between two sets of value systems that he believed were compatible, even if others did not. One value system was a subset of Puritanism to which early Boston's most influential leaders adhered, including Governor John Winthrop, Minister John Cotton, and Keayne's brother-in-law, Minister John Wilson. These figures distinguished between what Cotton called "diligence in worldly business" and ungodly business practices – "oppression" in the language of the day. They retained a vestige of medieval fears concerning undue profit. Merchants, they believed, could not engage in trade without sin unless they placed their priorities on piety rather than profits.[24] London merchants embodied the other value. They assigned virtue to activities, including business, that served the civic society and its prosperity. Their humanist world-view had shaped Keayne as a member of London's Merchant Taylors' Company, an elite guild that reached its height of prestige, wealth, and influence during his years as young man on the rise. In the first sentence of his will he identified himself as "Robert Keayne, citizen and merchant tailor of London by freedom and the good providence of God now dwelling at Boston in New England in America ..."[25]

Guided by these often competing values, Keayne believed that he had lived righteously according to both his guild and his church. However, of all occupations, Puritans considered trade most likely to imperil souls because merchants operated in marketplaces wherein people procured and sold life's necessities, which sorely tempted even the godly. Keayne struggled against what Bailyn called "insupportable pressures" to achieve a righteous balance through "self-discipline that only great faith could sustain." His will testifies profoundly to this struggle and its costs. His anguish was apparent throughout "what I have here writ out of the grief and trouble of my heart." As it turned out, Keayne embodied the increasingly dominant acceptance of merchants and their practices – the London humanist view – that would characterize Anglo-American culture as it drifted further from its medieval past. But his place in the vanguard clearly anguished him.[26]

Notwithstanding their differences, both sets of values in Keayne's life aroused in him a strong sense of community obligations. The elite Merchant Taylors' Company required that members swear loyalty to each other and to the guild's discipline, instruction, and rituals, and also to participate in the guild's considerable charitable activities. The latter included funds to support disabled workers, deceased members' widows and orphans, and the local poor, as mutual aid societies continue to do today. Even more deeply, Keayne's Calvinist faith insisted on community solidarity, reinforced by the ever-present threat of rebuke from neighbors and leaders. John Winthrop insisted that their inaugural "Covenant" bound Massachusetts Puritans to "strict performance" of its articles of solidarity. To avoid the Lord's wrath, "we must be knit together in this work as one man." Winthrop continued: "We must delight in each other, make others conditions our own, rejoice together, mourn together, labor and suffer together, always having before our eyes our commission and community in the work, our community as members of the same body."[27] Winthrop was repeatedly elected as the leader of Massachusetts, which was not merely a political position but also one of great religious importance. Therefore, his call for devotion to the body of the faithful was to be taken seriously, and Keayne's will affirms that he did. Thus, despite their differences, Keayne's worldly and spiritual value systems both insisted on self-agency – but in service of the common good.

This ambitious merchant believed that everyone's fate depended on external factors, especially Providence and communities. As a corollary, he believed that his success increased, not diminished, his responsibilities to the community, to which the successful owed gratitude, loyalty, and taxes. Doing his duty, Keayne claimed to have shared the "first fruits of all my increase" over the years. He also distributed nearly one-third of his estate to both church and town public projects and approved of public taxation based on fair assessments of men's assets. "For as it is the Lord out of His free bounty that gives us our estates, be they more or less, (for it is not our own hands' diligence or wisdom but His blessing only that makes rich) so He may justly challenge a part and interest in the same; and," Keayne insisted, "also the commonwealth or place where we live and where we have got more or less of that estate is also to be considered." Keayne argued that success in worldly endeavors manifested God's favor. Hence, his affluence followed from "the free mercy and kindness of God alone who raiseth up and pulleth down as He pleaseth."[28] All blessings flowed from God's grace, and all obligations were owed to God's communities.

Keayne's all too human frailties and faults make him seem very much like ambitious and self-righteous people of any era. He was arrogant and ostentatious. He may well have been insufferable, too, for he frequently reminded others about God's favor to him, and he incorporated that claim into his will. He faced both internalized and ever-present community pressures to abide by cultural and social authorities that constantly reminded him of debts and obligations. The achievement of material success, especially because it seemed to come at others' expense, did not make him a hero in the town's eyes so much as a target for condemnation from neighbors, court, and church. Success did not relieve him of tax burdens, or make him wish that it would. Instead, he accepted that New England's needs and values caused him to be "rated" higher than his peers in London.[29] Over centuries, the myth of self-made success would obscure if not erase such reminders to the successful of the communities and institutions that make their success possible.

Keayne's apologia indirectly shows that being self-made in the sense of rags-to-riches was not a source of satisfaction. If it had been, and given Keayne's desperate quest for justification and approval, his apologia might have highlighted his climb from modest circumstances in a butcher's household to wealthy merchant. He would have underscored that he had received "no portion from my parents or friends to begin the world withal." Instead, this simple observation was so low a priority to him that it appears only on page 82 of the ninety-three printed pages in Bailyn's edition of this long "last will and testament." And even here, he merely used this observation to describe his estate as achieved "through the favor of God." There was no pride then in a modest birth. His admission was regretful, a lament not a boast. He acknowledged his modest beginnings only in order to rejoice that "all may be attributed to the free mercy and kindness of God alone who raiseth up and pulleth down as He pleaseth."[30] Uninherited wealth and power were suspect then. Acquiring them through ambition could signal social folly and risked spiritual damnation. Better to credit the hand of God than one's own, especially if one has acquired critics along the way. Even better to acknowledge debts and share the fruits of success.

The myth of the self-made man would evolve over the centuries as contingent, first and foremost, on the idea that success *could* be achieved by the self, an impossible idea in Keayne's era. In turn, imagining self-made fates required a belief that people could affect their lives' outcomes, and also a standard by which their efforts could be judged. A shift in attitudes about work and idleness away from those common in medieval Europe provided the ethical system that became the foundation for the myth of self-made success.

MEASURES FOR JUDGMENT: WORK AND IDLENESS

John Smith, Robert Keayne, and their contemporaries took part in the early modern evolution of the Anglo-American meaning of work, a reconceptualization that eventually made possible the conviction that people determined their own fates and, therefore, could be judged accordingly. At their stage in that evolution, work approached the status of a sacrament: it was the outward and visible sign of an inward and invisible grace. It was bound up in individuals' dependence on God and community, and, just as important, their obligations to the same. Gendered notions of goodness emphasized communal duties.[31] Providentialism, even its extreme form as predestination, which asserted that God had determined individuals' salvation or damnation at Creation, did not relieve Calvinists or other Protestants from their personal responsibilities to act.[32] Self-improvement and action to change the world were profound obligations, whether to nourish souls with prayer and literacy, to benefit their communities, or to rid the world of papists and other infidels. As John Smith put it, everyone must "doe their utmost and best endevour." The great scientist and philosopher Lord Francis Bacon explained this charge and the balance of human efficacy and obligations in 1605: "Men must pursue things which are just in present, and leave the future to the divine Providence."[33]

In light of this powerful sense of personal accountability, a "calling" provided the direction and motivation for dutiful action, and its aim was "the publike good" according to the Reverend John Cotton.[34] He summarized this culture of improvement as striving to be "busy like ants, morning and evening, early and late, and labor diligently with their hands and with their wits, and which way soever as may be the best improvement of a man's talent, it must be employed to the best advantage." As well, "faith, *in serving God, serves men, and in serving men, serves God.*" Service must be the goal, and other tempting measures of success resisted: "*Care about the success of it*" is one of the "burthens that befall a man in his calling." Success in one's calling was not cause to be "puffed up," Cotton cautioned, because all outcomes "rested in God's gracious dispensation."[35] The glorification of self-made success was unthinkable because the notion of a "self-made" success itself was impossible.

The middling folk of early modern Anglo-America placed a high value on work that evolved parallel to an equally high aversion to its opposite: idleness, or, more accurately, what they perceived and interpreted as idleness. Not the same as rest or contemplation, "Idleness is," according to influential Puritan Richard Sibbes, "the hour of temptation, wherein Satan joins with our imagination, and sets it about his own work."[36] Or, as we now say, "Idle hands are the Devil's workshop."

This moral aversion to idleness was something new, and a vital prerequisite for the self-made myth as it would later evolve. In medieval English culture, leisure, not work, signified status. Marking his era's move away from that standard, Robert Keayne ceaselessly recorded his investments in time, effort, and materials, living this emerging attitude, the spirit of driven action. Pages of his will itemize "a particular account of my daily or weekly expenses and charges for diet, apparel, and housekeeping, which is summed up every week from year to year," in copious books "which I have writ with my own hand." He hoped that "all that I have read and done" would "testify to the world on my behalf that I have not lived an idle, lazy, or dronish life, nor spent my time wantonly, fruitlessly or in company-keeping." He never had "in my whole time either in Old England or New many spare hours to spend unprofitably away or to refresh myself with recreations" other than "reading and writing." Nor had he ever indulged in "folly, prodigality, or vainglory."[37]

Keayne's soulful declarations that he considered "time as a thing most dear and precious to me" reveal him to be a paragon of a new world in which work was a tool to display in seeking esteem as well as profit. This so-called Protestant work ethic was inspired as much by Renaissance-era worldly experiences as by religious beliefs. Protestants famously left their thoughts behind while merchants simply acted, which has encouraged the work ethic's misnomer. For at least a century before Keayne, European merchants had been gradually differentiating themselves from their medieval counterparts who sought profit but did not consider work as inherently good or as a measure of virtue. Europeans, especially merchants in the Netherlands and Italy, had likewise begun to discard the medievalists' Aristotelian contempt for labor and esteem for leisure, steadily replacing them with pride in filling their time usefully, with pride in work, even in work for its own sake.[38]

Thus, the modern sacralization of work was not a simple product either of religious faith or material change.[39] When two abstractions – in this case beliefs about work and faith – evolve together incrementally, it's all but impossible to assess which led and which followed. Moreover, trying to figure out the order of influences obscures the more important relationship between them and the ways that these ideas reinforced each other as they moved synergistically against the

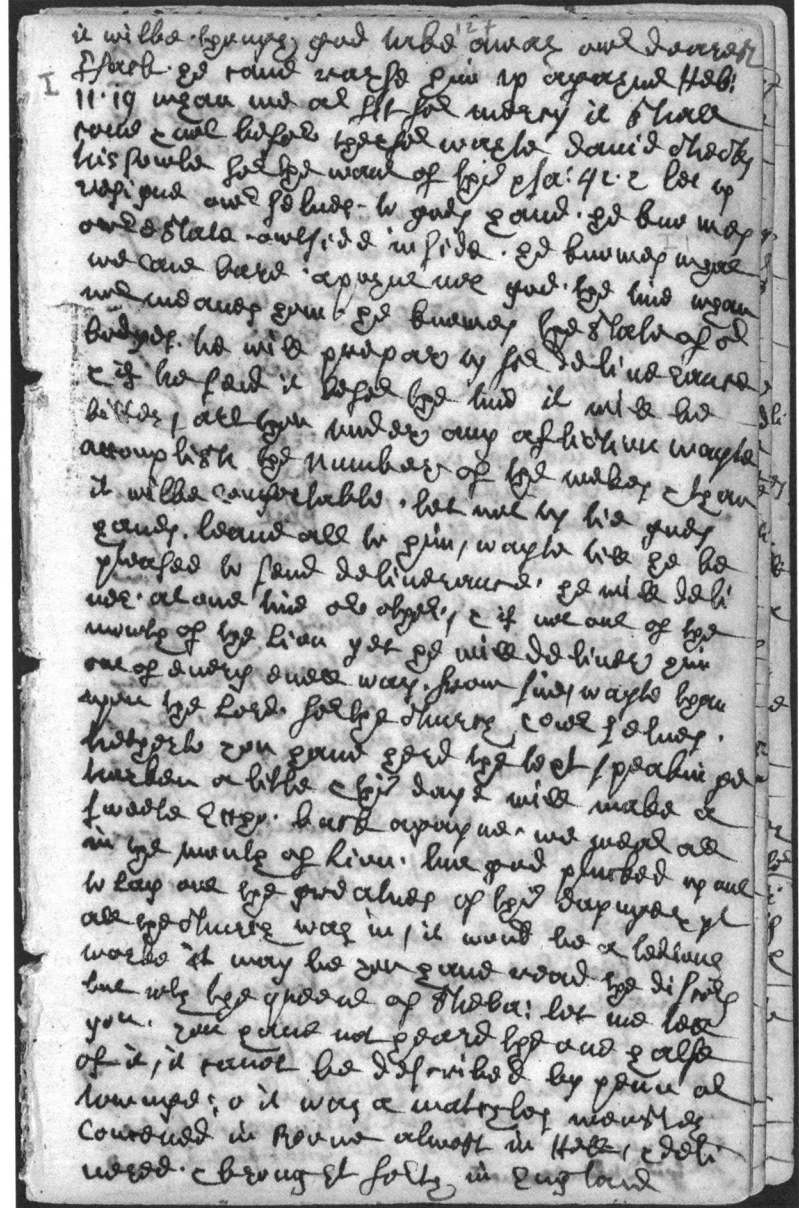

Figure 1.2 Robert Keayne, a wealthy Puritan merchant in Boston's earliest years, struggled with the tensions between his material ambitions and his commitment to serving God and his community. Hundreds of pages of dense notes on sermons attest to his intense religious devotion and his belief in the importance of constant work. ("Robert Keayne Sermon Notes, 1627–1646," vol. 3, p. 73; MS. N-1518. Courtesy of Massachusetts Historical Society)

medieval grain.[40] Larger historical changes inspired and fueled their reciprocal evolution: the rise in economic imagination and opportunities that marked the era and the decline of traditional respect for both poverty and aristocracy.

Together, these developments consecrated work and time in dramatic departures from medieval practices and biblical roots. References to work in the 1611 King James Version of the Bible generally suggest that work should be practical ("if any would not work, neither should he eat"), a benefit to others ("that he may have to give to him that needeth" and "Let all your things be done with charity"), or performed to glorify God. It was not valued or inherently sacred. In the book of Genesis, work is a burden from which both God and the faithful must rest on the seventh day. It is also the ever-present ordeal that God imposed on humanity as a punishment for Adam and Eve's Original Sin. In the Gospels, Jesus called "all ye that labour and are heavy laden, and I will give you rest." Jesus also summoned men away from their work to be his disciples. As a guest in Martha's home, he told her not to be distracted by serving her guests, not to be "troubled." Better that she join her sister Mary and listen to his words. In his Sermon on the Mount, Jesus confirmed this message, not only insisting that "Ye cannot serve God and mammon," but also encouraging believers not to worry about food or raiment: "Consider the lilies of the field and how they grow; they toil not, neither do they spin." Even the most recited prayer in Christianity asks, "Give us this day our daily bread."[41] For centuries, church leaders such as the saints Augustine, Thomas Aquinas, and Francis of Assisi continued to present work as merely necessary unless in God's service, such as prayer, evangelizing, or caring for others.

If the Bible did not revere work for its own sake, neither did it encourage judgment on the poor. During the Middle Ages, Christian believers could serve their faith and their own souls by charity toward poor persons. European medieval cultures urged admiration for devout believers who gave up wealth to seek salvation in poverty and to live by begging or in religious institutions such as convents and monasteries, as in the iconic medieval story of St. Francis of Assisi's voluntary poverty. His legacy sanctified poverty and encouraged elites to identify with the poor and make common cause with them. Yet status inequalities affected work's value as medieval chronicles in general lauded elites who renounced, but not those with nothing to renounce. This tradition denied the claims of the involuntary poor to righteousness because they had no worldly resources to sacrifice. When these poor people labored for monasteries or convents, they did so to earn a livelihood, not for salvation.[42] According to that ethos, there was no glory in work that people did if they had no other options.

Thus, Protestants did not invent judgment against poor folks; they just hardened it. In the early modern era, tolerance for poor people in England, whether voluntarily or involuntarily poor, had already begun to dissolve. The enclosure of arable land that began in the twelfth century had reduced commoners' access to traditionally open lands and initiated a series of demographic crises. The resulting loss of traditional ways of subsistence living hit particularly hard people who too often lacked skills to be employed productively elsewhere. Later, overpopulation and rising food prices compounded the effects of enclosure in the sixteenth century. Impoverished and without options in the countryside, some took to the road as beggars, vagabonds, and thieves. As early as the fourteenth century, English municipalities and other authorities had begun passing ordinances against begging by the able-bodied. These ordinances were largely ineffective, but they produced a compelling record of frustration with the problem of the poor. Guilds and other private secular groups also started to restrict access to their charity according to supplicants' proper behavior.[43] As the moral status of work gradually increased, tolerance for the poor gradually decreased; judgment became more narrowly dependent on their behavior and their capacities.

In this context of widespread concerns, Richard Hakluyt the younger, the most well-known early English promoter of colonization, saw the New World as an outlet for the unsettled poor. In 1584, he argued that colonies would do double service, to spread "the gospell of Christe" and also build an "enterprise ... for the manifolde imploymente of nombers of idle men" because England's "trades are growen beggarly or daungerous." He lamented that without colonies England "cannot deliver our commonwealthe from multitudes of loyterers and idle vagabondes."[44]

So it was that North America's founding colonizers headed to the Chesapeake and New England from an Old England in which widespread and visible victims of dispossession and malnutrition struggled for survival. As John Winthrop wrestled with his own decision about whether or not to migrate to New England, he seemed to have lost hope for Old England: "Why meet we so many wandering ghosts in shape of men, so many spectacles of misery in all our streets, our houses full of victuals & our entryes of hunger-starved christains? Our shoppes full of riche wares, & vnder our stalles lye our owne fleshe in nakednesse."[45]

Those who left the historical records judged what they could see. And what they saw persuaded them that idleness was a sinful choice. The failings of people who begged, stole, cluttered towns and villages, and burdened more productive citizens were easy targets for self-righteous criticism. Moreover, the lives of people just getting by can look undisciplined regardless of how hard they struggle to cobble together a living.[46] Thus, John Smith's experiences in Virginia reinforced his own penchants. Like others, he told stories about how he worked to avoid such troubles. Condemning listless victims of malnutrition, ignorance, or despair seemed obvious when others seemed blessed with opportunity, energy, and ability. Such contrasts built a sturdy foundation for the myth of self-making.

Hakluyt believed that poor people were willing to work if they had opportunities, but others were less generous. The ascendant middling sorts – trades people, artisans, small shopkeepers, professionals, and yeomen – experienced this rising tide of poverty as a blight and a burden. Existing on the edges of prosperity themselves, ambitious to advance, and hopeful enough to be willing to work at it, they added their voices to those in authority who wanted to distinguish between "deserving" recipients of charity and apparent ne'er-do-wells. Robert Keayne's will included several generous provisions for "the relief of the godly poor." But, as did many others then and thereafter, he expressed a growing sense that some unfortunate people were ungodly. Hence he approved of ungenerous provisions for "public, profitable, and general good" that included a "workhouse for prisoners, malefactors, and some sort of poor people, stubborn, idle, and undutiful youth, as children and servants, to have been kept at work in either for correction or to get their living."[47] For many, improving God's earth included improving others' behaviors in workhouses. In these harsh settings, communities could provide for basic needs but at the price of compelling labor in the name of training skills while constraining wicked ways. Centuries of praise for voluntary poverty, such as that modeled by St. Francis of Assisi and practiced by nuns and monks, gave way to criticism and ordinances, and then to damnation. Alms to the unworthy lost their value as vouchers toward one's own salvation. With each step toward judging and punishing idleness, English society on both sides of the Atlantic accepted that individuals could and must shape their own lives through work.[48] Respect required it.

At the other end of the spectrum, the idle but powerful whose wealth came from inheritance also provoked the ire of the middling English. The mid-seventeenth-century civil wars that Oliver Cromwell and others fought against the monarchy and that resulted in King Charles's execution in 1649 were only the most obvious of many upheavals against aristocratic cultural and political authority. For these "lilies of the field," that is, aristocrats, idleness still provided a positive sign of status, as it had traditionally. From royalty on down, aristocrats and gentry might well have worked – many engaged in politics or managed their estates – but if the strains of that labor were obvious to others, it would have diminished their stature according to ancient standards of elegance. Their dominant appearances had to be of leisure: embroidery as artistry, not mending; hunting as sport, not provisioning.

Elites' haughty condescension toward others beneath their status stirred deep resentment, including toward taxation that supported luxurious and repressive courts. Therefore, new opportunities for advancement in both Old and New England corroded respect for people whose wealth and power came from the luck of the genealogy lottery. Others who benefited from their race, rank, and gender but who worked diligently to make the most of their privileges and opportunities were especially intolerant. For example, in about 1616, William Perkins described as doomed those "such as live *in no calling*, but spend their time in eating, drinking, sleeping and sporting, because they have ... lands left by their parents." They had rebelled against God, he concluded. Likewise, Thomas Taylor reproached elites whose "rents come in ... whether they sleep or wake, work or play." He warned in 1653 that "only Doers shall be saved."[49]

Reflecting this cultural setting, Captain John Smith had little patience for aristocratic idleness. In 1608, when he took command in Jamestown, he forced residents to work, quoting St. Paul's exhortation that "if any would not work, neither should he eat." As the son of a prosperous yeoman farmer, Smith knew how to make a living from the land, and he determined that he would teach Jamestown's migrants how to do what needed doing: to build, to plant, and to train as a militia. In one instance, he selected thirty men, including two "proper gentlemen," to learn to cut down trees and make clapboard for buildings. After a week of work that "blistered there tender fingers," the thirty became able lumbermen, and even "delight[ed] to hear the trees thunder as they fell." Smith devised what he called "a remedy" to cure their "sin" of cursing while they worked, namely counting "everie mans oathes" during the day and at night pouring that many cans of water down the offenders' sleeves. Like others of his middling status, he knew well the wasteful and foolish elitism of gentry and aristocrats. Transplanted to Virginia, that elitism soured from foolish to fatal, and the stories Smith and others spread about it back in Old England reinforced the middling sorts' frustration toward the aristocracy. Smith, for one, relished satirizing the famed and once influential Sir Walter Raleigh and other elites for foolishly searching for gold, both under Virginia's turf and in Spanish ships, instead of recognizing the riches in American waters and soil – fish, timber, and corn, to name a few.[50] Because too many of Virginia's first English colonizers, and all of Jamestown's original leaders, resembled Raleigh more than Smith in their origins, ambitions, and practice, Smith could not rely on a work ethic and had to enforce toil.

Winthrop and Smith were certain that work would suffice to build a colony, but Englishmen in Jamestown starved in its early years. The question for four centuries has been how could grown men choose death over planting edible crops and foraging? Standard lore has condemned those men as cavaliers who crossed the Atlantic to find easy fortunes and then refused to degrade themselves doing the work of peasants or laborers. John Smith was quite sure of this explanation, especially because he was able to enforce work for a time, during which the colony fared reasonably well. In his 1624 *Generall Historie*, Smith asserted that the renewed famine after his departure resulted from "want of providence, industrie and government," all of which his leadership had previously provided. Smith and other witnesses described much wasted time looking for gold and demanding Native compliance. Yet should not hunger have motivated diligence quickly enough? Smith was perplexed: "I know not what punishment could be greater than that they indured."[51]

Modern knowledge about malnutrition, hopelessness, and isolation yields insights into that enigma, as do comparisons of Jamestown malingerers with victims of concentration camps and prisoner of war camps. The symptoms of beriberi, scurvy, and pellagra look very much like symptoms of laziness and poor character: weakness, lethargy, anorexia, leg cramps, irritability, despair, and, especially, apathy.[52] Whether or not the starving colonists were malingerers or suffering from desolation and malnutrition, their behavior has mostly attracted a mix of scorn and bewilderment – and further praise for work.

Smith and Puritan leader John Winthrop agreed about the value of work and the evil of idleness and how those principles correlated with social status. Winthrop sought out Smith's colonizing expertise before he set sail to New England in 1630. Like Winthrop, Smith saw the possibilities for building a thriving colony of freeholders, of families, of men with skills and purpose, each one desirous to prosper, to "be master of his owne labour and land."[53] Both Smith and Winthrop had countered objections against starting a New England colony, pointing out, as Winthrop put it, that "None of the former [colonies] susteyned any great damage, but Virginia, which happened there through their owne sloth & securitie." Although Smith did not attribute the failure to the fact that "their main end was Carnall & not Religious," as the Puritans declared, he agreed with their conclusion that the Virginia ventures relied on "unfitt instruments a multitude of rude & misgoverned persons, the very scumme of the people." Later, Winthrop explicitly discouraged aristocrats who expressed interest in joining the Massachusetts Bay Colony, forewarning them that their rank would not automatically entitle them to leisure or positions of authority. He knew not to expect those aristocrats to work on behalf of common interests. Smith admired the "noble Governour," who immediately set the standard in Boston by working "with his owne hands," reinforcing his spiritual and civic leadership in pursuit of the communal good. Winthrop's example made it clear that work was not only necessary but suitable for all residents.[54]

Idleness resides in the eyes of the beholder. When land-hungry English colonizers turned their gaze to indigenous people, they were already accustomed to condemning both the poor and the idle rich. They, therefore, found it easy to condemn as idle the people of a culture so alien that it could not fit into their understandings. Native Americans lived on their lands in ways that did not look like work to Europeans, and their relatively simple material world looked like poverty. Confounding their English sensibilities, neither hunting, an elite sport in England, nor the agricultural labor that Native American women performed seemed appropriate as work and did not earn title to the land in their eyes. Moreover, Native American women's labor earned high levels of cultural authority among their own people but threatened colonists' notions of patriarchy. Only rare observers, such as Thomas Morton, recognized the proficiency with which "the Salvages" supplied themselves with "all manner of needefull things for the maintenance of life and lifelyhood." He noted in 1632 that, instead of admiring an effective lifestyle amid natural abundance, most English colonists considered Native Americans to be "like our Beggers in England," that is, apparently idle. This fundamentally misguided perception and judgment of indigenous practices, in turn, became a weapon to justify expropriating Native lands and resources in the name of improvement.[55] That ideology evolved in response to what its creators experienced in the New World and what they wanted from it.

A calling to "improve" coveted land moved ethical mountains. Aristocrats had used similar, secular claims to "improve" lands when they enclosed England's commons and when the English seized land from Catholics in Ireland.[56] A keen observer, but insensitive to other people's perspectives, John Smith indulged in what became Anglo-Americans' standard self-exculpatory rationalization for centuries of colonizing the continent, namely that North America was an empty land, a wilderness awaiting improvement, "were it manured and used accordingly." John Cotton phrased it more elegantly in 1630 as Massachusetts Bay Colony migrants prepared to depart for New England. His farewell sermon assured them that it was "a Principle of Nature, That in a vacant soyle, hee that taketh possession of it, and bestoweth culture and husbandry upon it, his Right it is." John Winthrop and colleagues similarly contended with profound cultural insensitivity: "That which lies common, and has never been replenished or subdued, is free to any that possess and improve it."[57] In other words, suitable work on the land is what validated claims to it.

Converting indigenous peoples to Christianity also ranked high among religion-based callings and among the standard justifications for European colonization, avowed by Spanish and Portuguese colonizers as well as their English competitors. However, what lasted for centuries instead – and the most relevant point for the myth of the self-made man – was the fixation on ethno-centric ideas of work and "idleness" as a pretext for expropriation and exploitation of people whose labor and gendered roles perplexed Euro-Americans.

In earlier centuries, wealth had been a great barrier to passing through the eye of the Christian needle, at least in principle. "Slime," some had called wealth's burden on the soul, and charity was the primary way to remove it. However, by the time Robert Keayne, John Smith, and other English women and men embarked to the New World, wealth and the ambition to acquire it no longer condemned souls – provided it was circumscribed and directed in particular ways. That is, done properly in service to God and country, as the Boston merchant Keayne learned when he violated that norm. The standard was changing when Europe broached the New World and all the ambition and opportunity it supported. By then, hopeless poverty signaled disgrace and was becoming the mark of the unvirtuous.[58] Poverty chokes hope, dignity, and opportunities to self-improvement, and at that time its spiritual and social burdens became heavier, too, as the poor were expected to take charge of making themselves socially respectable, or risk doom. The wealthy once also bore spiritual burdens, but at least they had their worldly comforts and power as consolation.

It's easy enough to understand why striving folks in the middling ranks of early modern Anglo-America would find poverty and the appearance of idleness among the hopeless or alien an easy way to judge others. Without failures, what would success mean? Without idlers or wastrels, who is worthy? Likewise, they used self-righteous claims of moral superiority relative to Native Americans and Africans to justify expropriation and enslavement. Why, though, devise a world view to attack the idle rich? They could instead strive to take their places, to aspire to the prestige and power of the wealthy who did not need to work. Oliver Cromwell might have eagerly sought the crown once it had no royal head on which to sit. John Smith might have felt less resentment about Walter Raleigh's stature and gloated less about his downfall. However, these hard-driving people came to their ambitions with feelings of resentment and even rage against those who had insulted them with haughtiness. How better, then, to justify their own ambitions to prevail over others above and below them than by making their own work a sacrament, a measure of godliness and worth? They could then attribute their growing stature and worldly powers to God's support. In the colonists' eyes, this self-righteousness justified their ambitions and goals, and their self-serving deeds.

THE WICKEDNESS OF SOCIAL MOBILITY AND THE BOUNDARIES OF COMMUNITY

Robert Keayne and John Smith rose impressively, as had Oliver Cromwell, but all three either denied or neglected to mention their "obscure origins," in Cromwell's phrase. Theirs was an era of new geographic mobility, and it was also an era of new social mobility, downward and upward. Unless that mobility could be attributed to a higher power, such as an earthly patron or God, it implied sins either of sloth or ambition and, thereby, invited spiritual and social condemnation. Popular stories balanced those considerations, too, such as a trove of popular, allegedly biographical tales about Richard Whittington, a merchant who had served as Mayor of London multiple times around 1400, funded many public projects, and left his fortune to a charity that still operates today. Although Whittington was born into a wealthy gentry family, ballads, theatre, and chapbooks that praised him from around 1600 told a different story, that of a poor country lad, "obscurely bred," who prospered by luck and by marrying the boss's daughter. Although the fictional protagonist worked diligently, his wealth came not from work but from supernatural interventions and luck.[59] This was a rags-to-riches story, to be sure, but not at all a self-made man story. All of these stories, however fictionalized, rewarded striving and self-improvement yet also grappled with tense ambivalence around the idea of mobility during this major cultural transition. In the New World where expropriated land was more available than labor, an abundance of opportunities for merchants, tradesmen, and free laborers overrode the legacy of medieval values that eschewed mobility and worldly ambition.

Reticence about social mobility and symbols of status reflected their potential for disruption. Sumptuary codes, for example, which have ancient and global roots, targeted those who aspired beyond their station in attire, food, carriage, sport, and housing, restricting who could wear such grand items as silk and velvet garments or silver and gold buckles and buttons. Unsurprisingly, the greatest number of sumptuary laws in England coincided with the political turmoil and economic disruptions of the sixteenth century that threatened elites' stature and sense of propriety. Those codes were models for attempts at regulating consumption in English North America, which peaked in the seventeenth century. Virginia showed little interest in constraining extravagance but enacted codes to maintain proper social ranks. Massachusetts authorities quickly targeted both extravagance and climbing to enact a 1619 law "Against Idleness, Gaming, Drunkenness and Excess in Apparel." In 1638, Boston's court expressed concern about a "great disorder" due to "following new fashions." Then, in 1651, as Boston's economy picked up again after a lull, income became a criterion for allowing gold or silver lace and buttons. The 1651 rules explicitly "declare[d] our utter detestation and dislike that men or women of mean condition, educations, and callings should take upon them the garb of gentlemen." Although the language of sumptuary codes was typically gender neutral, enforcement most aggressively challenged women's pretensions to mobility. For example, an unusual spate of persecutions in 1653 Massachusetts convicted fourteen women but only three men; of the four other people charged, three men were acquitted but only one woman.[60] Self-fashioning seemed especially dangerous when practiced by women, whether they displayed their husbands' ambitions or their own.

Nonetheless, before the end of the seventeenth century, mobility and its engine, ambition, were slowly losing their stigma in British America as material and cultural resources often rewarded those who heeded relentless calls to strive and improve. Sumptuary codes faded as quaint attempts to contain status seeking. Although many dedicated people, like Winthrop and Cotton, had hoped to lay down foundational principles for a godly New World, the commonwealth that they fashioned would soon stray from their early emphases on communal obligations and constraints. Winthrop had even tried to justify a stable inequality in the name of community solidarity because it would ensure that "every man might have need of others, and from hence they might be all knit more nearly together in the bond of brotherly affection." This perverse mechanism for building community would have left no room for mobility. In a few decades, the increasingly fruitful New World economy encouraged accepting wealth as a legitimate ambition, increasingly the "chiefest good" of labor, against Cotton's warnings.[61] But that evolution away from community didn't come easily, and it did not yet include the blasphemous, community-denying notion of self-making.

The legal, social, and religious constraints that Boston's founders tried to enforce did not halt ambition's lure, but they did set limits on acceptable behavior and directed ambition toward citizens' obligations while minimizing claims that the prosperous could make on the community.[62] As John Winthrop explained, "the care of the public must oversway all private respects." Not only was this God's will, but there were worldly consequences to violating that principle that resonate poignantly today: "for it is a true rule that particular estates cannot subsist in the ruin of the public." Robert Keayne understood this. He complained that his taxes were higher than those of his peers in London, but he also acknowledged that Boston and the Massachusetts Bay Colony needed to build and nurture in order to grow. John Smith had long argued for practical benefits when citizens linked their ambitions to their local and national communities. His last book turned to religion, as well, to call on his fellow English men and women to serve their country: "seeing wee are not borne for our selves but each to helpe other, ... seeing our good deeds or bad, by faith in Christs merits, is all wee have to carry our soules to heaven or hell." A profusion of sermons and jeremiads against the destructiveness of self-love and self-regard echoed Winthrop's hopes for centuries to come.[63]

The utopian vision of a loving and prosperous community that John Winthrop, John Cotton, and their congregants cherished for the Massachusetts Bay Colony had a profound dystopian flaw at its core. Limits on who qualified for community membership and its benefits blinded them to the worth and contributions of women and others marginalized because of origin, race, ethnicity, or faith. In addition to the seemingly idle at both ends of the wealth spectrum – the "undeserving poor" and the wasteful aristocracy – Christian heretics of all sorts could be cast out and even executed. The ancient "warning out" tradition showed another dark side of narrowly defined community obligations to care for the ill and indigent. From the first English towns in Massachusetts until the early nineteenth century, town authorities could notify newcomers, who were sometimes considered life-long outsiders, that they would receive no aid if they ran into difficulties.[64] Gender presented other limits, for although women could garner respect for appropriate work and piety, they were excluded from most governance and other privileges of male citizens, including control of property if married. And despite declarations of missionary goals, Native Americans and Africans were never fully accepted into Anglo-American communities, whether enslaved or not. Even if "heathens" converted and adopted European ways over the ensuing centuries, that never ensured their respect, property, or lives. Perhaps the most egregious of all expressions of limits on community was one of Winthrop's earliest arguments for expropriating Native American land: "God hath consumed the natives with a great plague in those parts, so as there be few inhabitants."[65] Such sanctimoniousness rode on Winthrop's genuine belief in God's purposeful benevolence toward his own chosen people, even if that meant devastation by disease, degradation, or violence of everyone else. The demanding bonds of a community so tightly circumscribed prevented recognition of a common humanity.[66]

Drawing the boundaries of community narrowly also limited the extent to which the work ethic could bestow rewards. Not all work is created equal, much less rewarded equally in a culture that so disrespects others and their cultures. Allegiance to the work ethos made labor a requirement for esteem, to be sure, but not at all sufficient for esteem. Cultural and political authorities valued workers and work differentially according to how closely the workers and work resembled them and their own work. People ineligible for favorable recognition along this measure have been, as many remain, confined to work as specters: they are essential but invisible. For instance, John Smith boasted that Pocahontas had saved his life, as had, allegedly, a Turkish princess before her. Yet, as typical in a patriarchy, neither Smith nor Keayne recognized the roles women played in making possible their day-to-day lives or their thoughts and pursuits. Nor did Keayne, again typically, acknowledge the benefits of marrying well as the means to advance worldly fortunes. Likewise, the enslaved, indentured, or otherwise constrained people who took care of life's most unpleasant tasks remained outside of the ranks of esteemed workers. Denying respect and opportunities to so many people by law or custom and then disparaging them as inherently incapable or as failures left a costly and devastating legacy. Eventually, their work made possible the illusion of others' self-making. At that time, cultural and political norms required that ambitious and accomplished men credit Providence and patrons for their successes. In later centuries, when they began to credit their own self-agency, the people whose work made their own work possible remained in the shadows.

Through this early period of Euro-American history, service to community and faith remained the highest priority that one could openly declare. Adventurers sought support by contending that the community and their patrons would benefit, even if they made those assurances disingenuously. Their stories highlighted obligations to act and serve their communities, country, and faith as their cultures required.[67]

Almost two centuries of rising comfort with worldly ambition and individualism had to pass before an ethos of self-making could begin to reverse the cultural order and bestow esteem on enterprising individuals freed from obligations. St. Augustine's aversion to acting on self-interest had dominated the medieval Church and its cultures, but his warning, "Try to build up yourself, and you build a ruin," had begun to lose its authority.[68]

2

Self-Improvement for the Common Good in the Eighteenth Century

How much do life and the afterlife depend on the heavens and how much on earthbound actions? Wrestling with that eternal mystery – which is, essentially, the mystery of human agency, itself a prerequisite to self-making – seventeenth- and eighteenth-century Euro-Americans patched together an array of cultures in which the idea of self-making could begin to take hold. Admitting to such a belief would have been heretical both spiritually and socially in the early years of English colonizing. Seventeenth-century adventurers like John Smith and Robert Keayne strived to control their purposes and actions, but could only pray for their fates. In those centuries, Europeans on both sides of the Atlantic grappled with cosmic and worldly questions, and as they did, they grew their faith in human agency, in their potential to influence their fates. They hewed paths toward self-agency, and along the way they forged new mindsets and stories about self-fashioning, ambition, the value of work, materialist consumption, and whether individuals or communities were the proper beneficiaries of improvement.

The new mindsets and the stories that reflected them evolved in the complicated, coupled contexts of the Old and New World. The storytellers' only constant was judgment, either in praise or condemnation of themselves or of others. The dominant cultural movements of the eighteenth century, the Enlightenment and the First Great Awakening, were both the context for and products of the growing legitimacy of human agency, although in very different ways. Therefore, examining that transition period can help us to understand the early stages of self-making's evolution. The processes and outcomes of the era's competitions for cultural authority were full of ambiguities and conflicts, but they all in one way or another converged around the core question of human agency, whether in spiritual or secular realms, that would later make it possible to imagine self-making.

ENLIGHTENMENT AND AWAKENING

In starkly different ways, the Enlightenment and the First Great Awakening challenged people to take responsibility for the outcomes of their lives and eternal souls and thereby broadened respect for self-agency. The people active in the era's Enlightenment believed that the physical, social, and political world operated by consistent and coherent laws that are discoverable through trial and observation. For them, self-improvement required a deliberate process of education, informal just as well as formal, that was centrally about the human capacity to discover, experiment, solve, and understand. Meanwhile, another type of self-improvement and agency engaged attention and passions across much broader and disparate swaths of the population. Multitudes participated in the religious revivals now known as the First Great Awakening that offered salvation and inflamed popular culture during the 1730s and into the 1750s. Despite their differences, participants in both approaches, Enlightenment or religious revival, advanced the cultural authority of human agency, self-improvement, and the goal of community betterment.[1] This consensus set the stage for the idealization of self-making.

By far, the most important point of agreement between the Enlightenment and the Great Awakening was the admonition that participants take responsibility for self-improvement of one kind or another. Participants in each moved toward heightened beliefs in individual responsibility, even if they did not yet defy providentialism – belief in God's ongoing engagement with the world and human experience. As complex movements that engaged tens of thousands of people, they appear more coherent looking back on them than they did at the time. (A century afterward, the eighteenth-century revivals became known as the "Great Awakening," and the "American Enlightenment" was named two centuries later.[2]) Neither had a single point of origin, nor did their participants pursue their goals in the same way. Even so, singly and together, they advanced the idea of individual improvement intended for the common good. They also fostered demands on individuals that began to forge the double-edged sword of worldly achievement as the measure of human worth, especially of White men. One edge would later encourage ambition and demand worldly success as the criterion of worth; the other would diminish non-material measures of esteem.

The profound differences between adherents of the Great Awakening and the Enlightenment correlated with differences in wealth and learning, and interactions between their participants typically took place across a robust class divide, such as that between servants and employers. Participants' demographics also contrasted strikingly. Whereas "the enlightened" resided in or communicated with metropolitan regions, revival attendees were everywhere, including frontier areas, such as western Massachusetts and Georgia. Revivalists were also vastly more diverse in status and ethnicity than their rationalist contemporaries. Revival preachers generally welcomed Native Americans and African Americans, both free and enslaved; and women's experiences were not dismissed as evidence of hysteria any more than men's.

Like Benjamin Franklin and his fellow Founders, most Enlightenment adherents assumed that God had created a world that operated in an orderly manner that humans could understand with enough effort and acumen. Although advocates often differed in what they thought about godly authority and power, they all agreed on reason as the standard for judging anything, including religion. In contrast, revivalists judged success through highly emotional conversions and "enthusiasm." In both approaches, "self-making" in our current sense of going it alone and succeeding alone remained an alien concept, even as they inched gradually in its direction. For one thing, dismissing Providence still endangered one's soul. Closer to the ground, everyone understood that everything about their lives depended on other people, including families, secular authorities, patrons, peers, and subordinates. Every adult understood, just as Oliver Cromwell, Robert Keayne, and John Smith had, that dismissing their debts to others was unrealistic and foolhardy. Reputation was an adult's most important asset, regardless of gender or status. Although people's sense of individual efficacy would grow over the century, individualism did not yet seem natural or proper. Nor was it reasonable to judge anyone by such a measure.[3] Genius and dedication only went so far in achieving or assessing fates. Benjamin Franklin, for one, always made known that his accomplishments took shape within social and professional networks, such as the Junto, a group that he founded in Philadelphia in 1727 to expand his intellectual, business, and social interactions.[4]

New World lands and resources enticed enterprising colonials, while witch trials, Native American resistance, soul-wrenching fears of damnation, lightning strikes, and epidemics terrified them. Surrounded by these experiences, stories of earth- and heaven-bound ambition and self-determined action could be positive in tone, although only – and this remained a major qualification – if framed in service to God or God's community. Revivalist preachers intended to frighten their audiences into humility before God's awesome power over them, but only as individuals could anyone escape that fear. This required a personal choice, not a community action, and serving God's glory in this way did not necessarily serve a community as it incrementally advanced individualism. Meanwhile, the enlightened sought to discover the laws of nature and society to satisfy curiosity and, they believed, to benefit the common good. Success in any of those efforts could also accrue cultural and political authority for them, as well as personal wealth and power. In these ways, each movement offered participants incentives that appealed to traditional values while they also edged toward individualist cultural innovations.

ON THE BRIDGE TOWARD HUMAN AGENCY

John Winthrop, Jr. (1606–1676) and Cotton Mather (1663–1728) were both secular and religious leaders in New England who developed beliefs about human agency that bridged their forefathers' perspectives and Enlightenment-era ideas. Son and namesake of the first Massachusetts governor, Winthrop founded English communities in Massachusetts and Connecticut and became the latter's first long-term governor. He believed that scientific and technological developments could serve community wellbeing, including economic growth. Unusually broadminded for his time regarding ethnicities and cultures, he negotiated in good faith with indigenous people and protected Quakers and others condemned by Massachusetts. Mather, John Cotton's grandson, carried on his family's Boston legacy of devotion, religious and political leadership, and intellectual productivity. But he also took a step toward individualist ambitions when, as we will see, he praised William Phips, an aggressively ambitious man of "obscure" origins. As Winthrop and Mather responded to inoculations, social mobility, ambition, and witch trials, they were cultural bridges, looking backward and forward.

Two stories of alchemy illustrate their changing contexts. The first is Christopher Marlowe's drama, *The Tragical History of Doctor Faustus*, which appeared at the end of the sixteenth century and was popular through the seventeenth. Well known to literate English-speakers of the Renaissance era like Winthrop and Mather, it contemplates the profound dangers faced by seekers of worldly knowledge. The opening chorus introduced Faustus as from "parents base of stock," and his overweening ambition and discontent ultimately struck him down, exposing a lingering medieval belief that striving for knowledge and power beyond one's station was treacherous and invited evil bargains. Rejecting pursuits in theology, medicine, and law as insufficient to satisfy his ambitions, he turned to sorcery. Although warned that the "God thou serv'st is thine own appetite," Faustus succumbed to the Evil Angel's call to "think of honour and wealth." In hubris and greed, he chose "Wealth!" Ambitions that stretched human knowledge in this pre-humanist view required occult assistance, and for that Dr. Faustus sacrificed his soul.[5]

In a contrasting story of alchemy, John Winthrop, Jr., was an acclaimed alchemist who was decidedly not a magician. Alchemy was harder work than magical conjuring and artifice because it required experimentation to find and manipulate materials through natural observation and trials, not pacts with nefarious beings. Even so, Winthrop believed that his arduous efforts could only succeed with God's blessing, and those blessings only flowed from serving God's people. He made a very different pact than the Faustian one, although it also paired the quest for knowledge with deference to spiritual authorities. Winthrop believed that God guided his efforts to master the natural world through study and action in service – a course of improvements that prepared for Christ's second coming. With support based on his international reputation as a skilled and knowledgeable chemist, Winthrop led the construction of iron works, mills, and mines, while aiding others as a highly regarded healer. Like other Puritans, he had nothing against economic gain so long as it honored God and improved God's communities. Winthrop's strategy was to combine colonization and a religious mission through mundane and profitable industrial projects such as salt extraction. Unlike Faustus, a lone wizard, Winthrop sought to build New London, Connecticut, as a haven for collaboration among like-minded humanists to advance practical knowledge of the natural world in fields as diverse as metallurgy, agriculture, and medicine. He was so esteemed that in 1661 the British Royal Society elected him as its first colonial member.[6]

The cultural foundations for human agency in the natural world were still tenuous. Therefore, although Winthrop and most other educated elites rejected magic, ordinary folks often attempted magic or consorted with spirits on smaller scales than Faustus, usually more out of desperation or revenge than hubris. Traditions such as divination and casting spells continued as attempts to reduce anxieties when people could not understand or control what afflicted them; everyone blended natural and supernatural explanations for health, luck, and troubles.[7] Superstitions could, therefore, disrupt communities, as when people explained their own misfortunes by accusing neighbors of wickedness and even of witchcraft.

During New England's episodic scares and witch trials, Winthrop and Mather exercised very different leadership, but both illustrated emergent, tenuous beliefs in human agency. The alchemist Winthrop, governor of Connecticut for all but one year from 1657 to 1676, insisted that to have legal standing, evidence of witchcraft had to be observed by at least two witnesses – a foundational standard for empirical science. Because the most dramatic and damning "evidence" at witch trials was "spectral" – that is, based on ethereal experiences such as ghostly sightings – a minimum requirement for two witnesses to testify about it alike almost entirely eliminated convictions. It's not that Winthrop and his peers rejected the possibility of satanic interference in human affairs, but, rather, that they required more reliable evidence. Under Winthrop's leadership, Connecticut went from being New England's most aggressive witch-prosecutor to its least. According to this worldview, supernatural forces still reigned, but people could judge between the good, evil, and illusory among those forces.[8]

Like John Winthrop, Jr., Cotton Mather was a prominent leader in colonial politics, religion, medicine, science, and witch trials, who also valued noble work on behalf of communities that could only succeed by grace: natural science worked through godly actions to yield "useful Inventions," whereas the devil relied on superstitions that impeded beneficial discoveries. Therefore, during Boston's 1721–1722 smallpox epidemic, Mather urged inoculation based on medical evidence from Africa and Europe. Not ready to deny otherworldly influences, however, he also turned to spiritual arguments to oppose medical authorities who were afraid to deny divine powers as the sole factor in illness. He countered the naysayers with accusations that they did the work of the "Destroyer" by not seeing that inoculations truly revealed God's grace. By 1723, Mather, too, earned a place in the Royal Society.[9]

In another arena, however, Cotton Mather's fears of the supernatural overwhelmed him, namely the tragic Salem witch trials of 1692–1693. He joined other prominent religious leaders, including his father, Increase Mather, to lend his imprimatur to the proceedings, which they interpreted as a necessary cleansing. Mather expressed the urgency of the crisis in *The Wonders of the Invisible World*, which he published in 1693 "to countermine the whole PLOT of the Devil, against *New-England*." In this account, "the Devil is *come down unto us with great Wrath*" attempting to drive Christians from the land through "things confessed by *Witches*, and the things endured by *Others*." So little control did people have over their lives, he believed, that witches or their "wicked *Spectres*" could "seize poor people about the Country, with various & bloudy *Torments*." Some victims even became "*Self-destroyers*." The only choice was to accept or reject diabolical temptations, so he urged "a speedy and thorough conversion to God." At least twenty-five people died from lawful prosecutions during that crisis, and more than two hundred were accused of demonic complicity, many despite their long-standing church loyalties. Engulfed by his fears, Mather could not take Winthrop's humanist path to trust humans' observations and their ability to gauge evidence.[10] Even so, as they tried to meet their communities' earthly and spiritual needs, these two New England leaders inched away from their fathers' fears and traditions and haltingly, differently, advanced ideas of human agency as the means to serve God and humanity.

CREATING A NEW WORLD HERO

In another realm of human agency and one that heralded the worldly myth of self-made success, Cotton Mather forged ahead more confidently and decisively, namely in his promotion of the New World as a land of unprecedented opportunities for Christian men with ambition, ability, and patriotism. He dramatically reassessed the merits of material ambition and success, proclaiming in 1697 that social and economic mobility could reward the deserving, but *only* in the New World.[11] Mather announced this revelation in *Pietas in Patriam: The Life of His*

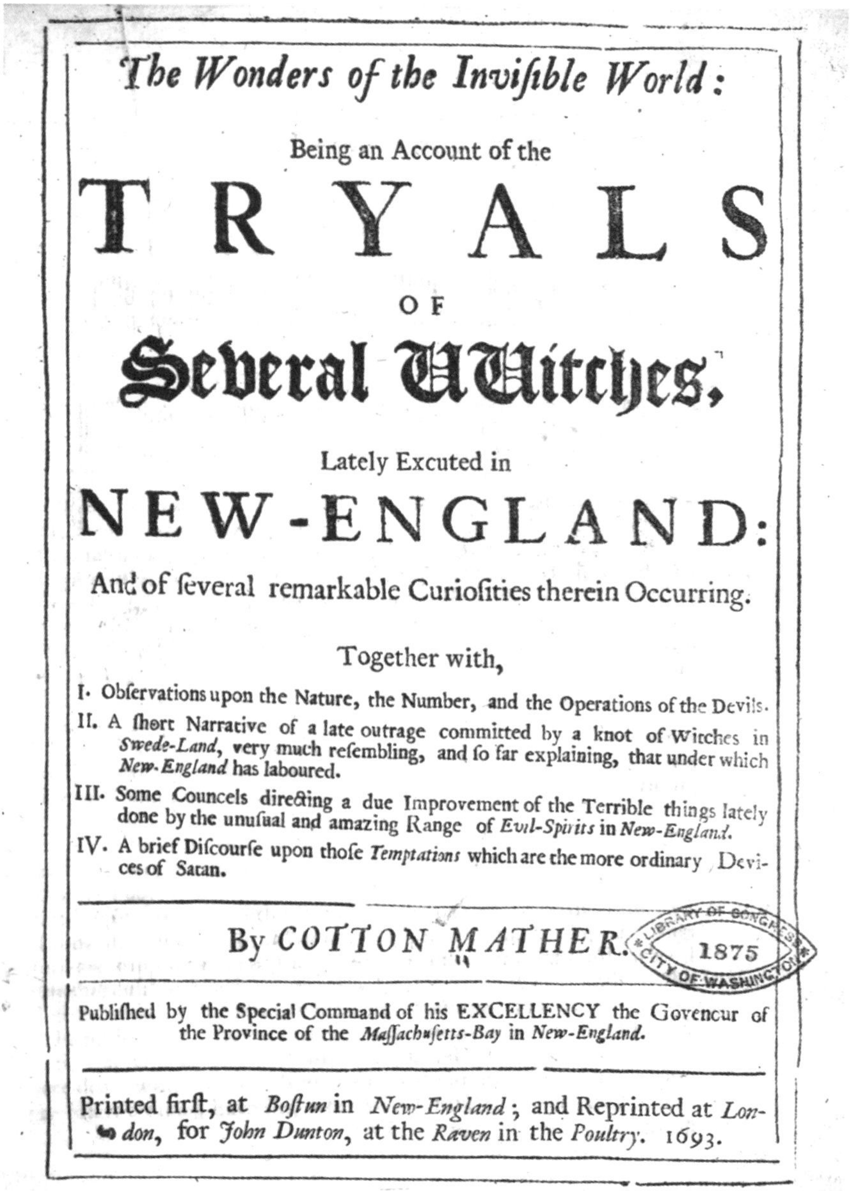

> *The Wonders of the Invisible World:*
>
> Being an Account of the
>
> # TRYALS
>
> OF
>
> # Several UUitches,
>
> Lately Excuted in
>
> # NEW-ENGLAND:
>
> And of several remarkable Curiosities therein Occurring.
>
> Together with,
>
> I. Observations upon the Nature, the Number, and the Operations of the Devils.
> II. A short Narrative of a late outrage committed by a knot of Witches in *Swede-Land*, very much resembling, and so far explaining, that under which *New-England* has laboured.
> III. Some Councels directing a due Improvement of the Terrible things lately done by the unusual and amazing Range of *Evil-Spirits* in *New-England*.
> IV. A brief Discourse upon those *Temptations* which are the more ordinary Devices of Satan.
>
> By COTTON MATHER.
>
> Published by the Special Command of his EXCELLENCY the Governeur of the Province of the *Massachusetts-Bay* in *New-England*.
>
> Printed first, at *Boston* in *New-England*; and Reprinted at *London*, for *John Dunton*, at the *Raven* in the *Poultry*. 1693.

Figure 2.1 "Self-making" is impossible to imagine unless people have self-agency. Cotton Mather, one of the most important Puritan leaders in New England during the late seventeenth and early eighteenth centuries, truly believed that both supernatural forces and human choices operated in the world. To his sorrow, he was, therefore, complicit in the executions of people in Salem who were convicted of succumbing to the devil's temptations, which he explains in this 1693 treatise on "the TRYALS of Several UUitches." (Photo by Library of Congress / Corbis / VCG via Getty Images)

Excellency Sir William Phips, Knt., a laudatory biography that he first published anonymously but then included in his 1702 magnum opus, *Magnalia Christi Americana, or, The History of New-England*.[12] In this story, Mather presaged future American partisans who reconciled individual agency with the common good by cloaking Phips's ambition in patriotism – the love of country pointed to in the title, *Pietas in Patriam*. Furthermore, he asserted, Phips triumphantly proved the New World's exceptional opportunities.

Born in 1651 on a "despicable plantation" in Maine, Phips's father was a poor gunsmith who died young. William herded sheep until he was eighteen, when, according to Mather, the "*providence* of God" inspired "further dispositions of mind." Phips's "unaccountable *impulse*" inspired him to leave Maine because, as he "would privately hint" to friends, he believed "*that he was born to greater matters.*" To pursue those greater matters, he made his way to Boston where he worked as a ship carpenter for a while and married well to become yet another wife-made man. His "enterprizing *genius*" and disdain for "*littleness*" then led to a variety of adventures that, aided by considerable luck, yielded a fortune in sunken Spanish treasure. Phips took this trove to King James II, who in 1687 rewarded him with a portion of the treasure, knighthood, and honors befitting a true Anglo-American patriot. He was appointed governor of Massachusetts, but after more military and political adventures, he acquired enough enemies to doom his career, especially among the well-born who disparaged him as an upstart. Undone by "*villanous libel*," the "*self-denying*" Phips died in 1695 while back in Old England to defend himself to the crown. Like Faustus and Icarus of legend, Phips had overreached. Mather mourned, "A PUBLICK SPIRIT'S GONE."[13]

Not just any stirring adventure story, Mather's tale of Phips's rise and fall was remarkable for its rejection of medieval social stasis in favor of the dynamism and energy of individual ambition that he hoped would build New England. John Winthrop, Sr., and John Cotton, Mather's grandfather, had wanted their communities to thrive, but to thrive *as* communities, even if that austere standard of a godly "city on a hill" was hard to attain and maintain while trying to prosper in a new colony, as Robert Keayne's troubles showed.[14] In contrast, *Pietas in Patriam* was a paean to New World opportunities that promoted a cultural innovation, adding worldly gain through individual agency as an indicator of moral superiority. Phips's story, as Mather told it, promoted the land of opportunity. There was no equivalent to Phips in either "the *archives* of antiquity" or "that [European] *hemisphere* of the world." Surprisingly, but in keeping with his ambitions for the New World, Mather featured as a second example none other than the Spanish conquistador Francisco Pizarro, who rose from poverty in Navarre to conquer Peru and thereby enrich himself and Spain, but whom the English typically reviled.[15] This intriguing inclusion in Mather's storytelling fortified his New

World boosterism for the low-born and ambitious. Later centuries invented the terms "American exceptionalism," "American Dream," and "self-made success," but the myths predated the phrases and typically reinforced each other, as we can see in Mather's volume.

Phips emerged from "obscure" origins, according to Mather, rising to fortune and power through boundless ambition, bravado, and good luck. "Reader," Mather insisted about Phips, "enquire no further who was his *father?* Thou shalt anon see, that he was ... *a son to his own labours!*" Mather also reported that Phips expressed pride in his "*low beginning* with as much freedom and frequency, as if he had been afraid of having it forgotten." Phips "would on all occasions *permit*, yea, *study* to have his *meannesses* remembered." Not too many decades before, John Smith, Robert Keayne, and Oliver Cromwell had either ignored or denied their "obscure" origins, and only their adversaries described them as upstarts, a term of derision rather than praise. But Mather praised Phips's rags-to-riches story and the determination that drove it. Despite the long Christian tradition of disparaging worldly ambitions, a tradition to which Mather otherwise contributed frequently, he praised as a genial, god-fearing patriot this hot-tempered and arrogant man whom others called a pirate and a rogue.[16] In other words, Mather and Phips himself were proud of this rise in the New World, impossible to find, so it seemed, in the Old World. Mather, thereby gave shape and voice to a narrative of American exceptionalism that paired the ethical and material rewards of ambition, while still adhering to the two essentials of the Puritan ethos: claims to community service and providential support.

Importantly, *Pietas in Patriam* was not the product of a dissident or a rebel against dogma, spirituality, elitism, nor against the qualities that Mather praised in "the second Winthrop" – those of a "*studious, humble, reserved* and *mortified* [that is, disciplined] person." Mather made clear that obscure origins did not ensure greatness because obscurity limited opportunities for ordinary people. But this caveat only underscored Phips's strengths: "*I never saw three men in this world that equalled him.*" Mather's unreserved tribute to Phips as "meritorious" and "an example of *heroick virtue*" seems a better fit now after centuries of bluster about self-making than it did then, hence his hesitancy to own it, publishing it anonymously at first.[17] Broadly extolling someone as rough, volatile, and nakedly ambitious as Phips risked encouraging others to drift away from properly balanced spiritual and worldly callings. Nonetheless, Mather was ambitious *for New England*, and he was grateful for Phips's service.

Tellingly, Mather's uses of the words "ambition" and "ambitious" in other works likewise chipped away its presumed sinfulness. A person could have a "laudable ambition," for instance.[18] In the 573 pages of *Magnalia Christi Americana*, there are only four instances of "ambition" or "ambitious," and all of them were positive.[19] Less brazenly than in his tribute to Phips, in the 1701 essay "A Christian at His Calling" Mather encouraged ambition in more traditional language: if a man follows his calling "with *Diligence* [he] may do marvellous things." Even a "poor man, that minds the *Business* of his Calling, and weaves a Threed of *Holines* into all his *Business*, may arrive to some of the highest Glories at the last." A degree of self-making and mobility, yes, but conditional: "When you follow your *Business*, have your DEPENDENCE on God, for the succeeding of it."[20] Given Mather's willingness to execute people convicted of witchcraft, and his need for spiritual argument on behalf of smallpox vaccinations, that he credited worldly success to providence was not merely a rhetorical gesture or an orthodox façade.

Justifying raw individual ambition in the name of God's cause and community advancement was the thin, leading edge for legitimating self-interest. It was all the more potent when that edge was sharpened by a prominent minister who presumed providential support for worldly success. Rather than worrying about arresting social mobility in this burgeoning New World, as his forebears had with their vestiges of medieval ethics, Cotton Mather envisioned new criteria for social stature that the ambitious and fortunate could achieve in the New World, moving away from age-old aristocracies of birth toward new hierarchies. To justify that shift and imbue ambition with cultural authority, service to the community remained Mather's top criterion. As he explained in 1701, "We are Beneficial to *Humane Society* by the Works of that Special OCCUPATION, in which we are to be emply'd, according to the Order of God."[21] If someone seemed to meet that measure of service, "obscure origins" should not preclude his rise. Few people anywhere, at any time, have met Mather's standard more spectacularly than Benjamin Franklin, the future patriot and model for self-fashioning whose life has inspired stories and misinterpretations for centuries.

SELF-IMPROVEMENT FOR THE COMMON GOOD

Before there was an American nation, the young Benjamin Franklin – a contemporary of the elderly Cotton Mather – epitomized many Enlightenment ideas, especially self-improvement as a process of rising and serving. As a teenager in 1722, Ben wrote a series of letters under the pen name of Mrs. Silence Dogood and slipped them under the door of *The New-England Courant*, his older brother James's Boston newspaper. It's hard to imagine even the wiliest sixteen-year-old boy successfully disguising himself as a middle-aged widow with three children. It's easy, though, to see the inspiration for the name: the Calvinist minister Cotton Mather, with whom James was then battling, had written *Bonifacius, or Essays to Do Good* in 1710 and *Silentarius* in 1721. James gladly published Ben's intriguing letters to boost lagging readership and, as a bonus, to poke at Mather, all the while not knowing that the author was his own apprentice. In these fourteen essays, the young Franklin displayed his budding wit and erudition and also foreshadowed his adult inclinations. Targets of his mockery included pretensions of all sorts, such as Harvard College, the "Temple of Learning" that produced "after Abundance of Trouble and Charge, as great Blockheads as ever, only more proud and self-conceited"; the use of "learned Languages, which will not only be fashionable, and pleasing to those who do not understand it, but will likewise be very ornamental"; and "*Pride of Apparel*" that undermines the solvency of "persons of small Fortune ... striving to appear rich [who] become really poor, and deprive themselves of that Pity and Charity which is due to the humble poor Man, who is made so more immediately by Providence."[22]

Although Ben's Mrs. Dogood scoffed and scolded aplenty, her voice also expressed principles that Franklin followed his entire life, including reading and patriotism. Although the youthful Franklin parodied Cotton Mather's titles, his content actually reflected much in the preacher's *Essays to Do Good*, but without the heavy hand of religious exhortations. Fittingly, at the other end of Franklin's life, in a 1779 letter to Cotton Mather's son, Samuel, he praised *Essays to Do Good*, which "gave me such a turn of thinking, as to have an influence on my conduct through life; for I have always set a greater value on the character of a doer of good, than any other kind of reputation." Franklin concluded that "if I have been, as you seem to think, a useful citizen, the public owes the advantage of it to that book."[23] This generosity overstated the debt: had the young Ben not been so inclined, he would not have taken to heart the preacher's calls to service.

Long after Franklin retired Mrs. Dogood, his principles on the value of communal efforts held remarkably consistent, a testament to his youthful insights and thoughtfulness. Later, Franklin even credited Mather's *Essays* for inspiring the Junto, the study and debating society he organized in 1727 in Philadelphia as a young man and that was a precursor to the American Philosophical Society. His early goal to do good, to be a "*Doer*," moved the young Ben to purchase as his own "first Collection" of books *The Pilgrim's Progress* as part of "John Bunyan's Works in separate little Volumes." Therein, the seventeenth-century Puritan preacher explained that the "Soul of Religion is the Practick [practical] part," and at the "end of the world" only actions are the "Fruit" by which souls will be judged.[24] This "Practick part" encapsulated Franklin's lifelong calling.

THE ENLIGHTENMENT AND RODS OF IRON

Dreams of celestial beings and their powers have animated human fantasies as far back as we can tell, and how various eighteenth-century Americans thought about lightning, the heavens' most dreaded force, says a lot about the different ways that they balanced, or reconciled, human and celestial agency. Benjamin Franklin's Enlightenment-era approach to studying electricity, his development of the lightning rod out of those studies, and others' reactions to it highlight some of those different ways of weighing natural and supernatural dangers. Most relevant for our purposes, they show how self-improvement and the resulting esteem could benefit both individuals and the common good. Thus, the people we most remember from that century, such as Benjamin Franklin, George Washington, Thomas Jefferson, and Tom Paine, prized self-improvement, collective knowledge, and dedication to community.

Franklin's initial goal in studying electricity was not to invent a lightning rod. Instead, he followed his perpetual curiosity at a time and in a social context that was eager to explore the natural world and to share and apply what they learned. It wasn't that he abided by Enlightenment principles laid down by others; he profoundly embodied the underlying inquisitiveness and priority on advancing the human condition. Despite popular fantasies then and still of the isolated mad scientist or inventor like Faustus or Dr. Frankenstein, science and invention are social processes, as Winthrop knew, well. This reality put to good use Franklin's life-long practice of forming networks, such as the Junto, and nurturing them in social settings or by extensive correspondence. Accordingly, his first exposure to the allure of electrical sparks was in 1743 at a social gathering, a demonstration in Boston by Archibald Spencer (1698–1760), an itinerant lecturer. This was five years before Franklin retired to pursue his non-business ambitions, but he was so intrigued that he soon brought Spencer to Philadelphia for public demonstrations and then bought Spencer's equipment. Conducting trials with his Junto colleagues and corresponding extensively across the Atlantic, he quickly learned what he could about "electrical fire" and also acquired more equipment in order to expand that knowledge. Although European scholars did not always appreciate Franklin's endeavors, some doubting that a mere "Colonial" could be so clever, increasing numbers of highly respected people like Londoner Peter Collinson (1694–1768) admired his creative experiments and thoughtful ruminations about their possible significance. A Fellow of the Royal Society, Collinson shared Franklin's excitement, and the two corresponded at length, Collinson serving as a conduit between Franklin's team of Philadelphian enthusiasts and the Royal Society's elites.[25]

Franklin sent Collinson and others long reports of experiments and observations, often concerned that he and his Philadelphia colleagues had not yet yielded anything practical. They kept at it, though, with dozens of experiments and detailed observations, including number 18, creation of "what we call'd an *Electrical Battery*." Philadelphia's experimenters could not find much use for this

Figure 2.2 This 1763 portrait of Benjamin Franklin as a thoughtful Enlightenment-era scientist includes vignettes that show his lightning rod protecting a building while unprotected buildings are damaged. Committed to public service, he made this and other inventions freely available. Franklin's broad correspondence, which the artist Edward Fisher features here, contributed to knowledge of natural laws on both sides of the Atlantic. (Courtesy of National Portrait Gallery, Smithsonian Institution NPG.70.66)

device, however, and Franklin closed the letter "Chagrin'd a little that We have hitherto been able to discover Nothing in this Way of Use to Mankind." To console themselves "humorously in a Party of Pleasure," they planned to kill and cook a "Turky" with the aid of various electrical devices.[26] Social merriment is always "of Use to Mankind" when it enriches solidarity within a community of practice.

In July 1750, Franklin sent Collinson a manuscript detailing thirty-seven experiments and their results, along with the insights and questions they raised. Uncertain of the significance of all this, but mindful of the ethics of work, his cover letter assured Collinson that "if no valuable Discoveries are made by us, whatever may be the Cause, it is not a Want of Industry and Application." Among the Philadelphians' observations were the striking similarities between the electricity they generated on a small scale and lightning bolts on a colossal scale: the discharges' crooked shapes, smells, color, ability to melt metals, and – most important for imagining the lightning rod – conductivity. From those observations, Franklin speculated that drawing lightning to a conducting object would prove the identity of the heavens' "electrical fire" and render it harmless, as well. "If the Fire of Electricity, and that of Lightning, be the same" then "may not the Knowledge of this Power of Points [to attract electricity] be of Use to Mankind; in preserving Houses, Churches, Ships &c. from the Stroke of Lightning"? He then proposed mounting grounded "Rods of Iron" on buildings in order to "draw the Electrical Fire silently out of a Cloud before it came nigh enough to strike, and thereby secure us from that most sudden and terrible Mischief!"[27]

Franklin was not self-sacrificing. He didn't need to make money from the "Franklin rod" either for a livelihood or for scorekeeping. Instead, he earnestly aspired to recognition for his leadership in science, especially electrical science, and, like modern scientists, he sought this as part of a collective effort on behalf of a collective benefit rather than his alone. Ebenezer Kinnersley (1711–1778), for instance, was one of Franklin's main collaborators in experiments and deliberations. Some critics charged that Franklin did not give Kinnersley adequate credit, but Kinnersley himself refuted that both privately and publicly. Moreover, Franklin listed his colleagues and their specific activities in later editions of his book, *Experiments and Observations*, which is now standard practice.[28]

Franklin also continuously shared his speculations about electricity and lightning, and everything else, with many others before he took the time from his business duties in June 1752 for what became his iconic kite-in-the-rain experiment. His French admirers tested his theories that lightning is electrical discharge from clouds in May of 1752, before he did, using an experiment of his design but more complicated than he thought he could manage. Because of the glacial pace of transatlantic correspondence, however, he hadn't heard of their success until after his own experiment that June. Even then, he didn't invite a neutral witness to document the event; only his son William (1730–1813) was present to assist. As he concluded another long paper of observations and speculations to Collinson in 1753, "if I were merely ambitious of acquiring some Reputation in Philosophy, I ought to keep them by me, 'till corrected and improved by Time and farther Experience. But," he noted, perhaps alluding to the broad benefits of having shared his speculations on lightning previously, "since even short Hints, and imperfect Experiments in any new Branch of Science, being communicated, have oftentimes a good Effect, in exciting the attention of the Ingenious to the Subject, and so becoming the Occasion of more exact disquisitions (as I before observed) and more compleat Discoveries." Franklin signed off saying that Collinson was "at Liberty to communicate this Paper" to whom he please. Franklin was content that it was "of more Importance that Knowledge should increase, than that your Friend should be thought an accurate Philosopher."[29]

The "Rods of Iron" soon vindicated Franklin's persistence many times over. The descriptions that Franklin shared with Collinson were published in England and Europe where they inspired more experiments and applications. However, elite journals and sophisticated pamphlets could not reach the wide American audiences Franklin reached every year with his almanac. The 1753 edition of *Poor Richard improved* was in press by October 1752, and Franklin described in detail "*How to secure Houses, &c. from* LIGHTNING." Tens of thousands in his audiences learned how to install these "Rods," through straightforward, easily shared, and easily followed instructions.[30]

Public demonstrations could also educate the public and expand appreciation for the wonders and benefits of exploring God's orderly nature. Therefore, although Franklin had worried that his experiments too much resembled showmen's tricks like Archibald Spencer's, he did not dismiss showmanship per se. He encouraged and aided his "ingenious Neighbor" and collaborator Ebenezer Kinnersley to travel around the colonies, attracting and educating audiences with displays of electrical fire. Franklin drafted Kinnersley's lectures, helped to design his demonstrations, and provided start-up costs for "elegant Apparatus, in which all the little Machines that I had roughly made for myself, were nicely form'd by Instrument-makers." Through both of these public channels, lightning rods spread quickly throughout the British colonies, faster than in Britain itself.[31]

Benjamin Franklin knew all too well the tolls of superstitions. The Salem witch trials of 1692–1693 preceded his birth by just over a decade, and one of his mother's sisters accused a victim who was subsequently executed. Growing up fifteen miles away in Boston, he was not far removed in time or space or family from this disaster in which troubled people profoundly doubted the human capacity to assess or withstand the threat of satanic powers. Franklin had other connections with that tragedy, too. His father attended South Boston Church where Samuel Sewall, one of the condemning judges, later repented of his decisions.[32] It's easy to see why Franklin joined many of his era in urging religious tolerance and the separation of church and state in the law. He and they sought to balance an understanding of what human agency could do and know in a world where providential laws operated in an orderly and discoverable way, befitting a Supreme Being that judged human beings according to their service to the common good. Like Franklin and his faith in the value of the lightning rod, "the enlightened" could have confidence in the value of their efforts, they believed, if *other* people were generally better off because of them.

The lightning rod, with other puzzles and inventions, challenged eighteenth-century Euro-Americans to sort out the balance between providential causes and human agency. The article in *Poor Richard improved* that introduced the "Iron Rod" to the American public began: "It had pleased God in his Goodness to Mankind, at length to discover to them the Means of securing their Habitations and other Buildings from Mischief by Thunder and Lightning."[33]

This deference to providential purposes, however, did not ensure acceptance among the many who feared defying God's power to act in anger through lightning and scourges. In America and Europe alike, many worried that hubris about human efficacy, for example by using smallpox inoculations or lightning rods, risked God's wrath. This seemed a reasonable concern to many people who were not ready to trust that God intended human intelligence to observe and control nature as the best way to improve the human condition. Gradually, experience showed that lightning rods saved lives, ships, and buildings, especially houses of worship with their tall steeples. Fears turned to appreciation for the devices' benefits as evidence themselves of providential grace. Ebenezer Kinnersley had been an itinerant Baptist minister before he joined with Franklin to collaborate on experimenting and disseminating electrical wonders. He knew well the obstacles to persuading frightened believers that God's creation was orderly: he had already failed at convincing congregations of the Enlightenment's vision.[34]

REVIVALS AND SPIRITUAL AGENCY

The Great Awakening emerged out of early eighteenth-century cultural concerns across a broad spectrum of people from Georgia to New England, across Protestant sects, across race and gender, across free and enslaved, across devout practitioners and people who didn't own a Bible. It was no coincidence that a religious revival movement fostering strong emotional "enthusiasms" coincided with the Enlightenment's pursuit of rationality: each confronted in its own way traditional restrictions on thinking about human agency. One sought observation-based knowledge and mastery in the material realm; the other sought faith-based revelation and mastery in the spiritual realm. As religious revivals flourished, they reinforced trends toward self-agency and shaped an incipient model of self-making that advanced individualism, which troubled some and empowered others. The transatlantic revivals spread the fire of individualist salvation with the lure that believers could be "reborn" through a personal conversion experience and thereby gain some degree of influence over their souls' fates. In this paradigm, only individuals could choose conversion, offering up their own souls but no others' – except possibly, and indirectly, by example. Their fervor spoke to social tensions and worldly hopes, especially concerns about salvation amid the temptations of rising materialism, social and geographic mobility, expanding towns, public improprieties like drunkenness, declining dedication to older religious rigors – all concerns that evangelists energetically amplified.[35]

A terrifying pestilence between 1735 and 1740 trapped New England towns in a crisis and exposed the practical limitations of reason. Despair and appeal to the supernatural seemed the only possible responses to the swift and devastating mortality of a diphtheria epidemic whose toll, especially on children, destroyed so many families. No methods of prevention or treatment or inoculations staved off death. Short of magic, only preparation for eternity and submission to an omnipotent God seemed to offer any comfort for the bereaved and frightened. Attempting to avert despair in the absence of natural explanations or remedies, local ministers stepped in. They offered rebirth in faith – an emotional catharsis – as a way to elect peace with God and to accept his authority. They gave believers a chance to exercise agency over their souls when it seemed no one could affect anything else that mattered. The price was surrendering themselves to faith through an emotionally wrenching conversion experience. In that raging epidemic, the alternative was to "be left to die in Horror and Despair," as minister John Brown of Haverhill, Massachusetts, decreed in 1738 during local revivals. Salvation was, as always, subject to God's grace, but individuals could choose between certain turmoil and damnation or the possibility of peace on earth and beyond.[36] Contemplating a spiritual rebirth was not a simple appeal to a supernatural power. It required a choice – a choice to assert agency over the fate of one's soul.

A horrible epidemic can prime preachers' audiences to consider desperate spiritual measures, but, short of that, revival preachers must inspire despair in their audiences with hellfire and brimstone drama. While some people attended revivals in earnest to save their souls, others attended primarily for the entertainment and social value of the large gatherings and lively preaching. Preachers had to persuade *all* of their listeners, regardless of their reasons for attending, to fear eternal damnation, and to offer a path, a hope for salvation through a personal choice. The most skilled revival preachers provoked fear while also offering relief through the possibility of conversion and salvation. One such preacher with a deep Calvinist pedigree was Jonathan Edwards (1703–1758), the era's most important theologian, who in 1733 and 1734 led forceful revivals in Northampton, Massachusetts. For a guest sermon in Connecticut in 1741, he composed the most well known of the era's fear-evoking sermons, "Sinners in the Hands of an Angry God." Although its imagery of the "God that holds you over the pit of hell, much as one holds a spider, or some loathsome insect, over the fire, abhors you, and is dreadfully provoked" became a classic among hellfire and brimstone sermons, his delivery was always quiet and deliberate. Most of his sermons were gentle. When the power of his words elicited cries of spiritual torment, he asked for quiet, unlike preachers who relished and encouraged "enthusiasm." Whatever their styles, revival preachers all measured their successes by rebirth conversions, especially conversions that endured and improved behavior.[37]

Whether preachers depicted a kind God or a wrathful one, their revivals raised the cultural authority of spiritual agency and moved toward the possibility of self-making. All preaching emphasized personal choice as the best chance for salvation, but this was new. Original-edition Calvinists had not envisioned any way to affect spiritual fates, only a hope of gauging God's favor as measured by success in earthly activities. Latter-day Calvinists, and revivalists in general, tempered that, as did Edwards, by indicating that an all-powerful God *might* have mercy, but only for those who were "born again, and made new creatures." Any who "remain in an unregenerate state" would be "*left behind*" to be "swallowed up in everlasting destruction." If the hopeful acted immediately, "this is a day of mercy; you may cry now with some encouragement of obtaining mercy: but when once the day of mercy is past," Edwards warned, "you will be wholly lost and thrown away of God, as to any regard to your welfare."[38]

For many but certainly not all contemporaries, the American revivals of the 1730s through the 1760s proved a remarkable "work of God," explicable only as a "pouring out of the Spirit of God," in Edwards's words.[39] Yet these outpourings coincided with secular beliefs about human agency in the natural world that Enlightenment circles advocated expanding. The revivals also coincided with, and encouraged, an emergent consumer culture in a growing economy that was already fueling ambitions and individualist approaches to pursuing them. Choices proliferated around apparel, food and drink, eating and drinking utensils, and domestic furnishings; only the poorest and the unfree, whether indentured or enslaved, could not indulge in some discretion around taste.[40] The revivalists themselves promoted printed materials from pictures to pamphlets and sometimes books, and the social gatherings implicitly invited attendees' most fashionable displays. The revivalists' thorny mixed messages about individual choice and God's omnipotence allowed preachers and their audiences to cling to long-standing traditions of God's power in a transitional pact that gave the revivals their force.

Within this pact, adults bore responsibility to choose their moral paths, to be what Jonathan Edwards labeled "moral Agents." Unlike "meer Machines in Affairs of Morality and Religion," people possess "Moral Agency," that is, "the Power of Volition or Choice." In contrast, the "brute creatures are not moral Agents"; they "don't act from Choice guided by Understanding, or with a Capacity of reasoning and reflecting, but only from Instinct," and, therefore, "their Actions are not properly sinful or vertuous." Instead, a person's "Liberty and Agency ... to act according to his Choice, and do what he pleases" makes him or her "capable of moral Habits and moral Acts." People possess "a Power of chusing."[41]

SPIRITUAL CHOICES AND MATERIAL AGENCY

Jonathan Edwards and other Calvinists fought a rearguard action against the rising acceptance of material ambition and self-making fostered by the New World's growing opportunities for free men to exercise individual agency in worldly and spiritual affairs. The proxy arena for that broad competition for cultural authority was Christianity's perpetual question: how can humans possess free will in a universe governed by an omnipotent God? Yet, without free will, it is meaningless to think about – or judge – sin. By the eighteenth century, original-edition Calvinists' assertion of predestination, that humans could do nothing to influence God's preemptive judgments, was weakening, as was church membership. Edwards's own first parish, which he had inherited from his grandfather, turned him out. Appealing to listeners' fears of their personal damnation may have been the only sure tool to recruit converts, but urging a personal conversion encouraged the very individualism that Edwards and his fellows loathed.[42] As the New World's geographical and occupational frontiers expanded, it beckoned free men and even some free women to imagine and follow new ambitions. To tell people that their actions could not prevent damnation, and that even their faith might not suffice, became increasingly hard to sell in that cultural marketplace. Spiritual passivity declined in cultural authority as a more pragmatic emphasis on worldly action grew.

As material and spiritual choices expanded for most White males during the eighteenth century, revivals offered choices about salvation to those who had fewer or no other choices: enslaved people, indentured servants, Native Americans, and women, including married women who were constrained by the laws and customs of coverture by which their husbands "covered" their rights and property. Preaching in this mix, most revivalists were eager to save souls of all sorts, unfree and free, female and male, poor and rich. They reached out to people of all educational and religious backgrounds, including indentured servants, enslaved African Americans, and dispossessed Native Americans, promising the blessings of a Jesus who cherished everyone, including the downtrodden. Regardless of identity and cultural background, all who accepted any part of the revivalists' messages blended those into their own belief systems and practices. For example, among the Narragansett Indians in southern New England, conversion could bring self-respect and collective respect to people from whom most everything else, including dignity, had been ripped. In yet other areas, Native American exposure to Christian revivalism nurtured indigenous spirituality by inspiring connections between spiritual and earthly wellbeing. In other instances, Native Americans harnessed this new spiritual empowerment to defy assimilation into the culture of aliens who had so devastated their heritage.[43] Out of all these reactions to revivalist messages some patterns emerged, notably the appeal of a salvation that did not require wealth, power, or even personal freedom from bondage – an inner salvation that was not subject to secular authority or judgment. A choice, and a form of agency and self-making, for everyone.

A soul is a believer's most precious possession. For some, it may be their only sure possession, and the opportunity to influence its fate may constitute the extent of their freedom. Many eighteenth-century revivalists welcomed enslaved people, offering salvation as their one shining possibility, but White evangelicals did not typically encourage any other sort of freedom, generally accepting slavery within a hierarchy approved in scripture and that required obedience. George Whitefield, for example, was one of the Awakening's most widely traveled preachers on both sides of the Atlantic. He and most other Great Awakening preachers eagerly sought to guide enslaved people to spiritual grace. Abusive enslavers, especially those who kept evangelical preachers away, they warned, would suffer punishments both spiritual and worldly. Like too many others, however, Whitefield blamed individual enslavers' failings, not the system, for these evils.

Despite the limits of its promises and enslavers' growing resistance, African Americans around the colonies pursued the spiritual agency that evangelicals offered. In seeking some influence in their fates, they also relished opportunities to learn to read from evangelists and in the schools some evangelists built because literacy was a tool for achieving grace and self-agency. Some were even able to follow their desires to write, most famously Phillis Wheatley (d. 1784), the brilliant

Figure 2.3 George Whitefield often preached outdoors to reach large audiences, as in this 1754 depiction. Like other First Great Awakening preachers, he urged listeners to choose dedication to God, thereby endorsing their spiritual agency. In this way and in parallel with the Enlightenment, the Great Awakening advanced the cultural authority of self-agency. (Photo by Universal History Archive via Getty Images)

Boston poet whose works included a 1770 elegy to Whitefield that began "Hail, happy saint! on thine immortal throne." Other African Americans taught and preached, although constraints against literacy and preaching increased apace with enslavers' concerns about uprisings. The spiritual freedom to choose salvation, they feared, risked infecting enslaved people with notions of earthly rights and aspirations to worldly agency.[44]

With anxious mistrust about encouraging agency among the marginalized, contemporaries who disapproved of the revivals often dismissed them as filled with women and their histrionics, along with those of other lowly folks, despite numerical evidence about sizable White male attendance. Such dismissals presumed that vigorous female participation discredited any public event or process. A leader among Boston Puritans and heir to generations of ministers and merchants, Charles Chauncy (1705–1787) proclaimed his opposition to the Great Awakening in his 1742 sermon "Enthusiasm described and caution'd against." In particular, he built on scripture to express his distress that women in revivals were not properly passive. "*Let your* WOMEN *keep silence in the churches*," he demanded, "*for it is not permitted to them to speak – It is a shame for* WOMEN *to speak in the church.*" Disturbing the "*just decorum*" of a proper church through "confusion and noise" violated God's commandments. Whether by men or women, such "extravagant conduct" revealed "proud imaginations" such as "men pretending to be under his extraordinary guidance and direction" to experience the "veryest fancies, the vainest imaginations, the strongest delusions." Yet those very extravagances attracted and converted more men than women, reversing gender ratios common at the time in mainstream congregations. The more dramatic the preaching and the more dire its threats of damnation, the more it persuaded male converts.[45] The typical formal lectures that characterized early eighteenth-century sermons in traditional congregations had offered parishioners few emotional challenges, except to stay awake.

The emergent individualism of Great Awakening revivals seems paradoxical because it unfolded in highly social settings and yet called for private, not collective action. Individual souls among the crowds could try to save themselves, but that would save no others. In contrast to this innovative approach to saving souls, the Reverend Chauncy insisted that salvation "does not lie in *sudden impulses* and *impressions*." Chauncy worried that "private revelations" would overtake "publick ones" that were, he thought, properly based on elites' interpretations of scripture. Yet, much of the revivals' appeals lay precisely in bypassing these elite channels, reaching out to audiences that were often marginally literate or altogether illiterate, putting all listeners on their own as spiritual beings and imbuing them with their own spiritual agency.[46]

Cotton Mather blamed profane apathy for the decades-long decline of White males' participation in traditional congregations, whereas revivals energized the apathetic of all sorts by igniting fears and calling for courage. A spiritual choice could empower women despite their constrained legal and cultural options. This was true for other marginalized or unfree people as well. For many, these gateway experiments with their own spiritual agency contributed to a growing and more expansive sense of universal responsibility for their own salvation. Looking at Chauncy's haughty and disagreeable admonitions from another angle, however, we can see that they struck a profound and foreboding note. "Private revelations" and individualized choices would increasingly leave "publick ones" behind, in some ways for better, but also with a loss of shared goals and processes.

AN UPSTART NATION – LOOKING AHEAD

As Americans of the eighteenth century participated to various degrees in sources of cultural excitement – the Great Awakening, the Enlightenment, and the beginnings of a materialist consumer culture – their regard for individual goals, choices, and agency expanded. These diverse experiences advanced the cultural authority of ideals about individuals' opportunities and, importantly, resistance to elites and institutions that tried to restrict those opportunities. In different ways, these cultural innovations soon drew together many otherwise disconnected and usually not likeminded colonists to a common goal of revolt and liberty. In turn, angry protests about citizenship rights in the 1760s and 1770s boosted the legitimacy of personal self-determination and self-interest. Experimentation with new ideas about governance reinforced new ideas about pursuing economic opportunities. The complicated causal connections between the War for Independence on the one hand and these clusters of cultural changes on the other have inspired an abundance of compelling, if sometimes discordant, analyses. Rather than untangle the many causes and effects of such important historical processes, we can appreciate how they interact with each other, sometimes reinforcing, sometimes impeding each other.[47]

In that tangle of historical strands, we can see that as these trends fostered self-agency and individualist ambitions, they contributed to a growing resistance to the centuries-long cultural and political sway of birthright aristocracies. As we have seen, these legacy elites had long used the scornful label "upstart" to deride people who presumed to pursue worldly ambitions beyond their assigned stations. That label served as a tool of social control to preserve elites' stations and benefits. However, as Englishmen pursued their fortunes in the New World, *work* acquired cultural authority as a succinct retort to birthright and a measure of merit. In the New World, human agency – spiritual through revivals, secular through Enlightenment, and material through economic opportunity – achieved new status and made the insults, hierarchies, and rebukes of the Old World that much more intolerable to the colonists.

3

Work and Merit in a New Republic

Philadelphia's renowned physician, educator, reformer, and ardent patriot Benjamin Rush (1745–1813) declared in 1786 that the "late American war" had ended but that was only "the first act of the great drama." He insisted that the "*revolution is not over.*" To complete the revolution and forge a true republic, "every man in a republic is public property" obliged to serve and drive out corrupt "monarchism." Rush and most of the founding generation sought a strong and resilient republic of citizens who improved themselves and their nation, free of unearned aristocratic entitlements and burdens. They knew that order required authority and structures both political and social, but after jettisoning Britain's hierarchies, cultural and political authority were in disarray. It all felt so precarious that many believed that only George Washington's personal stature and gravitas were holding the new nation together. Instability and fluidity seemed rampant, fostering an unfamiliar mobility – a dream for some and a nightmare for others.[1] Should mobility be controlled? Abetted? How should citizens' mobility relate to political participation? All these questions were especially worrisome because of the uncertainties about governance. In ways that would have been unimaginable prior to the Revolution, the new nation's invention of electoral politics created the incentives for telling stories of self-made success.

In building their new republic Rush and his contemporaries were preoccupied with competing ideas about who deserved cultural esteem and other earthly rewards, especially political leadership. As the Enlightenment moralist Adam Smith observed in 1759, people wish "not only praise, but praiseworthiness."[2] In post-Revolutionary America, beliefs about who deserved praise were diverse and unsettled, but the urgency of those cultural and political uncertainties rewarded stories that ambitious men told of self-making, while rejecting traditional stories of legacy stature. As a consequence of new competitions for political authority, a new standard for cultural authority emerged that only later made its way into the sphere of economic power. In keeping with notions of self-making, as the end of the eighteenth century approached, storytellers increased the cultural weight of self-improvement and work to address challenges in a nation that had rejected birthright aristocracy. In doing so, they built on the work ethos that English colonizers had imported since the early seventeenth century to construct a pillar to support ideas of self-making that would come into their own in the nineteenth century.

British colonists had also imported legal and cultural presumptions and constraints that marginalized wide swaths of the populace. Women, racial and ethnic outsiders, enslaved people, and poor people were subject to harsh physical and social penalties if they attempted to claim their self-agency. During the eighteenth century, while mobility became possible and even expected of White men, constraints on everyone else continued, and often hardened. Further, as we will see, the types of work and self-improvement that "praiseworthiness" required and that shaped the nascent self-making ideal remained unavailable to people on the margins. Compounding the harm, those standards were increasingly turned against people on the margins in a self-fulfilling cycle to justify withholding resources and opportunities for improvement.[3]

In keeping with rising expectations of self-improvement for White men in the new republic, inequalities that had traditionally been explained as God's will or merely tradition could increasingly be attributed to individuals' supposed flaws. Such justifications of inequality intensified as the myth of self-made success and its converse, self-made failure, took shape through the nineteenth century.

TO GOVERN WITHOUT ARISTOCRATS

The Revolution's expulsion of the monarchy and affiliated aristocracy cleared the stage for intense contests over authority, both cultural and political. Because no one knew how to govern a republic, citizens deliberated about what measures of merit, reputation, and ability should replace the ancient aristocratic standards for honor and influence. How could the new United States govern itself without the old hierarchies to separate the governing from the governed and to guide the acquisition and distribution of power?[4]

The New World's exceptional opportunities for Euro-Americans had long emboldened the ambitious to strive for honors and affluence, which threatened those who feared for stability and their own stature. Since John Smith's days in Jamestown, the colonies' aristocratic hierarchies had aggravated tensions in all spheres, and they eventually inspired America's revolutionaries. Like Benjamin Rush, many of the founding generation understood that pushing out British military control was only the start of building a new country. Beyond that, removal of an aristocracy from political authority required removal of its cultural authority as well. To achieve this goal, the nation needed new criteria for stature while converting "aristocrat," the old touchstone of stature, from a term of deference to one of derision, a rhetorical weapon against unearned claims to wealth, esteem, influence, and power. In political contests then and forever after, partisans have thrown this insult indiscriminately to accuse opponents of failing to work to improve themselves, their communities, and the new nation.

Yet at the same time, many, including Benjamin Franklin, John Adams, and Thomas Jefferson, believed that a republic could only survive and flourish under the leadership of a virtuous and capable elite. If Americans no longer looked to a birthright aristocracy for leadership, their new republic somehow had to devise a means to build and constantly renew a worthy elite. There were no ready models for such mobility. In 1813, for example, corresponding with Adams, Jefferson urged support for a "natural aristocracy ... for the instruction, the trusts, and government of society" as counterweight to an "artificial aristocracy founded on wealth and birth."[5] The extraordinary Franklin had trailblazed his own path, which helped to inspire others, but could mobility function more widely? Should it? The founding generation worried about both a descent into chaos and a return to monarchy. As they grappled with this conundrum, they laid the basis for what we now imagine as a meritocracy.

Amid all of this agitation, two seemingly simple measures of personal worth rose to replace birthright status: self-improvement and work in the public interest. As the opposite of idleness and parasitic gentility, prevalent religious and cultural values already bolstered the status of self-improvement and work, as we've seen. Service to God and community provided a set of gauges to evaluate them. The work ethic that the New England Puritans and other British colonizers brought with them was an early tool for criticizing elites not accustomed to physical labor or community building. John Winthrop, Massachusetts's first governor, worked "with his owne hands," earning admiration from the upstart John Smith.[6] Whether or not someone worked seemed to offer a clear measure of individual worth, although what and whose labor should be esteemed was a matter of values, not measurable effort. Therefore, work might encompass physical or mental efforts, praying or planting, supervising or harvesting, and so on, but its rewards have depended on those with the authority and resources to assign rewards. Success at work and improvement seemed equally ambiguous as fame, fortune, and power rivaled contributions to the common good for esteem. Further complicating the measure of work, eliminating honorific titles did not eliminate the unearned advantages that people in some ranks and demographics held while others were not even allowed to improve.

IDLE ARISTOCRATS AND CITIZEN WORKERS

Abundant preaching about work, whether in traditional aphorisms and sayings of the sort that Franklin repeated or pronouncements from pulpits, promoted a secular faith that became as deeply ingrained as any religion. This secular faith drew on ethics that glorified work, as John Smith and John Winthrop espoused it in the seventeenth century, a glorification that was an essential precursor to the myth of self-made success that began to take form after the Revolution. It also served as the main tool for people in the middle of the wealth and power spectrum to discredit the ranks at the opposite ends.[7] Birthright aristocrats resided at one end of the spectrum, and destroying their cultural authority was key to attacking Britain's political authority in the Revolutionary era. Meanwhile, the work ethic allowed middling merchants, yeomen, and tradesmen to blame people at both ends of the spectrum for their misfortunes. Because Euro-Americans' outcomes seemed to hinge more on their own efforts than they had in traditional European settings, failure to exercise initiative and self-discipline emerged as a potent explanation for poor people's struggles and adversity. Like any other faith, this secular zeal for work fostered self-righteousness, intolerance, and moralizing. Idleness was the ultimate, if not the original, sin against the upstart colonials' increasingly dominant ethos. Aristocrats and paupers alike seemed to make unearned claims on collective resources.

The colonists' experiences of building new lives and outposts in the New World felt heroic to them. Transforming the land and driving out its original occupants in order to recreate European societies demonstrated to them their moral superiority over anyone who stayed behind and yet profited from the work. Court-sanctioned monopolists and mercantilists became targets of moral outrage because they leveraged their political and social influence to limit New World enterprise and autonomy through policies forbidding most manufacturing in the colonies and limiting economic development.[8] More damaging and broadly frustrating, however, were policies and practices that constrained colonial trade while promoting British monopolies, asserting English control over local governance, and, of course, levying taxes. Objections to limits on enterprising colonials' opportunities typically alleged threats to their liberties. When Bostonians dumped 342 boxes of tea into their harbor in 1773, for example, they did so as part of a longer resistance against Britain's power to deny them economic autonomy, policies that benefitted the already rich by subsidizing the British East India Company, a corporate monopoly.[9]

Indignation reinforced immodesty about what colonists had achieved and what they could achieve once freed from the British yoke. Typical of self-made myths, these illusions ignored the advantages of colonial status, such as the help colonialists received from British military and naval forces to subdue indigenous peoples and to resist French and Spanish imperial interests. Other neglected benefits included the world's largest merchant marine; easy access to credit; education through schools, publishers, churches, and organizations such as the

Royal Society; cheap manufactured goods; and a constant stream of people, free and unfree.[10] Seeing only the costs of patronage, only the difficulties and not the benefits, gave rebels a national origins myth.

The myth of a self-made nation nurtured the myth of the self-made man that would emerge after the Revolution. It nurtured an idea of individual self-making based on ideas of American exceptionalism that prominent voices like John Smith and Cotton Mather had begun to formulate long before independence.[11] Many Americans perceived a synergy between individual improvement and national improvement, an ideal often described in terms of republican virtue: only a nation of honest, hard-working, and self-sacrificing patriots could survive as a republic. Those patriots could flourish individually, but they would have to prioritize the public good over their personal ambitions to fulfill the Revolution's ideals. This new, upstart nation had to exercise great vigilance not to fall back under the influence of monarchism and aristocracy.[12]

Because work was central to the cultural battles against an idle aristocracy, artisans and yeomen farmers participated early and wholeheartedly in many of the revolutionary actions, with Thomas Paine, author of the enormously influential *Common Sense*, inspiring much of the fervor. One such artisan patriot was Bostonian George Robert Twelves Hewes (1742–1840). His first brush with history was an obligatory visit to the wealthy John Hancock at the prominent man's invitation. Twenty years old but not accustomed to conversing with elites, Hewes stumbled awkwardly through the visit, making his escape as quickly as possible. Not too many years later, however, Hewes participated in Boston's harbingers of rebellion, most notably the so-called Boston Massacre in 1770 and the Tea Party in 1773. He believed that he had tossed tea into Boston Harbor next to none other than Mr. Hancock himself, unlikely as it was that the patriots would have risked losing Hancock and his funding during that evening's adventure. Hewes fought during the ensuing Revolution in militia and on privateers. A shoemaker who toiled throughout his ninety-eight years, he followed the free artisan's path to a proud citizenship, and expectations of mutual respect between fellow citizens replaced his former deference. As a spry elder, he proudly proclaimed his status as a citizen who "would not take his hat off to any man," according to a late-in-life biography that lauded this rare survivor of the nation's origins.[13] The secular faith in hard work had made it possible to redefine the criteria for worth. Deference now had to be earned.

Citizens who believed that America's own elites and their ambitions to govern threatened the promises of the Revolution found the label "aristocrat" an especially useful invective. Anti-Federalists in rural Pennsylvania, for example, opposed the new US Constitution as a manifestation of "proud & Lordly Ideas." On occasions when local elites toasted Federalist leaders, such as George

Washington and John Adams, they also called Anti-Federalists a "vile rabble" and the like. Conversely, a Federalist mocked his opponents' remarks in Pennsylvania's press in late 1787 by a simple calculation: "WELL-BORN, nine times – *Aristocracy*, eighteen times... *Great Men*, six times." Such battles-by-insult inspired lively essays from a Massachusetts farmer, William Manning, who called his 1798 essay "The Key of Libberty." He addressed it "To all the Republicans, Farmers, Mecanicks, and Labourers In Amarica your Canded attention is Requested to the Sentiments of a Labourer." Manning's first paragraph unabashedly pointed out his deficiencies in learning and travel, proud that "I always followed hard labour for a living." Throughout his long exposition, Manning repeatedly condemned those "ordirs of men who git a living without labour" and who "ingure the interests of the Labourer." Not an outlier, Manning was a loyal reader of the Anti-Federalist press and a respected member of his community who had taken up arms as a militia sergeant at Concord in 1775 "in the Cause of Libberty" and later served two terms as a town selectman.[14]

In the same vein, over 1,400 artisans from twenty Connecticut towns participated in a 1792 tax protest by petitioning as "worthy labouring Citizens" trying to protect their "hard earnings." Proudly referring to themselves as "Mechanics and Citizens," these artisans made up a substantial portion of the state's voters at the time, and they understood the advantage it gave them. They hinted that this "valuable labouring part" could remove "into other States," taking their skills, products, and spending. In the state's newspapers, Walter Brewster, who co-organized the petitions on behalf of Connecticut's "Mechanick's," asserted, "Whatsoever is repugnant to the Labouring interest is also repugnant to the general or common interest of the whole state, which is the labouring interest." This young shoemaker also objected to subsidies that granted "exclusive privileges" to large "manufactories" controlled by "knaves and robbers" who would drive out skilled workers to create "a Birmingham and Manchester [England] amongst us."[15] A new aristocracy was on the rise, and Brewster already recognized its dangers to workers. Similarly, throughout the 1790s, New York City artisans defended their visions of post-Revolutionary America, contrasting their useful wares with the fruitlessness of the "consuming speculator, who wallows in luxury," unlike "the productive mechanic, who struggles with indigence." At the same time, New York City Federalists called members of the Democratic Society "the lowest order of mechanics, laborers, and draymen."[16] Artisans laid claim to their citizenship by virtue of their work, while elites' insults relied on status.

John Smith had fulminated against aristocrats almost two centuries before these post-Revolution clashes erupted between elites and the newly enfranchised middling ranks. He had complained about aristocratic sloth, arrogance, and hauteur, and he claimed moral support from the emerging work ethos. Casting out the British monarchy and other legally ordained elites gave a powerful new legitimacy to both anti-elitist frustrations and the supporting work ethos. The debates that preceded the Revolution and the arguments that had recruited soldiers and finances to expel British authorities produced a well-developed set of rhetorical tools that combined patriotism and anti-aristocratic sentiments with the work ethos. After the Revolution, "ordinary" citizens had these forceful ideas at their command to put elites on the defensive in political contests.[17]

SHAPING MERITOCRACY AND MOBILITY IN THE POLITICAL ARENA

With the Revolution, the foundations of political authority became uncertain and unstable. The ensuing electoral upheavals propelled the eighteenth century's acceptance of self-agency and ambition toward the next century's creation of the self-making notion. This evolution followed from the new political reality in which electoral contests determined who governed, and successful candidates had to gain the allegiance of enfranchised White males who had never before had a voice beyond local governance. Elites had to reach outside of their ranks, whatever they might feel about the process and their audiences.[18] It was this electoral innovation that first incentivized ambitious Americans to downplay their origins and exaggerate their rises. The myth of self-made success was, thus, driven by electoral politics in the anti-aristocratic culture that was the Revolution's legacy.

New York State's gubernatorial contests under this new regime illustrated the new competition for cultural authority that would come to dominate competitions for political authority, nourishing the roots of the self-making myth. In the 1777 election, the state's elites fully supported Albany aristocrat Philip Schuyler. Yet, in an upset, George Clinton (1739–1812) won a majority of votes among a pool of six candidates that included Schuyler, who came in second. Clinton owed his victory to voters of modest means throughout the state, including 963 of the 1,250 soldiers who voted. A secret ballot had replaced voice votes, which also weakened the pressure to defer to elites. Friction between republican ideals and the aristocracy was deepening, and in Clinton's 1789 campaign for reelection his supporters claimed that opponents disapproved of his success "with the great body, not with the great folks of the community." Elites allegedly resented this "obscure *Plebeian*" who could prove "a firm barrier against the boundless ambition of *Patrician* families."[19] Among these opponents of New York's long-term elite, a man's rise from "obscure" origins deserved praise.

Such stories about George Clinton's origins contributed to a pattern that would become notorious in political contests of the first half of the nineteenth century because his roots were not at all obscure or plebeian. He hailed from an affluent and well-connected yeoman family north of New York City, had been tutored at home, and then educated into the law in the office of a prominent New York City lawyer. Like so many ambitious men Clinton received a major boost from an advantageous marriage, and as a young man, he was already a force in local politics. The Revolution and its impact on cultural attitudes, though, made possible his rise to national prominence because he was willing and able to present himself as a man with whom the state's newly enfranchised yeoman farmers and rural artisans could identify. Well-regarded, sober, capable, and intensely patriotic, even Clinton's rivals generally acknowledged his merits, if begrudgingly. For instance, two weeks after Clinton's first electoral victory, Schuyler wrote to John Jay, also a New York aristocrat who had come in a distant fourth, to admit that "Altho' his family and connections do not entitle him to so distinguished a predominance; yet he is virtuous and loves his country, has abilities and is brave." Many patricians assumed that this election was a wartime fluke which the next round would correct. However, Clinton carried six more elections for governor, and then two for the nation's vice presidency, serving in that office under presidents Jefferson and Madison from 1805 until his death in 1812.[20]

As Clinton's story suggests, elites would henceforth have to contend with abundant vitriol against them. The Constitution eliminated legal, birthright aristocracy, but many voters sought also to erase its centuries-deep cultural residue. The electorate was still less than 10 percent of the population, the free, White, male property holders and taxpayers who made up the portion of the nation responsible for making political choices. Among them, yeomen and artisans vastly outnumbered those previously accustomed to deference, and the language of political campaigns began to recognize this new political force.

This electoral revolution favored stories of social mobility, with new standards for merit and esteem at the expense of tradition. When Kingston's Reformed Dutch Church congratulated Clinton on his 1777 election, the ministers urged on him "vigilance, impartiality and firmness" because "nothing can more promote the general good than ... raising merit to distinguished power." "Raising merit to distinguished power" – this was a fitting benchmark for an upstart nation, a revolutionary idea about how to govern. Whereas merit was once God's to judge, by way of secular and clerical authorities, judges of *political* merit were now everywhere. Those newly eligible to vote could elect people who resembled them, or, at least, *seemed* to relate to them and their concerns. Many elites cringed at this inevitability; as one critic of the broadened franchise put it, "Every man thinks himself a judge."[21] Merit became the product of self-improvement and work, a new standard for culturally acceptable success, and political incentives drew out stories about well-earned mobility. Thus, it was the political arena that saw the initial rhetorical and ideological movements toward mythmaking about self-made success, but its spirit would suffuse American culture more broadly in a few decades.

WORK AS WORTH AND TONIC

Whereas seventeenth-century Anglo-Americans had praised work as evidence of religious and moral virtues, in the late eighteenth century, ambition and work incrementally acquired secular virtue as appreciation for self-agency took hold. Praise for worldly success was still tempered by precautionary doses of providentialism and respect for social debts, but vilification for failure fell increasingly on individuals and their flaws. Moreover, poverty and idleness threatened the ideals of an industrious, prosperous republic. Whether by implication or declaration, materially comfortable individuals' assertions that they had worked hard accused able-bodied people of scant means of failing to work hard enough to prosper, with little regard for their actual efforts or conditions. Such assertions of moral superiority became rhetorical weapons to turn against people who were tired, hungry, ill, hopeless, or just not motivated to work under conditions of servitude. Self-righteousness often also defended the violence, life conditions, and suppression of opportunities that could cause despair and disorder, and that, in turn, prevented improvement and mobility for many.

Citizens and policymakers up and down local governance ladders confronted poverty constantly and debated its causes and solutions. Poverty had troubled New World colonists from the start, and the Revolution did not eliminate those troubles. Instead, expectations about self-agency and individual responsibility advanced at this time just as providential explanations receded. "Hard work" itself came to be seen as a tonic of sorts, enforced when ambition did not inspire it. To that end, religious and civic institutions established various types of poorhouses to provide sustenance and shelter for the indigent and helpless. Rationales for poorhouses ranged from the benign to the punitive: taking care of children and the infirm; training in discipline and gainful trades; imposing order on paupers and vagrants; and removing beggars and other eyesores from the streets where they scraped by. In the eighteenth century, Boston and Philadelphia, both still culturally dominated by their religious leaders, followed British models to invest in poorhouses for the elderly and infirm and massive workhouses for able-bodied paupers.

Wealthy elites funded and often directed institutions that aimed to reform the poor while they provided relief. Tellingly, commercially successful people in New England organized groups with names like "Societies for the Suppression of Disorders." Making that same aim unambiguously, Quaker merchants organized and completed the Philadelphia Bettering House in 1767, a huge facility that was America's grandest "Almshouse and House of Employment" for decades to come. Donors, whose financial and administrative contributions made the workhouses possible, could thereby legitimate the worldly successes they believed that they

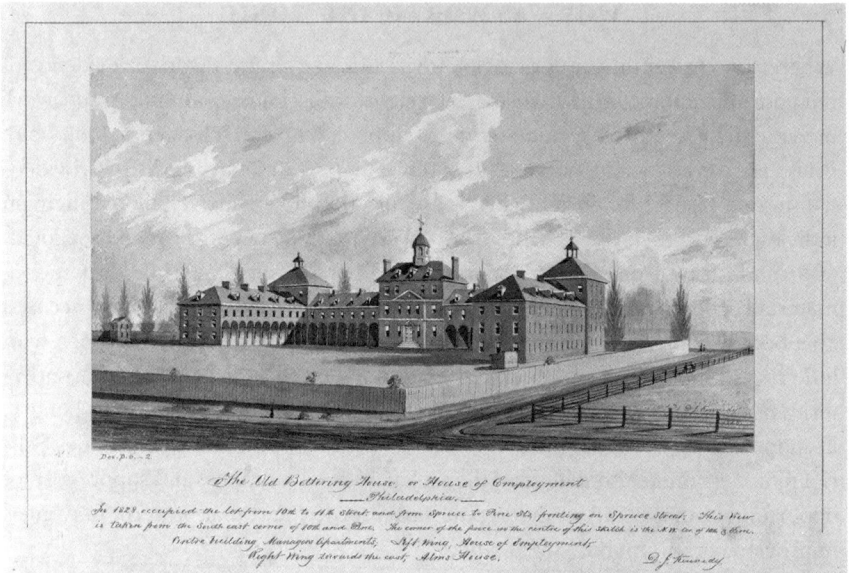

Figure 3.1 Workhouses, such as the Bettering House completed in 1767 by wealthy Quakers in Philadelphia, undertook to impose good work habits on people struggling to scrape by. This approach assumed that poor people were poor by choice – that they were self-made failures – the ever-present complement to the myth of self-made success. (*Bettering House or House of Employment*, 1828. David J. Kennedy watercolors (collection #V61). Courtesy of Historical Society of Pennsylvania)

had achieved by discipline and work while they grandly distanced themselves from the middling ranks. Establishing such hierarchies with service through philanthropy was one facet of the long project of justifying and rationalizing wealth. Meanwhile, relief stigmatized the poor as either helpless and, therefore, worthy recipients of aid, or idle and morally flawed and, therefore, unworthy recipients. Either way, eighteenth-century poorhouses subjected their inmates to indignities and demands as the price of any training or sustenance that they afforded, setting patterns for future attitudes toward the unfortunate.[22]

According to the expanding work ethos, hard work was necessary and sufficient for individuals to advance and better themselves. But a core paradox underlay this emergent work ethic: not all workers were alike, or free, or had the same resources. No amount of preaching about soul-gratifying work and its rewards could erase those differences. Euro-Americans' attitudes toward work from colonization's earliest times had tended toward stark judgments, such as John Smith's and other European colonists' demeaning views of the livelihoods of Native Americans. In reality, no amount of hard and purposeful work could raise the stature or rewards of people who were enslaved, or others denied opportunity due to gender, race, or rank. They might find salvation, but not prosperity or esteem. The paradox of a work ethic of self-making in a culture that explicitly denied chances for self-making, or even self-ownership to the enslaved, meant that the ethic made the advantaged more respected and the disadvantaged more judged and reviled.[23] If "hard work" truly sufficed to win esteem, the world of hard workers would look much different. Notably, wherever gross inequality, enslavement, raw bigotry, and their legacies, including Jim Crow, exist, the notion of "self-made success" is a self-fulfilling, logical contradiction.

Colonial Georgia's origins in the early eighteenth century illustrate the underlying speciousness of the work ethos. In an exceptional effort, the British planners who sought royal and parliamentary support for Georgia's initial colonization argued *against* allowing enslaved African labor. In part, their reasoning was strategic. Britain sought control of that region as a buffer against the Spanish-held territory to the south, and they worried that enslaved people could escape to the Spanish who would arm them. Also, the Parliamentary Gaols Committee and Georgia's gentlemen Trustees hoped to build an empire with the labor of people who could not earn their keep in Britain. Therefore, in 1732, they proposed a "Humanity and Charity" that would send to the new colony former prisoners and "all poor families as might be desirous of it." Their "Georgia Plan" argued that the opportunity for England's "miserable wretches" and "drones" to work on their own lands in the New World without rents or debts would prove a tonic to instill moral fiber and offset the evils of "idleness" to inspire improvement. James Oglethorpe (1696–1785), a prominent military leader and philanthropist, argued for this "single Act of prudent Beneficence" to replace perpetual charity with migration. He feared that conditions in the Old World made it impossible for many "unhappy People" to "earn above a Fourth Part of their Sustenance at Home." Even those "who are bred [trained] in low Life, and well versed in such Shifts and Expedients, find but a very narrow Maintenance by them." Rather than "an heavy *Rent-charge* upon the Publick," their productivity in the New World would "be made an immense *Revenue* to it" in "an happy Exchange of their Poverty for an Affluence."[24]

Importing enslaved Africans into the new colony would thwart this aim. Their forced labor threatened the moral improvement of both the indigent Whites sent to the colony and the more affluent "adventurers" who could afford to invest in human chattel. Within a slave economy, the former could not and the latter need not imbibe the moral tonic of hard work. Enslaved laborers' work in that moral economy did not qualify for merit or esteem by the paradox of the work ethic in an enslaving society; the limits on their self-agency deprived them of that. Slavery had already promoted luxury and idleness among enslavers in the Carolinas and reduced the opportunities of less advantaged migrants for gainful employment.[25]

South Carolinians eager to "adventure" in the new territory even tried to bribe Oglethorpe when they could not convince him that White laborers were too expensive and unfit for the work necessary to turn swamps and forests to profit. Intense debate roiled into the 1740s, but Oglethorpe and his allies could not prevail over arguments for the financial merits of enslaved African labor, with its profits to enslavers and to the imperial project. By 1761 more than half of Georgia's population was enslaved. As slavery's advocates had predicted, productivity rose dramatically over just a couple of decades. As the humanitarians had predicted, inequality also rose. South Carolina and West Indies planters who could invest in land and human chattel controlled not only Georgia's economy but also its social and political spheres.[26] Hard work did not advance those people, free or unfree, who actually did the physical labor that generated planters' incomes.

Not only were enslaved people deprived of self-ownership, a predicate of self-making, their skills, acumen, and labor were buried over time by a work ethic that was openly racialized: it held that only Europeans had the energy, inventiveness, and abilities to work successfully. Rice cultivation, for example, was at the core of development and prosperity in colonial South Carolina and Georgia, and planters depended on enslaved Africans, especially women, for much more than their labor. Captured Africans brought both the technologies and skills necessary to bring swamp lands into productivity. However, memories of that past disappeared over time, buried by mainstream presumptions that only Europeans could have been clever enough to make that happen. For instance, in 1936 in the depths of Jim Crow, a Carolina planter celebrated his forefathers' "skill" and "engineering ability" for creating a cultivation system despite "seemingly insuperable difficulties" with "only the axe, the spade, and the hoe, in the hands of intractable negro men and women, but lately brought from the jungles of Africa." The next year, another planter's heir asserted that White Americans had astutely adapted Chinese methods with only the crude labor of enslaved Africans at hand. Other stories credited Dutch or Portuguese colonizers with the necessary technology transfers and ingenuity. Only in recent decades has rigorous historical research exposed this ancestral deceit. Meanwhile, deeply entrenched, demeaning judgments of Africans' work efforts have continued to reinforce excuses to obstruct their descendants' education and opportunity.[27] Destructive forgetting of African Americans' crucial skills and problem-solving supported enslavement and, later, separate and unequal treatment.

A PATRICIAN'S WORK ETHIC

George Washington's attitudes toward enslaved people evolved to reveal how the values of self-improvement and the work ethic can affect prejudices and inequality differently according to cultural and legal contexts. While he accepted the ambient culture of enslavement, he showed how the work ethic can aggravate prejudices and inequality in deeply and structurally inequitable societies. It promotes judgment against people who have no possibility of fulfilling expectations and, in turn, uses that judgment to withhold resources and respect. However, after Washington broadened the reach of Enlightenment ideas about human rights and self-agency, he saw the paradox and sought to break it. His conversion followed from deeply absorbing the eighteenth century's transition to valuing individual self-agency.

For most of his life, Washington accepted and practiced enslavement in which people could only rarely earn either a decent living or esteem, regardless of how hard they worked.[28] His forebears had arrived in Virginia during the 1650s to evade Oliver Cromwell's wrath, and the men married well. By his generation, the family had risen into the top tenth among Virginia's Anglo-Americans. As a teenager, Washington inherited an estate that included twenty-two enslaved people, including children. His extremely advantageous marriage to a wealthy widow, Martha Custis, plus additional purchases, brought more people under his charge, approximately 670 over his lifetime.[29] This capital in human beings made his other major asset, land, profitable. He was fully aware of that interdependence and constantly worried about costs and inefficiencies; the practical flaws of the system exasperated him, but he saw no viable alternative within his culture's assumptions. Crucially, only in his last years did he consider the enslavement of African laborers in light of the Enlightenment principles of liberty and dignity that he prized for his fellow Euro-Americans. Until he made that connection, enslaved people were merely troublesome property, and he sometimes referred to them among "things" on lists of possessions, alongside livestock.[30]

American slavery's different regimes across time and regions all depended on enslavers' legal and cultural rights to enforce their authority by violence and its threat.[31] Washington and his peers saw him as exacting but reasonable: he insisted on compliance and advised his managers to apply methods ranging from threats of demotion from house to field, physical restraints, and beatings as punishments and deterrents. Washington's commitment to his own duty as an enslaver manifested itself in a dark paternalism. For instance, in 1794 while president, he told a manager that "I never wish my people to work when they are really sick, or unfit for it; on the contrary, that all necessary care should be taken of them when they are so." He warned, however, "none ... would work if by pretexts they can avoid it" through "rogueries," "old tricks," and "slothfulness." Likewise, objections to theft failed to account for inadequate diets. Guests complained about dirty children running about, criticizing their families rather than the lack of facilities or parental time for washing.[32] Impugning the character of people forced to live under degrading conditions exposed a common and chronic insensitivity that Washington shared until he began to apply the Enlightenment's ideas about liberty and humanity beyond Euro-Americans.

For most of his life, George Washington did not grasp why his human chattels did not, could not, share his work ethic and sense of duty. He deplored how they failed to measure up to his standards of discipline and self-improvement. He had invested his life, beginning in adolescence with intensive self-training, in the Enlightenment virtues of learning, self-control, graciousness, civility, and duty.[33] He rose at dawn to work and expected all of those in his employ, free and enslaved, to do so of their own accord and to "be diligent while they are at it," as he put it in 1789. He could not fathom how capable adults, enslaved or otherwise, did not share his standards for merit. Like most of his class, he considered enslaved people incapable of adult decision making and functioning, notwithstanding the substantial and purposeful work that they invested in their own gardens, animals, and business dealings whenever they had the opportunity. In short, he judged enslaved people by the criteria of self-improvement even as he denied them the very means – self-ownership and agency. Even though Washington often objected to the time laborers spent on enterprises of their own, he also believed that they had "no ambition to establish a *good* name" and were "too regardless of a *bad* one."[34] He did not take into consideration that they cared more about their fellows' opinions than about his or his overseers' opinions. There was, for example, more pride to be gained among peers, as well as practical benefit, from a well-executed theft than in meeting a field driver's quota.

Moreover, from any laborer's perspective, Washington's toil at his desk and his managerial exertions looked safe and easy, not at all like their work. A visitor to Virginia talked with enslaved people and recorded their interpretation of the work ethic and its implications: "Massa does not work; therefore he has not equal right; overseer does not work; he has no right to eat as we do." Years later in 1866, a recently freed woman who had worked for the last Washington to own Mount Vernon told a visitor: "You know the Bible says every one must live by the sweat of his own eyebrow. But John A. Washington, he lived by the sweat of my eyebrow."[35]

The Revolution's ardor for liberty and arguments from slavery's opponents, such as George Washington's friend and comrade in arms, the Marquis de Lafayette, changed his thinking about enslaved labor. In 1786, he praised Lafayette's pursuit of free labor alternatives as "generous and noble proof of your humanity." Overcoming his earlier attitudes, Washington was the only large slaveholder among the leading Founders to arrange for broad emancipation. His carefully crafted 1799 "Last Will and Testament" recognized the

Figure 3.2 After George Washington retired from the presidency, he returned to Mount Vernon, where he thought deeply about the principles on which the nation was founded. He came to understand that slavery violated those principles and that he could do his own work only because enslaved people took care of his estate's practical operations. This drawing portrays him talking with enslaved workers at Mount Vernon in 1797. (Engraved by Nathaniel Currier, 1852; MPI / Stringer Archive Photos via Getty Images)

contradictions between enslaving people and the era's proclamations about rights and liberty, as well as the growing belief in a work ethic to measure cultural merit. Many wrestled with these contradictions, including Thomas Jefferson and James Madison, but Washington alone acted broadly, if posthumously. Notable in his will was his devotion to the principles of service and self-improvement in order to disrupt the circular logic by which enslaved people were overworked, under-resourced, and deprived of self-agency and opportunity, yet derided as inadequately hard-working and lacking in purpose.

In addition to providing a "regular and permanent fund" for emancipated people unable to support themselves, which a 1782 Virginia law required, Washington also obliged his heirs to teach those under twenty-five to read, write, and "to be brought up to some useful occupation." Education, he understood, offered the best hope for freed people and others whose only asset was their capacity for labor. Therefore, he also bequeathed a generous sum to Alexandria's Academy to establish a "Free school ... for the purpose of Educating such Orphan children, or the children of such other poor and indigent persons as are unable to accomplish it with their own means."[36]

Washington came to believe that the Revolution's ideas about liberty and obligations had real and broad implications for work, authority, and duty. His determination came through poignantly in a much earlier statement that he had made in 1788 or 1789, before becoming president, in conversation with David Humphreys, who was a guest at Mount Vernon and had been an officer and aide. An accomplished writer, Humphreys had written letters and drafted speeches for General Washington, and he received permission to write a biography. Notes from their conversations reveal Washington's post-Revolution thinking about slavery that presaged his 1799 will:

> The unfortunate condition of the persons, whose labour in part I employed, has been the only unavoidable subject of regret. To make the Adults among them as easy & as comfortable in their circumstances as their actual state of ignorance & improvidence would admit; & to lay a foundation to prepare the rising generation for a destiny different from that in which they were born; afforded some satisfaction to my mind, & could not I hoped be displeasing to the justice of the Creator.

In 1794, halfway between his 1789 self-reproach and his 1799 will, Washington reversed his earlier equation of enslaved people with animals and objected to a relative's query about their monetary value: "I am principled agt. [against] selling negros, as you would do cattle in the market." That year he also hinted at preliminary arrangements for emancipation when he informed his private secretary of his intention "to liberate a certain species of property which I possess, very repugnantly to my own feelings."[37] He had come to understand that the behavior that he had disparaged in enslaved people was the result of the "unfortunate condition" of their lives, and "that the rising generation" should have a different "destiny." The Revolutionary era's republican virtues, if consistently applied, insisted on work, service, and personal improvement. Taking all of this to heart, Washington's values, if generally adopted, could have made the notion of self-making more of an egalitarian tool and less of a myth to justify inequality. Similarly, if mythmakers had abided by the life and words of their most misused hero, Benjamin Franklin, we'd have inherited a more honest narrative to guide us.

STORIES ABOUT A NOTABLE RISE

Franklin's lifelong principles contrasted with later myths about him as a self-made man, and comparing what he wrote and the distortions most famously misattributed to him makes that clear. In the first paragraph of what we now know as Franklin's *Autobiography* but that he called his "memoirs," he explained his purpose for writing:

> Having emerg'd from the Poverty & Obscurity in which I was born & bred, to a State of Affluence & some Degree of Reputation in the World, and having gone so far thro' Life with a considerable Share of Felicity, the conducing Means I made use of, which, with the Blessing of God, so well succeeded, my Posterity may like to know, as they may find some of them suitable to their own Situations, & therefore fit to be imitated.[38]

This very dense, often-quoted, and, more to the point, often-misquoted sentence invites closer scrutiny, especially to understand mobility and self-making in the early republic. For perspective, 65-year-old Franklin drafted this passage in the summer of 1771 and revised it several times between 1788 and 1790, after his nation-building duties had ended. Franklin himself revised his word choices at least once, for example, exchanging "Fame" for "Reputation" in describing how far he had traveled from "Obscurity." Then, in 1818, his grandson, William Temple Franklin, revised "Reputation" to read "celebrity," which actually reversed his grandfather's intended meaning.[39] While Benjamin Franklin certainly was and remains a celebrity in the sense of a prominent figure in popular culture, that term trivializes the centrality of reputation to esteem. That is still true today but was even more true then.

Franklin underscored the importance of reputation throughout the *Autobiography*. For instance, he explained that "to show that I was not above my Business," as a young man starting out he "sometimes brought home the Paper I purchas'd at the Stores, thro' the Streets on a Wheelbarrow." He also observed that "In order to secure my Credit and Character as a Tradesmen, I took care not only to be in *Reality* Industrious & frugal, but to avoid all *Appearances* of the Contrary." Therefore, he did not participate in frivolous fashion or sports. Franklin emphasized this point by next revealing that a less prudent competitor had lost his printing business to creditors and died in Barbados "in very poor Circumstances." Before modern credit agencies and formal, impersonal banks, financing and other scarce resources required social capital based either on family connections or solid reputation.[40]

Franklin's first clause in that long sentence about origins likewise deserves a close comparison with his grandson's 1818 alteration. Ben Franklin originally wrote, "Having emerg'd from the Poverty & Obscurity in which I was born & bred...." His grandson, Temple Franklin, revised this to "From the poverty and obscurity in which I was born, and in which I passed my earliest years, I have raised myself... ." "Having emerg'd" in contrast to "raised myself" speaks volumes about the mindsets and norms that separated these two generations. Despite Benjamin Franklin's determined and successful self-improvements, he did not see fit to claim that he had "raised" himself. His grandson, however, altered the text to describe a self-made man just as the myth was entering American usage. This revision reinforced Temple Franklin's substitution of "celebrity" for "Reputation," and, together, they jettisoned the senior Franklin's appreciation for diligent attention to the social factors that enabled success. No one is self-made in the sense of being made alone, and Benjamin Franklin understood that.[41] Temple Franklin, however, with all of his own advantages of wealth and colossal social capital, apparently did not. He fit his grandfather's texts to later times and beliefs, and his revisions have fostered two centuries of misconceptions about success, about Benjamin Franklin, and about how others might emulate him. Those misquotes and other ahistorical interpretations have contributed to mistaken sanctification of Franklin and his *Autobiography* as foundations for the American myth of self-made success – counter to his own beliefs.

Furthermore, looking retrospectively on Franklin's origins from the heights of colonial wealth and respect that he had reached has exaggerated his original "poverty and obscurity." True, he and his family members had to work at trades for their livelihoods. His father certainly had to pursue his business diligently to raise seventeen children, but he routinely invited to dinner "some sensible Friend or Neighbour" for the benefits of "some ingenious or useful Topic for Discourse, which might tend to improve the Minds of his Children." As well, the senior Franklin was "frequently visited by leading People, who consulted him for his Opinion on Affairs of the Town or of the Church he belong'd to & show'd a good deal of Respect for his Judgment and Advice." A prominent twentieth-century historian even considered Franklin's "origins" to be "middle-class" relative to the times.[42]

Especially in the early decades of the century when Franklin grew up and made his way, everyone, even elites, traveled mostly on foot through town. Therefore, a bright young fellow of appropriate race and ethnicity who worked in printing, the main communication medium, had a good chance of coming to the attention of prominent people within local networks in business and politics. Add to that the advantages of a well-connected father in his home town and a ship's captain brother-in-law who convinced the governor of Pennsylvania to visit the young printer in his newly adopted town. To be sure, Franklin made superb use of his social capital advantages in both towns, impressing others with his charm, brilliance, and industry along the way, just as he would later in London and Paris. In short, Franklin was a skilled and purposeful networker who required patronage to advance, as did everyone not born a king. Looking back on his vigorous networking with business and political leaders as an ambitious young man, he later observed that "These Friends were afterwards of great Use to me, as I occasionally was to some of them." He also recalled that his new printshop's first customer arrived at the door thanks to a friend's recommendation.[43] Success in any business arena cannot be a solitary process, and the *Autobiography*, like Franklin's other writing, is full of stories about building and making the best of connections and alliances. They, along with his technical skills and business acumen, made for his successes – all necessary and none sufficient alone.

Ironically, Benjamin Franklin himself would have thought it meaningless to say that he was self-made, but by the time many Americans came to embrace and praise the possibility of self-making in the next century, it was less possible to achieve what he did, even with his social advantages. It takes nothing away from his remarkable genius, his determination to improve himself, his innovations, his business sharpness, and his towering citizenship to say that national growth made comparable climbs less likely. Through his long life of close to a century, the colonies grew more populous and wealthy, making it more difficult to stand out in the two towns he called home. By the time he died in 1790, almost seven decades after leaving Boston for Philadelphia, each of those towns had grown markedly and reconfigured their neighborhoods. Boston grew from about 12,000 to 18,000, with adult White males at 4,325 according to the first federal census in 1790, a 50 percent increase since he left. Philadelphia had grown even more, becoming the largest city in North America by the 1770s. In 1790, Philadelphia had 7,739 White adult males and 28,522 total residents, having almost quadrupled since his 1723 arrival when there were about 1,500 free White men. A decade later, Philadelphia's population of White men reached 11,883.[44] Moreover, neighborhoods became less diverse by class, as residential areas separated from commercial and work sites, so that contact across classes became less frequent.[45] Therefore, the notion of self-making gained traction just as people were less likely to be able to build the social capital among leading businessmen and political leaders necessary to climb to fortune and fame. Pushing a wheelbarrow through Philadelphia's streets in 1790 or later would not have garnered much favorable attention from potential customers or elites.

The practical challenges of Ben Franklin's climb were in and of themselves often arduous, but he took them on eagerly and well. He took pride in devoting energy and ingenuity to improving himself, using his resources well and enhancing them.[46] For example, he described his woeful and weary condition when he arrived in Philadelphia in 1723, ahead of his trunk of clothes and books, so that his readers could "compare such unlikely Beginning with the Figure I have since made there." As a youth, he compiled detailed lists of "Virtues" by which he intended to improve, such as temperance in eating and drinking, avoiding "trifling Conversation," carrying out resolutions, observing frugality and industry, and being sincere. He figured out early on that self- and community-improvement made prospering possible. One of his favorite books, Daniel Defoe's *An Essay on Projects*, explored ways to improve society and economy through collective works – making a profit along the way, to be sure – and Franklin picked up early the value of improvement on a scale beyond the individual.[47] Franklin's correspondence and memoirs never denied his ambitions. Neither did he make private or public claims to having risen on his own. However, his grandson's injudicious revisions of the *Autobiography* almost three decades later, along with many others' references to an amended Franklin icon over time, show that the values he held were fading from popular view. He was enlisted retrospectively into the myth of the self-made man but did not and would not have described himself as such. Franklin was self-taught and self-improved, but not self-made.

FRANKLIN'S RISE AS IT LOOKED IN 1790

How did Benjamin Franklin's remarkable rise look to him and others in 1790 at the end of his life? Franklin not only participated fully in the rapid economic growth of his era but also outpaced pretty much everyone else along the way, even other well-known climbers such as Alexander Hamilton and John Adams. His deepest ambitions, however, were social and cultural. He retired from business at forty-two and, most famously, dedicated the second half of his long life to scientific study and public service. He moved to a fine house away from the trade district but never patented his inventions. Twenty-six years earlier he had mocked those who took on airs and fashions that embarrassed them socially and financially, and some critics considered him an "upstart" by traditional standards.[48] Most important, however, when he took on the responsibilities of a gentleman of leisure able to engage in public affairs without business concerns, he fulfilled his youthful pledge "to do for the future all that *lies in my Way* for the Service of my Countrymen."[49] By the middle of the eighteenth century, worldly ambition had lost its damning medieval associations with "selfish," "self-interest," "self-loving," and the like, but only if associated with self-improvement and "hard work."[50] As ambition became respectable, that cultural shift affected how he and his "countrymen" interpreted his rise.[51]

After his death, Franklin's biography was told in many ways. As we've already seen, some narrators revised his life story into an epitome of the self-made man myth. Immediately after his death, however, this was not the predominant narrative of his life. Franklin's stature certainly warranted tributes, and Philadelphia honored him with a memorial attended by many thousands and punctuated by an eighty-five-gun salute, equal to his years, while ships in the harbor from other nations joined American ships in showing their colors. The *Independent Gazetteer* declared that they paid "every possible mark of respect" to "this venerable and illustrious citizen and philosopher." All death notices recognized his elite stature, even brief ones, such as this from Boston, his birthplace: "At Philadelphia, the venerable and celebrated Philosopher and Patriot, his Excellency BENJAMIN FRANKLIN, LL.D. with whose amiable virtues and eminent

Figure 3.3 Benjamin West's dramatic painting *Benjamin Franklin Drawing Electricity from the Sky* portrayed Franklin as a classical hero, circa 1816. Unlike the 1763 portrait in Figure 2.2, West posthumously depicted Franklin's discovery of celestial electricity as spectacular but not as a practical tool to save buildings. The later image fit with other nineteenth-century descriptions of him as a self-made hero, contrary to his own ideas. (Courtesy of Philadelphia Museum of Art: Gift of Mr. and Mrs. Wharton Sinkler, 1958, 1958-132-1)

services the world is too well acquainted to need any attempt of ours at a recital." Or this from Philadelphia, the city Franklin had long since adopted: "The world has been so long in possession of such extraordinary proofs of the singular abilities and virtues of this FRIEND OF MANKIND, that it is impossible for a news-paper to encrease his fame, or to convey his name to a part of the civilized globe, where it is not already known and admired."[52] The most relevant point here is that these brief obituaries made no mention of origins, obscure or otherwise, or a climb upward.

Longer notices did recognize Franklin's origins and rise, usually without embarrassment but also without particular veneration. Among tributes to "his Excellency," a "short account" from Franklin's "Attending Physician" became the basis for most death notices and conveyed Franklin's own dying concerns. As his condition worsened in the last two weeks before his death, his doctor, John Jones, reflected Franklin's dedication to service by concluding that he had "made no doubt his present afflictions were kindly intended to wean him from a world, in which he was no longer fit to act the part assigned him." Dr. Jones also recorded that "when the severity of his pains sometimes drew forth a groan of complaint, he would observe – that he was afraid he did not bear them as he ought – acknowledged his grateful sense of the many blessings he had received from that Supreme Being, who had raised him, from small and low beginnings, to such high rank and consideration among men."[53] Had either Franklin's doctor or any of the many editors who republished this description objected to its reference to the "small and low beginnings" or to the rise that he attributed to "that Supreme Being," they might have filtered any or all of it out. Instead, they circulated it without comment.

In a departure from most posthumous honors, the American Philosophical Society, which Franklin had founded in 1743, published a lengthy eulogy, composed and delivered in a desultory manner by a long-time foe, the Reverend William Smith.[54] Smith exposed personal antagonisms and resentments to be sure, but also resentments and tensions between ranks. The spectacular rise and success of a man who once wore the tradesman's leather apron and yet came to tower over all but a few of his contemporaries on both sides of the Atlantic could not help but fuel frictions. Patricians of the period and those with pretensions to patrician status, such as John Adams, disliked Franklin's manner and may have begrudged his international stature.

In contrast to patrician aversion, tens of thousands of copies of *Poor Richard's Almanack*, along with Franklin's other published amusements and aphorisms, had sold annually for decades to middling folks, including tradesmen and their families, and had won him widespread popularity among those who took their newfound citizenship seriously and challenged political traditions of deference.

Franklin's homespun, folksy aphorisms and parables entertained readers and also, importantly, offered encouragement and advice for their self-improvement. His own story also shone a beacon of mobility to free men and the less-free women of the literate middling and artisan ranks. Printers and publishers began reaching for such audiences with serialized pieces within a month after Franklin's passing, with varying degrees of fidelity to what he had actually written. Overall, as literacy and personal independence grew among White Americans in a cultural and economic context that encouraged ambitions, an increasingly iconic Franklin served well as someone to emulate in a nation that imagined itself a bastion of freedom and opportunity.[55] In that novel and rapidly evolving setting, it was easy for storytellers to convert Franklin's life story as he wrote it during the nation's birth into a story that better fit the post-1800 nation and its denizens' aspirations. That revised story was the one that Temple Franklin told about his grandfather in 1818, a story that described a self-made man, a man who had "raised" himself rather than, in Benjamin's words, one who had "emerg'd."

From his youth, Franklin built institutions, public and private, to advance the common good. Three decades before helping to construct the US Constitution, he crafted the perpetually reprinted "Way to Wealth" essay of 1758, weaving into a story advice that he had published in *Poor Richard's Almanack* over years. In this allegory, the crowd awaiting a market's opening asked a respected old man what "think you of the Times?" They complained about "these heavy Taxes" as threatening the country's "ruin." Father Abraham's response rehearsed many of Poor Richard's stock of tradition-based aphorisms about hard work, as well as about saving time and money. He disagreed, though, that taxes were the source of people's frustrations. "We are taxed twice as much by our *Idleness*, three times as much by our *Pride*, and four times as much by our *Folly*." He urged, "If you would be *wealthy, think of Saving as well as of Getting*." Throughout, Father Abraham chided his audience for their resistance to taxes and their preference for spending on "the *artificial* Wants of Mankind" and "other Extravagancies." In the end, the "People heard it, and approved the Doctrine, and immediately practised the contrary, just as if it had been a common Sermon." Franklin's avatar, Richard Saunders, then decided against purchasing "Stuff for a new Coat" and finished with this advice: "*Reader*, if thou wilt do the same, thy Profit will be as great as mine." Fittingly, Franklin's "Poor Richard" signed the "Way to Wealth": "I am, as ever, Thine to serve thee."[56]

Just as Father Abraham's audience approved of his homily and then ignored it, so have most readers of the "Way to Wealth" ignored Franklin's argument on behalf of taxes and community service as relatively modest demands on citizens necessary to maintain and build a commonwealth. The essay's lure was money, but its tone most resembled the ubiquitous homilies that for centuries had defined "wealth" non-monetarily, such as salvation or the satisfactions of doing right. At the founding of the new nation in 1783, Franklin wrote to Robert Morris (1734–1806) out of concern about the "Remissness of our People in Paying Taxes." Morris was a prominent financier of the Revolutionary War, a signer of the Declaration of Independence and the Constitution and helped to create the nation's financial system. When citizens claim that taxes take "*the People's Money* out of their Pockets,*"* Franklin argued, they "mistake the point." Moreover, "All Property, indeed, ... seems to me to be the Creature of publick Convention." The public, through state institutions such as Congress, "has the Right of Regulating Descents & all other Conveyances of Property, and even of limiting the Quantity & the Uses of it." Anyone "that does not like civil Society on these Terms ... He can have no right to the Benefits of Society who will not pay his Club [levies] toward the Support of it."[57] Once citizens had acquired the privilege of taxation with representation, they also acquired responsibilities.

The eighteenth-century ideal of character emphasized reputation, public life, civic duties, exercising discipline, and overcoming temptations in service of society's highest principles. Only by dint of intense and self-conscious self-improvement and community-improvement, often by building public institutions, could anyone leave an indelible legacy of esteem, of worth. Everyone knew then that isolated self-making was impossible. Achievements worthy of honor could not be made alone. The ancients' flaws should not diminish the value of retrieving their vision for a more perfect union of individual and collective improvement.

Ideas about individual worth changed markedly and in diverse ways during the second half of America's eighteenth century. In turn, those changes laid a foundation for constructing the myth of the self-made man in the next century. Initially the myth's storytellers stayed within the contested spheres of culture and electoral politics, which dominated the early Republic's ideological disputes. As elites sought electoral victories in the early Republic they confronted incentives to obfuscate their advantages in order to appeal to the bulk of voters. Pursuing that electoral advantage fostered an illusion of self-making, rather than a reality of self-improvement. As the myth evolved, its nineteenth-century storytellers developed it as a tool for judgment in economic spheres, as well, valuing some people's contributions to the common good while dismissing others' contributions. Territorial and economic expansion accelerated geographic and social mobility that complicated those debates. By the early decades of the nineteenth century, pretensions to individuals' self-making would seem to be possible in what seemed to be a self-made nation.

4

The Politics of Self-Making in a Self-Made Nation

With no monarchs to set the nation's course, Americans have had to keep remaking it. To marshal political assets in the first decades of the nineteenth century, rival factions learned to appeal to an expanding population of voters who held competing ideals and interests. In these contests, stories – often mythical – helped to recruit and hold allies, shape ideals and identities, foster hopes, and galvanize action. Preachers and moralists also produced stories by the hundreds to persuade children and adults to follow one or another path of righteousness and avoid temptation. As the myth of a self-made nation took shape – self-made from a wilderness, it seemed to some – so did another myth, that of the self-made man. At their core, both myths are and have always been fundamentally judgmental: praising some and disparaging others, if only by implied comparison. Whether storytellers appealed to the myth of self-made success to applaud heroes, inspire others to strive, or rebuke some as self-made failures, they judged. They presumed a parity of choices and opportunities, plus their right to judge. The Republic's aspiring leaders and their advocates developed and applied this new judgmental rhetoric of self-making to build cultural authority – and the political authority it endowed.

In the cultural, political, and economic churn of the first decades of the nineteenth century, storytellers shaped and reshaped the meanings of self-making. Moving away from traditions that viewed individualist tendencies as threats to spiritual, personal, and community wellbeing, new stories emerged in which ambition and self-making became signs of merit, of self-improvement and achievement – especially notable if their protagonists claimed to overcome obscure origins. Initially in the realm of politics, "self-made" began to shift from a descriptor of anti-heroes to heroes.[1] As mythmakers moved away from the Founders' republican virtues, their new stories stripped away their heroes' foundations in society and community. Instead, many narratives glorified the archetype of a "solitary oak," as admirers said of Andrew Jackson. In turn, each grand oak's purportedly self-made success obscured the forest that supported him. Yet, the myth's hidden forest did not disappear in reality. The women, servants, enslaved persons, working-class toilers, clerks, and accountants still did the work that allowed heroes to be visible, to appear as solitary oaks.

IMPROVEMENT IN A SELF-MADE NATION

In 1825, the *Boston Monthly Magazine* published "Patriotism... A Sketch" that reinforced the link between "public and private virtues" and the country's "*self-achieved* independence." America could not rest on its "*prior* claim" to revolutionary "glory." Not only were other republics arising in that decade, but the aid that France and Spain had earlier given to "vex and humble" their rival Britain was no longer available. As with individuals, national self-improvement was necessary to grow, to prosper, and to be worthy of esteem. The article underscored that the country had to improve on its own, through its citizens' efforts: "we must be our own patrons, our own agents." The article's author, Nancy (Anne) Kingsbury Wollstonecraft, sister-in-law to the women's rights advocate Mary Wollstonecraft, observed the country anew after a time away and joined with other Euro-Americans to rejoice that where but recently "the dark and gloomy forest stretched its deepening shade... new and handsome buildings ... have sprung up," along with roads, canals, farms, and manufactories. She was astonished at what "seems a dream, a vision of fancy, and not the gradual and natural progress of ... improvement."[2] The nation's first half century saw such "improvement," as Wollstonecraft called it, everywhere, fueled by ambitions and fostering opportunities and choices.[3]

Wollstonecraft was not alone in her astonishment at the "dream" of rapid change. That the dream for some was a nightmare for others did not diminish the vast and ongoing expansion of individual and institutional choices. Frontiers beckoned, and not only in the "dark and gloomy forest" Wollstonecraft described in lands Euro-Americans imagined as wilderness empty of respect-worthy people.[4] Commercial, technological, cultural, material, and religious frontiers also lured many Americans toward new choices, thus advancing their sense of self-agency. Growing cities held multiple frontiers within them, with disparate opportunities and risks. Confronting these frontiers required countless individual choices that were cumulatively momentous: whether to enter; how deeply; alone or alongside kith or kin; for wealth, community, or power; out of desire or desperation? Every one of these frontiers hazarded destruction, perhaps by violence, alcohol, loneliness, or financial ruin. But to be without ambition, to lack a goal beyond subsistence in this new era and republic, meant to stand aside as the nation paraded by. Therefore, every free man, and most free women, had to choose a path – at least one, at least once – regardless of their risks. The cumulative effect was a nation that the loudest voices proclaimed as uniquely self-fashioning and also uniquely demanding of that self-fashioning.

Wollstonecraft declared, "We have risen faster in the scale of nations than any other people were ever known to have done," and she insisted on patriotic dedication to improve further. As this culture of prideful nation-making evolved, combatants in the competitions for political authority told stories of self-improvement, self-fashioning, and self-making – with or without those words – to align themselves, their visions, and their heroes with what they imagined as progress for their republic as well as themselves. As Walt Whitman wrote in the mid nineteenth century, "An individual is as superb as a nation / when he has the qualities which make a superb nation."[5] Of course, eligibility for being a "superb" hero was hardly universal. It paralleled eligibility to vote and eligibility for other choices, opportunities, and self-improvement.

SELF-MADE MANIACS

Across this new, self-created, self-governing nation, so much *could* go wrong. Within rapidly expanding opportunities for labor, finance, migration, innovation, culture, and consumption on personal and community levels, so much *did* go wrong. The phrase "self-made" entered slowly into jeremiads, appeals, and inspirations as Americans considered overcoming deep but fading traditions about providential and worldly constraints. Thus, early nineteenth-century parables of self-making were erratic as their storytellers navigated cultural transitions embedded in transitions toward urbanization, industrialization, mass communication, religious upheavals, and political campaigns. They did not so much herald the future's glorious myths of individualism to come as they highlighted the risks and opportunities of decisions in a land overflowing with choices and expectations.

Choices, of course, are a prerequisite to being self-made. No one was exempt from the challenges of ongoing cultural, economic, and political transitions, including geographical movement. After all, the Latin root for "ambition" means moving around, and move Americans did, in every sense. Many moved west for land, but, after 1800, they increasingly moved into urban areas as well. According to the 1850 census, almost a quarter of White native-born men did not live in the states where they were born.[6]

Stasis and calm became rare as ideals or realities and increasingly drew disapproval because the loudest voices in mainstream culture expected and demanded change, movement, action – some version of improvement and control of self, others, communities, and nation.[7] Only the churn was certain, but its temptations raised the risks of going astray. Those who left their origins behind could wind up as fools or heroes according to whether they foundered or flourished, sold or salvaged their souls, brought disgrace or credit to themselves and their communities. Peddlers and barkeeps knew this, and so did preachers. Madness could result if people succumbed to alcohol, but also if they got lost in debt chasing fantasies of abundance, or withered from social isolation after leaving their origins to pursue new ambitions.

In this fluid context, storytellers adopted new phrases to convey encouragements and warnings, to judge successes and failures. Variations on "self-made" entered the language as cognitive handles to grasp and convey new attitudes. Some older phrases, such as referrals to Franklin and others as "self-taught," continued and reinforced positive associations with self-agency. But traditional phrases that combined "self" with negative descriptors, such as selfishness or self-serving, continued unabated. Consistent with residual mistrust of personal independence and the likelihood of failure, early references to self-making very often described those who had gone astray – who seemed to have willfully chosen to leave the path of righteousness to challenge social or religious conventions. In other words, the earliest "self-made men" were likely to be anti-heroes, not heroes. Thus, early expressions warned of "self-made maniacs" who succumbed to the growing lure of alcohol as the populations of towns increased.

Temperance advocates asserted through sermons, pamphlets, and newspapers, as did one in 1815, that "one third ... of all the maniacs in our country are self-made." By "drinking to excess" once fine people "have literally made themselves mad by intemperance." By poor choices, "rational creatures can thus trifle with their eternal interests, and with tremendous perseverance work out their own destruction!" "Perseverance" in this jeremiad referred to the effort of self-destruction rather than achievement. An 1822 diatribe against "self-made idiots" explicitly described alcoholism as the result of self-defeating, self-isolating choices, such as "If you seek to prevent your friends raising you in the world, be a drunkard; for that will defeat all their efforts." Self-making from this view was a deliberate rejection of the benefits of social networks that otherwise help "to raise you to character, credit, and prosperity." Underscoring individual agency, each of its dozen warnings began with "If you wish..." or "If you would be..." Choosing to reject community standards and engagement would "starve your family," make you poor and easy prey for "knaves," and "blunt your senses."[8]

Various disparaging references to self-making abounded in other arenas, as well. Political partisans might be called "self-made mushroom patriots" who pop up overnight on a pile of waste, and whose "Sham-Patriotism ... dwindles to nothing before the glare of reason." Likewise, "self-made, bloated patriots" appeared as targets in many 1812 newspapers. An 1813 allegory emulating John Bunyan's classic seventeenth-century *Pilgrim's Progress* named every character for a trait, such as "Humility" and "Guilt." Among the flawed residents of the "*Hill of Conceit*" were "self-made philosophers and doctors" whose "madness" was infectious. In 1820, a man sent an open letter to his local newspaper to defend his own dignity against another's "self-made ridiculous tales." Even counterfeiters got derided as "self-made coiners." Europe, especially Napoleon, provided self-made anti-heroes for the American press. An earnestly partisan but not very elegant poem for Independence Day 1808 insisted that "All you who love the fed'ral cause" will not "crouch before a self-made king" such as "Buonaparte." Likewise, "The Warrior," an 1813 poem, condemned that same "self-made Emp'ror" who "when he falls, he meets a tyrant's end." Warning of the perils of such ambitious, self-driven heroes, it began "Of all the plagues whence mortals can be curs'd, / The mad'ning *hero plague* is sure the worst!"[9] These harsh judgments condemned anyone inclined to violate the Republic's principles, but they ironically foretold America's own, and imminent, *"hero plague."*

Among the most prolific and influential storytellers in the early Republic, Mason Locke Weems (1759–1825) lavished praise and imagination on American heroes, most notably George Washington and Benjamin Franklin, but none as self-made. This enterprising publicist was keenly attuned to the lower- and middle-rank audiences among whom he traveled as preacher and bookseller, and he correctly surmised the appeal of his tales, including his most famous fabrication, the tale of the boy Washington chopping down a cherry tree and then confessing because he couldn't tell a lie about it.[10]

It is significant, therefore, that in 1815, only a few years before Benjamin Franklin's grandson, William Temple Franklin, turned the illustrious self-improver into a self-made man when he revised the *Autobiography*, Weems produced a popular Franklin biography that instead looked back to tradition. His "self-made" references follow what was still then most prevalent, namely critiques of willful violations of norms. He paired "self" with "self-conceited" to describe a brandy-addled "self-made brute," and again to describe "lazy self-made paupers" whom Franklin generously aided. Making his case about the value of Franklin's self-improvement and good choices, Weems came down particularly hard: "O you time-wasting, brain-starving young men, who can never be at ease unless you have a cigar or a plug of tobacco in your mouths, go on with your puffing and champing . . . – go on I say; but remember it was not in this way that our little Ben became the GREAT DR. FRANKLIN." Weems was dedicated to self-improvement, but not at all to the notion of self-making: he expounded on the benefits Franklin received from his extended family and its ancient artisan roots, for "Ben was uncommonly blest in a father" and family.[11] Franklin would have approved of Weems's insistence on individual responsibility for wise choices, coupled with appreciation for social and community debts.

SANCTIFIED BY RELIGION AND PATRIOTISM

Out of these inauspicious precedents, "self-made" would shift gradually toward positive connotations that sanctified individualism and ambition. When this shift began, the only certainty was that religion and patriotism were paramount sources of worth, while "aristocratic" was the most wicked anti-American trait. Storytellers who grasped the power in these three axioms applied them to transform self-seeking and ambition from dangers into bulwarks against aristocracy's evils. Traditions of honoring and encouraging self-improvement broadly, as before, dominated stories intended to inspire citizens to advance the nation. Some phrases, such as references to Franklin and others as "self-taught," became more frequent and central in the new republic. Learning through informal means continued to rise in stature, again with frequent references to Franklin and Washington, whereas formal education could signal elitist advantages. Spiritual growth as well as patriotic service received praise as signs of self-improvement. As the electorate widened during the 1820s, anti-aristocratic appeals increasingly carried elections, to the dismay of both the well-born and those who had modeled their own improvement on traditional standards. Old-time combatants John Adams and Thomas Jefferson embodied such traditional hopes. To advance those hopes, they looked past some of their differences in 1813 to imagine the possible benefits and likely challenges of a patriotic "natural aristocracy," based not on inherited station but on individuals' talents and self-improvement through schooling.[12] However, their intellectual and nostalgic musings did not survive exposure in a culture imbued with anti-aristocratic rhetoric.

When we think of "self-made" heroes today, religious leaders do not spring to mind first. Two centuries ago, however, stories about just such figures began to dignify the concept of self-making. For example, an 1810 magazine lauded Samuel Miller (1764–1810): "more truly than of almost any other man, in all those respects, in which he rose superior to the common rank of men, he was self-made." Not only did he rise in worldly stature from his family's obscure roots, but, the story went, he applied his self-improvement to God and community in true Puritan fashion. That storyline wasn't new, but attaching the concept of "self-made" to it was. "Few men," his biographer explained, "have ever united so much business with so much reading, so much attention to friends and so punctual a discharge of all the relative and social duties." In 1789, Miller had moved from western Massachusetts to Middlebury in the Republic of Vermont, hoping to prosper by surveying and purchasing tracts of land while serving as the village's first lawyer. Two years later Vermont joined the United States, and by 1800 Miller had become a leading citizen and co-founder of Middlebury College. In another five years, "when surrounded by worldly prosperity" and with "no earthly motive," he experienced conversion and thereafter increasingly focused his efforts on affairs of the church and the Vermont Missionary Society, which was active in the era's revivals. His heroism came from the cultural authority of old-time religion, namely work that served faith and community and set "a pattern for imitation" for the young. This "humble follower of the Cross" who had risen above life's hardships through "habits of industry" was "diligent in business, fervent in spirit, serving the Lord" – a standard that religious storytellers would continue to assert for their heroes as they contributed to the contested meanings of self-making through the century.[13]

An 1822 religious publication out of Baltimore, Maryland, reviewed an 1818 biography of Andrew Fuller (1754–1815), a highly regarded and influential preacher. Although Fuller was British, American storytellers spread his reputation as a godly man worthy of esteem. A printer in Charlestown, Massachusetts, published the biography and between 1790 and 1840 Fuller appeared in American newspapers hundreds of times, either as an author or a subject. The 1822 reviewer was glad that the book presented Fuller as "a man of strong manly good sense" who was "a man of integrity, industry, perseverance, and disinterestedness." Without making a lengthy claim that Fuller rose from material obscurity other than to note that he started "without extensive learning," the reviewer remarked that "it is a matter of great curiosity and consequence to fall upon an eminent self-made man (that we may use a common phrase)" such as he. Fuller pursued spiritual and intellectual, not worldly, rewards, and the lesson for "young ministers" to follow was devotion to "enterprise and action" within a support system that was both providential and social.[14] These kinds of deeply religious blessings helped to move what was a "common phrase" with mixed connotations toward a consistently positive meaning, away from self-made errors and narratives of individual ruin and toward models for serving faith and community, albeit models only applicable to men with opportunities.

In addition to religion, politics and citizenship were another increasingly prominent arena for the consecration of individual ambition and, therefore, self-making, as the term transformed from adverse to heroic. It seems that the phrase "self-made men" was first used in Congress to argue for "the necessity of electing men of talents, morality, industry, and integrity" to the House of Representatives. Representative Alney McLean of Kentucky (1779–1841) argued on the floor in 1817 that members of the House, unlike Senators, were "elected directly by the people" and that voters could best find such men "in the lower and middle walks of life (I mean as to property) than among the more wealthy part of the community." Unlike "those who had been dandled in the lap of fortune," McLean explained, "these men, who might be styled self-made men, were generally more acquainted with the views, the wishes and desires of the great mass of the people." McLean did not point out that these men had advantages of race and gender, of course, but he was very clear that constituents would suffer if "represented only by men of wealth" rather than by "men of moderate circumstances" who had risen in their communities' esteem.[15] McLean's reference to self-made men in this example was a modest harbinger of much louder political dramas and rhetoric to come.

HEROES ON THE WESTERN FRONTIERS

Two key cultural arenas – faith and patriotism – thus began to refashion self-making from a sin to a virtue. This new, seemingly self-made nation intended to keep growing, although what that meant was hotly disputed. Some, most notably Alexander Hamilton (1755–1804) and Henry Clay (1777–1852), thought it best to hold tight within the nation's original borders and to concentrate on building cities and industries, roads and bridges, schools and libraries – what we now call infrastructure. Others followed Thomas Jefferson's intuition to expand into territories they believed were theirs for the taking, just as Euro-Americans always had. The storytellers who advocated for each set of frontiers heralded heroes and disparaged villains in order to advance their partisan claims on collective resources and to conquer: sometimes to conquer business and technological problems; sometimes to conquer the lands of indigenous peoples or of Spanish and French colonizers.

Throughout the nineteenth century, storytellers praised merchants and soldiers, inventors and explorers, but in the century's early decades the adventurers who inspired the most fervent mythmaking did so at the nation's geographic frontiers. Those "untamed" fringes – with their mysteries and seemingly wild animals, forests, and people – afforded the widest opportunities for ambitious men of obscure origins to refashion their life stories into romances of triumph over practical challenges, which also garnered them acclaim unlike those who had stayed safe at home. As a young man, for example, Middlebury's Samuel Miller left what seemed a crowded Connecticut for the open lands of Vermont and a community that welcomed his legal skills. Also on that social frontier, he could become a local hero and find his soul. For others, becoming a national hero on the frontier required bravado and a good bit of help from professional storytellers who had their own political goals.

Heroes had made the Revolution, and a half century later the Founders' stories could still satisfy patriotic appetites and provide exemplars such as those Parson Weems featured. However, as the country grew, that generation lost its monopoly on heroism and heroic tales. Along the way, the Founders' ideals of community-directed selflessness – "republican virtue" – began to fade as prime criteria for esteem. Patriotism and service, however, never became as quaint as powdered wigs and buckled shoes.[16] Even the most cynical still had to appear to act on patriotic, community-oriented motives on regional and national scales. Frontier tales with their spirited heroes found audiences who appreciated a rough-and-ready masculinity that the Founders had diligently disdained. By the War of 1812, stories about frontiersmen Daniel Boone, David Crockett, Andrew Jackson, and even Abraham Lincoln, as we will see, increasingly set the pace for Romantic heroism in the new west, much to the dismay of traditional elites of that same generation, such as Henry Clay, who preferred the Founders' elegance and eloquence. Even so, Clay and other ambitious elites of that era would ultimately adopt a frontier narrative because they too needed stories, however contrived, that carried the fragrance and romance of western self-fashioning and self-making. Masculinity itself was reshaped along the way – no more lace, breeches, or Latin.

Among the most basic factors that contributed to the frontier variation of the self-making narrative were distance and novelty. Fantasies and narratives of all kinds flourish within mysteries. When people live out their lives in small communities, there are few mysteries among them: they know who owes whom; who taught, guided, disciplined, or harmed whom. No one can claim to succeed independently in such a setting. As the nation grew through the early nineteenth century, the geographical distances between protagonists of self-made stories and their audiences grew. Yarn-spinning escaped the constraints of familiarity. Although most Americans still lived in rural areas before the Civil War, they largely lived in "settled" areas without mystery, except for newcomers who were subject to suspicion. On and beyond the fringes, however, everyone was either a newcomer or a newcomer's target, and imagination bred mysteries and adventures that were sent back to or imagined among eastern audiences. Self-reliance increasingly seemed a condition of prosperity and became a cultural standard for judgment; it would provide a foundation for self-made myths to follow. New generations of colonizers and their champions built new realities and new fantasies.

At the same time, the means of spreading stories multiplied. Mysteries of the nation's fringes filled endless books, newspapers, pamphlets, and sermons, as well as theaters, lecture halls, and legislatures, even when those tales flowed from comfortable abodes back East.[17] Commercial incentives attracted mythmakers to tell stories of frontier adventures, and their successes, conversely, indicate the rise of literate audiences who safely enjoyed vicarious thrills of adventures in a "savage wilderness." John Filson's immensely popular 1784 biography of frontiersman Daniel Boone (1734–1820), supposedly told in the hero's words, aimed at attracting people to Kentucky where both men owned property, "one of the most opulent and powerful states on the continent of North America." Filson reported Boone to say of his final years, "I now live in peace and safety, enjoying the sweets of liberty, and the bounties of Providence, with my once fellow-sufferers, in this delightful country, which I have seen purchased with a vast expence of blood and treasure" through "all my toil and dangers."[18]

Perhaps the most notable of frontier romance authors was James Fenimore Cooper, whose five *Leatherstocking Tales* were retrospective novels published between 1827 and 1841 about eighteenth-century upstate New York back when it was on the fringes. Their enormously popular protagonist was Natty Bumppo, whom Cooper may have modeled on Boone. Fascinating as literature and valuable as literary reflections, these tales amplified Romantic-era notions of heroism as individualist triumphs that revealed a Nature superior to "civilization" but, inevitably, overtaken by civilization. No less than the British Romantic poet Lord Byron acclaimed Daniel Boone in his epic poem *Don Juan*, as a figure to assail civilization: "Who passes for in life and death most lucky, / Of the great names which in our faces stare, / The General Boon, back-woodsman of Kentucky, / Was happiest amongst mortals anywhere." Although Byron's poetic tribute to Boone, first available in 1819, wasn't widely read, abundant other conduits for the West's romance carried the theme broadly in fantasies of conquering mysteries, peoples, and a continent. Many of these masqueraded as history but added lavish embellishments to their heroes' adventures.[19] Fiction writers such as Ned Buntline cranked out formulaic dime novels with rough-and-ready themes. Not particularly artful but commercially successful, they likewise portrayed their White male heroes as powerful, free to roam and to triumph over adversity by virtue of their will, fortitude, and capacity for violence. The dime novel genre continued through the century as a lucrative channel for disseminating the myth of the self-made man.

While these individualist, mythic tales were produced solely for commercial gain, other storytellers spread heroic sagas for both commercial and partisan gains. The most prominent product of this genre was David Crockett's long-lived celebrity that combined the frontier's exoticism with party politics. His fame illustrates how a narrative of frontier self-making converged with political self-making in the young Republic. Crockett's life has been so energetically and colorfully recounted over two centuries, not always even resembling genuine biography, that the historical Crockett is difficult to uncover. We do know that he was born in 1786 in what is now Tennessee. He was a tall, clever egalitarian who relished regaling audiences, and a genial sharp-shooter who called himself David – not Davy. He won local elections, including to Congress, against those he called his "educated opponents" and perished in 1836 at the Alamo Mission in what soon thereafter became the Republic of Texas.[20]

Crockett's origins were truly obscure and lean, which lent credence to his and others' future claims for him as a self-made man. Indentured at twelve to help pay family debts, in his teens he started school but played hooky to avoid a beating by his schoolmaster, and then ran away from home to avoid a beating by his father. After wandering around to various jobs, he returned home to help work off his father's debts. He soon set off to serve under General Andrew Jackson in 1813 and again in 1815, but preferred to exercise his marksmanship to feed troops rather than to shoot people. After returning home, he acquired his "colonel" title in the local militia as he began his climb in local politics.[21] These documented basics form the skeleton for subsequent tales about Crockett. As the well-regarded historian James Parton concluded in an 1870 article, "the merest outline of a life so full of strange and romantic adventure" called for "universal attention" through "a permanent addition to our literature," that is, a fuller historical study. Parton pointed back to Crockett's immense popularity decades earlier as a "hunter, story teller and general good fellow," a "gallant pioneer" who, the reigning tales said, perished a hero.[22]

Wildly variant stories about Crockett fed that popularity and expansively tied frontier fantasies to an ethos of individualist self-making, beliefs in American exceptionalism, and partisan politics. Significantly, during the mid twentieth century's Cold War, Walt Disney and John Wayne told their versions of Crockett fables to bolster fantasies of stalwart patriotism and individual heroism through romantic adventures that, they declared, ended nobly at the Alamo. Long before that, politically motivated admirers in 1831 had described "the celebrated Col. Crockett" as "a self-made man – a practical Legislator." According to that tribute, his education came from his frontier adventures, "which gave him so many opportunities of studying human nature in the lower walks of life" and "laid the foundations for his future course in the halls of congress."[23]

As a frontiersman turned politician, Crockett truly was self-taught according to traditions that valorized men like Washington and Franklin, whose educations also took place outside of formal schooling. Unlike them, however, Crockett earnestly embraced deliberate self-fashioning to compete in electoral politics in 1823, applying his penchant for energetic storytelling to campaigning. Although he indulged in plenty of exaggerations of his own, accompanied by a wink and a hearty laugh, he rejected some of the stories that others told about him. For example, he initially complained about an enormously popular play, *The Lion of the West*, that opened in 1831 and ran for many years, making a farce out of his backwoodsman's persona even as it enlarged his celebrity. But, to the delight of an 1833 audience that he joined in a box seat up front, when the show's star, James Hackett, who was decked out as the caricature Colonel Nimrod Wildfire, came onstage, he bowed to Crockett. To top off the merriment, Crockett returned the bow, first to the buckskin-attired Hackett and then to the cheering crowd.[24]

The importance of Crockett's ascent into legend came from how his career highlighted the growing intensity of partisan politics and the way that myths of self-making rose within the political arena. While representing his Tennessee

Figure 4.1 David Crockett's origins were much rougher than Andrew Jackson's, but he did not exaggerate or flaunt them. Therefore, this sharpshooter preferred not to be portrayed in buckskin or to be called "Davy." He autographed this engraved print with his motto, "I leave this rule, for others when I am dead / Be always sure, you are right, then go, a head." (Library of Congress: Popular Graphic Arts, Item 2003666771; no date)

district in Congress, he shifted his allegiance away from Andrew Jackson – a shift that not only added zest to the mix of history and fancy surrounding him, but also starkly illustrated the disingenuousness of partisan mythmakers. In 1827, Crockett began the first of his several terms as a Jacksonian, and as long as he favored Andrew Jackson, advocates for the more powerful Westerner portrayed him as a humorous, lesser version of their chief. During that stage of Crockett's political career, anti-Jacksonians saw nothing to praise about his education or values; as they told it, he was merely a loud and uncouth bumpkin who was good with a rifle and a tall tale. All this reversed once Jackson became president and Crockett began his second Congressional term in 1829. Jackson's Indian Removal Act and other policies, such as his refusal to support squatters' rights legislation, disillusioned Crockett, and so he switched loyalties. "Although our great man, at the head of the nation, has changed his course, I will not change mine," he proclaimed in Congress. "I would rather be politically dead than hypocritically immortalized."[25]

The Jacksonians' turn against Crockett was predictable and not so intriguing as the anti-Jacksonian turn toward him. Suddenly Crockett was their man. In 1831 they praised him as a self-made man, having apparently discovered the principled frontiersman who "had forsaken Gen. Jackson finding he was not the man he expected him to be" and could "discourse most marvellously" on all matters. In the 1830s, those who formed the Whigs, along with their allies in the press and other popular media, churned out accolades for this marvel of the frontier. They even trotted him around New England to win over voters enamored of the frontier, hoping to show that a truly rugged Westerner could oppose their nemesis, Jackson.[26]

Disregarding ghost-written publications, including *Davy Crockett's Own Story: As Written by Himself*, we can glean Crockett's own preferred narrative from a Congressional speech in 1830 in which he described himself as "one of those who are called self-taught men." Importantly, here and elsewhere, his version of the self-made story hewed to some of the older traditions of community service for the common good. Very much in keeping with Benjamin Franklin's expressions of debt to his friends and community, he explained that "by the kindness of my neighbors, and some exertion of my own, I have been raised from obscurity without an education." In that same speech, he also presented himself as a farmer rather than hunter or frontiersman, aiming at large electoral targets. The year before he had concluded a speech with "humble efforts in support of his poor fellow-citizens" in the West, a "plain farmer" representing "the humble but virtuous men" who had sent him.[27]

Crockett always spoke respectfully in Congress, even eloquently after a fashion, intent on serving as an even-handed champion for the West's citizens and their common good rather than the privileged. He argued, for instance, that funding for West Point Academy favored "the rich and influential" and "aristocratic" instead of "the destitute poor" who deserved public funds. In a robust anti-aristocratic spirit, he argued on behalf of "the sons of the poor, [who] for want of active friends" could not attend or afford travel to West Point. He filled his speech with class-based criticisms of "the sons of the noble and wealthy, and of members of Congress, people of influence" who should not benefit from money "raised from the poor man's pocket." In other speeches, he complained that "Eastern gentlemen" could not understand the concerns about land distribution and ordinary people working on the frontier.[28] Crockett freely contrasted ordinary people's circumstances with elites' advantages. Nonetheless, his egalitarian, community-oriented anti-Jackson stance lost Crockett reelection and were never prominent in the fables about him. Policy speeches about the common good lost to Jackson's powerful storytelling machine, which propelled bombastic heroism and anti-aristocratic acrimony to enthralled voters.

OLD HICKORY AS A SOLITARY OAK

Bringing Crockett into the anti-Jackson camp as an authentic frontier antidote did not slow the electoral advance of Andrew Jackson, the first president from the western territories and the only general to be elected president since George Washington. Supported by the votes of men enfranchised since the Revolution, Jackson was fiercely loyal, demanded loyalty from others, and exacted retribution without hesitation. He seemed to have two personas, one forceful, raging, and deadly; the other affectionate, polished, and charming. His dual identities encompassed military leadership and being a skilled lawyer and land speculator who often quoted the Bible.

Jackson was born in 1767 and raised by his widowed mother until her death when he was fourteen. He lost his brothers during the Revolutionary War and received a head wound as a boy from a British officer in punishment for defiance. This background enabled Jackson and his advocates to credibly construct his childhood as harsh. In reality, however, his mother's family was prosperous, and he grew up in an affluent uncle's home. He attended a private academy and taught for a while, receiving enough schooling plus legal training under the guidance of influential lawyers to practice law by 1787. At fifteen he even inherited about £400, approximately $85,400 in 2024, which he quickly squandered.[29] Invaluable connections among the small group of professionals in the territory that became Tennessee made for highly profitable land dealings, including in regions of questionable legal status, plus a successful entry into politics in his early twenties. Despite so many advantages – unusual in western regions – he and his advocates later highlighted the tragic elements and ignored the blessings. In other words, they narrated Jackson as a self-made and self-fashioned frontier hero, which attests to the growing force of that mythology and the corresponding weakening of narratives about community support.

Jackson built his reputation for resolute discipline and relentless patriotism by leading volunteer troops effectively against indigenous peoples and veteran British forces in the Southeast, culminating in January 1815 with a remarkable victory in New Orleans that brought him fame and made him an attractive candidate for national office. An assortment of storytellers then took up the challenge of making this war hero into a president, and the mythmaking began. "ANDREW JACKSON was born a great man – he was born free," concluded an 1818 biography that rapidly went through multiple editions. Not only did Jackson benefit from his free birth, according to S. Putnam Waldo, but as a westerner he could ascend unencumbered by "a monied or a landed aristocracy" like that which dominated the nation's "settled" regions. There, "an insulated being, . . . without the influence of friends to aid him, or without funds to procure them, can hardly

Figure 4.2 In commemoration of Andrew Jackson's death in 1845, Nathaniel Currier printed this image of the late president as a polished gentleman standing in front of his mansion. The caption calls him "The Hero, the Sage, and the Patriot." This image portrays him as having nobly risen from the rough frontier origins that he and his storytellers exaggerated to appeal to an expanding electorate. (HUM Images / Universal Images Group / via Getty Images)

hope, with the most gigantic powers, to place himself in eligible circumstances." In "the new states," however, Waldo asserted that "each individual may almost be said to make a province by himself." There, Jackson could "rely solely upon intrinsic worth and decision of character, to enable him to rise rapidly with a rapidly rising people." Waldo depicted a drama of "arduous toils, the severe privations and the excessive fatigues, by which he acquired his fame."[30]

Despite Jackson's good fortune through mentors, inheritance, and professional partners and connections, Waldo asserted that Jackson entered adulthood "entirely alone" and without "extrinsic advantages to raise him into life." Continuing with that theme, "he sought no aid out of himself, and he received no aid but what he commanded by his own energy."[31] Neither Waldo nor anyone else mentioned Jackson's squandered inheritance or numerous advantages. Waldo's narrative contained all the elements of self-making praise, plus plenty of drama and links to "a rapidly rising people," but still did not use the phrase itself. Jacksonian era political combatants would soon thereafter utilize the phrase as they competed for the cultural authority that could support political authority.

Pacesetting those competitions, Jackson's allies devised a concerted storytelling campaign to make a president out of the "Hero of New Orleans." Aiming for 1824, they built a network of supporters based in Nashville, Tennessee, but connected throughout the country to local political committees and newspapers. Sometimes, where favorable newspapers did not exist, they established them; their stories had to get into the wind. They raised partisanship to new heights, and in the hotly contested four-way presidential race of 1824, Jackson achieved a plurality in both the popular and electoral counts, only to lose the race in the House of Representatives. Allegations that a "corrupt bargain" had cost him the victory became a powerful rallying cry for the next four years, marshaled as evidence of the need for a hero who could reform national politics. The innovative and brilliant workings of that long campaign constructed and broadly disseminated the image of a self-made hero who could revive the true, pure spirit of America's revolutionary generation, and who, like George Washington, was willing to sacrifice his peaceful rural retirement to serve the nation. Much of Jackson's persona was refashioned for this campaign, including the fiction that he was a reluctant candidate. The outcome was a landslide victory in 1828.[32] Stories – this story – mattered, not realities, and the election rewarded the mythmakers.

Along the way to 1828, candidates' supporters began to tell stories in a language that had seen little use outside of moral judgment – condemning drunkenness or praising godliness – but was available to judge worthiness for the national stage. William Crawford of Georgia, one of the four leading presidential candidates in 1824, received the newly honorific term "self-made" in a lengthy 1824 essay Thomas H. Hall addressed to "The Freemen" of the North Carolina district he represented in Congress. Signaling that the phrase "self-made" was still germinal and unusual, he self-consciously attempted to define and elaborate it: "Crawford is what we call a self-made man; has risen from obscurity by his own exertions." Hall contrasted Jackson with Crawford, who was a man of "integrity and ability" and whose "manners and deportment were always those of a polite gentleman." According to Hall's diatribe, Crawford could be self-made as self-improved even if not self-taught in Jackson's rough manner. A space-filler "*Maxim*" highlighted at the end of this campaign piece declared simply: "Merit should be the only passport to office." In that same North Carolina newspaper, an unsigned essay illustrated how the phrase could still be used to denounce rather than praise. Although the "nation owes him a large debt of gratitude," a long list of Jackson's actions exposed him as either "ignorant or despotic," with "uncultivated notions of military tactics" and a mere "smattering knowledge of law."[33] From some perspectives, of course, those very attributes were beginning to sanctify Jackson as self-made in what was becoming its positive sense – but not in this partisan enemy's camp. What is significant here is that the status of "self-made man" was still conditional, tentative, and subject to partisan debate: it was possible either to praise or deride with the concept. Self-making did not yet assure an indisputably heroic or positive narrative.

The next year, as the campaign accelerated toward 1828, an essay on Jackson's behalf appeared in many venues, loaded with melodramatic descriptions of origins and triumphs that forcefully advanced the self-made myth, both as regards Jackson, and generically. It began, "If the present age can boast an ornament for whom history furnishes no example, ... that man is *Andrew Jackson*." Because he had been "deprived in his boyhood" of his family, "he stood alone, and unassisted" like a "solitary oak that stands forlorn." With "neither the pride of ancestry, nor the patronage of office – he was not the fondling of a dominant aristocracy, but had to struggle for subsistence in the darkest hours of adversity, and to encounter vicissitude after vicissitude" with only the forces of his "energy and self-possession." Intriguing reflections mixed causal factors between the "Nature [that] designed him for a great man" and the *"force of circumstances."* Neither influence alone could form a hero of such magnitude: "poverty, and self-reliance" had to combine with "natural qualities." Thus, although "the ancients would have attributed the successes of Napoleon Bonaparte to the decrees of destiny," in an era with "kings and sceptres alike sinking into unimportance, and non-entity," it would be inappropriate to attribute Jackson's rapid march "to honors, and popularity" simply to "fortune, ... [a] capricious deity." Instead, "*Talents*, and not the auspices of supernatural protection" provided the foundation for both Napoleon's and Jackson's achievements. Fortunately, however, unlike "the conqueror of Europe," Jackson was "the friend of man, the soldier of liberty" who would not "prostitute his principles at the unhallowed shrine of ambition."[34] Unlike the anti-aristocratic praise typical of the time for men who educated and improved themselves to serve, this hyperbole relieved its conquering hero of debts to any community. Instead, self-making appeared here, as it would increasingly in stories to come, to be the lonely success of a solitary oak that eclipsed the forest. Just as strikingly, this encomium to Jackson also denied that he had benefited from "supernatural protection," which would have been heretical not too long before.

SELF-MADE: THE STORIES THAT FORGED AN AMERICAN MYTH

Two years after the fateful 1824 election, the heat of anti-aristocratic polemics on Jackson's behalf continued to rise. A Jacksonian from Kentucky, Joseph Le Compte, told his Congressional colleagues that Westerners worried that the practice of selecting presidents from previous Cabinet appointments as in 1824 was "likely to grow into a dangerous precedent." The "hero of New Orleans" deserved esteem because he "was self-made; he rose by merit alone." Not only had he "made" himself, but by saving "the great commercial city of New Orleans," Jackson had "saved the Union." Beyond the puffery, Le Compte contrasted his candidate, who "owes nothing to patronage," to the elites who owed everything to it.[35] That anti-aristocratic contrast animated the core of self-making's force and appeal as it migrated outward from the moral spheres of preachers, educators, and public servants and into spheres of political power.

This budding political genre of stories about self-making rarely aimed to set godly examples for youth, whether positive or negative, and focused instead on polemics about ambitious men. By the 1820s, the self-made man concept had begun to acquire enough cultural authority to make it an attractive rhetorical tool to enhance men's portrayals and their claims on public resources, including esteem and votes. A story of self-making, however disconnected from fact, was becoming a form of political certification. It also highlighted contrasts between people who mattered in the public sphere and those who did not. Of course, White males alone had the potential for self-making in these myths and fables. Necessarily, everyone else and their contributions were rendered invisible. In stories of self-making that foregrounded the solitary oaks, the forests constituted by almost everyone else – women, people of color, the working classes, the poor, and even the putative "oak's" own family and connections – were invisible, except as figures protected or subdued by the hero himself.

As a surprising reminder that nothing is fixed, intuitive, or self-evident about the ideology of self-making in America, in this early stage of its evolution people who were merely rich but did not engage in political competitions were also invisible as subjects of the myth. For example, John Jacob Astor built astounding wealth during these decades but had no religious or patriotic credentials and, therefore, did not qualify as self-made despite his relatively obscure origins. His time for those accolades would come in a few decades. Elites competing for political authority, on the other hand, were visible but ineligible for praise as self-made if their opponents identified them as aristocrats. In this new genre of folklore, elites' self-improvement to serve, following the Founders' models, did not guarantee prestige. A candidate's initial advantages created toxic political disadvantages and had to be hidden. Thus, elites initially served anti-elitist mythmakers only as foils – until, that is, they figured out the game, as we will see, and turned it against their rivals in the coming decades.

But who were these "aristocrats" who, by contrast, ennobled the self-made? The category could include any number of figures, not just beneficiaries of inherited wealth or social benefits, but also formally educated people; businessmen who sought government subsidies for transportation projects, such as roads and canals, that would help them profit from their own investments; boosters who sought federal aid for projects that would advance their regions and the nation; or political appointees. Anyone might qualify as aristocratic, essentially, who stood as an obstacle to someone else's ambitions. "Aristocrat" was becoming a catch-all political pejorative, contrasted against "self-made" as a catch-all political encomium. By the 1830s, one's allies were best defended and promoted as self-made men, poaching the respected meanings of this phrase from the realms of preachers and public servants to justify ambitions and claims on public resources.

The Revolutionary patriot Roger Sherman had long ago been laid to rest when he rose again in 1828 to serve as a model for young men and as a Founding Father whose politics and conduct could support anti-Jackson partisans contending with anti-elitist attacks. One of the four who worked with Thomas Jefferson in drafting the Declaration of Independence, Sherman signed more of the nation's founding documents than anyone else. He also served as mayor of New Haven, Connecticut, for almost a decade and in the federal House and Senate. Descriptions that made their way through the press starting in 1828, however, emphasized less the details of his state-building than his rise from shoemaking and farming into the legal profession and beyond.[36] Lavishly praised during early nation building for his wise counsel, this later praise emphasized other things, including that he had achieved such stature without a formal education, that is, as self-taught and, therefore, self-made.

Not that Sherman's birth in 1721 was impoverished by any means, but his origins qualified as obscure in the sense of having been ordinary in stark contrast to his eventual wealth and prominent national profile. His 1828 revival, long after his 1793 demise, seems to have begun with an address by a Professor Newman that Boston's *Youth's Companion* quoted extensively with the title "A SELF-MADE MAN." Newman was here using an emergent phrase, and so he used Sherman's life to define it. He began, "it may tend to the definiteness of our view of a self-made man, to fix the attention on an individual instance." In this telling, Sherman had lacked "kind, liberal patrons, or generous associations" to help, and he "saw that all his resources were in himself." With "the strength of this resolution... he rose from the bench of the shoe-maker" and eventually "took his place with the first" in the nation. "And yet," Newman affirmed, "this same man was a SELF-MADE MAN."[37] Newman's "and yet" conveyed a residual ambivalence about the merits of being self-made as some were using the term at the time. Sherman was not a "self-made maniac" or a rough frontiersman or a "solitary oak." As an element of polemic, "self-made man" had a long way to go before approaching a consensus on its meanings and uses, but it was on its way.

Along that way, in 1832, while training to become a Congregational minister, New Englander B. B. Edwards (1802–1852) published a *Biography of Self-Taught Men*. His stated purpose was to inspire the nation's young men "who are endeavoring to rise to respectability and usefulness, by their own efforts and resources," but his partisanship linked the emerging rhetorical value of self-making with the era's politics. The collection was a hybrid of rhetorical genres: partisan contests and praise for godly men as self-taught. As such, it embodied self-making's transition from moralizing to the public spheres in which worldly fears and ambitions drew on competitions for cultural authority in order to attain political authority. Accordingly, Edwards featured Roger Sherman on the frontispiece and in the collection's leading essay because the anti-Jacksonians claimed him and his legacy of "great usefulness" through "INDUSTRY and PERSEVERANCE." In contrast, Edwards only included a single brief and flat aside about the sitting president Andrew Jackson. Instead, Henry Clay, Jackson's adversary in that year's presidential election, received a full and glowing chapter although his educational and other advantages meant that he was not at all "self-taught." Moreover, highlighting his partisan intentions, Edwards began the book explicitly expressing concerns that the "strength of our political system is beginning to be tried."[38] In that election year, no reader would have missed the reference to Jackson's incumbency.

Elites with ambitions to govern a republic, then as now, face the challenge of gaining voters' acceptance.[39] In the early Republic many addressed the problem explicitly, some seeking to level leaders down, some to level citizens up, and others not inclined in either direction, choosing instead to persuade as needed. Thomas Jefferson, James Madison, and John Adams, among others, proposed shaping a "natural aristocracy" of republican virtue in which youth of talent and discipline could rise into a pool of leadership that would serve capably and selflessly. That was a hard sell when so much political and cultural rhetoric targeted any sort of aristocracy as the nation's worst danger. Instead, competition between factions, what George Washington called the "spirit of party," doomed dreams of genteel governance because, as he warned in his Farewell Address, it "agitates the community with ill-founded jealousies and false alarms."[40]

And this is precisely why, and how, the unabashedly partisan presses of the new Republic shaped the early political utility of self-making myths, an oratory augmented by theater and books. In doing so, they generated a notion of self-making that could serve ambitious men even as that notion strayed away from the clergymen's and educators' continuing moralistic and instructional messages of self-improvement put to selfless ends.

Along the contested and bumpy road to validate ambitions in the Republic, the myth of self-made success was an innovation that gradually delegitimated what we now call class – structural social and economic inequalities – as an explanation for differences in human conditions and outcomes. It wasn't always so, such as when the egalitarian David Crockett spoke against elite advantages. Yet, already in Crockett's time, endorsing self-making as a shield against class-based tensions was beginning to find a place within public conversations. For example, two almost identical 1829 articles reviewed a cluster of "self-made" Americans, starting with Benjamin Franklin, then moving on to Roger Sherman and a dozen other notable men of public service "who are expressively termed *self-made men*." The first article proclaimed that all had "arisen from obscurity to the highest posts of honor and respect by powerful and persevering effort," overcoming their lack of formal education. "Emphatically styled, 'the architects of their own fortunes' . . . [these biographies offer] the strong voice of successful example to the young men of our country, who are aspiring to posts of usefulness, and who have no patrimony but indigence, and the genius which the God of nature has given them." This anonymous pontificator then denied the value of community responsibility for conditions that brought only indigence to some youths' lives. He decried "any system of charitable aid, which should have the tendency to repress a single energy of such minds."[41] How or why aid would repress the energy of ambition was unclear. What was clear, instead, was the message that communities had no obligation to diminish inequities. Self-making was a solitary achievement in this telling.

A month later, the *Daily National Journal* reprinted sections of that article but left out the objection to aiding worthy minds. Nonetheless, just below it, a brief essay reprinted from the *Boston Palladium* referred to the original article and insisted that there was "but little individual wealth in this country." A man's "wealth is divided and subdivided" until all descendants "must be poor, unless they are themselves successfully industrious." As well, the "means of education are also so abundant, in this country, and the path of political and professional distinction is so open, that it is in the power, even of the poorest, to obtain the one, and advance himself in the other."[42] Through stories like this, the myth of self-made success has supported the profoundly American fantasy of universal opportunity that has long since weighed against dreams of truly universal, community-supported education and opportunity.

As the 1830s began, "self-made" and similar phrases were in the air. Self-making's meanings and uses would remain contested and mixed for decades to come, but they were uniformly applied in judgment – sometimes positive, sometimes negative. Some stories, such as the two 1829 articles above, also foreshadowed the use of self-made success as a talisman against policies for equitable distribution of resources: what truly worthy person would possibly need a boost? What self-made men did not deserve public esteem and resources?

Although electoral politics may have first animated rivalries among ambitious men vying for credentials as self-made, soon the politics of economic power would inspire competitions for cultural authority to convince the electorate of rich men's worthiness. Ideas of self-making have since contributed to judgments of ambitions, abilities, opportunities, choices, and outcomes, as well as their failures. White men of disadvantaged classes were particularly vulnerable to judgment as the myth grew and advanced fallacies of equal opportunity. The rest of the population – women and people of color – were not judged so much by this storytelling as simply erased and obscured by those solitary oaks, appearing as heroes' beneficiaries or victims, but not yet as visible agents in their own stories.

5

Forging Origins in Antebellum Stories

If ever someone rose from obscure and harsh origins, it was the wealthy art collector Eliza Jumel, who told her story as if she had not. If ever someone did *not* rise from obscure and harsh origins but told his story as if he had, it was presidential aspirant Henry Clay. Born two years and worlds apart as the American Revolution began, both worked intently at self-fashioning to make the most of the young nation's cultural, political, and economic developments. Each also inspired storytellers throughout the nineteenth century, and their stories' differences reveal how the evolving myth of self-made success simultaneously epitomized and widened the nation's social and cultural chasms. Storytelling about Jumel, Clay, and others shows how uses of the phrase "self-made" evolved after 1810 from a term of moral judgments – recall the "self-made maniac" or "self-made man of God" – to increasingly secular accolades. These new accolades were still more or less irrelevant to Eliza Jumel's rags-to-riches story, as we will see, but Henry Clay and his partisan storytellers saw them as essential and seized upon them.

Within the nation's breathtaking economic and territorial expansion in the first half of the nineteenth century, a powerful Second Great Awakening, Romanticism, and electoral politicking shared the cultural landscape. Together, these antebellum movements accelerated individualism, encouraged refashioning, and thereby advanced acceptance of self-making, which developed vigorously in the religious realm of the Second Great Awakening; the material, economic realm of fortune-building; and the political realm of power seeking. In each realm, the idea of self-making served storytellers' interests and goals differently, and, therefore, a focus on the gendered stories of self-making and, in particular, the self-made *man* considers exclusion as well as inclusion in the pantheon of self-making as a way to trace self-making's evolving meaning and criteria. Stories about Eliza Jumel, Henry Clay, and Dorothea Dix, a major figure in the era's reform movements, and stories by leading Great Awakening preachers Joel Hawes and Charles Grandison Finney illuminate the shifting and contested narratives of individualist self-making that were taking shape.

BURGEONING CHOICES AS CONTEXT FOR SELF-MAKING

Choices and challenges multiplied for America's nineteenth-century denizens. Towns and printed media expanded rapidly and magnified the cultural and political impacts of commercial, technological, industrial, and territorial expansions. Industries did not appear everywhere, but their effects did. Young women left farms to operate loud and dangerous machines in New England mill towns to produce yarns and cloth, and others produced the thread and buttons needed to turn colorful calico fabrics into clothes. Literate young men flocked to cities to earn livelihoods as clerks in shops and other small businesses, leaving the hard and repetitive work of farming behind them as they dreamt of owning their own firms. Some of the rapidly growing pool of store clerks sold manufactured dry goods, while other clerks sold groceries, and still others kept their employers' account books. In cities women operated and cleaned boarding houses, while food preparation and purveying became sources of income as well as family provisions. Less literate young women and men also came to the cities to work in rougher jobs with fewer dreams because artisans with traditional skills had dwindling opportunities to establish themselves in honorable livelihoods. Meanwhile, although almost all businesses were still very small, employers and employees were growing apart socially as well as economically. Plantations, which were among the nation's largest businesses, operated with hundreds of enslaved laborers who lived at a purposeful and obvious remove from enslavers. Moreover, in addition to internal migration from smaller to larger towns, immigration from Europe began to accelerate, which added ethnic diversity and cultural distances within towns and cities.[1]

All this change generated a surge of choices, some trivial, others monumental. Free men and many free women had to decide where to live: whether to stay put, venture west, or succumb to cities' gravitational pull. Some young women and men could consider their options for formal education or training to prepare for a livelihood. Souls also warranted notice as another Great Awakening spread, even more broadly than the first, calling on individuals – unfree as well as free – to save themselves because no one else could do it for them. Many pondered what their conversions meant for their earthly obligations, and some explored reforms to meet those obligations.

And then there was money. Sometimes it seemed there for the taking by anyone who was at all clever and industrious. At other times, money and the prospects to earn it seemed to vanish into the downturns of economic cycles that could surprise everyone. Amid these uncertainties, earlier negative judgments about self-making and self-agency continued to recede, replaced by anxieties about deficient ambition, talent, or self-reliance. Even as most people struggled with the era's financial precarity and unpredictability, mainstream culture increasingly insisted on individuals' responsibility for life outcomes, regardless of their circumstances within those challenging and unstable times.

PREACHING SELF-AGENCY

In this antebellum America, a sea of novel choices and perils beset everyone. In response, from the 1790s into the 1850s the preachers and converts of the Second Great Awakening promised an anchor – a single choice that could put the others into perspective and offer some calm and solace. Even Americans with profound if not total limits on their earthly choices could sometimes find comfort in spiritual choices and the social benefits of gathering together. More than its precursor, this Awakening offered new ways for individuals to relate to their nation and their communities, as well as to providence.

Doctor of Divinity Joel Hawes (1789–1867) was prominent among the many who contributed to a stream of sermons, lectures, and publications to guide the Republic's "Young Gentlemen" through what he called an "age of great mental excitement." These easily digested guides show the persistence of pairing self-fashioning with service. His widely distributed 1828 *Lectures to Young Men* detailed options and consequences of the decisions they had to make. He put the stakes bluntly: to improve "habit and character" or to "misimprove" them, in which case, "you are undone for ever." Hawes warned his young audiences against navigating so many choices "without plan and without order." To avoid "loss of peace of mind – loss of self respect – loss of the respect of others – loss of success in life," and so on, they must determine their course. To simplify, he split the possible choices into two categories: "all the pleasures and advantages which you can expect from the world" on one side of the scale, and "the present consolations and future rewards of religion" on the other.[2]

Hawes and other preachers could not avoid contradictions when they warned free Euro-American young men about worldly temptations while they also extoled the Republic's worldly opportunities. In this bind, no one was self-made: "God and your country are *your* patrons," Hawes reminded readers, and ambitions to be solitary "heroes" must fail. Young men had to attract social approval to ensure success, which, in turn, required the advantages of upbringing and demographics to attract "the patronage and favor of the respectable part of the community." National exceptionalism had its place in these stories, as well. Temptations to pursue wealth were "especially true of the young men of this country" because "all are born equal, and are alike left to make their way in the world by their own exertions." But, he cautioned, the "great object that fills the eye, and fires the heart, and engrosses the thoughts" is wealth. The "process of rising in the world, as it is called," could drown anyone in "destruction and perdition."[3]

Despite these traditional caveats, Hawes's idea of ambition and self-making differed from that of his predecessors. He used the call of worldly ambitions as a lure to good behavior, as had Benjamin Franklin in his renowned "Way to Wealth" essay, but Hawes went further. The "field of enterprise is widening and spreading around you," he declared. "The road to wealth, to honor, to usefulness and happiness is open to all, and all who will, may enter upon it with the almost certain prospect of success." Why was he so confident? "In this free community there are no privileged orders. Every man finds his level." Put more forcefully, "*you may be, whatever you resolve to be. Resolution is omnipotent.*" He urged his audiences to "Determine that you will be something in the world, and you shall be something." In this fantasy, no one needed more than "fixed purpose and persevering exertion." Therefore, any young man "can hardly fail of his purpose." His "irresistible energy" will "render success, in whatever he undertakes, certain."[4] He held fast to that story, even on occasions when he admitted it might not fit people whose lives overwhelmed any "fixed purpose and persevering exertion."

Hawes was no obscure preacher. His 1871 biographer, Edward A. Lawrence, explained that Hawes had a favorable transatlantic reputation and had often been recruited to take up other parishes. His *Lectures* were printed widely beginning in 1828, with six editions by 1832, plus revisions into the 1850s – at least 100,000 American copies in all, in addition to British editions. He appeared in newspapers of his day at least 1,000 times, including announcements of lectures, book dealers' ads for his various publications, and notes from abolition or temperance society meetings. Others asked to list him as a reference; even the publishers of *Webster's American Dictionary* solicited his public recommendation. Many ads resembled an 1828 notice for *Lectures* in South Carolina: "Every parent ... would wish his son to peruse this most excellent little work." In Hawes's eclectic messages there was something for everyone, from traditional Calvinists and advocates of republican virtue to entrepreneurs eager to forge into the future, all written in "a plain, manly, and business-like style."[5]

Hawes's texts, like Franklin's, or the Bible itself, provided a reservoir from which readers could draw selectively to support their own dreams and visions. For example, in 1830 a Kentucky newspaper article featured Hawes's optimistic individualist lessons, such as, "No young man, however humble his birth, or obscure his condition, is excluded from the invaluable boon. He has only to fix his eye upon the prize ... and it is his." This article also described Hawes as "a self-made man, i.e. a man, who has risen from obscurity, poverty, and through many difficulties to honourable eminence as a scholar and to great usefulness as a preacher," although Hawes never used the term "self-made" or claimed it for himself.[6] The *Lectures'* mix of cautions and cheerleading sold it, encasing maxims for youth and their elders alike within traditionally earnest calls to serve God and country through discipline and good character.

Despite Hawes's assertions about the Republic's opportunities for all, he addressed his *Lectures*, in reality, only to literate "Young Gentlemen." He made no apologies for his limited perspectives but rejoiced that "every man here is a freeman. He has a voice" in political decisions "and may be called to fill important places of honor and trust, in the community."[7] Although a member of abolitionist societies, he did not mention that race or sex or class might limit anyone's options. Seeing only the world of his relatively privileged audiences, and dazzled by the nation's opportunities for them, he did not acknowledge the inherent limits and inequity of his boosterism. His promises, therefore, conveyed the judgments that have since made the emerging myth of self-making so invidious. The view that individual choice and effort alone determine success implies that every successful man merits his rewards while every unsuccessful man, regardless of circumstances, forfeited his opportunities and deserved his outcomes.

Figure 5.1 Charles Grandison Finney preached to huge crowds as a leader of the Second Great Awakening, and the Broadway Tabernacle in New York City, portrayed here in 1856, was built two decades earlier to house his congregations. He promoted the idea of self-agency by exhorting believers to commit themselves to a life of serving God by serving their communities. (Photo by Sepia Times / Universal Images Group via Getty Images)

As the Second Great Awakening's waves of intense religious revivals washed over the country from the 1790s into the 1850s, its most influential revivalist across classes was Charles Grandison Finney (1792–1875). Hawes once answered a query about whether his own horse was "kind and gentle" by saying, "Perfectly so. I call him one of Brother Finney's perfectionists: he hasn't a fault." Few literate people of the era would have missed the droll reference to that powerful religious figure. Finney aroused the nation through decades of revivals and soul-searchings, amplifying the previous Awakening's message of choice and individual agency in accepting duty to God. He declared in 1835, for example, that "God Has no Slaves." That is, serving God merely out of duty or obligation could not satisfy the call to faith. Again and again: "when an individual actually *chooses* to obey God, he is a Christian. But all such desires, as do not imply actual *choice*, are nothing." Finney did not even credit God for the success of revivals, for they, too, resulted from human efforts. Each person is "a voluntary, responsible agent in the business" of conversion. Moreover, revivals resulted from human "cause and effect," not miracles but "the result of the *right* use of the appropriate means." Nor should the hopeful rely on miracles for conversion: "Set yourself to the work now." Defying many old-school Calvinist beliefs then prevalent in mainstream churches, Finney and many other religious activists held that the "perfectionism" to which Hawes wryly referred was possible through intense human dedication, not to *be* perfect or to be without sin, but to engage in ongoing, unselfish labors in God's communities.[8] Self-agency was ascendant, and, in keeping with earlier values of republican virtue, its purpose was to serve.

The Second Great Awakening helped many Americans orient themselves in the tumultuous first half of the nineteenth century, and in this way influenced the nation's course and culture. While electoral politics then fostered an inflated sense of equality among the eligible minority, revivalists aimed to reach all populations with equality of faith.[9] Whatever their differences, Finney and Hawes shared the mainstream's ever-growing sense of human agency, which for them carried obligations for self-improvement and community improvement. They joined others who urged Americans unmoored from the constraints of home communities to constrain their own behaviors as they pursued ambitions on urban and hinterland frontiers. In this cultural context, temperance campaigns arose in parallel everywhere, while some reformers also attacked tobacco and caffeine or promoted "moral reform" to oppose "lewdness." Preachers earnestly asserted that, as Finney put it, "a converted soul takes the deepest interest in all benevolent efforts to reform and save mankind," which for him included abolishing slavery and providing for the poor. In this vein, Hawes's 1828 lecture, "Claims of Society on Young Men," highlighted traditional republican virtues of self-improvement in service of "God and your generation." This theme of service ran throughout his writing, as it did through Finney's, emphasizing that only by fulfilling "the duties you owe to society" could anyone become "a public blessing."[10] Self-making had not yet become self-serving. Far from it, in fact. Instead, in that antebellum age of purposeful improvement, revivalists urged believers to venture beyond their own improvement into community improvement.

Evangelism's challenges often appealed keenly to young people, and benevolence gatherings attracted young women and men eager to be good and to do good. Notably, they appealed to young women of every ethnicity and economic status, who typically had fewer worldly choices than young men. The call to decide the course of their spiritual lives acknowledged their individual identity and worth in the spiritual arena, and that call to conversion brought with it a call to serve, often to serve outside the bounds of domestic duties. Thus, while many social and cultural authorities directed privileged women to withdraw to their homes, evangelism could draw them into opportunities outside, at a minimum to gather at each other's homes for prayer. At the same time, society's relentless needs to care for orphans and the poor seemed ever more urgent with the accelerating pace of urbanization and industrialization. The reforming zeal drew female and male activists alike, either alone, in informal groups, or, more likely, as members of the voluntary associations for which the era became notable.

Importantly, evangelist leaders were more likely than traditional churchmen to empower female believers to participate actively in the world. Finney, for example, not only allowed women to pray aloud in his services but encouraged them, incurring considerable opposition from traditional pastors. Lydia Andrews Finney organized women's prayer meetings as she traveled and worked with her husband, a full partner in preparing communities for revivals by organizing women and leading house-to-house visitations. Faith and reform, self-improvement and service could foster both purpose and community, especially treasured by women who were losing other opportunities to build and assert their individuality and capabilities.[11] Thus, the Second Great Awakening continued earlier revival traditions of linking self-agency in the spiritual realm to worldly service and benevolence. More than reinforcing traditional lessons, this Awakening expanded the reach of that linkage and actively extended it to women, who were usually excluded from the emergent possibilities of self-making.

FANTASIES OF SELF-RELIANCE

Meanwhile, in the realm of secular culture, the idea of self-reliance, a necessary element in the myth of self-making, grew more prominent. Whereas preachers in the revival movements preserved reliance on God, secular thinkers could move away from such restrictions toward self-reliance. The phrase "self-reliance" appeared in period newspapers and books a handful of times in the 1820s and reached nineteenth-century high points in the 1850s and 1870s in secular literature, sometimes to bolster political heroes, and at other times to condemn the impoverished.[12] Advocates for President Andrew Jackson, for instance, praised him, the "present Chief Magistrate," in 1829 as "Severely schooled in those stern virtues which poverty bestows," to develop habits of "laborious industry, decision, integrity, fearless energy, sustained by a spirit of self-reliance rarely found in men." For more ordinary people, an observer who objected to community assistance commended, instead, the application of "'steady, persevering industry' – a buoyant self reliance – a looking to one's own energies – and not to relief laws, lottery tickets, or some chance luck." Others more sympathetic to poor people typically sought "to exercise over them a moral influence, to urge the necessity of self-reliance, to encourage industry." Even those who supported "Reform" of "our Social System" in order "to avert the ills of Poverty" believed that, in the meantime, assistance from "hands stretched forth in kindness and love" should include "such sympathy and counsel as may tend to foster virtuous habits, and a spirit of self-reliance."[13]

At the same time as the Great Awakening, Romanticists told stories of heroism that beckoned Americans to travel along the path of self-agency toward self-making. Their idealized level of personal independence paralleled national independence and sense of exceptionalism.[14] The antebellum era's most widely known proponent of these fantasies was New England's Ralph Waldo Emerson (1803–1882).[15] Like other storytellers in pulpits, lecture halls, and the press, he assumed the right to judge other people's level of self-reliance. His confident, refined tones applied a softer, intellectual, even quasi-spiritual polish to his audiences' personal and national ambitions of aggrandizement, linking material progress with the national mission to reject traditional and European sources of wisdom.[16]

Emerson's writings and lectures – especially "The American Scholar" (1837), "Self-Reliance" and "Heroism" (1841), and "The Young American" (1844) – powerfully evoked self-fashioning and manliness in service of American nationalism. "The American Scholar," for example, declared that Americans had "listened too long to the courtly muses of Europe." He wanted to liberate the "spirit of the American freeman" who should "plant himself indomitably on his instincts, and there abide." In his own declaration of independence, he asserted that "We will walk on our own feet; we will work with our own hands; we will speak our own minds." This philosopher-poet extended his audience through public lectures and publications, such as the morsel from "Self-Reliance" reprinted in many 1841 newspapers to scold young men who "should be ashamed of our compassion" should they fail. If, instead, they take on "a greater self-reliance" and a "new respect for the divinity in men," surely their lives would take on "splendor."[17]

Practical – or at least more practical and less romantic – advice was everywhere for literate young men. What Emerson's popular lectures and writings provided instead was a highbrow worldview that valorized independence and worldly ambitions and allied these traits with masculinity. A key audience for these inspirations were young men seeking their way in the bustling, expanding cities as clerks, hoping to thrive in business but mostly struggling to earn a respectable livelihood. Like migrants to hinterland frontiers, young migrants from small towns to urban frontiers left behind support systems and traditional constraints. Loneliness may have saddened them, but the Romantics – most notably Emerson, Henry David Thoreau, and Walt Whitman – told them to relish that freedom and exploit its opportunities. These ambitious young men read the Romantics and attended lectures at local libraries and lyceums in their quest for essential self-improvement on the path to bourgeois manhood and social standing.[18] Emerson's 1841 excerpt that appeared so widely also proclaimed that a man who did not "lose all heart" upon a failed initial foray into the world but who exercised "self-trust" was "worth a hundred of these city dolls" who became "disheartened."[19] The economic hard times still ongoing since 1837 might well have disheartened many of his readers, but not Emerson, who was a wife-made man, having sued his in-laws after his first wife's death to secure a substantial legacy.[20] He was thereafter able to abandon employment in order to freelance as an essayist and lecturer. As such, he produced many words on many topics, but his most enduring, famous words were "self-reliance."[21]

As an advice giver, Emerson preached to his audiences' interests, not to expectations of serving the common good. He directed decades of lectures before the Civil War to people who sought inspiration and guidance less in the intellectual or spiritual realms and more in the cultural and social ones that might enhance their worldly prospects. More often sponsored by city boosters and businessmen than churches or schools, especially in the 1840s and 1850s, Emerson favored streams of aphorisms in praise of individuality and heroism, advancing elements of self-making, rather than ethical challenges to his audiences. In promoting self-examination and self-improvement, he assured audiences that they were in the presence of a great mind who had equipped them and the press with appealing and possibly useful phrases and terms. It made sense to tell stories to his public that were more inspiring than those recorded in his journals. For example, during the disastrous financial crash that surged in 1837, he lamented in his journal, but did not publish, the grim observation that "the land stinks with suicide." An ethos of self-reliance that blamed people for their economic failings even when the whole system collapsed provoked that bleak note. Five years later, he noted in his journal that "The merchant evidently believes in the State street proverb that nobody fails who ought not to fail. Always there is a reason discoverable in the man for his good or ill fortune." Was this Emerson's view or was he paraphrasing one or more merchants? The revision he published in the 1860 essay "Wealth" for the world to see – and to purchase, which the world did through numerous editions – pronounced this judgment as a truth, unmediated by anyone on State Street: "There is always a reason, *in the man*, for his good or bad fortune, and so in making money."[22] Emerson's private thoughts were more complicated than the clipped public phrases, but those were the ones that stuck.

SELF-RELIANT WOMEN WHO ROSE FROM OBSCURITY

Emerson and others in secular American culture increasingly aligned self-making with ideas of masculinity, leaving women largely invisible in antebellum stories of self-reliance and self-making. Those belonged to men, both as protagonists and storytellers, not to the free and unfree women who managed men's households, fed and clothed them, raised their children, and encouraged them so they could be "self-made" and "self-reliant." In this secular realm, woman's strongest claim to credit for self-reliance, according to an 1848 observer, followed from carrying out her wifely duties with "self-possession." That is, if she could "meet an emergency with calmness and nerve, ... rule her own household, and take care of her husband's home, property and children."[23] Legal constraints compounded social and cultural constraints to limit women's honorable opportunities for mobility to making advantageous marriages or doing business behind the veil of their men's names. Being self-taught, which qualified many men for respect as self-made, did not secure the title for women. Even women who made astounding achievements could not yet be considered self-made or self-reliant. Improvement and failure were possible, but not self-making. Individualism, likewise, was theoretically impossible for women, who were legally and culturally – if not in reality – men's dependants.[24] Hawes and many other antebellum religious leaders vigorously advocated education and exercise for women, but primarily for domestic success, as he explained in 1845 through *"A Looking-glass for Ladies," or the Formation and Excellence of the Female Character*. This address to the Mount Holyoke Female Seminary urged women to direct their energies and educations toward their homes and families, though he also joined other religious leaders to encourage careers in teaching and missionary work, especially for single women.[25]

Hawes and other proper authorities assigned women to an "honorable station" as a "help-meet for man," but that did not suit Eliza Jumel (1775–1865) or Dorothea Dix (1802–1887), who challenged all such presumptions, although in opposite ways. Their driving ambitions and successes collided against their era's presumptions about women as agents of their own lives. They purposefully forged their identities, as did men, to achieve their ambitions.

Eliza Jumel began as a beggar child but died at ninety in her very own New York mansion. Few people, and precious few women, found their way in America's unstable antebellum culture to the level of fortune and self-taught knowledge she amassed. Born Elizabeth Bowen in 1775 to Phebe Bowen and her husband, a sailor by whom Phebe already had two children, Betsy spent an unsettled childhood in Providence, Rhode Island. Her illiterate mother had been indentured to at least five families by her first pregnancy at fourteen, and, like many women with few options, Phebe took up prostitution when Betsy was a child. Betsy and her siblings begged for food and dodged law keepers, often without their mother's help as she was periodically jailed for working in a "disorderly house." Until Betsy was old enough to be indentured, her shelters were most often brothels or workhouses for the indigent.[26]

The rapid changes on the antebellum urban frontier ruined some, as Betsy's mother experienced, but they opened opportunities for others to refashion themselves and prosper. Poor but ambitious and determined to make her way, Betsy Bowen left Rhode Island for New York City as a young woman, where an 1803 directory listed her as Eliza Brown. For a beautiful and brilliant woman with dismal origins, moving into a large city enabled dramatic refashioning that would have been impossible had she stayed in her hometown. Strangers were commonplace in nineteenth-century cities, which afforded novel freedoms alongside the challenges of novel roles in unfamiliar settings.[27] In this case, the new Park Theatre was a short walk from Eliza Brown's residence, and it provided rich opportunities to develop the arts of self-fashioning, not only as an extra in its shows, but also as a witness to the social arts enacted on stage and in the audience.[28] Learning those lessons helped her to "pass" above her station in a social environment full of strangers.

Many mysteries remain about Eliza Jumel. No records exist of how she described her origins. Unlike the men who vied for electoral victory in the new Republic by feigning obscure origins, she had nothing to gain by telling her real story as she sought social acceptance among elites proud of their pedigrees. Nor do we know how Eliza Brown met Stephen Jumel, a wealthy French merchant with whom she cohabited before marrying in April 1804, when she was twenty-nine and he thirty-eight. With her husband's indulgence she continued refashioning herself. Before their marriage, Stephen hired a French tutor for Eliza to help her fit in with his French community, but she joined the Episcopal Church to align herself with New York's Protestant elites rather than her husband's fellow Catholics. She donated Stephen's riches to charity in her own name and spent money aggressively chasing her never-fulfilled wish for social acceptance among

American social elites, who typically declined her invitations. Eliza intently improved herself all the while, reading voraciously, including classics, theology, and high literature in French as well as English. Her campaign of self-improvement went further, and she becoame an accomplished art collector. During two years in France that began in 1815, she purchased over 200 paintings dating back into the sixteenth century with expertise quickly acquired from high-ranking connections she formed there. When she returned to New York, the American Academy of Fine Arts recognized her discernment and featured ninety-seven of her paintings, almost half of its fall 1817 exhibition, in what was then a rare display of European fine art in America.[29]

Eliza Jumel sought admiration for her collection, so she preferred grand paintings attributed to Old Masters that were large and visually stunning rather than those of contemporary artists. She applied similar standards for remodeling the Harlem Heights mansion she and Stephen purchased in 1810, which had once served as General Washington's New York headquarters. She was so successful in this project that First Lady Elizabeth Monroe conveyed her admiration in 1819 and asked if President Monroe's architect might visit when he designed their new house. Fine carriages and elaborate gardens also served her ambitions.

Her broadest fame, however, resulted from a grievous miscalculation. A year after Stephen's death, the charming and well-born Aaron Burr courted the Widow Jumel, and they married in 1833, when Burr was seventy-seven, and she was fifty-eight. The former vice president held abundant honors, along with the dishonors of having killed Alexander Hamilton in an 1804 duel and having stood trial for treason for another offense three years later. Despite their initial attraction to each other – her money and his elite status – she expelled him from her house within four months. Thirty years after Burr's duel with Hamilton, Eliza filed for divorce, outraged at his shameless raids on her fortune, to which he was entitled as her husband. With legal assistance from Alexander Hamilton, Jr., she triumphed. Aaron Burr died shortly thereafter in a boarding house, disgraced and insolvent, and the Widow Burr's celebrity grew.[30]

Eliza Brown's marriage to Stephen Jumel did not ensure a lifelong fortune, any more than Eliza Jumel's marriage to Aaron Burr ensured social status. Although she could do nothing to achieve high-level social acceptance, after her husbands' deaths she salvaged and rebuilt her fortune twice. In this regard, therefore, she was not just a kept woman, or merely a "husband-made woman." Economic downturns, most notably in 1819, then in the mid 1820s in Europe, required that she curtail her extravagances, but also that she sell assets, preserve what she could, then restore them. A shrewd real estate investor and manager, she rebuilt after Stephen died in 1832 and, again, after freeing herself from Burr.

Figure 5.2 Eliza Jumel did everything she could to hide her truly dismal origins. Born in a brothel and raised on city streets, she refashioned herself into a stately, well-versed lady, who also became one of the early Republic's major art collectors. This larger-than-life painting of her with her great-niece and great-nephew in 1854 now hangs in the mansion she and her husband, Stephen Jumel, refurbished after it had served as General George Washington's New York City wartime headquarters. Despite her remarkable self-improvement and business achievements, chroniclers of that century never credited her with self-made success. (Alcide Ercole, *Jumel Family Portrait*, 1854. Oil on canvas, 97 × 68 inches, MJM 1980.429.1. Courtesy of Collection of the Morris-Jumel Mansion. Photograph by Bruce Katz)

Nothing among her achievements could, however, overcome the stigma of her deliberately obscured origins and premarital cohabitation with Stephen Jumel, both of which thwarted her rise among the people she most wanted to impress.[31]

To fill the vacuum of Eliza Jumel's mysterious origins, innuendo and outright fabrications abounded in the press, especially during decades of litigation over her estate that filled US and French newspapers after her death. Stories in court testimonies and the press failed to recognize her as either a powerful businesswoman or an astute art collector. Instead, they measured her worthiness in the era's usual terms of womanly virtues. By that metric, her achievements, self-improvement, self-reliance, and self-fashioning gained her nothing. Among the wild array of stories, the *New York Observer* titled an 1865 death notice "The Widow of Aaron Burr," featuring her brief marriage to the "notorious" Burr. It also referred to her "immense" real estate holdings and, quite fancifully, to her "conspicuous part in social life in this city, fifty years ago." A lengthy *New York Times* obituary spun a strange tale that began with birth to an English mother on a French frigate whose captain placed the instantly orphaned baby in the custody of a pious woman who raised her "amid good influences." The rest of that whimsy was even more detached from reality, imagining close friendships with Benjamin Franklin and Thomas Jefferson among the men she allegedly captivated as a young beauty. This extravagant fantasy may have been the only public rendition of her life that Eliza would have relished. In contrast, hundreds of newspaper articles told malicious stories invented by claimants to her estate, quite willing to defame Eliza's reputation to claim her fortune.[32]

At the most basic level, Eliza Jumel's story, like every other in the evolution of the self-made myth, reinforces that the myth was non-intuitive and mutable. She could not qualify as "self-made" in the religious sense during the Second Great Awakening, in which the term connoted a devout servant of God or community. In that light, Jumel was invisible. Likewise, she certainly could not qualify as self-made when a woman's raw and undisguised ambition was unacceptable, and when even a man's ambition had to be cloaked in service, which she could not feign. The self-made myth was not yet a paean to material or political success that conferred esteem regardless of a protagonist's means or benevolence credentials. In reality, no one can succeed alone, but self-made success was unthinkable – even as a fantasy – for a woman.

Newspaper coverage on the lengthy litigation of Eliza Jumel's estate starkly illustrated the era's gendered limits to the idea of self-making and also conveyed the presumed limits on women's opportunities. In 1873, eight years after her death, the *New York Times* reported a lawyer's denial "that she was a loose character, but admitting that her early life was veiled in obscurity." "Obscurity" was something in a wealthy woman's origins to be *admitted* rather than offered as evidence of her self-improvement and remarkable rise. That same year, a long front page article inflated her social successes, noting that Jumel had commenced "existence amid the squalor and filth of the vicious classes" but "came to mingle in the highest society, both in this country and Europe." It reminded readers that "from a penniless child," Madame Jumel "had become one of the richest women the country has known." However, there was no praise here, either explicit or implicit. There was no mention of how she rose, her extraordinary self-improvement, or her business acumen, only an allusion to "the old Frenchman" who may have married "with his eyes shut" but who "died with them open."[33] In these tellings, Jumel's ascent could only have come through deception and scandal, nothing to be admired – certainly not "self-made" by any positive standard of the time.

Finally, in 1935, after a half century of cultural transitions, a sympathetic biographer, William Cary Duncan, could introduce her differently: "If ever there was a self-made woman, that woman was Eliza Jumel. If her story is worth writing, it is she, and no one else, who made it so."[34] Here, again, a story about self-making is a story about judgment and, therefore, dependent on the values of the judge, which are always context bound. The rags-to-riches tale of a woman of dubious sexual morality could not earn esteem in the nineteenth century. After the relaxed mores of the 1920s and in the dark days of the Great Depression, that ascent to riches looked better, and Jumel's intellectual and business achievements could emerge from behind the cloud of Victorian strictures.

Whereas Eliza Jumel did not qualify for esteem as a self-fashioned and self-made godly servant, Dorothea Lynde Dix famously did, refashioning herself to pioneer a course across frontiers of culture, politics, and lost souls. Born in 1802 to indigent and itinerant parents in Maine, Dix was recognized as a hero when her long life ended in 1887: newspapers throughout the country referred to her "national reputation for efforts to relieve the condition of the pauper, criminal and insane classes."[35] Her own childhood was inauspicious, marked by poverty, instability, and vicious discipline aimed to beat her into salvation. At twelve years old, she escaped to the safe but icy sternness of her Calvinist grandmother in Boston, where, among New England's elite, Dix discovered cultural models that better suited her, and she resolved to fit into their quiet and cerebral elegance. Refashioning herself, like Jumel, she posed as an orphan to clear the stage for her self-construction. Beyond that, and fiercely determined to exercise self-reliance, she resisted her grandmother's insistence on traditional proprieties and supported herself by teaching and writing children's instructional literature.[36]

Despite Dix's obvious self-reliance, she seems not to have received the term's respect until a posthumous 1890 biography by Francis Tiffany, who frequently referred to Dix's "self-reliant and indomitable nature." As a child, Tiffany explained, Dix was "rudely awakened to the necessity of resolutely fronting the world and fighting her way on her own resources."[37] Dix truly fought for her own independence and improvement. She also applied religious fervor and enormous energy to improve the nation by serving its most vulnerable. This qualified her for high praise, but not as self-reliant or self-made in her own lifetime.

As part of her self-fashioning, Dix isolated herself from most of "society" rather than be reminded constantly of the era's gendered constraints. For example, a highly regarded minister, professor, and active abolitionist, John Gorham Palfrey, knew Dix and admired her reform work, but, true to his era's stereotypes, he thought of self-reliance in gendered terms that excluded her and other women. In an 1834 newspaper excerpt from a sermon with the title "Brother and Sister," he described the "beautiful" relationship between siblings that gave full play to the "delicacy, dependence, and retirement" of sisters as well as the "energy, self-reliance, and enterprise" of brothers. A sister relished "watching the brother's growing virtues and consequence with a modest pride, while she checks his adventurousness with her well-timed scruples, and finds for him a way to look more cheerfully on his defeats." In turn, he enjoyed fondly "looking on the sister's graces," appreciating her "gentle guidance" to his ambitious and "impetuous spirit."[38]

Dix rejected this ideal of gendered roles, but she did not envision herself as a solitary oak. She felt "that I had no right to live for myself alone; that there was much work to be done in the world."[39] By the time of her death, stories of self-made men of God were appearing less frequently than earlier in her career, but they had not disappeared. If the journey from obscure origins to godly communal service qualified anyone in that century for esteem as self-made, then Dix would have been exalted with that title alongside so many men with less strenuous lives and fewer accomplishments. Similarly, by the time Eliza Jumel died in 1865, stories of self-made, rags-to-riches men had begun to appear with considerable frequency, evidence that the term's meanings had begun to shift toward material success. Yet neither woman received inclusion in either sense of "self-made" – the spiritual or material – during the nineteenth century despite the increasingly active presence of women in public. By the criteria of the century, neither saintly dedication to godly improvement nor extreme rags-to-riches accompanied by cultural improvement admitted women to the pantheon of the self-made.

Comparisons like these of inclusion and exclusion show us, again, how the meanings of "self-made success" are culturally contingent and, therefore, fluid according to storytellers' purposes. There is nothing objective or constant about how storytellers assign the term. Even the concepts of self-reliance and self-agency vary across realms. Enslaved people, as an example, were cruelly constrained in what they could do in the secular realm and denied credit for what they still managed to achieve, yet the two Great Awakenings offered them the possibility of self-agency in the spiritual realm. Meanwhile, a very different set of stories within the high-stakes and entirely masculine arena of antebellum electoral politics illuminates how the evolving criteria for "self-made success" depended on cultural authority and the vicissitudes of political ambition.

FEIGNING OBSCURITY IN THE QUEST FOR ELECTORAL SUCCESS

In response to expanding electoral rolls in the pre-Civil War decades, ambitious politicians vied – and lied – to be considered self-made rather than the beneficiaries of aristocratic origins. Along the way, they energized and shaped the myth of self-made success, forging origin stories as needed to pursue their ambitions, deepening the status of so-called self-made men as a vital form of anti-aristocratic certification. Andrew Jackson and David Crockett were the most prominent political beneficiaries of prolific anti-aristocratic storytelling in the 1830s, as we saw in the previous chapter. Jackson and his allies had already set the bar for cynically exaggerated accolades, which he and they had begun to propagate shortly after his 1815 military victories in New Orleans. As the cultural authority of well-born elites slipped away, "obscure" origins, rather than elegance, increasingly bestowed political authority. Their stories thus agitated and transformed electoral practices beyond anything the Founders could have recognized and, in doing so, sometimes stretched the limits of credulity to the point of absurdity.

The electoral challenge for American elites and elitists in the nineteenth-century's second quarter was to dodge anti-elitist sentiments and present themselves and their deputies as men of the people.[40] In that context, Jackson's melodramatic legends of starting as an impoverished and orphaned victim of British imperiousness and then rising to wealth and heroism on the western frontier, keeping his youthful advantages well-hidden, were hard acts for presidential candidates to rival. One exception was William Henry Harrison (1773–1841). Although born in Virginia, Harrison helped capture Native lands in the Northwest Territories in the 1790s and again as Indiana's first territorial governor in the next decade. Most politically relevant for his status as a colonialist hero, he had led the 1811 Battle of Tippecanoe against Tecumseh's confederation. These credentials made him attractive to anti-Jacksonian Whigs who were in disarray in 1840 and unable to settle on a presidential candidate who took strong policy stances, such as Henry Clay or Daniel Webster. They turned, instead, to Harrison – a western military celebrity with a low policy profile – to defeat the easterner Martin Van Buren. The nation was deeply distressed in 1839, still mired in the economic disasters that began in 1837 and that might have sufficed to oust the incumbent Van Buren, but the Whigs did not feel confident about that alone.[41]

Days after Harrison's December 1839 nomination, a Jacksonian newspaper, the *Baltimore Republican*, hurled a by-then antiquated insult at him that backfired and inspired an electoral upheaval: "Give him a barrel of hard cider, and settle a pension of two thousand a year on him, and our word for it, he will sit the remainder of his days in his log cabin." Initially, Whigs wailed indignantly about this disrespect of their "successful general who never lost a battle" and "exemplar of all the virtues," as one of their own, editor Richard Smith Elliott, recalled later. After all, Harrison was a gentleman. Log cabin, indeed! He was born in 1773 into a wealthy, patrician Virginia family. His father had been a governor of Virginia and signer of the Declaration of Independence who educated his children well. William received college and medical training, but worked his family connections to pursue a military career instead. The newspaper would have done better if it had attacked Harrison's *elite* origins, given the Jacksonians' campaign innovations of the previous two decades. It didn't take long for Elliott and other Whig activists to exploit the mistake. Early in the new year, and with gusto, they spun the insult into compelling slogans and symbols of log cabins and hard cider jugs. The brilliant but bizarre 1840 campaign produced rollicking doggerel and ballads; banners, flags, and large backlit transparencies; miniature log cabins and cider jugs to hang on watch chains, earrings, and harnesses; and a party newspaper called *Log Cabin*. Elliott pronounced it all as "irresistible as a Kansas tornado." Other patrician Whigs also shed the appearances of their relic elitism to pirate their foes' strategies and triumph over Old Hickory's chosen successor, Van Buren. Novices also joined the fray, including none other than Abraham Lincoln early in his political career. Like Lincoln, these newcomers to the national scene were often westerners and rough around the edges but, for that very reason, more effective in their electoral climate.[42]

Jacksonian Democrats indignantly retorted with their own use of the self-made moniker, and a blistering rhetorical battle raged. "Who is Martin Van Buren?" a Pennsylvania headline asked during August's heat. The answer? "He is a self-made man, and . . . rose by his own exertions, and by his own talents, to be the President of the Union." A "short sketch" explained his origins in a "reputable" but modest family in Kinderhook, New York. Jacksonian newspapers scorned any "band of men robed in coo[n]-skins, and riding on cider barrels, trying to get votes of the people as the keeper of a monkey-show gets pennies from the children!" They quite rightly charged Whigs with duplicity. How could Whigs boast "of the 'noble descent' and 'illustrious ancestry' of their *old hero* of a candidate, at the same time they attempted to make log-cabins his exponents and representatives"? They objected to Whig attacks on Van Buren's "*Kinderhook obscurity*" – "the obscure and humble birth of the poor self-made boy of Kinderhook." Democrats held only disdain for Harrison, "who owes his prominence to his *birth*, and who, if born in that '*obscurity*,' would have remained there forever!"[43]

Looking back on the "Log Cabin" campaign four decades later, Elliott expressed reservations about "the wisdom" of the "jolly" campaign that tossed argument and reality to the winds: "All we wanted was to win the election."[44] Perhaps, amid ongoing economic troubles, frivolity itself carried the day. Whatever its ethics or tastelessness, or assumptions about voters' judgment, the notorious 1840 campaign accustomed the public to declarations of self-making that served worldly ambition rather than godliness or the common good.

All the while, Kentucky Senator and long-time presidential aspirant Henry Clay (1777–1852) had watched the Federalists drown in their eastern elitism for years. Then he saw Harrison succeed by claiming obscure origins. Although Clay hesitated to step off the Founders' dignified path of republican virtue and into this blustery fray, his ambition ultimately got the better of him. After twenty years of frustration, Clay's ambitions and his dedicated supporters persuaded him to bow to the self-made myth's growing potency and rewrite his own story to recount a rise from obscure and impoverished origins on the western frontier. He had already resorted to such an account at least once, back in 1822 in a congressional debate with the powerful patrician John Randolph. Defending himself against the condescending Virginian's attacks, he mourned: "I was born to no proud patrimonial estate; from my father I inherited only infancy, ignorance, and indigence. I feel my defects; but . . . they are more my misfortune than my fault."[45] In 1842, this spontaneous lament got refashioned into a premeditated boast.

Born in 1777, Henry Clay was raised in a well-connected Virginia family that supported itself more than comfortably on a 464-acre farm, a gift from his maternal grandfather along with about twenty enslaved people. When his father died, four-year-old Henry inherited three enslaved people of his own, and his mother shortly remarried an even more prosperous gentleman. Clay grew to be polished and elegant, relatively well, if informally, educated (for a time he was a university professor who taught, among others, Abraham Lincoln's future father-in-law, Robert Smith Todd), and would come to impress even his foes as one of the country's towering speakers. Like Crockett, Jackson, and Harrison, he also laid claim to the West, having followed his family to Kentucky as a young man to make his fortune there as a lawyer already trained by elite Virginia jurists. By the time he arrived, however, Lexington had grown well beyond a frontier settlement, and Clay enjoyed the benefits of family and their extensive networks there, as well as a university and opportunities for a flourishing legal career. He also found a bride there within a wealthy and well-placed family. Clay fit the waning and by then almost antiquated sense of the self-made template: he had diligently trained from boyhood for patriotic service through politics, law, and, especially, oration.[46] Yet he had too many worldly advantages to be self-made in the sense of rising from obscure poverty, and he knew it. Nonetheless, he adopted the fashionable charade of having risen on his own, obscuring his multiple advantages with outlandish fictions.

"Mill-Boy of the Slashes" was chief among those colorful fictions Clay and his allies embraced in 1842 – as did his foes in parody. Although Clay's family had a mill on its properties and at least twenty-five enslaved people to do its hard labor, he and his advocates portrayed him in his Virginia home region, the Slashes, as a guileless, barefoot boy on horseback, without saddle or proper bridle, carrying grain to and from a distant mill at his mother's behest. This conjured portrait of the lad was widely circulated, and the phrase "Mill-Boy of the Slashes" still has currency in Kentucky today.[47] The fiction deeply infiltrated public storytelling with Clay's 1842 speech when he retired from the Senate. He refashioned his youth and move from Virginia to Kentucky this way: "I went as an orphan boy who had not yet attained the age of majority; who had never recognised a father's smile, nor felt his warm caresses; poor, pennyless, without the favor of the great, with an imperfect and neglected education, hardly sufficient for the ordinary business and common pursuits of life." Upon arriving in Lexington, and in front of an audience that knew better, a less self-pitying version began "I have great reason to be thankful." Even so, he still exaggerated his youthful situation, highlighting a "neglected education [that] was improved by my own irregular exertions." Denying powerful family-based and professional social capital, he claimed to have "established myself... without patrons, without the favor or countenance of the great or opulent, without the means of paying my weekly board." Despite these deficiencies, "my hopes were more than realized. I immediately rushed into a successful and lucrative practice."[48] That, at least, was true.

Clay's supporters quickly took up the "Mill-Boy" slogan in songs, speeches, toasts, and newsprint in preparation for the 1844 presidential election. Whig newspapers explicitly referred to their 1840 "glorious Harrison campaign" and going "into the canvass ... with stronger hopes of electing the MILL BOY OF THE SLASHES than they had, *at first*, of elevating the FARMER OF NORTH BEND." Clay's "friends ... call upon *all* the PEOPLE ... to rise up and come to the help of the PEOPLE'S MAN." Some proclaimed unanimity among Whigs for the "Mill-Boy of the Slashes," aka "Harry of the West," as "always the champion of the people's interests, and the defender of their rights." Some Whigs gleefully poked at their opponents' "aristocratic habits" in opposing Clay as a true mill boy, "naked as to feet and breech." Some Whig papers predicted that replacing log cabins with mills, and coon-skins with Clay's meal bags, would "produce ... perfect horror" among their opponents by parading "the democratic origin of the greatest man in America."[49]

Democrats, of course, did not retreat from the anti-aristocratic game, calling the Whig antics "vulgar humbugging." This left them open to accusations that they disdained "log cabins" and "mill boys." Should "the whole American people ... be regarded as '*vulgar*'"? Surely it was a matter of pride "that the humblest 'mill boy' in all the country, if he have merit, may reach the highest post of honor."[50] Here we see an American political cliché in its early stages within campaigns empty of policy substance.

Amid this blustering, "A Song for the Man: A Henry Clay Ballad" asked in 1844 "Was his heritage wealth?" The answer: "Integrity and health / Were all that to the mill boy fell!" The young man's luck began "when to noble old Kentuck' / Unfriended and poor he turned." The sheet music cover was designed to appeal to every variety of voter with a large center engraving of "the Man" looking strong and confident in formal attire, partially wrapped in a black toga. The four corner vignettes pictured the "Mill-Boy," Clay as lawyer and orator, and his genteel Ashland residence.[51] Calvin Colton penned a campaign biography of Clay in 1843, which its subject modestly critiqued as "too much commendation and panegyric."[52] Colton's passages on Clay's youth told the usual stories of working "barefooted for his mother" and receiving his "first rudiments of education ... in a log schoolhouse," and so on. In another section's heading, Colton bestowed upon Clay the title "*The self-made man.*" All his "distinction ... was *achieved* – achieved by his single arm, by his own lofty aims. Such is the self-made man." Nonetheless, Clay lost to "Young Hickory," Tennessean James Polk, Andrew Jackson's protégé. Polk's promoters portrayed him as a Tennessee "corncracker" who would proudly "serve up to 'my lord of Ashland' ... a dish of our homely fare." He was, their stories pronounced, "a plain, honest, energetic, and able companion, who has risen to high position in the country; who knows what it is to encounter all the hardships of life; from the capacity of a mill-boy and cotton-ginner."[53] This was no more true of Polk's origins than of Clay's, but it was becoming an obligatory claim for political certification, nonetheless.

And so it was that stories about rising from obscurity and self-making as the epitome of anti-aristocratic principles increasingly colored America's political competitions. Heat from those electoral struggles energized and accelerated the evolution of the self-making concept beyond the realm of electoral politics. For example, Clay's ideas about political economy extended the aura of self-making to businessmen. Halfway between his 1822 public lament alleging childhood indigence and the 1842 launch of his desperate "Mill-Boy of the Slashes" campaign, he embedded the phrase "self-made men" in an 1832 high-profile,

Figure 5.3 Henry Clay's western origins were relatively privileged, yet this sheet music for his 1844 presidential campaign depicted him as having risen from an impoverished farm boy to an accomplished and wealthy statesman. Like Andrew Jackson and William Henry Harrison before him, Clay hoped that this "self-made man" image would appeal to recently enfranchised White male voters and fulfill his ambition to become president. (Sheridan Libraries / Levy / Gado via Getty Images)

three-day speech on the Senate floor. This master orator had an especially tricky point to make, and he addressed it adroitly by tying nationalism to the emergent cultural and political authority of the self-made man. This fiscal-policy speech defended what he had introduced in 1824 as a "genuine AMERICAN SYSTEM" of policies that would ensure prosperity by supporting domestic manufacturing through internal improvements, such as building bridges, roads, and canals – in other words, infrastructure. Sectional interests differed widely, however, and Clay responded to a "charge … against the manufacturing system" that its growth would favor "the growth of aristocracy." How better to refute such a charge than to assert that in his home state of Kentucky "almost every manufactory known to me, is in the hands of enterprising and self-made men, who have acquired whatever wealth they possess by patient and diligent labor"? Furthermore, he asked, "is there more tendency to aristocracy, in a manufactory, supporting hundreds of freemen, or in a cotton plantation, with its not less numerous slaves, sustaining, perhaps, only two white families – that of the master and the overseer?" Clay, reluctant to challenge his southern colleagues, and himself an enslaver, was not about to allude to harms against enslaved people.[54] Instead, he echoed James Oglethorpe's reason a century earlier for arguing against slavery in colonial Georgia, namely that it offered too few opportunities for White men to rise and to be self-made, and, instead, fostered an idle aristocracy.

PRELUDE TO LEGITIMATING MAMMON

As the nation approached the mid nineteenth century, fewer and fewer storytellers stuck with the earlier patterns of praise for men who self-improved in order to fulfill godly and community service. More and more partisans acclaimed men with pretensions to solitary, unaided improvements in the pursuit of worldly ambitions. Electoral activists filled the press and the air with high-volume versions of this story, experimenting along the way. Since the promotions of Andrew Jackson's presidential possibilities in the 1810s, some of those experiments moved the rhetoric toward the metaphor of the heroic "solitary oak," while others scattered the seeds of self-making more broadly, into other realms of competition. Polk's Democrats prevailed in part not only by trumpeting his own claims to self-made worth but also by warning that opponents were "haughty and overbearing enemies to the advancement of self-made men."[55] By the time the farcical political repertory of the 1840s played out on the national stage, the term "self-made man" was secure as a widely, although not universally, accepted rhetorical tool for judgment. Those electoral campaigns – major media events of their day – had accustomed Americans to imagine individual successes without benefits of social capital or other unevenly distributed assets. With those stories, self-making gradually lost its spiritual and service dimensions and acquired a new one: worldly success. In this emerging spirit, Henry Clay's 1844 campaign ballad pictured the "Mill-Boy" vignette in one corner and Clay's plantation manse in another. Storytellers dangled the emerging myth of self-making before multitudes of men ambitious to climb ladders themselves and tacitly reproached them if they failed.

In the coming decades, as we will see, material criteria for success rose in prominence, although without securing a universal consensus. Religious, philosophical, literary, and nationalistic debates continued over what kinds of ambitions and achievements to value. As the cultural authority of worldly success rose in mid-century, intriguing comparisons appeared in literature and the press that reveal pervasive tensions. For example, stories about John Jacob Astor and his grand fortune appeared sometimes with, and sometimes without, reference to self-making during these years. An 1848 juxtaposition that would seem strange a decade or so later typified the concept's unsettled, ambiguous status. In this case, a reference to Astor's "great wealth" appeared on the same page as a lengthy story of a now long-forgotten member of Congress, Patrick Tompkins, whose "true sketch" credited him for rising from hardscrabble origins. In this story, Tompkins was "a self-made man, and his history shows what a humble boy can do, when he determines to *try*." Like many a story of self-made men, this was didactic, intended to inspire youth; apparently Astor's story could not serve that purpose here, joined in his story as he was by three European aristocrats, and no mention of self-making.[56]

That same decade, however, in a newspaper that eagerly boosted national expansionist ambitions – for Texas and Oregon territories in particular – Astor's western aggressions and eastern real estate fortune found praise. Placed prominently among news items and polemics, a long biography concluded that Astor, indeed, deserved a place among "all distinguished self-made men" as having "raised himself greatly above his compeers." The profile explained that in a "money-loving land of social equality like ours," when a man "owes his position entirely to his own labor and ability, most people are wont to lose sight of his humble origin, his early struggles" surmounted by "perseverance against obstacles and readiness to seize advantages," plus assorted other admirable qualities.[57]

In contrast, Eliza Jumel's rags-to-riches rise by the means most available to a destitute woman of her time would not qualify for status as self-made for almost another century, despite her success at self-improvement and building a fortune. Dorothea Dix's heroic work on behalf of God's most troubled children would continue to earn worldwide honors, but not for her as a self-made heroine. Of course, no one can truly be self-made in the sense claimed for Astor. However, the myth that an exceptional man could indeed succeed owing "entirely to his own labor and ability" grew more intense and frequent, but was not applied to women. The stories that *did* surface envisioned a fantasy of rising with no community, no family, no state subsidies, and, therefore, no obligations. That self-serving fantasy was the direction to which the myth of self-made success pointed at mid-century, gathering momentum apace with the nation's industrialization, commercialization, and glorification of worldly riches. Promises of affluence rather than threats of damnation came to spur ambitions.

6

Character and Money in Mid-Century

Mid-nineteenth-century American marketplaces offered more and more ways to spend and make money. Along the way, stories of self-making increasingly oriented toward material ambition rather than service to God or the common good. In these transitional decades, stories sometimes still articulated self-made success in the old ways, but new meanings evolved within cultural venues as diverse as advice literature, temperance advocacy, entertainment, business guidance, and phrenology. Despite continuing tensions within the competitions to shape self-making's cultural authority, the dominant meaning of self-made success moved irrevocably toward material affluence.

Conspicuous within everyone's experience was a steadily expanding variety and quantity of goods and services arrayed before them, whether or not they were able to partake of the growing abundance. In urban areas, store windows and outdoor displays did their best to lure anyone with a coin to spare or whose credit was acceptable. An almost constant din pervaded the urban soundscape: hawkers and peddlers cried out to attract attention, as did performers – it wasn't always possible to distinguish between them. Colorful printed messages competed for attention as they decorated the streets, adorned public buildings, and filled periodicals and scrapbooks. Small towns and villages, though quieter by far, were not at all devoid of commercial stimulations. Their general stores kept up with trends as best they could, and when residents traveled, they witnessed the wonders beyond their daily experience. Moreover, the marketplace came to them. Village-to-village, even farm-to-farm peddlers, sold industrially produced wares from ribbons to pots and pans to clocks to on-the-spot portraits. Religious revivals attracted vendors, and sundry entertainers ranged over roads, waterways, and railroads. Whether visual or aural, whether in public spaces or in acquaintances' private spaces, temptations everywhere demanded decisions, and, more often than not, fueled frustrations. In turn, those frustrations encouraged worldly ambitions.[1]

The means of pursuing those ambitions likewise expanded. There were more dressmakers and tailors, hat makers, boot and shoe makers, jewelry and trinket makers. More candy makers, bakers, butchers, distillers, breweries, tobacconists.

More types of places to live and to sin. More varieties of shops, and more industrial sources of goods in them, from farm equipment to decorations to patent medicines. There were also more professionals to tend to businesses, such as accountants, lawyers, bankers, and brokers; as well as professionals to tend to people, such as doctors with diverse credentials, teachers, undertakers, loan sharks, entertainers, and even more clergy than before. The numbers of civic leaders also grew, along with clerks and administrators, public and private. More cleaners, servants, and unnamed toilers, free and unfree, made all of this possible, but they inhabited the mainstream's backdrop. Those vast populations saw everything but risked debt or social derision to indulge in commercial temptations. And to spread widely divergent ideas about all of this there were more writers whose wares were available in more books, newspapers, magazines, pamphlets, plus other products of the printers' arts, such as posters and trade cards.

In the midst of these visions of abundance, frugality was less fashionable, and wealth, like ambition, was losing its moral sting. Already, in 1836, the Reverend Thomas P. Hunt (1794–1876), a well-regarded preacher and temperance crusader from the Chesapeake area, published *The Book of Wealth* with the subtitle, *In Which It Is Proved from the Bible, that It Is the Duty of Every Man, to Become Rich*. Unlike Benjamin Franklin's *Way to Wealth*, Rev. Hunt fully approved of individuals' material wealth, if properly obtained and generously applied to good ends. "*God has promised riches as rewards*" for following his rules, and, in any case, "it is almost impossible for men to do their duty without being rich" because, this indefatigable fundraiser argued, the poor and the church can only survive through the beneficence of the wealthy. More important for our purposes, Hunt anticipated the future of the self-made myth. He argued that "in the general [case], poverty is a sin; and it is always so, when it results from idleness, wastefulness, want of discretion, and [lack] of prudence." Despite admitting that "providential circumstances" could cause poverty and that not "all poor men are disobedient to God," Hunt put readers on notice that judgment and their own happiness were at stake. To be sure, many "robbers and liars" dwelt among the rich, but better to have the option to serve through charity than to defy God's will by voluntary or deserved poverty.[2] Money was looking better and less inevitably sinful.

Within this burgeoning consumer culture, in which there was always more to want and more to invite debt, traditional critiques of materialism persisted. They thrived in sermons, of course, as well as in fiction, such as in Mrs. C. H. Butler's "Looking Up," first published in the *Saturday Evening Post* in 1847 and then widely republished elsewhere. Here we meet William Wilmot, a respected and successful businessman, able to provide a "genteel" home in "one of the most fashionable streets" and furnish it expensively. Yet Mrs. Wilmot had married solely "to rise in the world" and lived in "a continued round of fault-finding and complaining," always "looking up" at the next rung on the ladder of material expenditure with "un-praiseworthy ambition." She even belittled the plight of seamstresses, "born for such drudgery whose place is in attics and cellars, and who are not supposed to require either food or sleep." After years of "wasting his fortune," Mrs. Wilmot drove her husband so deeply into debt that, despite his "years of untiring industry," he could not ride out a business downturn that destroyed his firm and their lifestyle. Scorned by his wife, Wilmot turned to alcohol and its companions. After a few turns of the dramatic screw, the family survived poverty thanks only to the good spirits, patience, and industriousness of their lovely daughter, Emily. She had never succumbed to the lure of consumer culture's excesses and had earlier refused her mother's pressures to "ape some newer novelty." Now she provided for the family in their "small, obscure dwelling." In a happy ending, Mr. Wilmot found a new position, and Mrs. Wilmot confessed her "wickedness and folly," rejected the wiles of the market, and rid herself of "the demon of discontent."[3]

Butler's fiction echoed multitudes of tales in the popular press that pushed back on the enticements of consumption and its outsized or misdirected ambitions. Not only did Butler attack wanton consumption and material ambition in this and other stories, she also employed the phrase "self-made" in an ever more unfashionable sense, describing Mrs. Wilmot as "this self made wretched woman." Likewise, the nation's hugely influential temperance movement maintained earlier meanings of self-making as a deleterious shunning of community help and support, and looked back to older ideas of the common good. But, increasingly, the stories of self-making became centrally about material gain and wealth in what was becoming an unapologetically materialistic culture.

COMPETING IDEAS OF SUCCESS

In the heat of the political battles of the 1830s, William Price (1794–1868), a highly regarded lawyer, businessman, occasional politician, and US Attorney for Maryland, secured a place in the history of the self-made myth through widespread reactions to his 1838 novel, *Clement Falconer, or the Memoirs of a Young Whig*. Dozens of references to it appeared as late as 1864, as newspapers and magazines published comments, reviews, or excerpts from it. Those entries fell into three categories: noting the novel's intense anti-Jacksonian partisanship; its passages on self-made success; or both. Price was an ardent admirer of Henry Clay, and, in that day of fervently partisan presses, references to his novel's politics were entirely polarized. Yet, *all* references to the novel's advice on self-making were positive.[4] Even though only about a dozen of the novel's 421 pages advise readers on building character and career, almost all reprintings featured Price's passages on self-improvement.

The *Daily National Intelligencer*, a leading Whig paper, simply copied passages that the *Boston Chronicle* had previously reprinted, describing the novel as "a sprightly and interesting" work, which they "commend[ed] ... as full of the keenest and acutest satire." At the other partisan extreme, *The Gentleman's Magazine* captured the opposing electoral and cultural politics. Its editors described this "political novel" as "the emanation of a violent partisan" who treats the "leaders of the democratic party ... with unlimited severity." And, yet, its "Review of New Books" section excerpted a long paragraph of guidance without reference to that partisanship, noting that it "exhibits a picture of successful industry and perseverance of a cheering nature to our young friends who are not blessed with a large share of the *aurum potabile*" [drinkable gold].[5]

The passage most often reprinted, and always favorably, relayed advice from the protagonist's wealthy uncle to young men about finding professional success:

> You take the whole population, select from it the fifty men who are most distinguished for talents or any description of public usefulness, and I will answer for it, they are all, every one of them, men who begun the world without a dollar. Look into the public councils, and who are they that take the lead there? They are men who made their own fortunes – self made men, who began with nothing. The rule is universal .... It is true of all the professions .... You must throw a man upon his own resources to bring him out. – The struggle which is to result in eminence, is too arduous, and must be continued too long to be encountered and maintained voluntarily .... He who has fortune to fall upon, will slacken from his efforts, and finally retire from the competition.[6]

"Fortune" here retained its traditional mix of meanings. It appears twice, once ambiguously in the phrase "made their own fortunes," which then often referred to controlling one's own fate. The second usage, however, clearly refers to wealth: he "who has fortune to fall upon" will "retire from the competition" and, therefore, is unlikely to take on challenges and overcome difficulties. Also sanctifying self-making here was the continued pretense of non-material goals, namely "eminence" as the reward for "struggle."

This popular passage fit nicely with the electoral rhetoric of the times that declared, if disingenuously, that wealth was a burden for heroes to overcome – or deny, as was often the case. In reality, of course, beginning "with nothing" most likely doomed anyone to continued "nothing," even in those antebellum decades that saw one of America's greatest eras of mobility. The economy's expansion generated a tide that lifted many boats, most modestly, many splendidly, but many not at all.[7] The myth's something-from-nothing fantasy flourished among enough examples of triumphs to chasten those left behind. Its storytellers could, as did Price, use it to make the case that the capable need only their ambition and abilities to climb out of "nothing."

Even so, resistance continued to push against the era's movement toward market-driven values, embedding cultural tensions in childrearing advice. For example, when the *Boston Investigator* repeated that admired paragraph from *Clement Falconer* in 1842, an adjacent passage copied from the *Ladies' Magazine* was quite explicit about the moral dangers of money. That important magazine's editor was, after all, leading reformer Sarah Josepha Hale. This excerpt cautioned mothers to "teach your children the art of doing good" by vigilantly *not* treating their homes as businesses or their children as workers for hire. It admonished mothers to "repress as much as possible, the *selfishness* of animal instinct and appetite," urging them to apply children's affections and their own "love, which is benevolence," to develop "the noblest faculties of your children." Mothers should "never hire them with *money* to perform their tasks of any kind," and "never pay them for being good." According to such traditions, character building was unambiguously not about money, and it was mothers' duty to prepare boys to leave their domestic "haven" and move into the "heartless world" without putting their souls at risk.[8]

The contemporary press coverage of Price's long-since obscure novel and this one of many messages from the *Ladies' Magazine* tell us about anxieties that accompanied the advance of material culture. That attention highlights this stage in the evolution of the self-made myth, which was marked by worries and tensions about the goals of self-improvement, sometimes catching advocates in contradictions. In Price's telling, individualist ambitions to make money and abuse power described – and derided – only the Jacksonians, whereas there is no mention of Henry Clay's ambitions, only that like "all our really great men," Clay was "a self-made man." He belonged "to a higher and better order of men."[9] Price was caught trying to claim self-making for his hero but without admitting to the deep ambition that compelled Clay into falsifying his origin story, as we have seen. By this time, it was too late to admit to genteel origins in pursuit of electoral ambitions.

In 1843, shortly after William Henry Harrison's successful Log Cabin campaign and in the midst of Henry Clay's last futile campaign, a widely popular writer, Emily Chubbuck (1817–1854), told the story of *Allen Lucas: Self-Made Man*. A glowing review in the *Saturday Emporium* summarized the widely reprinted book as "the history of Allen Lucas, who by dint of his just views, honorable principles and meritorious conduct, won his way to fame and honor." Lucas succeeded, Chubbuck explained, through "devotion to his art" of architecture, and "by industry and economy, he had amassed a little fortune." She contrasted her hero, who had "no time to be selfish, for every minute is employed in thinking of somebody else," with another young man, Robert Mays, who grew up in the same town, but whose manner had always betrayed that "he is ambitious, selfish." Both boys had studied hard, but our hero stayed in his community to serve, whereas, by the time that the men were in their thirties, Mays had reached the US Congress. To advance his career, he had left his penurious family and sweetheart behind and married the daughter of a judge. He not only lost his community, but also, in full Victorian melodrama, Mays had prematurely aged, plotting his "eloquent and subtle" speeches within "a web of sophistry." This man, for whom "self is the centre and circumference of his desires," was not an ideal of a self-made man for everyone. His power and wealth were not its proper measures.[10]

Chubbuck – like Butler, Clay, Hale, and Price – was on the losing side of the contest to define cultural goals for self-improvement and, therefore, self-made success. Worldly assets could still appear as a hindrance to self-improvement in some storytelling, but, in other stories, they were beginning to appear as its worthy goal.

A few years later in 1848, John Frost (1800–1859), a prolific compiler of biographies, published *Self-Made Men in America*. His first words declared: "'SELF-MADE MEN!' We use the term every day; and we use it without irreverence, because all understand its popular import." However, he ignored the phrase's still-diverse uses, and his collection included neither godly men self-made to serve the common good nor less godly politicians who drew on self-making's rhetoric to assert their anti-aristocratic credentials. Instead, for Frost, a "self-made man means one who has rendered himself accomplished, eminent, rich, or great, by his own unaided efforts." Frost had already published *Lives of American Merchants: Eminent for Integrity, Enterprise and Public Spirit* in 1846, which was reprinted dozens of times, as well as sundry histories of wars, mechanics, "great cities," an illustrated biography of Andrew Jackson, and another of George Washington, sketches of "heroes and hunters," and even of "heroic women." Most of these collections were heavily patriotic, and *Self-Made Men in America* was no exception. In his preface he proclaimed that "this is the country, the home of self-made men." Because "enterprises of learning, ingenuity, or industry, is [sic] not checked in every path by stupid, restrictive laws, enacted in ages of feudal barbarism, ... when the republic shall be no more, self-developed greatness will become a theme of past history." This was a fitting overlay of the idea of the self-made man onto that of a self-made nation in the very decade when some took on the self-serving and bloody mantle of "manifest destiny" to justify their colonialist ambitions.[11]

Each of Frost's eleven portraits described the usual rounds of overcoming youthful hardships and adult challenges diligently met – as claimed in older stories for preachers and politicians. However, some combination of wealth and fame was Frost's main criterion for selecting each hero. He looked all the way back to

William Phips in the seventeenth century, but found no preachers or educators worthy of inclusion. Once selected, Frost tried to make a case, although perhaps a pro forma one, for contributions to the nation, sometimes stretching to do so. The most egregious stretch, which Frost reprinted from *Hunt's Merchant's Magazine*, a leading business periodical of the era, argued for John Jacob Astor's "public character" (1763–1848). After a "moderate" estimate of Astor's "actual wealth at $20,000,000," this story lauded Astor for what were actually relatively small donations, the largest of which was $350,000 for "a great public library" in New York City. A lot of money, to be sure, but a trifling 1.75 percent of Astor's worth. The encomium to Astor concluded by reiterating "the essential features of the self-made man. The original talent which no opposition can restrain, the steady perseverance which no difficulty can dishearten, the unwearied enterprise which no success can satisfy or enervate." Together, all of these "mark him as a character of inherent power, not formed by circumstances." Lest anyone doubt, "Before such a genius, all obstructions vanish, and his march is ever onward."[12]

Hunt's Merchant's Magazine also provided Frost with his account of Gideon Lee (1778–1841), a shoemaker turned merchant turned politician who rose, as he must, "from poverty and obscurity." Embedded in Lee's biography was wonderment that "the countless opportunities which everywhere offer themselves to the enterprising, the industrious, the frugal, our surprise is excited, not that a few succeed, but that more do not."[13] Just as did pronouncing Astor's invulnerability to "circumstances," this rumination on Lee encapsulates the self-made myth's most harmful elements: an accusation against those who do not succeed and the growing presumption that financial success is the appropriate measure of the "enterprising," "industrious," and "frugal."

SELF-IMPROVEMENT FOR THE COMMON GOOD

America's leading intellectuals also joined in the era's discussions about self-improvement hoping to inspire and judge. *The Young American's Magazine of Self-Improvement* headlined authors who included William Ellery Channing, James Russell Lowell, Charles Sumner, Horace Greeley, Lyman Beecher, and his son Henry Ward Beecher (Harriet Beecher Stowe's father and brother, respectively); the editors also drew on works from other leading intellectuals, including Oliver Wendell Holmes, Henry Wadsworth Longfellow, and Wendell Phillips. The publication's "Prospectus" explained in 1847 that the editors aimed their messages at merchants and mechanics – "Practical classes" and "Republican citizens" – in order to "awaken a more general interest in SELF-IMPROVEMENT." Aptly, a promotion for the journal featured an engraving of Benjamin Franklin, the nation's model of self-improvement to serve the common good. With transparent presumption, these elites believed that they could and should "disseminate correct views of the *kind* of education" for young men and that "the more prosperous classes" should "take the most generous interest in the elevation of every branch of Society."[14]

The journal's first issue proclaimed the principle for "all persons engaged in the Practical pursuits of life" that "we must OURSELVES be the grand Instruments for accomplishing the purposes of our creation," and throughout young men were charged with similar directives. The December 1847 issue included praise for the 1846 edition of *Biography of Self-Taught Men* for its "sketches" of men "most remarkable, not merely for their genius and the extent of their acquirements, but for the disparity between their advantages and their success." The biographies were "calculated to inspire the most laudable ambition" among young Americans. The journal's first anniversary boasted of "opinions of the press" from across the country, one of which reinforced their gendered perspective: "a manly, hearty, well written journal, with no tincture of sentimentality."[15]

Although "self" appeared constantly, as in self-educated and self-knowledge, the term "self-made" did not appear at all. Yet the concept of self-agency reverberated throughout this transitional publication, telling the men in their audience that "our destinies are in our own hands," and so on. That was the central point of "The Pauper Lad of Woodend: Or, a Will and a Way: A Tale of Real Life," about the struggles of an orphaned boy whose "benefactor" enabled his studies while hiring him for "honest toil" in return. In the end, the unnamed hero became a famous mathematician, "a brilliant example of what may be done by determination, faithfulness, and integrity."[16] Unlike appeals to self-making increasingly prevalent in political or business spheres, however, this collection of essays credited sources of assistance, such as the lad's "benefactor." Their diligent heroes were not solitary oaks, and their measure was advancing the common good.

According to these New England elites, there was no shame in ambition, depending on its goals. The Rev. Leonard Withington urged that it be nurtured, declaring that "the only way to cure ambition, is to starve it to death." However, wealth and material riches were not at all celebrated in the journal, although impoverished origins were. Withington, for example, explained that "the great and good, in all ages" have experienced poverty, but true heroes did not "boast and glory" in it.[17] Few autobiographers could resist the self-promotion afforded by obscure roots, however. "In Imitation of Dr. Franklin" illustrated this tendency: "it was my fortune to breathe, for a long time ... the bracing air of poverty," it read, interlaced with platitudes about "the hallowed mysteries of poverty" to prepare for adulthood.[18] The judgment that rising from poverty was within everyman's reach ran through the journal, but it never praised wealth as a measure of success.

"Who Is Greatest?" was the first short story in a small family-oriented book with that same title, published in 1852, that kept to tradition's path in urging the common good as self-improvement's goal. Full of clichés that defended the older definitions of merit against newer, more materialistic ones, a family's conversations reminded readers, for example, that "It is the effort to benefit others that makes true greatness." It also urged appreciation for diverse occupations, regardless of status or income: the children's father assured them that "the humble artizan, or tiller of the soil, may be a greater man than ever was the most distinguished hero the world has seen." The children's quest that runs through the tale began with a brother's admiration for Alexander the Great. As their father explained, however, none of the "ambitious men" like Alexander, Caesar, or Napoleon could truly be great because they "loved themselves and cared not how much suffering they caused, so that they could be the highest of all and the rulers of all." In contrast, George Washington could be "one of the greatest men who ever lived" because he risked everything to defend his country. This "great benefactor" earned an affection that the conquerors could not. Even so, this wise father told his children that he would not wish to be Washington or anyone else. He "would rather be just what my Creator has made me." It "takes all to make a perfect world," hence the importance of all trades, of each man doing the work "for which he is best fitted."[19]

Who Is Greatest? was one of at least 100 books and short stories too numerous to count by Timothy Shay Arthur (1809–1885). Not one of America's intellectual elites, Arthur was one of the most prolific and well-known temperance and sentimentalist authors of the nineteenth century, and others amplified his words through copies and popular plays.[20] Fighting the temptations within the growing consumer culture, including taverns, Arthur and his ideological allies argued that if people limited their material ambitions to building comfortable lives, they could avoid getting drawn into debt or into fixation on relentless acquisition that could only lead to frustration. Individuals owed responsibility to develop their character and abilities, but always in service. As the sister in "Who Is Greatest" reminded her brothers, the biblical definition of greatness was "*And whosoever will be chief among you, let him be your servant.*" To this her brother replied, "But how can any one be chief of all, and yet the servant of all?"[21] This was a perfectly reasonable question, and an answer could depend on whether one looked backward or forward for models of self-improvement.

As we saw earlier, the phrase "self-made" often referred to "self-made maniacs" and "self-made drunks." No one under the influence of excessive drink could meet the expanding expectations for "self-reliance," "self-possession," "self-dignity," and "self-improvement," much less be self-made in any positive sense. Alcoholism became more dangerous as industrialization and urbanization expanded, and as commerce tempted everyone to take on debt. Thus, the same decades in the early nineteenth century when the early language of self-making developed were the decades when alcohol consumption peaked in the United States. Then, as if by miracle, by 1850, average consumption dropped dramatically, not so much because everyone cut back by half, but because large portions of the population had accepted the arguments that flourished through the anti-alcohol, sometimes anti-tavern, temperance movement working synergistically within and sometimes as part of the second Great Awakening. Untold numbers of women, preachers, civic leaders, and writers of all descriptions became temperance activists to save souls, families, communities, and, they believed, the nation. Arthur's most famous novel was his evocatively illustrated *Ten Nights in a Bar-Room and What I Saw There*, published in 1854 and prominent among the nineteenth century's vast temperance literature that portrayed the ravages of alcoholism. Fiction and nonfiction publications, plays, and sermons told tales of ruin when people abandoned self-restraint and lost self-control.[22] Their assumption that alcoholism was entirely a matter of personal choice and their calls for personal responsibility helped to move American culture toward accepting self-agency and, eventually, self-making.

"SELF-MADE OR NEVER MADE"

Calls for temperance found support in nationwide movements dedicated to the cause, such as the working-class Washingtonian Total Abstinence Society and the Women's Christian Temperance Union. They also found support among leading figures of popular culture we don't intuitively associate with temperance – phrenologists and entertainment entrepreneur Phineas Taylor Barnum. These influential promoters embedded advocacy for temperance within their promotions of self-making, and their broad reach into many arenas of popular culture reinforced the migration of self-made success toward worldly goals.

We generally think of human skulls as pretty much rigid by adulthood, neither subject to purposeful modification nor useful for assessing character. It seems, therefore, counterintuitive that phrenologists, who identify people's traits and potentials according to their cranial measurements, could have been prominent proponents of self-making. Yet the highly successful Fowler brothers, Orson Squire (1809–1887) and Lorenzo Niles (1811–1896), broadcast the phrase "Self-Made or Never Made" through their widespread lecturing, advertising, and publishing. They and other practicing phrenologists believed that the brain, like a muscle, could change dimensions and shape with proper exercise and thereby

Figure 6.1 The mid-nineteenth-century Temperance movement advanced the notion of self-making by framing alcohol abuse as entirely a matter of personal choice. This image appeared at the front of a popular 1854 book, *Ten Nights in a Bar-Room* by T. S. Arthur, and illustrates abolitionists' emotional appeals. This poignant tale of family loss was repeated into the 1920s through multiple editions, songs, and theatrical performances. (Courtesy of Cornell University Library)

alter the skull as well. After Europeans introduced this field to the United States in the 1820s, phrenological societies sprouted up and books proliferated, as did ceramic models and printed illustrations of the head, all with instructions for gauging traits such as secretiveness, acquisitiveness, destructiveness, parental love, benevolence, and so on. All of these phrenologists earnestly advised audiences on how to approach "perfection" strategically by developing, governing, and balancing traits. By the 1840s, the Fowler brothers and their publishing partner, Samuel R. Wells (1820–1875), operated at the center of America's version of this international movement, "practical phrenology" (called that for its emphasis on behavioral change rather than theory). Significantly, the Fowler brothers and Wells, along with family members and many fellow phrenologists, fervently advocated wide-ranging reforms, most notably abolition, women's suffrage, temperance, and vegetarianism, as ways to improve individuals and the nation. Not at all a marginal fad, phrenology argued for self-making within the core of popular culture for decades.[23]

The motto "Self-Made or Never Made" appeared on the title page of Orson Fowler's 1842 *Self-Culture, and Perfection of Character, Including the Management of Youth* and its later editions. As a Detroit bookstore advertised the seventh edition of the book five years later, they wished "it were in the hands of every young man and woman in America" because "it tells us how to cultivate or restrain the organs of the brain." Moreover, "Improvement is the practical watch-word of the age," and "No individual can read a page of it without being improved thereby."[24] The book's title recalled the eminent Reverend William Channing's widely published 1838 lecture, *Self-Culture*, which he directed to those "occupied by manual labor" because of his "joy in the efforts they are making for their own improvement" and his "firm faith in their success."[25] In contrast to Channing's attempts to persuade through complex arguments and genteel condescension, the Fowlers aimed to show everyone how to pursue self-culture in daily actions.

Capturing the mainstream's mood and the era's fixation on self-improvement, Orson Fowler began his lessons in *Self-Culture* by proclaiming that "IMPROVEMENT is the practical watch-word of the age." People "daily and earnestly" ask "How can I REMEDY my defects? By what MEANS can I increase my deficient organs, and diminish or regulate those that are too large?" He and his fellow phrenologists proudly, if rather naively, declared that they could address all these desires "scientifically." They could guide readers "who attempt to improve their higher faculties [but] know neither where to begin nor how to proceed." In just three pages of text, "improve" and "improvement" appear eight times. The book's final page ends with Fowler's declaration that he wrote this book to serve God's command to reach the "'greatest good' – HUMAN IMPROVEMENT."[26]

Phrenologists joined the ranks of those who neutralized ambition's sting in the nineteenth century, contributing to acceptance of individualism, worldliness, and illusions of self-making. Although eighteenth-century mainstream American culture had selectively nudged ambition from its medieval associations with

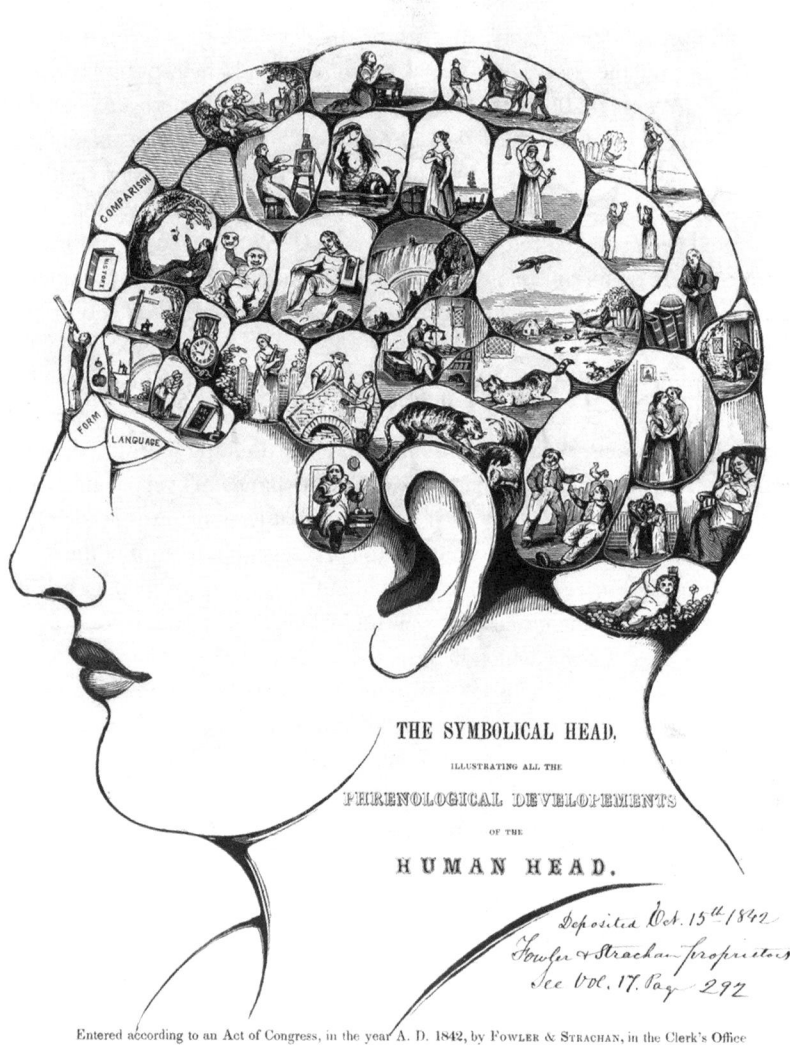

Figure 6.2 Phrenologists claimed that they could detect people's character and intelligence by the shapes of their skulls. Like other mid-nineteenth-century believers in reform and self-improvement, they insisted that people could improve their mental faculties through work and discipline and, thereby, reshape their skulls. Such faith in self-fashioning advanced acceptance of the myth of self-made success. To show what parts of the brain governed assorted activities, Fowler and Strachan published this 1842 print of "The Symbolical Head, Illustrating all the Phrenological Developments of the Human Head." (Library of Congress: Prints and Photographs, Item 90713998)

damnation and sin, free women and men still wrestled with the temptations and dangers of worldly opportunities. What were acceptable and legitimate goals? Among phrenologists ambition shed its moral load; it was neither a sin nor a blessing. It became instead one of the many human "faculties" that interact within an individual's personality. For phrenologists, it could energize action but could not itself determine action's direction.[27] Like every trait, such as magnanimity and destructiveness, ambition only functioned within a network of other traits. Therefore, "ambition always combines with those faculties which are the most active." For someone whose level of "Conscientiousness" is high, "it gives regard for MORAL character and correct MOTIVES." Ambition that empowers "Combativeness" and "the other animal propensities," however, would lead to harm. A favorable balance of "COMBINATIONS of the faculties" could "sanctify ambition, elevate motives, and ennoble the whole character." Phrenologists pledged to guide clients to that balance. They accepted ambition as itself morally neutral, a trait that should be "properly directed." Indeed, they detected a problem when someone's "flattened crown indicates a want of ambition, energy, and aspiration."[28]

To be clear, while leading phrenologists viewed ambition as morally neutral, they did not neutralize wealth the same way, adhering to traditional reproaches. Thus, Orson Fowler critiqued those who, "since the Revolution," have been "straining every nerve" to achieve wealth, "though [their] intellect lie waste, and moral pleasures are unknown." Moreover, the popular aversion to aristocracy still inspired disparagement of "money-made nabobs" who imagined themselves "far above their fellow-men." He asked, "Is the possession of wealth indeed so much above that of WORTH?" He also reminded readers that "Christ was no aristocrat." And in the spirit of the prevailing electoral populism, Fowler declared that the "mushroom, codfish, stockjobbing aristocracy of our nation is utterly contemptible anywhere, but a perfect OUTRAGE in this country." Instead, the Fowlers always emphasized the goal of their discoveries and instructions to help people reach "*happiness*. This is the one, single, only ultimate of both life in the aggregate, and of each of its individual functions." Common sense and bourgeois values permeate their encouragements and lessons to advance "social feeling; love of society" and "community of feeling and interest."[29]

Although phrenologists and their amateur enthusiasts relished illusions that they – not elites – could assess themselves and determine their lives' courses, they resisted the cultural movement toward a "solitary oak" version of individualism. "Self-Made or Never Made" did not mean "made" alone. While improvement required individual responsibility and action, Orson Fowler explained in *Self-Culture* that "Men should NOT wrap themselves up in the frigid cloak of selfish isolation." Without others, there would be "no companies formed for trade, mechanical, public, or other works," nor any other "religious, political, scientific, or other societies." With no "concert of action," achievement within "only an exceedingly limited arena" could result, along with "green-eyed jealousy, burning animosity, and dire revenge." After the Civil War, the Fowlers and Wells would continue to press for "co-operative, not isolated action" among and between Americans, as both God's will and something intrinsic to the "human constitution."[30] As with so many reformers of their day, they earnestly sought to encourage self-agency along with appreciation for social bonds and shared responsibilities for the common good.

The Fowlers attracted a mix of scorn and imitation – the price of their widespread success. Critics accused phrenologists of excusing bad behavior as beyond a person's control. Of all the perfectly reasonable criticisms of this pseudo-science, that one was completely off the mark. Self-agency and responsibility resided at the core of their worldview, however unrealistic it was. Birth and circumstance absolved no one. Even drunkards and criminals, they believed, could overcome their difficulties if they understood the physical origins of their waywardness and accepted responsibility to reform themselves. Cranial bumps, they thought, were diagnostic, not deterministic, useful to ascertain flaws and to calculate how to improve. The title of *Self-Culture*, after all, offered "Perfection of Character."[31]

Everyone was eligible for phrenology's benefits. Curiosity and hope drew people to a character reading, and many found the experience, the images, and the texts worthwhile in some fashion. The Fowlers and other practitioners captured the spirit of their times so successfully that prominent citizens and reformers of all persuasions were caught up in their enthusiasm. Some of the most notable proponents included Henry Clay, Henry Ward Beecher, education reformer Horace Mann, diet reformer Sylvester Graham, abolitionists and social activists Samuel Gridley Howe and Julia Ward Howe, abolitionists and women's suffrage activists Lucretia Mott and Elizabeth Cady Stanton, literary giants Walt Whitman and Edgar Allan Poe, and more. Middle- and working-class people, too numerous to count, found inspiration as well, as indicated by sales and attendance at lectures and other events.[32] However, beyond the literate and the mobile, the insistence that everyone could and should "know thyself" and improve accordingly was insensitive in the extreme to people whose enslavement made self-determination impossible, or whose poverty made accessing phrenology's lessons and practicing self-study highly unfeasible. Yet the Fowlers and fellow advocates truly believed that they were benign prophets of universal improvement. And many others agreed. Clara Barton (1821–1912), for example, founder of the American Red Cross who had experienced decades of denigration by men who stepped in to run organizations and projects that she had originated, described Lorenzo Fowler in 1886 as a professional whose "heart had in it the essence of kindness and broad humanity, with chords attuned to human needs."[33]

Phrenology's approaches to human perfectibility were far from unmixed. Its theorists and practitioners also supported later cultural foundations for "scientific" prejudice, including Social Darwinism's extreme champions of the myth of self-made success. Such approaches bolster pervasive racism and sexism by attributing what proponents see as inadequacies and flaws to what appear to be biological differences, what we now know to be superficial differences. Phrenologists' canon argued for everyone's potential to develop, but it set differential ranges within which various populations could do so. As it happened, the more a group resembled the phrenologists themselves – men of Northern European ethnicity – the greater the potential for advancement. Elizabeth Cady Stanton, for example, freely used phrenological language and logic to explain and improve her own and others' behaviors. She believed in it as a science and appreciated its support for increasing women's alternatives and opportunities, encouraging them to advance their abilities and to apply them in the world. Yet she resented the field's residual sexism, complaining in 1848 that "they call all the fine heads masculine and all the ill shaped feminine, for when a woman presents a remarkable large well developed intellectual region, they say she has a masculine head."[34]

Even so, such sexism was mild compared to the field's racist assumptions, even among abolitionist phrenologists. For example, Orson Fowler concluded about Sarah Kinson, an African, that "the forehead is large, sustained by a vigorous constitution. She is far superior to Africans generally."[35] As the Fowler brothers did not hesitate to explain and illustrate, the "various races also accord with phrenological science." Thus, in their view, "the Caucasian race is superior in reasoning power and moral elevation to all the other races, and, accordingly, have higher and bolder foreheads, and more elevated and elongated top heads."[36] The imagined ranges of improvement for all other groups were, therefore, determined by comparison to Northern European males. Other groups could overlap but never equal or exceed the presumed ethnic- and sex-based benchmarks. They were quite sure that everyone could and should improve, but improvement was only possible within the range prescribed by their sex, race, and ethnicity.

BARNUM AND SELF-MAKING FOR FUN AND PROFIT

Not all improvement and temperance activists were preachers, wistful romantics, enterprising proto-scientists, or resolute reformers wholly dedicated to inspiring goodness. None other than the century's greatest showman, Phineas Taylor Barnum (1810–1891), was a complicated person who promoted self-making as the means to profit as well as to sobriety. Although remembered mostly as a self-proclaimed trickster and creator of a famous circus, Barnum was a steadfast and high-profile temperance campaigner and advocate for self-fashioning, just as often for moral improvement as for profit. He agreed with fellow activists that families and communities would benefit from abstinence, but he mostly pitched sobriety to benefit ambitious men as an essential component of their self-agency. When invited to contribute to a *Practical Treatise on Business* in 1852 as "one who is known all over the world as the ablest tactician and one of the most successful business men of the age," he composed "Barnum's Rules for Success in Business," the fourth of which he labeled "Sobriety." He proclaimed that "no man can succeed in business unless he has a *brain* . . . and *reason* to guide him." Along with maxims more common in advice literature for self-made success, such as "Ambition, energy, industry, [and] perseverance," Barnum insisted that no amount of intelligence can overcome the "lassitude" produced by "the wine-cup" and its "neutralizing the energies so essential to success in business." A master storyteller, Barnum illustrated business failures and families lost to drunkenness, on the one hand, along with encouraging parables of men who chose temperance and became wealthy and respected for their "moral worth" on the other. Barnum later included these rules in his widely read 1880 book *The Art of Money Getting, Or Golden Rules for Making Money*.[37]

Barnum was also an engaged citizen who served his communities, especially as a local booster and one-time mayor (1875) for Bridgeport, Connecticut, and member of the state's House of Representatives (1866–1869). On a larger scale, he triumphantly linked individual self-making with nation making, urging individual improvement as a patriotic good. He staunchly supported the Union in the Civil War and often referred to his own patriotism, as in the dedication to his 1885 autobiography: "To the Universal Yankee Nation, of Which I Am Proud to Be One." Likewise, he declared both his patriotism and his belief in everyone's potential for affluence when he began *The Art of Money Getting* (based on lectures to British audiences in 1858) with a fantasy of easy money-making and self-made success available to everyone: "In the United States, where we have more land than people, it is not at all difficult for persons in good health to make money." Because of the nation's growth, he boasted that "there are so many avenues of success open, so many vocations which are not crowded, that any person of either sex who is willing, at least for the time being, to engage in any respectable occupation that offers, may find lucrative employment."[38] Like so many of his fellow nationalist boosters then and now, he either did not see or would not acknowledge the real world factors that constrained people on the margins.

A complicated man, Barnum was a welcome, earnest, and generous participant in many congregations, and he wrestled in later life with the tensions between his public persona and his private belief in the Second Great Awakening's sense of perfectibility. A contemporary recognized this paradox and described Barnum as possessing "double characters, one professional &

Figure 6.3 Phineas T. Barnum is best known as a promoter and entertainer, but this 1875 studio photograph shows him as a no-nonsense businessman. His promotion of self-agency departed from traditions of self-improvement for service alone, advocating enthusiastically for character-building that advanced *The Art of Money Getting*, the title of his widely read 1880 book. (Hutton Archive / Stringer / Archive Photos via Getty Images)

scoundrelly, the other private, church-going, decorous, and utterly abstinent from pocket-picking."[39] The showman's lectures and writings always contained moralistic messages. But, whatever his own intellectual and moral journeys, his *public* fame rode on his boosterism on behalf of self-achieved money-making – his own and his audiences'. His cultural legacy combined what he sent into the public realm with what his audiences there took from it. The most popular messages fed into the nation's burgeoning materialism and ambitions to succeed within it.

It was certainly hard to see anything else when "**MONEY!**" sprawled three times across the top of a broadside for an 1863 presentation of "The Art of Money Getting." Specifically, as the "Prince of Humbugs!" he promised to explain "How to make it. How to Lose it. How to keep it. How to spend it."[40] Subtlety was not his style. Even charity, to which Barnum contributed generously and that he avowed could be "a duty and a pleasure," should be valued because a good reputation would attract more business with a proper reputation – "a *profitable philanthropy*." To justify his boosterism, Barnum ended *The Art of Money Getting* with a series of tributes for "money-getting." Among them, he assured readers, "money itself, when properly used" is a "blessing" if "the possessor of it accepts its responsibilities, and uses it as a friend to humanity." Moreover, the "history of money-getting, which is commerce, is a history of civilization," no less. In effect, Barnum moralized, "as a general thing, money-getters are the benefactors of our race."[41]

Barnum was, thus, a transitional figure in the evolution of the individualist materialism embedded in the myth of self-made success. He seems to have appreciated his own advantages and, although he relished telling his adventures on the way to fame and fortune, he neither claimed a rise from obscurity nor used the phrase "self-made man" often. Nonetheless, he was devoted to the concept of self-making and promoted it to his enormous audiences in every venue of the era. Among his "Rules for Success in Business" he declared, for example, "*Do not depend on others*. Your success must depend on your own individual exertions. Trust not to the assistance of friends; but learn that every man must be the architect of his own fortune."[42] This was the essence of advice he offered frequently and in many forms.

With his storytelling largesse Barnum also hailed enterprise through tales of notable tycoons, John Jacob Astor, for one. In keeping with the self-made pattern, Barnum described this "poor farmer boy" who "died worth twenty millions." Likewise, "Cornelius Vanderbilt began life rowing a boat from Staten Island to New York ... and died worth fifty million." While neither of these gentlemen started off as disadvantaged as Barnum suggested, and Astor was never a farm boy, they both did end fabulously rich. Barnum insisted that every young man who aspired to riches and studied "the rules" – his rules – could get there. Inequality should not deter young men who "will find, as a general thing, that the poor boys get rich and the rich boys get poor." Starting off with money, he claimed, kept young men from knowing "the value of it by experience" and, therefore, they lacked motivation.[43]

Thus it was that P. T. Barnum genuinely, jubilantly, and profitably advanced the cultural authority of an emerging myth of self-making in an emergent version that had money as its goal and its measure rather than godliness or virtuous citizenship. In his tales, as in the era's budding genre of rags-to-riches fables that dime novels would spread far and wide, laced with tales of adventure, money was becoming a criterion of "worth," as he used that word to describe Astor and Vanderbilt. He was quite sure that "Nine out of ten of the rich men of our country today, started out in life as poor boys, with determined wills, industry, perseverance, economy and good habits." Barnum applied other booster platitudes taking shape then, for example, "There is no such thing in the world as luck," and, if a man does not succeed, "there are reasons for it, although, perhaps, he may not be able to see them." It seems that Barnum and others of the comfortable classes who joined him, intent on justifying wealth, could not see – or were unwilling to see – the contextual "reasons" for success and failure that lay beyond individuals' range of action. The prospect of being the architect of one's fortune offered little hope for people without property, assets, opportunity, or freedom. For example, in giving advice on how to "Use the Best Tools," Barnum referred to employees as "they," while directing advice on hiring "those men who have brains and experience" to "you," the people who decide whom to employ. Although he eagerly sought the trade of working-class folks, office clerks, and seamstresses for his entertainments, he aimed his advice for "money-getting" above their station to the burgeoning middle-class where he had begun.[44]

There is no evidence that Barnum repented of his boisterous insistence that all people were the architects of their own fortunes. Yet as he prepared for his cosmic reckoning, he relinquished his own self-agency. For his tombstone and funeral sermon, he requested the prayer "Not my will, but Thine, be done."[45]

COMPETING BIOGRAPHIES AFTER THE CIVIL WAR

The mid-century contests over self-making's cultural authority swirled around telling stories of noteworthy lives, including about P. T. Barnum himself. In December 1854, the *New York Times* carried two articles about Barnum's first autobiography, his *Life*. The first article good-naturedly tagged it "the Barnum Confessions" and described it as "really a *very* amusing book" that was "nurtured in humbug." The second, however, scathingly rejected the vision of American ambition and success that Barnum boosted, regretting that the "book will be very widely read and will do infinite mischief." This second article, "The Lesson of Barnum's Life," repeated the usual self-made success script that "From being poor and obscure, he has rapidly made himself very rich and very famous" – even though Barnum himself didn't make that claim. Its lament then targeted another concern, namely that "the vast army of our American youth" look to Barnum as a model. Humbug made money, but "*obtaining money under false pretences*" made him "the stupendous and magnificent master of the art of deception," an invidious model for young men "to seek fortune by other means than industry in the worthy pursuit of the honorable business on which the welfare of society depends." Distressed that Americans already regarded "Success ... as the test of worth," this skeptic was genuinely angry that Barnum, "the embodiment and impersonation of success," published his own story to boast and misguide others, while also belittling any act of his own or others that hinted at doing "an apparently noble and generous deed."[46] Wealth neither excused such folly, nor did it deserve merit from that traditional perspective.

Critics occasionally targeted biography compilers' uses of the self-making concept to argue about its meanings. For instance, a few years later in 1858, Charles C. B. Seymour (1829–1869), a well-regarded drama critic in New York City, took it upon himself to publish *Self-Made Men*. Popular enough to warrant multiple editions, it was an odd volume, with no obvious purpose other than to sell books. It lacked, for instance, any statement of purpose regarding either nationalist or moral edification. Betraying standard practice among the century's biographers, Seymour explicitly refused "to append to each sketch a little sermon to point out its moral tendencies." Contemporary reviewers noted that Seymour's clichéd pledge that subjects had "attained eminence in spite of adverse circumstances of birth and fortune" did not hold for many stories, especially about the numerous Europeans. One critic described the collection of sixty-two biographies as a "patch-work" with "no particular arrangement" of subjects. Another reviewer objected that "the use of the term 'self-made' has acquired a sort of technical import" that disqualified some men because of their privileges. A South Carolinian editor objected to the entire idea of self-making itself, not just to who deserved the title. Seymour's "very imperfect vision" of "what constitutes a self-made man [reflects] a superficial meaning attached to the phrase in every-day talk." Attacking the very core of the concept, this critic insisted that "all men are self-made, either for good or evil." This rare challenge to the myth as a whole argued that "All men depend on time and circumstance, and on other men." No mention of women's assistance here any more than elsewhere, its main purpose was to defend those born to affluence, not to argue for equality. "At least equal honour is due," in this view, "to those who have achieved distinction in spite of everything that could tempt them to sink into inglorious ease."[47] This southern rebuke on the eve of the Civil War showed that the concept of self-made success had diffused sufficiently into American culture to inspire backlash. Its defense of the well-to-do, however, would resurface later in the age of tycoons to justify their reputations and legacies and, in doing so, preserve the myth's hold.

On the other side of the Civil War, stories far and wide continued to offer some version of self-making – judging, prodding, urging, and sometimes rewarding. Even so, no consensus emerged yet on what it meant, what qualified someone as self-made, nor how to measure the worth of a self-made man. Stories about godly men and public servants who had lacked much formal education and other elite advantages had earlier given the concept rhetorical value. By the 1820s, as we have seen, political partisans followed Andrew Jackson's lead to angle for voters' loyalties within the popular aversion to aristocracy, proclaiming their worth as servants of the Republic but misrepresenting their credentials as having "obscure origins," in Oliver Cromwell's ancient phrase. Politicians of that era shaped self-made heroism as a lonely triumph, free of debts, thereby setting patterns that would continue to fuel the myth. By mid-century, cultural, military, and political heroes increasingly had to share the stage of public renown with businessmen, whose wealth and power drew public notice and storytellers' attention. Material success was becoming a measure of worth, as evidence of self-discipline and fruitful ambition that merely gestured to older standards. A historian's survey thirty years ago of mid-nineteenth-century autobiographies confirmed that trend and also that people with the affluence and longevity to produce a memoir highlighted the challenges they overcame, standard fare for stories of self-making, with or without the name.[48]

By the time that Harriet Beecher Stowe (1811–1896) published *The Lives and Deeds of Our Self-Made Men* in 1872, the label "self-made man" and the esteem that it carried were no longer the domain of godly men and community servants. Stowe, however, was not ready to give up that older standard. Instead, she earnestly enlisted in the competition to define the concept and resist the growing trend to affiliate self-making with worldly success. Among her heroes, "almost every one of these men sprang from a condition of hard-working poverty" to become "some of the leading public men of our times." Most important, their "frugality, strict temperance, self-reliance and indomitable industry" qualified all nineteen as models to inspire "the young men of America." As when Stowe wrote the tide-turning abolitionist novel, *Uncle Tom's Cabin*, two decades before, she aimed to inspire citizens. Therefore, she selected every one of her heroes for having advanced the cause of abolition, with Abraham Lincoln leading the list and Frederick Douglass included. Moreover, the only time Stowe referred to her subjects' adult wealth was to minimize that of Schuyler Colfax (1823–1885), vice president under Ulysses S. Grant: he "has earned a very comfortable living …, though he is by no means a rich man." Daughter of the century's premier Calvinist evangelist, Lyman Beecher, Stowe remained unconvinced of materialism's merits. She repeatedly praised her subjects for their willingness and capacity to make "sacrifices of tangible and material present values for abstract principles," as she said of Salmon P. Chase, who served as Secretary of the Treasury during the Civil War before President Lincoln appointed him Chief Justice, crowning a lifetime of duty.[49] Stowe meant for stories of self-made men to inspire individual improvement to take on family and community responsibilities, not for the acquisition of wealth.

Stowe had good reason to be defensive: she stood on the losing side of the Victorian-era battle against materialist measures of merit and success. In this respect, among the mid-century's notable compilations to laud so-called self-made men, her stories alone gazed decidedly back on tradition. That she was aware of the contest over the meaning of self-making seems clear when we compare this collection with a near-identical book she published four years earlier, *Men of Our Times; or Leading Patriots of the Day*. Neither that 1868 title nor its text included the phrase "self-made"; the time-honored idiom "self-educated" only appeared twice, once in the preface and again to distinguish Lincoln from the formally educated Charles Sumner.[50] In contrast, Stowe highlighted "self-made" with her 1872 title and, also, in the new biography she added at the end for B. Gratz Brown (1826–1885), a leading abolitionist in the border state of Missouri. Her story for Brown fit with the tone and language of self-making, even putting a key phrase in quotation marks in this sentence: Brown possessed the "pluck and daring, the ambition and energy" that "justify ... man's proudest claim that he is 'the architect of his own fortunes.'" In concluding Brown's story and the book, Stowe gave "credit to the self-made men of our times – men whose early advantages were limited" and to "those who have justified the pains and patience of a liberal early training by prudent and honorable lives." Each "class," she resolved, must struggle differently, but "personal responsibility" along with "faith and courage are equally relied upon for success."[51] Strong words of inspiration, although unrealistic for members of the many classes and stations unable to act on such inspiration.

Despite Stowe's earlier influence, the world saw only a single edition of her 1872 606-page *Lives and Deeds* until her son, Charles Edward Stowe, revised it in 1889. In striking contrast, the year before her 1872 edition entered the arena, James D. McCabe, Jr. (1842-1883) profitably took a more materialist approach in *Great Fortunes, and How They Were Made: or, The Struggles and Triumphs of Our Self-Made Men*. Its thirty-eight biographies filled 633 pages, and new editions appeared in each of the following two years from different publishers in different cities, followed by thirty more editions before the end of the century. There were plenty of capitalists by 1871 who had risen from obscure origins and whose exploits had built huge fortunes rising from obscure origins – John Jacob Astor and Cornelius Vanderbilt, to name two of the most prominent. None of these or other giants of material success found their way into Stowe's *Lives and Deeds*, but they dominated McCabe's *Great Fortunes* in which neither Lincoln nor Douglass appeared. Instead, he organized his subjects by vocation: "merchants" (eight), "capitalists" (four), "inventors" (eight), "publishers" (two), "editors" (two), "lawyers" (two), "artists" (four), "divines" (two), "authors" (two), "actors" (two), and "physicians" (two). A Virginian who had served in the Confederate War Department, McCabe avoided sectional politics in his reach for a national audience, omitting statesmen and military figures altogether.[52]

In his pursuit of commercial success, McCabe did not abandon entirely traditional values that tied ambition and self-making to service, especially not in his preface. He took pains to explain that "'Great Fortunes' is not used here to designate pecuniary success exclusively." He pointed out that "A few of the men whose lives are herein recorded never amassed great wealth." They qualified for inclusion among his accounts, however, if they "achieved the highest success in their vocations" and "achieved the greatest good," including that they "opened the way to fortune for themselves, but also for others, and have thus conferred lasting benefits on our country." Stowe's and McCabe's different notions of nationalism were also revealing. Whereas Stowe's nationalism gloried in America as a "Christian republic" and in her heroes as "graduates from the American school of Christian Democracy," McCabe's nationalism combined "the increase of the national wealth, the development of the national resources, and the elevation of the national character." He concluded his preface with an obligatory nod to ordinary people, assuring them that any man who contributed to these national ambitions, "though he himself be poor in purse, has indeed won a great fortune." Tens of thousands of those ordinary people purchased *Great Fortunes*, lured by sales pitches proclaiming that it "teaches how to succeed in life and at the same time benefit mankind."[53] This was an optimistic promise from a book praising men whose initial advantages, including those of ethnicity, gender, and class, would be impossible for most in America to match.

Although James McCabe never reached Harriet Beecher Stowe's reputational heights, *Great Fortunes* and its widely distributed storytelling helped to crystallize and carry forward modern fantasies of self-made success. Dozens of his editions, plus at least one other plagiarized edition, advanced mostly secular and material meanings of self-made success over and above the notions of self-improvement for God and community that had earlier given cultural authority to self-agency.[54] McCabe's preface articulated the emerging myth with romantic grandeur:

> The chief glory of America is, that it is the country in which genius and industry find their speediest and surest reward. Fame and fortune are here open to all who are willing to work for them. Neither class distinctions nor social prejudices, neither differences of birth, religion, nor ideas, can prevent the man of true merit from winning the just reward of his labors in this favored land. We are emphatically a nation of self-made men, and it is to the labors of this worthy class that our marvelous national prosperity is due.

In this evocative passage, McCabe captured the century's belief in the inspirational potential of biographies. As his next paragraph contended, "men are naturally cheered and encouraged by the success of others" if they carry "valuable lessons." As did Stowe and most biographers of that century, McCabe offered "the record of their lives as models worthy of the imitation of the young men of our country" as a patriotic gesture.[55]

McCabe seized upon – and valorized – much that is destructive in the myth of self-making. Although he recognized that "no one can hope to succeed in life merely by the force of his own genius," the remedy for anyone "still struggling" could be found in his heroes' stories. And though he did not deny entirely the reality of differential opportunities, he concluded that all "the man of true merit" needed to do to avoid failure "in this favored land" was to learn from the "valuable lessons" of other men. Like McCabe, other mainstream storytellers increasingly declared that anyone who did not achieve "fame and fortune" must not be "willing to work for them." This judgment sits at the core of the myth's modern justifications of inequality, namely that inequality simply reflects different degrees of individual merit and effort, not opportunities or constraints. Even more destructive was the presumption that "merit" encompassed not only abilities but also character and willingness to work. The myth of self-made success solidified over the coming decades as a tool for judgment to justify a social and economic system that demeaned many as it praised a few.

7

Gilded Age Heroes

Thomas Mellon founded a financial dynasty, inspired, he often declared, by Benjamin Franklin, whose *Autobiography* provided "the turning point of my life." In 1871, to honor that inspiration, Mellon placed a larger-than-life cast-iron statue of Franklin to preside over the grand entrance to his elegant four-story bank in downtown Pittsburgh, Pennsylvania. He also distributed hundreds of copies of Franklin's story and adages throughout his life to encourage others to better themselves. A grandson, William Larimer Mellon, confirmed that Mellon "revered Benjamin Franklin above all men and Franklin's name frequently was on his lips. The boys in our family literally were brought up on Franklin." Accordingly, "Franklin became a sort of genie of the Mellon family. I cannot exaggerate the influence." Thomas Mellon testified in his own 1885 autobiography that the "maxims of 'poor Richard' exactly suited my sentiments" and that he "read the book again and again."[1] In many ways, Mellon's career truly did parallel his hero's rise from modest origins. Nonetheless, the contrasts in their stories – those that each told about himself and those that others told about them – reveal vast differences between the men and their eras as chapters in forging America's romance with self-making.

Over the course of Thomas Mellon's long life (1813–1908), the very nature of American capitalism changed, leading in turn to new meanings and politics of self-making. Images of Pittsburgh over the century starkly illustrate that transition. When Mellon arrived there as a boy in 1818, it was a small town, "pleasant and flourishing," according to a visitor, nestled between still-green hills where the confluence of the Allegheny and Monongahela rivers forms the Ohio River. It looked like most other small hinterland towns then, although already "numerous" iron furnaces and forges presaged its sooty future. Businesses there as elsewhere functioned pretty much as they had for a century or so, producing and trading mostly on a modest scale. By the time Mellon started his bank in 1869, however, Pittsburgh had exploded into an industrial colossus with few American peers. Its population jumped from about 21,000 in 1840 to over 86,000 in 1870; and growth would continue apace, reaching 321,616 by 1900. When Mellon began banking in 1869, Pittsburgh produced half of the country's

Figure 7.1 Thomas Mellon, founder of the Mellon fortune, always credited Benjamin Franklin as his inspiration, so in 1871 he placed a larger-than-life statue of Franklin prominently over the door of his new bank building. However, he had only absorbed the material ambition elements of Franklin's message, and he exemplified a misleading individualist interpretation that became increasingly widespread in the late nineteenth century. (Courtesy of Carnegie Library of Pittsburgh)

iron. More than 400 factories produced munitions, railroad tracks, locomotives, and freight cars, along with one-third of the nation's window glass, and a large portion of its refined petroleum.[2]

Industrialists and their enabling financial institutions accelerated America's economic motion, forming and leading organizations so colossal that they not only commanded economic influence but also encroached upon the nation's cultures and politics. Together, they altered the public face of business, until then the purview of artisans, merchants, farmers, and planters. These large-scale industrialists wielded increasing quantities of money, laborers, political power, and technological innovations to produce railroads, telegraph, steamships, wagons, processed and packaged foods, machines, agricultural equipment, consumer goods, household durables like furniture and stoves, and even new ways to illuminate the night, among other wonders of the age. To many, this looked like progress, perhaps not on the road to salvation, but certainly in terms of choices for many and materialist lures for all, despite differential access to those lures. Not everyone was convinced that industrialization was the road to improvement, of course; contrarians included philosophers such as Henry Adams and Herbert Spencer, and artisans who lost their livelihoods, such as Andrew Carnegie's own father. However, the promise of industrialization was a juggernaut that rolled ahead to crush most other visions and possibilities.

Narratives after the mid nineteenth century increasingly portrayed businessmen as a new type of hero, blazing paths through new frontiers toward progress. As exemplars of both bewildering developments and material success, men doing business on unprecedented scales joined the nation's pantheon, and successful businessmen received the kind of local and national recognition once reserved for political, military, and spiritual leaders. They and their champions held up their acquisition of influence and wealth as proof of their superiority and, by implication, everyone else's shortcomings. They also proclaimed their rights to that influence and wealth, along with rights to general esteem and public resources, even when many of them, like Thomas Mellon, abandoned the norms of communal service that Benjamin Franklin had modeled, while others, like Andrew Carnegie and John D. Rockefeller, fashioned personas of munificence. In this context, the rhetoric of self-making acquired a new individualist grandeur that served them and their allies in new rounds of the competitions for cultural authority that forged the self-made myth.

NEW CHALLENGES, NEW NARRATIVES

Pursuing capitalist ambitions entails confronting challenges, such as political decisions on land use, corporate charters from states, labor policies, labor organizations, environmental regulations, and taxation, all the while building alliances and competing with other businesspeople. Nineteenth-century entrepreneurs angled to change the political landscape to build novel versions of capitalism in which wealth seemed to overwhelm political institutions and the influence of most people within them.[3] In the intense contests to influence policy and practice that ensued at local and national levels, their few ballots carried only trifling influence. Therefore, in those political competitions –electoral and behind the scenes – they and their advocates reinforced their array of claims, including self-making, as being the vanguard of material progress and, therefore, deserving of esteem and privilege.

The intense political and cultural competitions of those industrializing decades seeded a paradox: businessmen and their advocates portrayed entrepreneurs as self-made individualists although they increasingly operated within an environment of expanding corporations, financial institutions, trade associations, and business combinations then called trusts. At the same time, inequalities not only grew but became more apparent as the press displayed both tycoons' mansions and urban slums. Machinations within governmental bodies likewise highlighted differentials. Under these conditions, the myth of self-made success served elites' needs for cultural authority that they required for the political authority that maintained and expanded their assets. Many businessmen were not above exercising raw power and exploiting their connections with government authorities. Nonetheless, their rhetorical tools promoted their successes and resources as measures of their merits and, at the same time, minimized communal obligations. As Thomas Mellon judged the contest, "The world owes no one a living, but sooner or later rewards him fairly for his exertions in the proper direction."[4] This logic aimed to justify wealth and power, dismissing strugglers as inept while muffling opposition from pre-industrial elites as well as the laboring classes.

In this context, the frequency of the term "self-made" reached its nineteenth-century peak in the press around 1890, by which time the concept was well embedded in mainstream culture. Even when the term "self-made" was not used explicitly, its criteria for judgment prevailed. So at that same time the frequency of a related term, "individualist," was climbing rapidly, carrying forward rhetorical advocacy for the "solitary oak" who triumphs alone. Mellon, for example, did not use the term "self-made" in his writing, but its values suffused it with terms like "self-reliance," "survival-of-the-fittest," pecuniary hopelessness as a result of "bad habits," and poverty's double-edged sword – a "blessing" to the honest but a curse to "weaklings who are without courage or ability."[5] He judged individuals as fully responsible for their situations.

The notorious financier and railroad mogul Jay Gould was once asked bluntly and in public whether "the men who conduct business enterprises and wield the power of capital in this country to day … are what are called 'self-made men.'" He faced this question during 1883 hearings before the US Senate Committee on Education and Labor regarding "the Relations between Labor and Capital." Gould responded, "I think they are all 'self-made men.'" An unapologetic scoundrel who had little interest in courting public opinion, Gould also acknowledged the question's implication that "what are called 'self-made men'" may not be literally so, inserting the qualification that "I do not say *self*-made exactly, for the country has grown and they have grown up with it." Nonetheless, after this observation he immediately returned to the point of the myth – not the reality – pronouncing that in America, "Every man has to stand here on his own individual merit." Moreover, when asked about "the proportion of those men who have made their own fortunes pecuniarily," Gould replied, "I think they are nearly all of that class," the self-made. He continued, "nearly every one that occupies a prominent position has come up from the ranks, worked his own way along up." And, conforming to the myth's judgmental function, he volunteered that although there were "many cases of actual suffering, … generally if men are temperate and industrious they are pretty sure of success." Gould then echoed Emerson and other champions for the rule of individual self-reliance: "I could almost always go back behind the scenes and find a cause for such a person's 'misfortunes.'"[6]

Progress was becoming the mainstream's watchword, and the era's businessmen vied to become its heroes. In this perspective, strugglers and stragglers in all circumstances were "weaklings" or ne'er-do-wells.

BETRAYING FRANKLIN

Fourteen-year-old Thomas Mellon found a "dilapidated copy" of Benjamin Franklin's *Autobiography* while plowing a neighbor's field. He forever after retold the story that this serendipitous discovery had opened him to his life's choices. As Mellon looked back on that encounter with Franklin from the perspective of his seventies, "It delighted me with a wider view of life and inspired me with new ambition." After all, if "Franklin, poorer than myself, who by industry, thrift and frugality had become learned and wise, and elevated to wealth and fame," why should he not aim for that, as well? He, too, would "work his way up in the world" as "a merchant or a professional man." And yet, in his own vision of Franklin's story, nowhere does Mellon recognize Franklin as a community benefactor; instead, he curates Franklin's story to support self-making for self-aggrandizement. Mellon thereby severed the tie between self-making and the common good, so central to Franklin's worldview. Mellon's stories about ambitions and accomplishments relentlessly focused on his and his family's economic successes.[7]

Mellon read Franklin's *Autobiography* "again and again," but he merely took from it a narrow vision of what Franklin saw as a worthwhile life, pruning everything *other* than wealth in Franklin's stories. For example, after a bit of experimentation with "big-bellied bottles and glass fruit jars, which in its effects astonished the neighbors," Mellon abandoned electrical "researches" because "other and more useful practical branches of knowledge" better suited his "purposes," namely, to prosper. Civic service, in contrast, was a burden. He was grateful that when he was a county judge his "public duties were light and pleasant" so that he could focus on his growing family and his "private affairs [which] were prosperous." In the 1880s, he accepted election to Pittsburgh's city council but made it clear that he would not accept another term: "No more unsatisfactory position could be held by one of my disposition."[8] He founded and funded businesses aplenty, but no civic institutions benefited from his considerable abilities and assets. Moreover, and perhaps most relevant for our purposes, he saw no need to tell his story as other than that of a man who fashioned himself to rise to wealth and guide his sons to even greater wealth.

Despite these profound differences in their worldview and values, Thomas Mellon had good reason to see connections with Franklin's life. Mellon rose from a modest but prosperous family of farmers, just as Franklin had risen from his modest but prosperous artisan family. Each was eager to get more out of life than what he had growing up, what Mellon described as "the rude pursuits of farm life." They were voracious readers from childhood, benefiting from others' generosity, including access to private libraries and gifts of reading materials. In Mellon's case, the Philadelphia uncle for whom he was named often sent boxes of books and papers and also convinced Thomas's father to support a better education for the boy than what the local school provided. That enriched schooling experience included boarding with a family that wasn't wealthy but was "dignified and stately in their manners, exclusive of their companionship, high toned in regard to honor and morality!" These excellent role models fired the farm boy's ambitions, heightening his disdain for the "low sentiments and purposes of our neighbors at home." This early education, including college, notwithstanding, much of Mellon's life-long education came through the reading that was his constant "source of pleasure," as it had been for Franklin.[9]

Stark differences, however, between narratives about Thomas Mellon and Franklin show how the century between them had changed criteria for esteem. No longer was a claim to godly or patriotic or practical work on behalf of a community relevant. Such achievements might earn a man a respectful eulogy, but they no longer sufficed for self-made glory. Mellon took an extreme but not unique stand when he scoffed at professionals in law, medicine, or preaching who toiled "for the love of it"; he never saw any such "rare" folks and mocked them as "phenomenal," in the antiquated sense of something unnatural. Instead, he argued for money as the purpose of a profession, not "Name or fame [which] are incidental to well doing, not ends in themselves." Thus, "the natural principles of human affairs invariably result in rewarding each according to his merits; and the acquisition of wealth is really therefore a badge of merit and ability."[10] There were other badges, such as personal and family loyalties, that he valued, but he admired nothing professional other than money, and other prophets of self-making increasingly reflected this attitude, as well.

Accordingly, tributes to Thomas Mellon at the end of his life early in the twentieth century recounted how a boy from County Tyrone, Northern Ireland, arrived at great wealth in Pittsburgh by way of nearby Poverty Point. In keeping with the myth-making fashion, these stereotypical stories often contained inaccuracies, always describing his family's origins the same way: "They were poor, and even the advantages of the country school were denied young Mellon. He educated himself, however, and to-day is one of the best exemplifications of Pittsburg's self-made men." Other homages likewise identified him as "an example of a self-made man" whose "early life tells the story of a struggle against poverty and lack of educational advantages," but, of course, "it was this struggle that brought out all the latent power in the man and developed a character that shines forth as a beacon light to others."[11] All claimed the humble origins mythology of earlier tales of self-made success, but were entirely secular, lacking any reference to serving God or community. And they denied Mellon's considerable advantages as he began his journey to wealth and esteem.

These accolades often repeated a charming vignette of Mellon's first visit to Pittsburgh with only a dollar (actually, ninety-nine cents) in his pocket, all the better to heighten the contrast with his later fortune. His 1908 *New York Times* obituary told the story this way: "He was the founder of a fortune estimated at $125,000,000, but came to Pittsburg for the first time eighty-three years ago with $1 in his pocket." These narratives neglected to mention that he was only nine or ten years old at the time and on a three-day adventure, sufficiently well treated along the way that he was able to hold on to his money. By 1839 when he established his law practice in his mid-twenties, he had a college education, legal training, and a law license. He also had capital enough – saved from teaching Latin, working in the court's notary office, successful investments, plus $200 from his father – to spend "some seven hundred dollars" on a law library, well more than two years' wages for a working-class man then.[12] Similarly, each myth-inspired telling of his life followed the usual pattern and ignored Mellon's vast social capital resources, including marriage into a wealthy and connected family, even though he himself freely credited those social assets throughout his own autobiography, as had Franklin. Indeed, Mellon admitted to his youthful assets – resolutely and industriously applied – more than did those who eulogized him in the flush of the myth of self-made success.

Mellon's and Franklin's eulogies reveal much about the profound shift in the meaning and measure of self-making over the breadth of the nineteenth century that separated them: whereas none of Franklin's eulogies mentioned his considerable wealth, Mellon's mentioned nothing but wealth to measure his success. Likewise in Mellon's own narratives. For instance, his term on Allegheny's Court of Common Pleas earned him the life-long honorific "Judge Mellon." However, he didn't seem to have been especially proud of that civic work, even thinking at first that his nomination was "a practical joke." Mellon described his judicial duties from 1859 to 1869 as light compared with practicing law, but still they left him too little time for business ventures once the Civil War accelerated Pittsburgh's economic growth. Thereafter he resented the "pecuniary sacrifice" that resulted from "declining passing opportunities for making money." He was "eager to launch" his sons "on this flood tide of business prosperity," so he declined a second term.[13] Despite the statue of Benjamin Franklin that adorned his bank's entrance, he had no ambition to make his mark on Western Pennsylvania except as a successful businessman and the patriarch of successful businessmen.

Mellon's ambitions were neither new nor different from those of many Americans at any time. What had changed was the cultural and moral authority of wealth. John Jacob Astor had earlier acquired much more wealth than Mellon ever did, but that fortune did not earn him the esteemed "self-made man" label when most Americans honored with that label were preachers, scholars, scientists, military heroes, or politicians who at least created an appearance of foregoing personal prosperity to serve. From the audacious P. T. Barnum and the austere Thomas Mellon, Americans heard time and again that money on its own terms had become a perfectly valid and fine measure of merit. Although never universally accepted, money became the new default measure of worth over the half-century after the Civil War against which every other set of values had to struggle to be heard. To achieve this hegemony, the myth of self-made success emerged from its older roots as a tool to condemn drunks and praise preachers. With its emphasis on personal responsibility, self-reliance, and self-improvement, it helped to raise businessmen's status and, equally important, to diminish others'. As always, every story of self-making was an instrument of judgment, either to praise or to condemn.

A NEW HEROIC NARRATIVE

Across the nineteenth century's wildly expanding and unsettled economy emerged astounding fortunes. Americans before the mid and late nineteenth century had controlled great wealth, of course, such as John Hancock and George Washington. But before the days of John Jacob Astor, Cornelius Vanderbilt, Thomas Mellon, Andrew Carnegie, John D. Rockefeller, Leland Stanford, and Henry Clay Frick – to name a few with the highest profiles – that wealth was not so visible to most Americans, whose own observations and experiences were mainly local. In contrast, the new titans' grand mansions, art collections, and luxurious travel on private railroad cars and yachts captured broad, national attention in the press. Exemplifying this flourishing genre of press coverage, an 1887 column by widely published and syndicated journalist Frank G. Carpenter lauded "Self-Made Millionaires: A Score of Rich Men and Their Fight for Fortunes." Carpenter confidently attached an inaccurate statistic to the usual claim that most wealth came to men with obscure origins, namely that "Seventy-five per cent of the rich men of today began life as poor boys." Then he summarized a cluster of those romanticized "fights" to acquire fortunes.[14] We know very well that these "poor boys" were only poor in relation to what would become middle-class norms as the century progressed, just as Benjamin Franklin's boyhood conditions were poor by comparison to the nation's wealth when he was an adult.[15] As Jay Gould explained to the Senate, the country as a whole was rising. Nonetheless, applauding rising individuals as heroes served them and their allies well; and it sold newspapers.

The growing stature and national visibility of successful businessmen in the mid and late nineteenth century didn't just happen. The spectacular growth of industry made it impossible not to notice forceful new economic actors, or, for that matter, powerful actors with long pedigrees, most famously the mega-financier J. P. Morgan. However, wealth and power alone were not yet enough to ensure the cultural authority of people possessing massive fortunes. For one thing, factories or impressive bank buildings did not necessarily celebrate or reveal the people who founded, owned, or managed them. Moreover, to many, these powerful men were hard-hearted despoilers and exploiters. Winning over skeptics across the landscape was unlikely, which made building cultural capital among other voters essential. Expanding the reach of the self-making myth from religious or political service to business achievements was one tool in that contest, and one that also served local businessmen well who were not among the super-rich, thereby spreading its influence through the mainstream. It augmented middle- and upper-class self-regard while allowing their denizens to scorn members of the working classes as failures. The impoverished fared even worse in this cultural milieu.

The visible titans of capitalism both nationally and locally inspired tales of self-made heroism that found favorable audiences across the mainstream, especially among aspiring middle-class men whose professional lives increasingly

Figure 7.2 Thomas Hovenden's poignant 1890 painting of a young man *Breaking Home Ties* depicts ambition's emotional costs. This portrayal was the most popular painting at the 1893 Chicago World's Fair and received wide press coverage because it resonated so powerfully with the experiences of many American families. The theme of leaving home appeared in many art forms during the nineteenth and twentieth centuries as young Americans pursued mobility and worldly success. (Courtesy of Philadelphia Museum of Art: Gift of Ellen Harrison McMichael in memory of C. Emory McMichael, 1942-60-1)

dominated their personal identities. As urbanization and industrialization drew young men from farms and small towns, from artisan shops and small stores, their families, friends, and neighbors could no longer see them at work. To compound this shift as the century wore on, they could rarely achieve the traditional visible signs of masculine success, which were based on economic independence, such as a productive, debt-free farm, an artisan's shop, or a dry goods store that provided for their families. With the growth of ever-larger firms after the Civil War, most men's work was no longer visible, or even comprehensible, outside of the workplace. How could they explain and demonstrate their character or their masculine virtue? Variations of the popular biblical phrase offered some inspiration – "Seest thou a man diligent in his business? He shall stand before kings" – as did countless advice books, pamphlets, sermons, and newspaper articles about success and character.[16] But how could anyone know if a man was diligent? Most men in the new economy had no evidence for their work other than their incomes, especially if they were employees, which meant that their families' consumption became the measure of their earnest labors.

Despite the century's boom-and-bust cycles, the economic tide rose overall and lifted many ships, giving their middle- and upper-class captains reason to believe that their work advanced material comforts and the nation's prosperity. Although businesspeople, professionals, and white-collar employees were a modest portion of the population, they dominated mainstream culture and its media as both creators and audiences. Thus, powerful presses broadcast the prophets of affluence in words and pictures, including ubiquitous advertisements that glorified individual contributions to and gains from industrial and commercial progress. Through their purchasing power – of goods, labor, newspapers and books, advertisements, and politicians – those who claimed material success as evidence of virtue most widely defined what it meant to be valued as an American male. And this was the direction toward which self-making's storytellers moved. In a world increasingly dominated by business – without the rigors of farm life, exploration, or military exploits – heroism required seeing the market as an arena of intense competition that rewarded manly attributes. Hence, late nineteenth-century businessmen increasingly interpreted their activities as "campaigns."[17] Stories of heroism and heroes are solitary dramas, and so must businessmen's tales be told, despite all evidence to the contrary.

Ralph Waldo Emerson had earlier asserted in "Self-Reliance," his oft-reprinted 1841 essay, that "An institution is the lengthened shadow of one man." At the end of the century Andrew Carnegie told businessmen, "Your firm is your monument." Accordingly, surnames emblazoned on factories, office buildings, publishing houses, stores, and banks raised the public profile of businesspeople everywhere, even in the smallest towns, which made apparent and tangible their stature.[18] Naming businesses for their proprietors was nothing new. It was the scale that had changed. Tradenames could carry founders' and proprietors' names, which made their ways into consumers' homes on goods as diverse and numerous as packaged foods, kitchen tools, pianos, harmonicas, thread and buttons, medicinals, toys, beer, tobacco, sewing machines, and so on. Advertisements in newspapers, magazines, trade cards, catalogs, and posters added to public awareness of the businesspeople behind the products, often with their portraits embellishing ads and packages. Ads tell stories explicitly to persuade, and all those proliferating calls to consume performed a second persuasion duty: proclaiming their purveyors' merits and contributions. From the mid nineteenth century until about 1920, printers and publishers were glad to portray advertisers and their produces as contributors to progress. Back in 1710, the great English essayist Joseph Addison had pointed out that businesspeople could use this kind of paid publicity to build their status: "advertisements are of great use to the vulgar," he decreed, "as they are instruments of ambition. A man that is by no means big enough for the *Gazette*, may creep into the advertisements."[19]

Addison's observation helps to explain how pro-business ideas spread so widely and swiftly, not only through advertisements but also through a broad shift in revenue sources for newspapers and magazines toward advertisements. The religious press was in decline from its antebellum peak, and newspapers established after the Civil War reduced their open affiliations with political parties. For political parties or other overtly partisan entities, such as labor groups, to demand a publisher's loyalty, they had to provide financial support, at least through guaranteed subscriptions and often through patronage printing contracts. Yet as reporting, technologies, labor, and other costs rose, supports from political and religious organizations declined. Periodical publishers began to see themselves more as businesspeople, fending for themselves and relying increasingly on advertisements and subscriptions for revenue. To maximize those, they diversified their content and visual appeal to expand their audiences, promoting businesses and businesspeople along the way.[20]

The business luminaries and the throngs of middle- and upper-class men who identified with them faced obstacles of all sorts, dreaded "ruinous competition," and brooded about the hazards of doing business, all exacerbated by the century's economic instability. Naturally, they experienced their own challenges keenly and usually neglected to appreciate whatever advantages they had of gender and ethnicity, access to social capital, opportunities, expedient marriages, and other assets. Plugging ahead as they did, these successful men and their advocates could well imagine themselves as self-made, and used that myth to rationalize their exploitation of collective resources, labor, and political favors. They competed fiercely with each other, to be sure, and that added to their sense of valor, ignoring the reality that those who had access to their arena in the first place made up the small fraction of the population with "potential": a minority that was White, Protestant, male, literate, and had connections.[21]

Rousing stories of successful businessmen were too congratulatory toward their heroes and too oblivious to others' truly obscure or impoverished origins not to be challenged from other perspectives. More subtly, the power of mutually beneficial networks – essential to success but unequally available – challenged claims of self-making. Furthermore, businessmen often enjoy the advantage of law and state-based policing, especially when they demand that working-class employees negotiate as individuals against employers' collective strengths. Narratives from working-class sources and their supporters fervently challenged the "solitary oak" perspective of business successes and its rhetorical use against them. And, then, there was the problem of how to maintain cultural authority based on self-made success while preventing it from backfiring on privileged heirs. A return to Pittsburgh during its heyday as an industrial center allows us to explore these alternative perspectives.

MUTUALLY MADE MEN

When the young Henry Clay Frick entered T. Mellon & Sons' Pittsburgh bank in 1871 for a large loan of $10,000 (about $259,000 in 2024), he subjected himself to the senior Mellon's careful scrutiny. The banker recalled thinking, "That young man has great promise." Mellon concluded that Frick was "able, energetic, industrious, resourceful, self-confident." Moreover, Frick came from a moderately wealthy family with connections to Mellon. Passing what stood for a creditworthiness appraisal almost wholly based on social capital, as those judgments often happened then, Frick gained access not only to the financial capital he needed to chase his ambitions, but also to social capital. With that plus his brilliance and hard-driving ambition, he rose spectacularly by producing coke, a powerful coal-based energy source essential for steel making. Mellon's involvement in coal and his links to Pittsburgh's rapidly growing iron and steel firms had made him well aware of the importance of coke. Deciding that this young man was, as he put it, "of a character to succeed," later that year, Mellon granted Frick a second $10,000 loan for additional coke ovens, overriding a bank officer's rejection based on a more objective assessment of risk.[22]

Once within Mellon's orbit, Henry Clay Frick was on his way to becoming the "Coke Baron," a millionaire by the time he turned thirty, and soon one of America's richest men. Now known mostly for the superb art collection and mansion that he bequeathed to New York City, Frick was famous a century ago as a relentless businessman, a fabulously wealthy powerbroker, an art buyer, and a partner-then-foe of Andrew Carnegie. As we will see, he was also known as the man who precipitated the bloody Carnegie Steel Company lockout at Homestead, Pennsylvania, in 1892, and the target of an almost-successful assassination attempt during that crisis. More than 4,500 articles, obituaries, and editorials recognized his national renown within two years of his death in 1919 just weeks short of his seventieth birthday.[23]

Mainstream post-mortem entries were typically tributes that distorted his origins markedly but generally described his achievements accurately, as did the *New York Times*: "Born to salutary poverty, a Pennsylvania farmer's barefoot boy" who worked his way to a million dollars by the time he was thirty. This hardworking hero "belonged to a race of creators of industry and graspers of industrial opportunity." The widely read *Literary Digest* gathered depictions from a multitude of publications, mostly of the same sort, reflecting, it said with some irony, "an era" that believed in great possibilities for "every American boy . . . if he were only born poor." Thus, "Frick came up from the bottom . . . but he was a born fighter" who was "lucky in finding opportunities where he might make his fighting ability count." With Andrew Carnegie, he was one of "the greatest and last" of "a race of industrial supermen" among whom he was a "leader of the forces of capital." In an interview a few years earlier, Frick had told his rags-to-riches story himself, saying that "I was very poor and my education was limited, but I worked very hard and always sought opportunities."[24] Unquestionably, he worked hard and "sought opportunities," but the rest of the description was true only relative to his adult empire.

Eulogies generally celebrated and vindicated Frick's relentless ambition and accumulation. The *New York Times* notice ended by noting that, fortunately, the "very rich are so [ambitious] mainly for others, not for themselves." Almost all noted his grand, philanthropic bequests, which the *New York Times* announced in a front-page headline: "Leaves Art to City." From such perspectives, Frick's philanthropy, like Carnegie's and other titans', justified his wealth and added glory to his self-making; not everyone agreed, of course, as we will see. A long tribute in the popular and influential *North American Review* featured the subtitle, "Builder and Individualist." The editor, George Harvey, acclaimed Frick for the industries "his genius, toil and faith" built. He succeeded "Not by luck assuredly." With his "intrepid spirit," and with "no advantage whatever," Frick could "grasp the great opportunity when it appeared." Every American should feel proud "that it was our country, our free and just Republic, that not only held open the door of opportunity to the penniless lad, but guaranteed by her laws and customs the permanent possession of all . . . that skill and energy produced." Frick's success was, therefore, a "triumph of individualism"; he "personified self-determination"; he "was the most intense individualist"; "he was a man"; and so on. As an admirer in *The World's Work* expressed it, "Mr. Frick has yet the aloofness of the great commander, of the man able to stand alone."[25]

Like most self-made heroes, Henry Clay Frick was typically depicted as a solitary oak, a lonesome hero. However, the coke industry operated between the coal industry, on the one hand, and the iron and steel industries, on the other, and Frick operated among the "mutually-made men," in historian Judith McGaw's astute term for collaborative webs, who dominated both of those fields for the next half century. In no way could anyone acting alone build that network's collective capacity to innovate technologies and institutions, influence state actions, or control markets and labor. Together, Pittsburgh's mutually made men shared access to human capital and financial capital among the extended business, social, and political networks that each of them contributed to the larger

Figure 7.3 Henry Clay Frick became one of the nation's richest businessmen and a leading art collector. He built on his family's business background, affluence, and networks, which included the Mellon family, and he advanced his fortune alongside Andrew Carnegie. This autographed studio photograph of Clay as a young man, circa 1870, belies his allies' later claims that he had risen, self-made, from a poor farm boy. (Courtesy of West Overton Village & Museum Archives)

web. They could learn, assess, and take risks together. They could build what no individual could build alone, despite the common and misleading practice of identifying a product or an edifice by an individual's name, or designating them "self-made."[26] Legends of "self-made men" and individualists flourished as corporations, trusts, trade associations, and other formal institutions became inescapable in all but the smallest businesses.

Frick's cluster, for example, included Andrew Carnegie and the Mellon family, all key to his rise, and collectively these first movers exploited their initial advantages while holding others at bay. Their successes at building industrial, financial, and real estate powerhouses in western Pennsylvania and northern Ohio made them and others within their networks staggeringly wealthy. In an often repeated pattern, these first movers in successful industries rose in ways that appeared to be self-made successes, but on closer view were the triumphs of mutually made men, whether in Paterson, New Jersey, earlier in that century, or in Silicon Valley in our times.[27]

The words Mellon used to describe the young Frick – "able, energetic, industrious, resourceful, self-confident" – apply to most who climb in any field or pursuit. Notably, this list of qualities does not include ethics, perhaps because cynical strategies can abet ambition in any system. In any case, the one essential factor in business success is access to networks, the ability to connect, even if not initially connected. Therefore, had a young stranger with Frick's goals, intelligence, and knowledge approached Thomas Mellon but from an ethnic background other than that of Pittsburgh's decision makers, the banker's aversion to risk would have undermined the chance of a large loan. Such a man might not have even made it through the bank's lobby. Had a woman of any age or ethnicity broached the subject, the outcome may have been polite, but no more positive. The rationale for such exclusions is still couched in the language of "potential" – but it so happens that the more that candidates resemble the gatekeepers, the more potential they seem to possess.[28]

Highly useful networks can engage members' lives beyond directly professional activities. The mechanisms for that engagement help explain why connections and "connectability" have always enhanced opportunities for some while limiting opportunities for others. It's hard to trust people without shared cultural experiences and expectations. Moreover, so many professional transactions occur in social venues, even in casual conversations, that anyone who is excluded from those scenes is effectively excluded from opportunities to engage fully. Henry Clay Frick began building his networks among family and friends. He modeled himself after his prosperous grandfather, who mentored him and provided opportunities to learn the world of business. Through these experiences, Frick gained enough knowledge, savvy, and confidence to approach Thomas Mellon effectively. Once within the Mellon circle, Frick formed a strong friendship with Thomas's son Andrew Mellon, whose fortune and fame later exceeded his father's. A cluster of this network's wealthy families built homes outside Pittsburgh in a neighborhood that some called Carnegie Colony.[29]

Frick was also instrumental in setting up or supporting various social venues, such as the exclusive South Fork Fishing and Hunting Club and the Union Club in Pittsburgh, so that elites could gather without distractions from ordinary folks, except, of course, those who prepared and served their meals and cleaned up after them. Members of Pittsburgh's elite social clubs were predominantly Presbyterian with Scotch-Irish and Scottish ethnic roots, plus some of English and German origins. In New York City, Frick and a handful of other elites belonged to at least eight of the same clubs as J. P. Morgan, the nation's leading financier. These prestigious and exclusive social venues assimilated the acceptable nouveaux rich while filtering out those unacceptable for want of wealth or "good stock."[30] Political connections synergistically strengthened other ties. Thus, successful businessmen were second only to lawyers in populating the US Senate in the late nineteenth century. And, of course, politically inclined lawyers had their connections in the business arena, as well. None other than Frick's personal lawyer, Philander Chase Knox, was selected to fill a vacant seat in the Senate by agreement among some of Pennsylvania's wealthiest businessmen, including Frick. Elites did not have to like each other for these network dynamics to function, but they did have to feel culturally comfortable with each other, which inevitably excluded others.[31]

Beyond their offices and social venues, mutually made men organized and gathered explicitly for business. Trade and professional associations that businessmen organized by industry or other business activities proliferated as industrial and commercial activities themselves expanded. Like medieval guilds, these associations could improve business practices, support technological development, foster collaboration on labor issues, facilitate cooperation as well as interactions with state authorities, or persuade legislators.[32] The attractiveness of cooperation between firms on prices and other business practices in the nineteenth century also fostered a variety of mechanisms such as "trusts" through which firms cooperated. But neither businessmen's competitiveness nor public opinion favored trusts, giving rise to waves of consolidations to maximize cooperation and control within single entities that would not be subject to anti-trust restrictions.

In this context, the clichéd impetus for many rugged individualists to abandon their rugged individualism was "ruinous competition." From the 1880s through the next century's first decade, capitalists who prioritized profits and security over competitive individualism spurred the mergers of thousands of firms, often into corporations that required state-granted charters.[33] Combining firms within an industry enabled horizontal integration; combining suppliers and distribution systems integrated businesses vertically. Both types fostered economies of scale and enhanced controls over production, labor, distribution, and marketing. In 1909, economist Edward Sherwood Mead explained that "the *régime* of free competition was productive of manifold hardships to the manufacturer.

Competition," he observed, "might be considered the life of trade, but at the close of the last industrial depression [in the 1890s] it was regarded as the death of profits." Mead concluded that "this struggle ... benefited nobody save the consumers" and "the producers were tired of working for the public." Competition between firms also aided employees. Each firm's management "stands alone, struggling for business" against competitors while "united action" within labor's "well-organized combination" plays against "all his rivals." By combination, instead, "the menacing growth of the power of organized labor might be checked." Thus "freed from the hobbles of mutual distrust and suspicions," Mead assured, they "might stand firmly together against what they believed to be the unreasonable demands of the unions."[34] So much for rugged individualism.

Henry Clay Frick and Andrew Carnegie numbered among the many famed "self-made men" who, with associates and allies, used cooperative means to fulfill individual ambitions, acquiring astounding personal fortunes in the process. By July 1, 1892, Carnegie Steel Company was, already, the product of multiple acquisitions and mergers over previous decades, including one that had absorbed the H. C. Frick Coke Company. Then, in 1901, financier J. P. Morgan orchestrated yet another compact, consolidating Carnegie Steel Company and other firms into U.S. Steel. Cumulatively, Carnegie's strategies over decades, including that 1892 consolidation, created a behemoth within the steel industry that achieved, according to Mead, "the acme of productive efficiency." The officers "had risen from the ranks by dint of compelling merit," incentivized in part by "an interest in the business," that is, by partial ownership. Among both managers and workmen, Mead admired "the intensity of the effort and the strained attention evident in every department. None but the strongest, he noted, could stand the terrific pace. Breakdowns were frequent at thirty-five, men were old at forty-five."[35]

In pre-corporate capitalism, such competition between men may have been glorious, and competition between firms could yield spectacular progress, as it had with steel production. But Mead observed its limits in an economic system that values money over all else. The "financial industry," he observed, "dreads a reduction of profits" from competition, and, therefore, steel had not been "popular with the speculators." Consolidation appealed to capitalists, such as Morgan, who were less interested in production than in the prices of stocks. Consolidation "exorcised the forbidding specter of competition."[36] When thus tempted, both Frick and Carnegie exchanged personal control for colossal fortunes. Nonetheless, storytellers in the mainstream did not abandon the myth of tycoons' self-making, even in that era of high-level consolidation. Instead, they increasingly turned that myth against workers whose collaborative activities to improve their livelihoods put them at odds with capital and its allies.

WORK AND ESTEEM

In the marketplace of esteem, the working class has nothing to sell but its labor. Were the nation true to its declared esteem for work, then the men who toiled through twelve-hour shifts in the harsh conditions of Carnegie Steel Company mills would have earned universal respect. Or, had those steelworkers eked out more than a subsistence during those exhausting and dangerous twelve hours, their livelihoods could have purchased esteem as defined by consumer culture measures. As it was, however, their employers – among them the "self-made" Henry Clay Frick and Andrew Carnegie – thought of that labor as a mere commodity, to be purchased like any other raw materials as cheaply as possible in pursuit of efficiency and its profits. They advanced their reputations within the mainstream by sponsoring libraries and museums, all the while enforcing working hours and low wages that precluded either steel workers or their families from pursuing self-improvement there because whole families had to toil to cobble together livelihoods. Carnegie financed 2,811 libraries saying that these would make improvement possible to "the industrious and the ambitious," ignoring that most of his employees and their families could not use them. They would have preferred leisure and free time and a portion of the money he gained by working them so hard.[37]

As nineteenth-century industrialists reduced the most rewarding among working-class jobs through automation, some grew concerned about labor's commodification as just another cost of production. Iron production required much more expertise and more workers than steelmaking, therefore, the new Bessemer technology that Carnegie brought from Europe left laborers with fewer claims on their employers. Most of them became, in effect, interchangeable parts in the mills as skilled artisans increasingly joined the ranks of unskilled laborers employed only for their time and brawn. The barriers to prosperity were especially high for immigrants brought into the country to stoke the furnaces of industry. Deskilling jobs cost workers not only economic leverage but also the respect of being able to provide well for their families. To make matters worse, this new work in the mills was more dangerous and exhausting. As the economist Mead described a visitor's experience, "clothing would be burned into holes by flying sparks." People had to "dodge locomotive engines running at top speed around corners"; they would "be almost deafened by the noise, and often scorched by the heat." Toiling there day in and day out was extremely dangerous, and long hours made it more so. Therefore, even if men survived intact, they were worn out by the time they were forty, and company-based pensions did not exist until after 1900. Adding insult to injury, Carnegie designed his employees' pension fund as a "relief fund," a charitable kindness rather than an earned benefit.[38] Its beneficiaries had no claim as hard-working men, only as worn-out bodies.

In order to cling to the myth that they and their champions were self-made, middle- and upper-strata Americans constantly praised work, but remained insensitive to differences between types of work by different types of people. As it happened, the most active nineteenth-century promoters of the American work ethos spent their days in the cleanest and most quiet settings and returned to the cleanest and most quiet homes. This is not at all to say that members of the middle and upper classes did not suffer stressful lives, but simply that they could ignore or dismiss the stresses experienced by people without options for living and working in clean and quiet settings. Henry Clay Frick grandly pronounced that "There is no secret about success; it simply calls for hard work, devotion to your business at all times, day and night."[39] What he didn't note was that not all work is created equal. He had determined as a young man to get wealthy, and he tried several vocations, including bookkeeping in his grandfather's distillery and tending his wealthy uncle's store, until he found an activity that energized him enough to keep at it day and night. Others who preached the work ethos as the key to character and worldly success discriminated similarly. George Washington had only recognized late in life his good fortune at having work that benefited his assets and that was congenial to his class status. Benjamin Franklin famously ran away from his dreaded apprenticeship, and Thomas Mellon rejected his father's occupational preference for farming.

In 1909 Elbert Hubbard (1856–1915) proclaimed that "The synonym of the word 'Carnegie' is work." Moreover, "The reward for all good work is not rest, but more work, and harder work." (Hubbard had written the 1899 melodrama *Message to Garcia* that employers distributed by the hundreds of thousands for its message of unquestioning obedience to authority; he was well known for his own idiosyncrasies and intolerance of them among employees.) Hubbard did not point out that, as a youth, Carnegie had nightmares when he tended a furnace and loathed work in a bobbin factory. Or that Carnegie became one of the century's greatest preachers of the work ethos while insisting that other men with few options do the jobs he could not abide, and do them seventy-two hours a week in hell holes to make steel and profits. Similarly, Thomas Mellon opined: "Work is oppressive where nature, inclination, or education withholds the necessary qualifications, and in time becomes irksome where no other motive but duty exists for its performance." But then he preached, "There is a great deal of humbug and nonsense afloat about people breaking themselves down with hard work. I have never known hard work to hurt any one in good health and strength, if the work and will went together."[40]

Success for struggling people meant survival for them and their families, but that did not keep the advantaged from belittling it. Henry Ward Beecher

(1813–1887), Harriet Beecher Stowe's brother, was America's most extensively heard and read preacher in the last half of the nineteenth century. His words could move audiences even though consistency was not his strength in either political issues – most importantly abolition – or marital fidelity. However, he was consistent in his endorsements for material acquisition and his tolerance of ambition, both his own and his audiences'. His wealthy parishioners supported his prosperity with a grand salary, and kindred spirits enthusiastically purchased his sermons, articles, and books. His sympathies, however, did not extend to everyone seeking a livelihood. During the great labor upheavals of 1877, he brought his congregation to applause with what became known as his "bread and water" sermon. His own annual income approached $50,000 (about $1.5M in 2024) when working-class men did well at $500 (about $15,000 in 2024), yet he mocked strikers who complained that "a dollar a day is not enough to support a man and five children." A daily dollar was plenty for bread and water, he maintained, but not enough "if the man insists on smoking and drinking beer." His congregation even laughed along with the line that "the man who cannot live on bread and water is not fit to live." Digging deeper, Beecher declared that "God has intended the great to be great, and the little to be little." Digging even deeper, he reassured his affluent audience that the poor must by God's will and nature's way "reap the misfortunes of inferiority." In contrast, he relished his well-remunerated career, rejoicing that "Happily, my work is my play."[41]

THE SELF-MADE PLIGHT OF ELITES

By the last decades of the nineteenth century, various notions of self-made success were so widespread that the most powerful Americans called on this rhetorical talisman as they competed for cultural and political authority. That same self-made myth threatened to trap their sons, however, because they could not pretend to rise up from obscurity or poverty. They needed to find and navigate a loophole in the myth.

To persuade citizens that the Republic truly was the land of opportunity, it had to be possible for the high to fall as well as for the low to rise. This was a constant theme of patriotic boosters such as P. T. Barnum, who insisted in 1890 that in America "the poor boys get rich and the rich boys get poor." To defend elites' male progeny, by the end of the nineteenth century, self-making's cultural authority compelled some storytellers to praise men as "self-made" who had no claim whatsoever to having risen, but, instead, had survived wealth with their character intact. This twist on the myth suited scions of prominent families, who by no stretch of the imagination could contrive a façade of poor or obscure origins. To salvage second- and third-generation claims to cultural authority and deflect potential attacks on them as aristocrats unworthy of respect in America, their advocates drew on codes of self-improvement and self-reliance. To this end, Thomas Mellon proudly described how he had trained his sons to prosper. They did not have to work as he had, yet, somehow, young men "must in self-reliance travel the rugged road of experience," so he set them to a series of tasks.[42] Mellon's sons' worldly cushion, their top-tier access to social and financial capital and other assets, did not diminish his pride in their successes, which were considerable. In particular, son Andrew exceeded his father's fortune by far and led the nation as Secretary of the Treasury under three presidents.

Those born into privilege and wealth should, therefore, exhibit self-control, self-improvement, self-reliance – and they had to work. These were ingredients for idealized self-making, and much of the character-building literature relentlessly made this point, often to inspire, but also to justify the well-off and their (inherited) claims to public esteem. For instance, the *New York Times* argued in 1906 that "If an American theory of opportunity applies to the poor and to people of moderate wealth, so also it must apply to those who have the exceptional advantages that come with important financial affiliations, provided only the individual seeks to utilize them." Thus, "the law of survival of the fittest" determined which families *sustained* their fortunes, and such self-improvement and self-making could absolve those born rich. Fathers who "trained" their sons to work "in the harness" of the family business were to be admired, such as the Mellon, Rockefeller, Morgan, Guggenheim, and Vanderbilt sons whose work, brains, and dedication overcame temptations. The *Times* regretted that the "daily papers and magazines" find more to tickle their audiences' fancy in the "doings of the 'spenders' which, as a matter of fact, are a whole lot more interesting than those of the workers."[43] Not being a wastrel who threatened a family's fortune could, it seems, qualify a son for a variant of "self-made success," even if the drama of not *losing* a fortune paled in comparison to the drama of *making* one.

Just as sympathetic storytellers expanded the notion of self-made success to accommodate the descendants of men who had built fortunes, the sons of older wealth also felt the need to prove their worthiness in the industrial age. Their unease followed in part from competing for prestige with the nouveaux riches, compounded by a widespread fear among Anglophone men that their very masculinity was at risk. The comforts of affluence within the consumer culture combined with women's growing public presence to make them fearful of becoming effeminate inheritors of their forefathers' achievements. To assert their self-agency, their most prominent men reached back into earlier American traditions of self-improvement for service for what they saw as the common good.[44]

The most notable of that era's American defenders of masculinity was Theodore Roosevelt (1858–1919), whose adventures and achievements added up to a remarkable life, including African safaris, urging wars of imperialism, and serving as the nation's president from 1901 to 1909. He was a product of the anxieties about masculinity that the "muscular Christianity" movement reflected, and Roosevelt promoted self-improvement as part of a "strenuous life" that fostered a fitting manhood. But, as heir to centuries of New York wealth and influence, he could not measure success by wealth. Instead, as did other elites such as Henry Cabot Lodge, his measures were more traditional – work and duty. Thus, "I wish to preach," he declared in 1899, "not the doctrine of ignoble ease, but the doctrine of the strenuous life, the life of toil and effort, of labor and strife." People who were, like him, "free from the necessity of working for their livelihood, are all the more bound to carry on some kind of non-remunerative work in science, in letters, in art, in exploration, in historical research ... which reflects most honor upon the nation." He applauded "the strong men who toil for wealth with brain or hand" to build "material prosperity," but mostly he admired those who toiled for "loftier duties," such as George Washington and Abraham Lincoln. In this light, Roosevelt considered the Boy Scouts of America, founded in 1910 to counteract emasculation, to be "distinctly an asset to our country for the development of efficiency, virility, and good citizenship."[45]

Heirs to fortunes who actually worked warranted newspaper coverage. John T. Faris's 1912 *Men Who Made Good* included men "reared in homes of comfort or even wealth." Quoting a newspaper column, the "son of rich and indulgent parents" earned "even higher praise" than did the "poor boy who rises by his own exertions to a strong and useful life," for, without the "stimulus" of poverty, he had shaken off "the soft chains of luxury [to make] his life hard with self-denying toil." In this vein, the next year the New York *Tribune* eulogized J. Pierpont Morgan as self-made, although his family's prosperity extended back to the seventeenth century. Although he had "no traditions of the steerage," he possessed "the qualities of the self-made man." Linking national progress with individual effort, this and other tributes credited Morgan with archaic values of service to the nation's industrial growth and prosperity. In truth, Morgan genuinely believed in those values and saw himself as a public servant. However, to be expected, not every commentary on Morgan's life was positive. After all, like Andrew Carnegie, he had bought his way out of the Civil War draft. Later in his life and very publicly, Congress had questioned his outsized influence on the nation's economy, as he reshaped the nation's corporate landscape; even his management of the 1907 financial crisis seemed to manifest overbearing power.[46] Morgan embodied the industrializing capitalist nation for many, whether for good or ill. Judging him as "self-made" either added to his esteem or tainted the concept, depending on the audience. For mainstream audiences, drawing on the cultural authority of self-making to justify wealth among men who began with uncommon advantages and then, as mutually made men, added to their wealth and power had become a way to legitimate disparities that dominated the era popularly known as the Gilded Age.

DIFFUSION AND VARIETY

After centuries of evolution and diffusion, the concept of "self-making" remained malleable according to storytellers' goals and audiences at the end of the century.[47] Its deep roots in tensions about self-agency, self-improvement for saving souls, and service continued to color biographies and other advice literature, but those elements were in steep decline by then. Meanings jostled for attention, pulled forward and into the light according to storytellers' purposes, whether to guide, praise, or criticize. Its multi-faceted utility even brought it into high literature, such as William Dean Howells's 1885 masterful novel, *The Rise of Silas Lapham*, a sympathetic if condescending portrayal of a parvenu who struggled in vain to fit into the culturally elite world he could afford but could not understand. Howells presented Lapham as unable to hide "the pride which comes of self-making," but, even so, he was a poignant figure ultimately conquered by the business world's cruel churn and the elites who obscured in their snobbery the distant origins of their own fortunes.[48]

Rarely did narratives about "self-made success" reach Howells's literary heights in wrestling with its meanings and judgmental nature. Most storytellers continued to apply the self-made myth as a tool to criticize or praise in political and cultural competitions. Some just told jokes while judging, such as a 1900 "covert insinuation":

> Braggs – I am a self-made man.
> Waggs – You seem to have expended more effort on the dining-room than on the attic.[49]

Some earnest authors grappled with how the earlier grounding of self-making in patriotic or spiritual service could survive a world where worth was increasingly measured by materialism. The concept became so steeped in the idea of business success that by 1890 some, including William Larremore in California's *Overland Monthly*, could worry that the sort of "industry [effort] in one's profession or trade [that] usually brings success" would migrate into the realm of politics. Early narratives of self-made success had been a rhetorical tool in political competitions, but Larremore lamented that, now, the "hard commercial spirit which pervades the meetings of a joint stock company is the spirit in which most politicians speak of public business." Even respectable citizens had come to believe that "indefatigable energy" in political pursuits adequately justified political support. More distressing, "the misapplication of the saying, 'From the tow-path to the White House,' has done much harm." It inspired "ordinary Americans" to aim beyond "the humble spheres for which they are fitted," which served them and the nation ill.[50] Across the century, Henry Clay's fairly ignoble use of the "tow path" slogan still sparked political fires.

Adding to the cacophony of meanings for self-made success at century's end, three novelettes satirized the concept and tugged at its various clichés. The first was George Horace Lorimer's enormously popular *Letters from a Self-made Merchant to His Son*, first published in 1901 as a series of "letters" in the *Saturday Evening Post*. Despite its glib style, Lorimer was serious about the generational differences between "self-made" businessmen and their sons. Even more seriously, he applauded business's evolution to become America's dominant profession, with its practical approaches, opportunities, and challenges. He admired the old-fashioned standard for "self-made men," namely rising without a formal education, but recognized that that was an obsolete model. Charles Eustace Merriman quickly responded with *Letters from a Son to His Self-Made Father*. He satirized the fictional son's Harvard education, which emphasized "cultural" studies, such as a "topography course, in which we are making a careful study of Boston streets" at night. Amusing tales ended with a request for "philanthropy," that is, a check from dad, in one case "to keep your name out of the police court records." Maurice Switzer's *Letters of a Self-Made Failure* jabbed less and therefore amused less, but he dispensed realistic advice along the theme that "it is less important to know how one man attained great success than it is to understand why a thousand men became utter failures." First published in *Leslie's Weekly*, Switzer's epistles cautioned that, in "an age of big business," work still was key, "hard, prosaic, monotonous effort," neither heroic nor romantic. Most of all, "Take your work seriously, my boy, but not yourself; we are all of us jokes, more or less."[51]

As in earlier times, struggling in poverty without visible means of employment laid one open to charges of idleness despite working constantly in the interstices of an economy. Constant struggle, even foraging in hard times, left many working-class and poor families few moments or resources for the sorts of self-improvement, formal or informal, that observers could admire.[52] Even "regular" employment did not mean year-round employment. Yet, from the perspective of self-appointed arbiters of propriety, the working class could look "shiftless," as it did according to "Two Kinds of Workingmen" during nationwide strikes and labor–capital violence in 1877. This article began with a "puzzle" asking how, in "a country in which there is no class which does not work" and nothing "obstructs the humblest or the poorest from rising to the highest station and the amplest wealth," some "workmen were always shiftless, often intemperate, never saved anything and grow steadily poorer." Retelling the fallacy that "all started with equal advantages," the piece continued, "our national biography is made up of the lives of men who have raised themselves from poverty to eminence and fortune." Looking beyond the "great fortunes, ... the universal diffusion of moderate competence marks this country" as the only one "in which the path of labor to prosperity is clear and easy." Into this blinkered portrayal of shared opportunities but differential behaviors and fates fell "the whole secret of the class distinction, if any exists."[53] Such was, and remains, the judgment that the myth of self-made success supports.

Storytellers in the next decade who wanted to dismiss concerns about wealth inequality and the efforts of community activism also gravitated to stories of "self-made paupers." Some polemicists in the 1880s pleaded with their readers to avoid "communist" appeals, as did a sermon with wide distribution. It set those who "believe in making property in an honest way" against "a worthless set of self-made paupers and vagabonds, who are hourly being hurried on and on by foreign anarchists." Another essayist argued for restraints on firearms because of their danger to "chief magistrates" as well as to the "wealthy men [who] are now termed monopolists, oppressors, etc., by the lazy, unthrifty, and thieving, drunken, self-made paupers that make up a large portion of every large city." Another diatribe regretted that "these self-made paupers ... without character and as ignorant as a horse" could vote equally with "the citizen whose very soul is burdened with the great desire to advance the real interests of society." Likewise, "The Bondage of Land-Owners" contorted its narrative to present landowners as oppressed by poor people because they must support "all the self-made lunatics, paupers, and public beggars," all of the "broken-down victims of sensual indulgence." Upstanding taxpayers were bound to care for "impecunious, self-ruined imbeciles."[54] And so on.

All this variety of advice, humor, and admonition aimed at audiences among the middle- and upper-class mainstream. The labor press had its own perspective on self-made success, a complicated view that further attests to the diffusion of the self-made myth into America's various cultures.

"SELF-MADE OR MADE FOR SELF"?

In the decades around 1900, the labor press found its own uses for the concept of self-making, not only as a source of guidance but also as a way to judge and poke at elites.

An 1898 article in *The Labor World* out of Duluth, Minnesota, offered advice, leading with the title "The Self-Made Man." It thoughtfully balanced circumstances and self-agency as they affected the lives of ordinary people. "Thrift is still a virtue" that could improve lives despite the decline in American mobility with the advance of the corporate economy. "When the self-made man started forty years ago he had chances that are now closed." Men who had saved and "watched" for chances back in mid-century "could not get a foothold now." The days of becoming one's "own employer" and acquiring "a competence" had passed for the "average man," who must be an employee because too much capital was required to start modern firms, even small ones. Striking a balance between personal responsibility and diminished opportunities, the essay observed that ordinary men "know that they are industrious and sober," and, more to the point, "they resent the imputation that it is only through idleness and vice that they fail to become millionaires." Being "economical" might make them comfortable but could not make them wealthy: "The self-made man did not get rich simply by stinting himself." Thrift, like work, was necessary but not sufficient "to take advantage of the opportunities that made him rich."[55]

When pro-labor newspapers around the country appraised the wealthy who claimed to be self-made successes, they sometimes applied its judgmental functions to differentiate between men who seemed to have earned wealth and others who, essentially, had stolen or wrenched it from others' labors. A 1902 retrospective, "Self-Made or Made for Self," distinguished between "the highest type of true self-made men" and the "lawless plutocratic pirates and sluggers and scoundrels" who "were made for self." Few of the "highest type" could rank with Benjamin Franklin and Abraham Lincoln, of course, who "rose right up from the people by rugged toil" but also sought to lighten others' burdens. Yet, at that distance, even John Jacob Astor and Cornelius Vanderbilt seemed "legitimate business men." Although certainly no "humanitarians," according to this account they did not "pound the public" with their wealth. Instead, the current target was labor's foes who "dominated increasingly every year important corporate enterprises in America." Although the "spur of honest poverty" could well motivate "honest ambition," dubious claims of rising or self-making were no justification to "plunder the bodies of better men than themselves."[56] From the distance of years, labor advocates could look past Astor's and Vanderbilt's voraciousness in order to pass judgment on contemporary corporate antagonists.

Some pro-labor authors accepted the dominant values of individualism but rejected the whole idea of self-making. One such "natural born, ingrained individualist" insisted in 1908 that a man unwilling to acknowledge his debt to his community should find "some uninhabited island" where he can "indulge the delusion that he is a self-made man." That same year, the pompous, evil, and deceitful Josiah Bounderby in Charles Dickens's popular 1854 novel *Hard Times* inspired a comparison between that cruel fictional employer and "many of our boastful 'self-made' men who are grinding, heartless employers."[57]

In 1914, Samuel Gompers (1850–1924), one of American labor's strongest voices, expressed a wry grasp of America's popular legend of self-made success.

As was his custom, he did not mince words in describing John D. Rockefeller, "with his callousness, his indifference to public opinion, his secretiveness, his absolute disregard of the rights of others, ... his contempt for justice, and his sanctimonious cloak of religious vanity," and so on. Yet this co-founder and long-time leader of the American Federation of Labor surmised that the elder Rockefeller had not "aroused the resentment and indignation of the nation, partly perhaps because Americans forgive much in a 'self-made man,'" although "they may ardently wish that some wiser person had undertaken the job of making him." In contrast, John D. Rockefeller, Jr., seemed to make his demands as a "dictator by divine right" – in other words, as an aristocrat, that enemy of the Republic and the antithesis of true workers. Writing in the wake of that year's Ludlow Massacre, which had killed striking coalminers and family members at the climax of the Colorado Coalfield War, Gompers was incensed that "Rockefeller II" used his inherited wealth and power "to control men's living" through "violence and bloodshed."[58] This advocate for the working class extolled the work ethos and accepted that acquiring a fortune could secure public esteem. From his view, however, exploiting others' work was evil when conducted by someone who never had to work.

Here, Gompers rekindled the anti-aristocratic fires that had forged early versions of the myth of the self-made man in the young Republic. He, like other labor advocates who referred to self-making, showed just how deeply the myth had penetrated American culture. Strikingly, Gompers and his allies revealed that self-making's storytellers had succeeded to some degree in insulating their protagonists from criticism. Thus, even among labor activists, it was not obvious that self-making for the purpose of self-advancement and wealth was always subject to criticism.

In 1897, former president Grover Cleveland wrestled with the multiple meanings of self-making when he addressed Princeton University. To this audience of elites, Cleveland argued against a simplistic assessment of "the Self-Made Man" and confronted one of its constants: the element of judgment. True, a "romantic and sentimental glamour has enveloped" the self-made man, "magnifying his proportions, and causing him to appear much larger and in every way greater than other men." Yet Cleveland mocked the "fanciful notion that the difficulties that stood in the way of these self-made men were essential to their success." He also rejected the presumption that "all successes ... are of that useful and elevating kind that should excite our admiration." We are, he insisted, "at liberty to resent ... the attempt to cover a multitude of sins with the cloak of the self-made man." Instead, "the merit of the successful man ... must be judged by the kind of success he has achieved" and whether he meets "all the obligations of a liberal, public-spirited, and useful citizen." In contrast, "if he clutches [his success] closely for his selfish gratification, ... his struggles should not save him from contempt." He is "not worth the making."[59] A man made for self deserved no esteem.

8

Competing Stories of Self-Help Before 1936

"Properly speaking, there are in the world no such men as self-made men. That term implies an individual independence of the past and present which can never exist." No less a personage than Frederick Douglass delivered this caveat dozens of times in his speech "Self-Made Men," beginning in 1859 and continuing into the 1890s. This remarkable man was born into slavery in 1818 but escaped in 1838 to become one of America's foremost abolitionists, leaving an awe-inspiring legacy before his death in 1895. He was as "self-made" as anyone could be. And yet even he saw the label, "properly speaking," as absurd as a "self moving machine." What did he mean, then, later in this same speech, when he proclaimed that "America is said, and not without reason, to be preeminently the home and patron of self-made men"? Unlike Ralph Waldo Emerson, who felt entitled to disregard coherence, Douglass carefully worked through the logic of self-making, trying to balance self-agency with the causal influence of context, accountability, and circumstance. He admired Emerson's conception of self-reliance, but never lost sight of "the brotherhood and inter-dependence of mankind." Despite "self-conscious individuality and self-conceit," nothing "can lift a man into absolute independence of his fellowmen."[1] From his vantage point on the margins, Douglass saw the tensions of self-fashioning as few notably successful people have, and, therefore, he advocated for *collective* self-help. The mainstream, however, fostered an individualist genre of self-help stories that neglected both community resources and obligations.

By the nineteenth century, telling stories of self-agency had lost the taint of blasphemy that had weighed so heavily two centuries earlier on figures such as John Smith and Robert Keayne. New storylines flourished.

The phrase "self-made" had entered storytellers' lexicon to describe and judge the fallen as often as the risen – self-made drunks and self-made preachers. Soon thereafter, that rhetorical tool rang out in political arenas to praise "solitary oaks" such as Andrew Jackson and Henry Clay. As the zeal for mobility intensified in mid-century, an array of self-help recipes offered ways to achieve it. But "self-help" was never the same as "self-made." Stories about the "self-made" tell the *results* of lives and individuals' choices; stories about "self-help" feature the *processes* of improvement. Frederick Douglass applied both terms not as hammers but as levers, as did preachers and authors such as Harriet Beecher Stowe, to inspire self-improvement and service. Thus, he closed his oft repeated and reprinted "Self-Made Men" speech hoping to "have stirred in any mind, a courageous resolution to make one more effort toward self-improvement and higher usefulness."[2] Douglass's interpretation was more Benjamin Franklin than Thomas Mellon, and far more Charles Grandison Finney than P. T. Barnum.

A second genre of self-help stories evolved to offer entirely individualist recipes for success. More Thomas Mellon than Benjamin Franklin, and far more P. T. Barnum than Charles Grandison Finney, this outpouring of individualist enthusiasm continued the evolution and popularization of a blunt form of the myth of self-made success. It insisted on finding an inner "will" that assured success in all things. Little remained of self-making's earlier sources of cultural authority in self-improvement to serve God and community. In simultaneously demanding and boosting individual ambitions, its fables of "Acres of Diamonds" and *How to Win Friends and Influence People* could give hope along with advice and spurs to action, self-interested action.

Collective self-help blends individual responsibility for improvement with obligations between individuals and community. Unlike mutually made men, such as Henry Clay Frick, who swam in America's mainstream, and who worked and competed against each other too single-mindedly to appreciate their rare advantages and opportunities, outsiders like Douglass saw what marginalization denied them. Consequently, their self-help stories revealed how gender, ethnicity, and class too often blocked them from shaping and pursuing their own hopes and ambitions. The conundrum for well-intentioned advisors was to reconcile the individual responsibility urged by self-help platitudes such as the ones Douglass offered – including "Help Yourself!" and "Be the architect of your own fortune!" – with the legal, economic, cultural, and social barriers against outliers.[3]

To address that conundrum, labor organizations, other mutual aid societies, immigrant groups, as well as farmers' cooperatives known as Granges (active throughout rural areas since 1867), engaged in and promoted collective self-help. They built libraries and schools and conducted lecture series on both abstract and practical subjects for their communities.[4] Neither a mystery nor a contradiction, collective self-help is how effective individuals and communities function. It is how mutually made men prosper regardless of how individualist and self-made they and their advocates claim for them. In recognition of this reality, a genre of self-*help* encouragement emerged from the margins of American society that was quite different from the unabashedly individualist *self*-help genre. In his perspective, Douglass asserted, "the man who will get up will be helped up." In 1896, the National Association of Colored Women's Clubs captured this sense of mutual obligation in its motto "Lifting as We Climb." Labor unions, likewise, always rely on solidarity among individual members to improve their shared chances to prosper. Especially in hard times, community gardens, cooperative stores, and mutual aid societies all put into practice the principle of collective self-help.[5]

Unfortunately, as we will see, outliers engaged in self-help were undermined in the late nineteenth and into the twentieth century when their codes of how to prosper – collectively and as communities – clashed against those of powerful authorities. This was the case in Pittsburgh when its mutually made captains of industry suppressed labor activism with their collective resources of armed force and law in 1892, and when federal legislation further dispossessed Native Americans with the 1887 Dawes Severalty Act, all in the name of individualism. Collective self-help was also key to African Americans' efforts to improve their lives despite the enormous weight of law and bigotry after Emancipation. Storytellers in the mainstream have rebuffed and often pathologized the ethos of collective self-help while promoting the tales and recipes for individualist self-help that are most familiar now.

FREDERICK DOUGLASS AND MAKING A DIFFERENCE

Harriet Beecher Stowe led off her 1872 *Lives and Deeds of Our Self-Made Men* with Abraham Lincoln but emphasized in her entry on Frederick Douglass that he "had as far to climb to get to the spot where the poorest free white boy is born, as that white boy has to climb to be president of the nation."[6] Stowe featured Lincoln and Douglass among her nineteen self-made men, but most other biographical collections of the era featured men who had ascended to affluence. Stowe's criteria paralleled those that Lincoln and Douglass also valued: self-reliance, mobility, and community improvement. Moral authority was key. As Douglass concluded an 1860 version of "The Trials and Triumphs of Self-Made Men," to earn praise for rising, "some grand motive power other than the simple hope of personal reward must be present." No one is "so small, none so destitute, but that he is rich enough to make this great world a debtor to him for something in the way of example, word, or deed." His audience responded with "loud applause."[7]

As part of his resolute self-fashioning, Douglass became nineteenth-century America's most photographed person. During his first twenty years, other people had the legal right to mold him as they wished, but, thereafter, Douglass took charge of his image. "Negroes can never have impartial portraits at the hands of white artists," he explained in 1849. Photography, not paintings or drawings, could best carry his image around the world and into the future. Also, because photography was more accessible than hand-drawn imagery, he believed it was more democratic. He sought out photography studios as he traveled, and artisans of that new craft also eagerly sought out him. As he did with the eloquence of his words, he deliberately cultivated an august persona for cameras and their audiences.[8] In this medium and throughout his life, Frederick Douglass purposefully made himself.

Hoping to encourage others, Douglass declared that "WORK! WORK!! WORK!!! WORK!!!!" is "the true miracle worker" to make oneself. His calls for "exertion" plus "fortitude and perseverance" were standard fare, as was most of his other self-improvement advice. He told stories of White and Black men, such as Abraham Lincoln and astronomer Benjamin Bannecker, "who have come up from the depths of society" to show the fundamental importance of "well directed, honest toil." He intended each story to raise "the dignity of labor." Yet he also worried that "Labor can never be respected where the laborer is despised," a problem that persisted long after Emancipation. It also lay at the core of troubles in the industrial North, but he believed, optimistically, that in America, "the man of toil," if free and respected, could "meet the capitalist as the representative of an equal power."[9]

Douglass was not optimistic, however, about the prospects of respect for African Americans, their work, and their chances for mobility. Time and again he insisted that White America "Give the Negro fair play and let him alone." Yet, even beyond omnipresent violence and the threat of violence, fairness in the aftermath of "two hundred years heavy with human bondage" also required "a school house in every valley of the South and a church on every hill side," supplied with teachers and preachers for a century. At a minimum, every African American should be accorded respect for self-improvement and self-help "measured, not by the heights others have obtained, but from the depths from which he has come." He viewed that anyone who rose at all was "entitled to a certain measure of respect" and that each "such success is an example and a help to humanity."[10]

Not until 1878 did Douglass make his first trip as a free man to his Maryland birthplace. The *Easton Gazette* reported on this visit and depicted "This distinguished colored man" at such length that would be considered inappropriate now, while also noting that, "we presume," he was the first "colored man" to stay as "a guest in one of our principal hotels." Douglass presented his "Self-Made Men" address in Easton to a mixed audience's acclaim. The reporter noted that Douglass delivered what was an otherwise "hackneyed" theme with "so much originality and eloquence as to deprive it of its common place character." Moreover, Douglass looked directly at "the white portion of the segregated audience" when he amplified his standard calls for non-interference from Whites at the ballot box, churches, and schools: "let him alone." He appealed

Figure 8.1 Frederick Douglass, the renowned abolitionist and advocate for African Americans, spoke in 1892 at Tuskegee Institute, which Booker T. Washington co-founded and led. Like Washington, Douglass stressed self-improvement that bolstered communities, which would, in turn, support individuals' efforts and wellbeing. ("Hon. Fred. Douglass on platform in [the] Pavilion," Booker T. Washington Collection, Library of Congress)

to the audience's patriotism, assuring them that, if left alone, African Americans could live up to the nation's standing as "the soil to produce most abundantly self-made men." According to this report, Douglass showed "no pretension to have achieved any great things as a self-made man, but to have simply done the best he could, and to have made the most of himself."[11]

Like Abraham Lincoln, Douglass appreciated the merits of work and the value of their own stories as inspirations and credentials. Both of them also refused to shame the impoverished. President Lincoln had reportedly praised Douglass as "one of the most meritorious men in America" given the "conditions from which Douglass rose," and Douglass often repaid the accolade. In 1886, he attributed Lincoln's respectfulness and "entire freedom from popular prejudice against the colored race" to "the similarity with which I had fought my way up, we both starting at the lowest round of the ladder."[12] Douglass also resembled Lincoln in his dedication to community, which kept both of them true to Franklin's sense that self-improvement should serve the common good while serving as role models for individuals. They also recognized the necessity for people on the margins to band together.[13] Self-help, and even self-reliance were community projects and responsibilities in their eyes, to be supported and advanced to everyone's benefit.

A CONSPIRACY BY ANY OTHER NAME

When is collective self-help a "conspiracy"? This question emerged in the 1883 US Senate Committee on Education and Labor hearings on "the Relations between Labor and Capital." As we saw in the last chapter, businessmen were anointed as self-made men in the decades when collective action and association increasingly characterized capitalism, and, as we will see, those mutually made men turned their collective resources against their employees who attempted self-help by collaboration. Robert D. Layton, Grand Secretary of the Knights of Labor of North America, the nation's most prominent labor organization in the 1880s, was the first witness to testify before the Committee. Early in his testimony, Layton protested that "since the railroads are granted special privileges" by government policies, they should not be able "to form pools and rings against the interests of the people, so as to raise the price of the necessaries of life." Following up on Layton's comment, Senator James Z. George of Mississippi asked, "Among the capitalists that is called a 'pool,' or 'syndicate,' but among the laborers it is a 'conspiracy'?" Layton responded simply, "Yes, sir." Senator George also observed that "I think it has got to be pretty generally understood that the only safety or protection of the workingmen in these large shops and manufacturing establishments is by combination." Layton agreed and added that "a working man single and alone cannot protect himself; he requires the combined effort of all to protect him."[14]

When George invited Layton to conclude his testimony with recommendations for change, Layton's top priority was "the abolition of conspiracy laws preventing legitimate combinations of laborers." Those laws allowed imprisoning laborers for organizing, even for "conspiring" to quit their jobs on the same day. Other witnesses testified to the impact of such laws in most states that "expressly made it a criminal act for a workingman to combine with others even for the purpose of resisting a reduction of wages," even participating in an "ordinary labor strike, without violence or tumult." When asked what laws disadvantaged labor, another witness put the case plainly: "The most important law or laws ... are those which permit large corporations to combine, and ... permit the corporations and individual employers to do that which the law prohibits the workingmen from doing." He continued, "when it is done by them the law describes it as a 'conspiracy' to interfere with trade and commerce." In this legal and cultural context, Samuel Gompers, leader of the American Federation of Labor (AFL), called upon the "captains of industry" to cease their inconsistency and "see to it that the same rights of organization were accorded to labor which they demanded for themselves."[15]

Five years later in 1888, Senator George joined with other lawmakers, most notably Senator John Sherman of Ohio (1823–1900), to construct "An Act to Protect Trade and Commerce Against Unlawful Restraints and Monopolies," which became law in 1890. The Sherman Antitrust Act, as it is still known, addressed widespread public concerns about trusts and their growing power over the economy and politics. The future president and Supreme Court chief justice, William Howard Taft, no foe of business, described the law's targeting of trusts as "a step taken by Congress to meet what the public had found to be a growing and intolerable evil." Yet the Act was first and most frequently successful against labor unions, initially during an 1892 general strike in New Orleans and then the larger-scale 1894 Pullman strike. During that tumultuous 1894 conflict, Taft agreed with other authorities that "until they have had much bloodletting, it will not be better" because of the "demagogues and populists." Having heard that federal troops had killed thirty men, he was hopeful: "Though it is a bloody business, everybody hopes that it is true." Who was "everybody"? Certainly not laborers. The front page of the *New York Times* described labor actions in New Orleans as "conspiring against commerce." Labor's "manifestoes and notices" amounted to "an indictable conspiracy."[16] Conspiracy lives in the eye of the beholder.

Blacklisting workers requires that managers cooperate with each other, that they look past their claims as self-made individualists to enlist their networks against employees' efforts to do the same. Conspiracy charges against strikers resulted in relatively few long-term imprisonments, but collaborations among employers to blacklist workers cost untold numbers their livelihoods. A witness in the 1883 Senate hearings explained that in railroading any man "is at once blacklisted and discharged, and his name is sent to all the railroad companies of the country if he has taken any active part of the organization of labor." Another witness tallied outcomes of "blacklisting men who have the courage to speak their opinions." Of three men blacklisted by a Lowell, Massachusetts, manufacturer two years previously, one "is now dead; another is tending bar, and the other we do not know where he is." He cited thirty-four other instances in which men "are working now under assumed names" with private detectives on their trails. Yet another witness explained that the "system of 'blacklisting' prevails here to a great extent in the small trades, and in the large trades, also." It succeeds, he said, because "Men who are known to be active among the workingmen are singled out and made the objects of the special displeasure of the employers. Their names are passed around among the employers to keep them from obtaining employment."[17]

Despite their own collaborations – a capitalist's version of conspiracy and "collective self-help" – owners and managers typically agreed that laborers should have to act as individuals when negotiating and monitoring employment conditions. To compel employees' "self-reliance" and limit their capacity for cooperation, employers acted together through professional and personal connections, often abetted by the state. To oppose unions as bargaining and monitoring units, many insisted on what was often called the "open shop" system by the twentieth century, by which laborers came to terms individually with their employers, unaided by collective negotiations.[18] Shortly after Henry Clay Frick's death in 1919, his close friend George Harvey eulogized him as "Builder and Individualist." Among the standard hyperboles, such as that "he was the most intense individualist," Harvey highlighted that Frick "believed in the open shop for men and he established it." Harvey celebrated this mutually made "triumph of individualism" who doggedly opposed employees' ability to mutually make *their* working conditions. Frick "would brook no interference" with directing the "vast accumulations" that "he had earned and fairly won."[19] Harvey did not, of course, mention that Frick, like his peers, relied on very non-individualist collaborations all along, plus state-based aid when the going got rough.

Workers empower a union to act as their bargaining agent to balance their collective weight in negotiating against employers' clout. However, Pittsburgh's coal, iron, and steel bosses, like many other employers, resisted limits on their authority to deal directly with individual employees. Back in 1877, Carnegie and his managers had successfully fended off unionized bargaining at their new Edgar Thomson Steel Works because its technological innovations devalued workers' skills and reduced their leverage. The outcome was a contract that prohibited quitting without a three-day notice and branded as a criminal conspiracy any instance when ten workers gave notice the same day. Then, in 1889, Homestead Steel Works' management, with Andrew Carnegie at the helm, confronted labor with a three-year contract that not only disadvantaged workers but that they had to sign individually in order to hold their jobs. A lockout followed, but the workers held together in that last bastion of unionism in the area's steel mills. Most important, they bridged divisions that often separated them, such as those between native-born and immigrant groups.[20] For the next three years, that labor victory gnawed at management. When the next crisis erupted at Homestead, Pittsburgh's most powerful mutually made men would impose a crushing economic individualism on workers, deploying their own and the state's collective resources.

When workers struck in 1892 at Homestead, management was determined to thwart them. In Frick's words during the crisis, "Somebody has got to be a boss," and "as that individual," he applied collective resources to end the strike. Those

Figure 8.2 In 1892, Henry Clay Frick called for Pennsylvania National Guard troops to put down laborers' organizing at the Homestead Steel Works in Homestead, Pennsylvania, as pictured here. He and his fellow executives, including Andrew Carnegie himself, combined individualist rhetoric and taxpayers' resources to prevent workers from bargaining collectively. ("The First Troops in Homestead," wood engraving after drawing by Thure de Thulstrup, 1892. Library of Congress / Corbis Historical / VCG via Getty Images)

resources included funds to hire mercenaries from the notorious Pinkerton detective agency, to assemble an arsenal, and to build a three-mile wall some called "Fort Frick" in order "to protect the interests of the association." Beyond what money could buy – or, perhaps, including what money could buy – he called for policing from the local sheriff, and, when all else failed, demanded that the governor send Pennsylvania National Guard troops: more than 8,000 arrived at taxpayers' expense of about $500,000 (more than $17,226,000 in 2024).[21] Afterward, management had strikers prosecuted for trespassing and conspiracy. Completing the devastation, Frick and allies blacklisted labor activists, not only at their own factories but also across an industry-wide network of managers likewise eager to control obstreperous workers.[22]

In the midst of the Homestead crisis, Frick instructed a supervisor to tell union leaders that "when those works do resume, it will be as non-union, and former employees satisfactory to us, who desire to work there, will have to apply as individuals." For emphasis Frick added, "under no circumstances will we confer with the men at Homestead as members of the Amalgamated Association." Despite thirty-five violent deaths, Frick wrote to Carnegie, who avoided the Homestead difficulties while in Scotland, "we had to teach our employees a lesson and we have taught them one they will never forget." He also assured Carnegie that "I cannot see where we have made any serious blunders, or done anything that was not proper and right." The *New York Times* agreed, impressed with how "he remained cool and collected during the trouble." This "self-made man," this "man of iron will" had ensured that the company would "run the plant at Homestead."[23] But without the state's enforcement of his "iron will," this story could well have ended otherwise.

Many businessmen who, like Frick, presented themselves as self-reliant individualists genuinely believed that they were justified in holding otherwise contradictory stances toward individualism and collective self-help. Such logic was common within the National Association of Manufacturers (NAM), founded in 1895, which still speaks for business.[24] In 1909 John Kirby, Jr., began his presidential address to the NAM by affirming that "the labor question ... is the great concern of this Association." He urged support for the NAM's growing "concentration of influence" on legislatures because, he said with no apparent sense of irony, "in union there is strength." The NAM, Kirby said, represented men who, "like Lincoln, Grant, and Garfield and thousands of others started in life with nothing but principle and pluck." This "great army of men of wealth and influence" had raised themselves "from the humblest conditions in which men are born." Although "yesterday [they] were struggling to get the upperhand of poverty," they "will be numbered among the class of men who constitute the bone and sinew of the Nation's prosperity."[25] Accordingly, these people who saw themselves as self-made individualists had earned the right, not only to the nation's esteem, but also to its support.

PATHOLOGIZING NATIVE AMERICANS' COLLECTIVE SELF-HELP

Just as legal authorities and police forces acted collectively to limit labor organizing, they enforced "individualism" to combat the collective self-help that Native Americans practiced. Major threats of violent resistance from Native Americans had pretty much been suppressed by the 1880s, but many Euro-Americans interpreted Native communal systems as a cultural threat, especially if they coveted lands still occupied by indigenous people. Further complicating the political context, people compelled to live on reservations with neither traditional nor modern resources struggled to survive and typically required government provisions. Ignoring the causes for this condition, dependency made Native Americans vulnerable to derision such as "barbarians and beggars," as the *Boston Evening Transcript* characterized them in 1887.[26] By pathologizing surviving cultural patterns, the mainstream could require "remedies."

"There is no selfishness, which is at the bottom of civilization," pronounced Senator Henry L. Dawes (1816–1903) about Native Americans in 1885. He then explained that some Native American peoples "have got as far as they can go, because they own their land in common."[27] He and others who called themselves "Friends of the Indian" proposed to solve much of what they considered "the Indian Problem" by breaking up reservations and reducing the roles of tribal leadership. Soon thereafter, the 1887 General Allotment Act, more widely known as the Dawes Severalty Act, allowed the US government to impose individualism by law and, if necessary, by force.[28] Convinced of their own good intentions to remedy the malady of communal living, policymakers sought to compel Native people's assimilation by severalty – that is, by dividing reservation lands into small parcels that individual families would own and farm. As Senator John Logan, a renowned Civil War general, chided resistant members of the Sioux Nation in an 1883 meeting that included Chief Sitting Bull: "The Government feeds and clothes your children now, and desires to teach you to become farmers, and to civilize you, and make you as white men."[29] Logan and most others in authority did not question the wisdom or integrity of forcing Native children to attend schools for assimilation, or of remaking Native adults "as white men."

What did "make you as white men" mean? The stories revolving around severalty presumed that self-agency and self-reliance along Euro-American lines were essential for any man's stature in modern times. It might have seemed romantic that "boys from the captive band of Sitting Bull" who were "fresh from the wildest Indian life" and installed in a mission school had "asked only the privilege of ceaseless hunting and roaming." However, that variety of romantic individualism held no charm among mainstream thinkers because it violated "civilized" standards and ambitions for adult men. Civilization required small plots of private property and the responsibilities that came with making a livelihood from it. In line with countless similar expressions about the nature of acceptable civilization, a government agent summarized in 1881 the grand premise that "Separate individualized families and interests would seem to be the universal order of progression in human affairs."[30] The keepers of civilization took it upon themselves to enforce such progress.

With the closing of what had once seemed an infinite horizon of land there for the taking, what remained by the last decades of the nineteenth century was largely bound up by treaties or in federal lands. In that context, severalty took on

Figure 8.3 Advocates for the Dawes Severalty Act of 1887 claimed that they could improve the lot of Native Americans by stripping away their collective traditions and imbuing them with a strong individualist ethic. Apparently without irony, many of those same White reformers supported residential schools for Native American children that demanded regimentation, as photographed in 1899 at one of the largest of these schools, the Carlisle Indian School in Pennsylvania. (Photo by Choate / Library of Congress / Corbis Historical / VCG via Getty Images)

new urgency. It could open more territory for land-hungry Euro-Americans and, at the same time, impose "civilization" on Native peoples. (As it happened, the first goal was readily met by decree. Native peoples lost almost two-thirds of their lands in areas affected by the Dawes Act. Eighty-nine million acres out of 140 million became available for homesteaders to purchase.) Stories to justify both goals could express deep malice as did Arizona Territory Governor F. A. Tritle in an 1885 letter to the Secretary of the Interior: Native Americans in his view were "either diseased and filthy nonproducing vagabonds or cruel and treacherous beasts of prey in human form."[31] Most mainstream storytellers presented their cases more gently, but condescendingly. All based their cases on their own ideas of proper ambitions, self-improvement, and successful lives, disregarding cultural differences and circumstances.

At its core, the debates over the "Indian problem" manifested the clash of a by-then entrenched ideology and myth of self-making against a communal ideology of self-*help* and mutual obligation. Thus, the *Boston Evening Transcript* lamented that Native Americans who protested the Dawes Act "have failed ... to reach a genuine civilization, ... or to make anything like a full use of their resources."

Reminiscent of English colonizers' reasoning in the seventeenth century, this failure "is a conclusive impeachment of the tribal system." Therefore, "If their capacities are ever to be developed and ripened, it must be under a different system, more stimulating to individual enterprise and self-dependence." Not at all "a bill to destroy the Indians, the severalty act is a measure to give them a chance to become civilized men and citizens instead of barbarians and paupers," according to enlightened Bostonians.[32]

Likewise in the spirit of valiant individualism, the *St. Louis Globe-Democrat* assured readers that the Dawes Act would allow everyone, including Native Americans, "to celebrate the emancipation of the red man" because the law would allow the Interior Department to "wage extermination war on the old tribal communism." Secretary Schurz insisted that it was "certain that the introduction of industrial habits, that settlement in severalty, the foundation of permanent homes, the conferring of individual title, and thereby the practical individualization of the Indian" would "cultivate among the Indians the pride of individual ownership of property and the love of a fixed home, and thus to encourage a feeling of independence of their tribal relations." Senator Dawes reiterated this gospel of self-making confidently in 1886. Severalty, he assured the citizenry, would "take the Indians out one by one from under the tribe, place him in a position to become an independent American citizen, and then before the tribe is aware of it its existence as a tribe is gone." According to this law, American citizenship required "every Indian" in affected territories to have "voluntarily taken up ... his residence separate and apart from any tribe of Indians therein, and [to have] adopted the habits of civilized life."[33] Despite the illusions of progress, the disastrous results of this law and subsequent versions reverberated for decades, well beyond its repeal in 1934.[34]

"LIFTING AS WE CLIMB"

African Americans who valued collective self-help and advancement also found their efforts undermined in the late nineteenth century. One of the essays in *The College of Life, or Practical Self-Educator: A Manual of Self-Improvement for the Colored Race* began by emphasizing that "Our people have not been slow to see the advantages arising from combined effort." The book was first published in 1895 "to advise, encourage and educate," and, especially, "to inspire ... Self-Improvement." That essay also asserted the community's belief "in societies for mutual improvement, for dispensing charity to aid the unfortunate, for protecting their civil rights, for aiding one another in business and for elevating the race." A few years later, *The Negro in Business* reported on a conference to study "business ventures among American Negroes," part of a series on "the Negro problems." The attendees'

"Resolutions" asserted that "We *must* cooperate or we are lost." Then, optimistically, "Ten million people who join in intelligent self-help can never be long ignored or mistreated." Likewise, the Universal Negro Improvement Association (UNIA) was founded, first in Jamaica in 1914, then in New York City in 1918, to teach "our race self-help and self-reliance."[35]

Frederick Douglass's successors – Booker T. Washington (1856–1915), W. E. B. DuBois (1868–1963), and Marcus Garvey (1887–1940) – famously and vehemently disagreed about many issues, but they all agreed on the fundamental value of mutual self-help.[36] Like Douglass, they valued individuals' improvements that would, in turn, improve their communities and the nation. They reinforced Douglass's promise that "the man who will get up will be helped up," at least within their own communities. Calls for self-help and mutual aid ran through *The College of Life*, *The Negro in Business*, and writings of the UNIA, the first guided by Washington, the second guided and edited by DuBois, and the third founded and dominated by Marcus Garvey. Through abundant stories of challenges and successes, the phrase "self-made" appeared rarely. Instead, contributors contended that all should make every effort to improve themselves, but that no one managed alone.

The motto "Lifting as We Climb" expresses Black activists' dual goals of self-help. In 1896, the Colored Women's League and the National Federation of Afro-American Women, together representing women's organizations across the country, merged to form the National Association of Colored Women (NACW). They adopted this slogan to express their dual duties to climb and to lift their communities, fostering improvement along the way. Pittsburgh's Aurora Reading Club, for example, began in 1897 not only for weekly book discussions but also to support local charities, such as the Working Girls Home and the Aged Women's Home, shelters to preserve the safety and dignity of women in need. In tune with the NACW's mission, they, too, adopted "Lifting as We Climb" for their motto.[37] Educated African American women paired the pleasures of improving themselves with their duty to aid their less fortunate sisters.

Mary Church Terrell (1863–1954), daughter of formerly enslaved people and the NACW's founding president, brought that slogan in 1898 to the fifty-year anniversary of the National American Women's Suffrage Association, invited by no less a personage than Susan B. Anthony. In presenting "The Progress of Colored Women," Terrell pointed out that the obstacles all women faced then "to educate and cultivate themselves" were compounded for "colored women with ambition and aspiration" by "a cruel, unreasonable prejudice which neither their merit nor their necessity seems able to subdue." Nonetheless, she expressed pride at the progress achieved by people "liberated less than forty years ago, penniless and ignorant." Education brought to "the hearts of colored women an ardent desire to do good in the world." Teaching "the less fortunate of their race" and "public work of all kinds," such as medicine, trades, and domestic skills, were aimed to "benefit and elevate their race." Terrell concluded by affirming their "keen sense of the responsibility" to serve, "lifting as we climb, onward and upward we go, struggling and striving."[38]

Terrell represented many affluent and well-educated Black women and men who expressed complex sentiments about their "unfortunate sisters" and brothers.[39] The 90 percent who had been forced to remain illiterate while enslaved shared a widely recognized, clearly urgent desire, and need, for education. Churches and other cultural institutions blossomed throughout the South to build communities. Education for adults as well as children was a high priority for everyone.[40] Terrell and most female African American activists, including professional social workers, often focused on children's wellbeing and on building respect for women among both the White population and African American men.[41] Strategies varied widely, but the need to act collectively prevailed. Terrell echoed others regarding "the call of duty" to "go down among the lowly ... to whom we are bound by ties of race and sex."[42] Critics complained that this was a presumptuous and elitist stance, but Terrell and other social activists, like women in the Settlement House Movement, knew that holding "the lowly" at a distance would neither improve lives nor fulfill their own duties to abolish the vicious, derogatory stereotypes that disparaged all African Americans. Training and resources to help mothers raise their families healthfully and with pride could instill "self-respect which is both an incentive to effort and a safeguard against wrong-doing."[43] Mutual self-help offered hope for respect.

Not every person of color shared Terrell's and Washington's optimism about building cultural respect for both individual and community through self-help. African Americans had dramatically different expectations after emancipation about the chances of modifying others' attitudes, and internal tensions about class fed into long-running debates about strategies and goals for improvement. These differences cast into deep relief the strong consensus about self-help in the 1880s through the 1910s, unlike the mainstream's growing deference to the myth of self-made success. Thus, among thousands of pages of advice and prized examples of successful people published by African American leaders, the phrase "self-made" rarely appeared. For example, it appeared only once in more than 700 pages of 1902's *Progress of a Race: The Remarkable Advancement of the Colored American*. Deep within an abundance of stories about African Americans, the only person so described was the White abolitionist William Lloyd Garrison. He received that title to compare him to Wendell Phillips, another leading abolitionist, but from an elite Boston family. The term also appeared but twice in *The College of Life* with its nearly 1,000 pages of stories intended to inspire *Self-Improvement for the Colored Race*, according to its subtitle. The first instance concluded a biography of Frederick Douglass – a "noble specimen of a self-made man"; the second appeared merely in passing in a section on phrenology written by a White contributor.[44] Calls for self-help, in contrast, were ubiquitous.

Even an essay with the title "Carve Out Your Own Fortune" in *The College of Life* was not about money or self-seeking. It featured men whose life stories merited admiration for "industry and self-reliance," but it measured their successes in terms of public service to their "race's welfare" – as abolitionists, scholars, lawyers, political leaders, and so on. Its half-dozen stories illustrate the essay's opening sentence: "The world will not start of itself and go for you." True, they "carved out their own fortunes and have risen to eminence by the might of their own inherent ability and determination," but here the term "fortune" was less about money than life's outcomes. One among these "shining names," John M. Langston, was Virginia's first Black Representative to Congress, elected in 1888, a "popular leader and the powerful and true friend of his race and blood." A second, I. Garland Penn, "strives hard in the upbuilding of his race, and is meeting with unbounded success." The stories of these "rising men of the race" and those of hundreds of others celebrated in *The College of Life* mentioned riches only as tools – the means to a nobler end, not the end itself. They offered plenty of advice for worldly success, but aimed to "inspire us to noble actions." Another essay fervently objected to "the rule now" that prioritized "self-interest, without regard to others."[45] Again, nothing novel here within the era's inspirational narratives – except the absence of stories crediting and praising individuals for being self-made without regard for or obligation to their communities.

Regardless of who they followed or their approach to race relations, Black activists broadly proclaimed, as did Booker T. Washington in his widely reprinted 1905 essay "Negro Self-Help," that "the Negro is constantly displaying the quality of self-help – the most important and significant force in the uplift of any person or race." He began that essay praising "the individual struggles and sacrifices of colored youth to secure an education … and the knowledge they crave." He regretted, however, that "the aid given the Negro race by philanthropic white people" and government funds had received disproportionate public attention. The public should also know "what the Negro himself has been doing during the past forty years … thru [their] religious organizations." Two-thirds of Black adults belonged to churches, and all of those were "contributing something toward the expenses of the schools and colleges." He also highlighted as a "form of self-help" voluntary tax on "Negro communities" to extend the public school year.[46] Individual students should not have to struggle alone.

The first convention of the National Negro Business League (NNBL) in the summer of 1900 provided opportunities for about 400 businesspeople (mostly men but some women) from thirty-four states to share their stories, challenges, and successes. For all their pride in their accomplishments and communities, the almost 300-page *Proceedings* contained much about individuals' efforts at self-help and community improvement, but without any explicit reference to "self-made" as an individualist achievement. A leading African American newspaper, the *New York Age*, described the NNBL as "an organization which has accomplished inestimable good for the Afro-American people, by stimulating in them the saving principle of self-help in business matters." Dr. A. C. Dungee of Montgomery, Alabama, concluded from the stories "that the Negro has at last awakened to the idea of self-help." Observing that "though many of us feel that manly sense of independence which comes with self-reliance," he asked that everyone "feel our indebtedness" to each other, whether successful or "struggling," and, thereby, build "the strength developed by self-help and helping others."[47]

Well-known female African American historical figures include Sojourner Truth and Harriet Tubman (activists for abolition and female suffrage), Maggie Lena Walker (benevolent society leader, bank founder and president), Ida B. Wells-Barnett (author and anti-lynching activist), and Mary McLeod Bethune (education activist and school founder). Each of their private and public lives wrapped around and went through benevolent societies and churches – institutions with long traditions among African Americans that stretch back into the seventeenth century. Stories of these women's courage and achievements almost always unfolded in the context of the institutions they worked in and for. All were unwavering advocates of self-help for uplifting themselves and their communities.

This was equally true for Madam C. J. Walker (1867–1919); however, stories about her have typically neglected the social institutions that fostered and helped her as she built a fabulous fortune. Born to a formerly enslaved couple, Sarah Breedlove was the first among her siblings to be born after the Civil War. Orphaned at seven, she married at fourteen, but then found herself supporting a child alone at twenty when her husband died. She took her daughter, Lelia, to St. Louis, where her brothers had built their lives as active members of the St. Paul African Methodist Episcopal (AME) Church, which welcomed her and strengthened her religious faith. The Black middle-class ladies who founded and operated the St. Louis Colored Orphans' Home also welcomed her and Lelia. Along her difficult path, Walker regretted that she had received her only formal education during a few months as a child in a church school. She was determined that her daughter would have more, and agreed to allow Lelia to stay at the orphanage parttime in order to attend school. Walker never forgot those women's kindnesses and the opportunities they offered Lelia and her for education and community.[48]

In 1903, Walker met and began working as an agent for Annie Turnbo Malone, an African American woman who had developed an effective hair care product. This opened a path out of the harsh life of a laundress. That opportunity to climb was aided by occasions to observe and learn decorum from Black elites, such as the delegations attending the NACW's convention in her church during the 1904 St. Louis World's Fair, as well as the women of local benevolent societies. Although she was struggling financially herself, Walker followed their lead into the St. Paul's Mite Missionary Society, contributing what she could and raising money for people even worse off. When she moved to Denver in 1905, she established her life and budding entrepreneurship in a thriving Black neighborhood with an abundance of benevolent organizations and churches. She started in Denver as a boarding house cook while selling Malone's products but soon developed her own products and methods and advertised extensively. Before long, she adapted her new husband's name and became Madam C. J. Walker, befitting a lady of grace.[49]

Madam Walker thus began her way to a fortune. To build a national business, Walker traveled the country for almost two years in 1906 and 1907, reaching out to AME and Baptist churches and fraternal organizations in each town for demonstration venues and communication channels. While there, she trained agents in "The Walker System" and promoted mail-order sales. Over the coming years, her income grew at a phenomenal pace because she built networks and trained thousands of agents – Black women who could begin their own climbs toward respectable livelihoods. True to her dedication to racial uplift, as she traveled and attended conventions for the next dozen years, she also taught the value of social work, of self-help for women and their communities. Thus, Walker quite purposefully aligned with Booker T. Washington's message. Even at her pinnacle of achievement in 1918, Walker remained so attuned to the self-help ethos that when she spoke to the NACW's biennial convention back in Denver, she emphasized that "none of us may live our own lives because we are all dependent on one another." That same year, Walker spoke intently to a convention of her agents, reminding them of "my duty, your duty" to "advance the best interests of the Race" by helping the least fortunate, especially new migrants from the South. "Bring them into your clubs and other organizations where they ... can catch the inspiration of higher and better living."[50] She knew well the benefits of such outreach from her own hard years.

Madam Walker epitomized the self-help ideal. As she famously told Booker T. Washington and the 1912 NNBL convention, "I am a woman that came from the cotton fields of the South. I was promoted from there to the wash-tub. Then I was promoted to the cook kitchen, and from there I promoted myself into the business of manufacturing hair goods and preparations." Underscoring her point, she declared, "I am not ashamed of my humble beginning." There was no mythmaking exaggeration of obscure origins here. More to the point, she did not neglect the institutions and communities that nurtured her, in her own storytelling, guidance to others, activism, or resolute and generous philanthropy.[51] In other words, Walker purposefully honored all aspects of self-help. She lifted as she climbed.

Stories about Madam Walker have drifted closer, over time, into alignment with the myth of self-made success. No one ever questioned her rags-to-riches credentials, but as a Black woman she was not immediately or readily invited into the pantheon of the "self-made" among mainstream storytellers. In 1917, the *New York Times Magazine* devoted a full-page to her newly completed thirty-four room grand mansion as "one of the show places on the Hudson." Noting with some amusement neighbors' "astonishment" at her "color," the author enthused about Walker's achievements, wealth, and tasteful spending. Extensive quotations described Walker's rise through "perseverance, persistency, and hard work" as well as her ambitions to use her wealth "to help my race." Despite an abundance of admiration for Walker's character and self-improvement, which might well have earned the "self-made" honorific for a White man, this mainstream story merely pointed out that "She is self-educated, of course." In contrast, upon her death in 1919, an editorial in the African American *New York Age* emphasized that this "remarkable woman" had abilities and determination beyond "mere money-making." Only after outlining her dedication to "movements tending toward the uplift of the race" did it refer to "this self-made woman" who could inspire "all members of the race to work zealously and persistently." The result of such work "should not only be financial success for the individual but the ability to help the race on its upward stride."[52]

A century later, the myth of self-made success stands on firm ground, and broader swaths of humanity qualify for the status. In that spirit, Netflix brought Madam Walker to the public with its 2020 miniseries *Self-Made: Inspired by the Life of Madam C. J. Walker*. It purports to be "based on a true story," but it nonetheless downplays or overlooks much of what is inspiring in Walker's life. Instead, the production's official one-sentence description conforms to the now-standard templates of self-making, measuring merit by wealth and neglecting social contributions as well as resources: "An African American washerwoman rises from poverty to build a beauty empire and become the first female self-made millionaire." As if there were not drama enough in Walker's life from the racism and sexism she endured, *Self-Made* exaggerates clashes between individuals. In keeping with the "self-made" label, this portrayal minimizes the community supports essential to bringing Walker's brilliance and dynamism to fruition as well as her own generosity toward the community during and after her rise. The self-help that Walker and generations of African American activists have hoped to inspire gets buried by boilerplate individualist drama and cheerleading, further undermined by inexplicable bouts of dancing and psychedelic lights.[53]

Success stories like Madam Walker's and others' whom self-help advisors highlighted offered hope and guidance. The "rising generation" to which many self-help stories referred would surely build on the "Progress of a Generation," as Washington began his introduction to *Progress of a Race*. "Springing from the darkest depths of slavery and sorrowful ignorance to the heights of manhood and power almost at one bound," he noted, "the Negro furnishes an unparalleled example of possibility." The *Kansas City Sun* similarly urged its readers to witness Walker speak in 1918 at a local church for "inspiration for the great work which each individual member of the race must do." Progress was possible, and this "Noted Philanthropist, Lecturer, Traveler and Most Wonderful Negro Business Woman in the World" could inspire everyone. Tragically, that optimism fell victim to the evils of Jim Crow. Decades of harassment, derision, cruelty, legal constraints, and devastating destruction of successful Black businesses and even whole districts, such as in Atlanta, Georgia, in 1906 and Tulsa, Oklahoma, in 1921, turned self-help strategies from goals of advancement to defense.[54]

In response to worsening conditions, many African Americans came to see economic and cultural viability "behind the walls of segregation" as their best option, according to the Black economist Abram L. Harris during the 1930s. The competitive economy, lack of access to capital, coercive legal systems, and unchecked racism fostered small "defensive enterprises" in service businesses rather than in capital-intensive production businesses. Harris reluctantly accepted that the "hope of creating an independent black economy dates back to pre-Civil War days" and that it had revived because of "the differential disadvantages suffered by the Negro masses as compared with the white since the depression of 1929." Moreover, "Mob Violence" compounded Blacks' economic and legal constraints, making it yet more difficult to compete in the general economy. He regretted that while this parallel Black economy could be profitable for some and "made possible the development of black respectability," it also "effectively stifles the demand for social equality and civil rights," which gratified the South's "white leaders of opinion."[55]

Despite often fierce and violent opposition that was compounded by constant affronts, African American communities persisted, turning inward as needed, bolstered by self-help practices and stories. At all levels, activists recognized the necessity to pool individual and community resources and to push back against the mainstream's growing acceptance of individualist ideology.[56] And yet, within business enterprises, John Henry Harmon, Jr., regretted that in 1929 "more than ninety per cent of the Negro businesses of today are individual in form rather than cooperative." As a consequence, few outlived their founders, and they could not compete with "the larger syndicates" for capital or trade. Nor could they grow or "efficiently" conduct a "modern business," which often required "a corporate form." Instead, "as long as Negroes remain individualists so long will they remain weak and helpless in business." He encouraged "the co-operative spirit" among businesspeople and leaders because "a people who had once staked so much upon the exercise of civic rights, now had to work out schemes for solving their problems in another way," namely, through collective efforts. Too many businessmen succeeded only because of the "unrelenting toil of the wives and children ... [who] toiled all but slavishly to assure success."[57] Such practices could not sustain growth or longevity, unlike formal practices and corporate structures that can hold businesses together over time, providing opportunities for communities. Neither Harmon nor the other authors of the 1929 *The Negro as a Business Man* had any use for the term "self-made." Fantasies of self-made success did not carry much weight in this culture under assault.[58]

TURNING TO THE *SELF* IN SELF-HELP

Unlike the genre of collective self-help narratives, the stories now most readily identified with "self-help" balanced self-agency and context differently. They placed full responsibility on individuals as the agents of their fates, feeding fantasies of self-making measured by affluence. However, the earliest of the well-known advocates of what became known as "positive thinking" was Mary Baker Eddy (1821–1910), founder of Christian Science. Eddy grew up during the Second Great Awakening and taught troubled people to seek health and comfort through faith based on her interpretations of the Bible. Eddy's formulations were individualist – she had no patience for the social benefits of most religions – but not at all materialist. Yet her successors spread the power of mental determination into the realm of material success. Years later, Eddy's writing inspired the founder of Fuller Brush Company, Alfred Fuller (1885–1973), with "confidence" to enhance his salesmanship.[59]

Among the most prominent of the self-help masters, Russell H. Conwell (1843–1925) began giving his "Acres of Diamonds" oration in 1861 and published it in various forms, including as a book in 1915. This Yale-trained minister preached that people's struggles sanctified their material goals. Before more than 6,000 cheering audiences over a half century, he proclaimed that "the number of poor who are to be sympathized with is very small." Only a few had not made their own sorry fates. Opportunity was everywhere, and everyone "ought to get rich. Moreover, it is your duty to get rich."[60]

Less remembered now than Conwell, but hugely popular in the early decades of the twentieth century, Frank Channing Haddock (1853–1915) began the first chapter of *Power of Will: A Practical Companion Book for Unfoldment of Powers of Mind* quoting Conwell to insist that "Success has no secret." Haddock drew on that master's authority to explain, through more than two hundred editions after the book's debut in 1907, that "Your brain matter is your sole workshop for success in this world – and possibly the next, too." Because *"all rests with your will,"* he assured readers, as had phrenologists, *"we can make our own brains... if only we have Wills strong enough to take the trouble."* Therefore, "the real wonder-worker that builds your life structure in this world is – POWER OF WILL." According to Haddock and his successors, the ambitious person must undergo psychological self-fashioning before tackling the practical actions that success requires. Failure was, therefore, a mark of one's lack of will.[61] A self-made failure.

Another professional motivator, Orison Swett Marden (1848–1924), published over fifty books and the magazine *Success*, usually promoting individual efforts toward success for women as well as men. He often described how Britain's Samuel Smiles (1812–1904) had inspired him as a youth to imagine success beyond his origins. Smiles had sent *Self-Help* into the world in 1859, and it became very popular on both sides of the Atlantic. Smiles spent much of his life as a social reformer, and, like Franklin, he sought to inspire self-improvement that fostered community improvement. Thus, popular clichés about *Self-Help* dismayed him. As he explained in the 1866 second edition, the title had become more prominent than his message: the *self* more than the *help*. The public, especially people who had not read the book, misinterpreted it to suggest "a eulogy of selfishness." This was "the opposite" of his beliefs in "individual duty, which is the glory of manly character," and that "the duty of helping one's self in the highest sense involves the helping of one's neighbors."[62]

Marden found a copy of *Self-Help* in an attic and took it as a personal call to overcome worldly challenges for profit – very much as Thomas Mellon had (mis)interpreted Franklin's autobiography. The stories his biographer, Margaret Connolly, told in 1925 about him hewed to the standard self-made success line: Marden's "own victory over the hardest of circumstances and his remarkable accomplishments in the face of grinding poverty, bitter opposition and heartrending discouragement, furnish outstanding testimony to the soundness of his psychology." His "first-hand knowledge" through a life of "struggle and triumph," she affirmed, gave him credibility with which "he heartened and inspired ambitious strugglers in many lands." Connolly described Marden's most famous book, *Pushing to the Front* (1894), as "a veritable romance of success." She was sure that "it shows the sources of success, reveales [sic] to men their hidden strength – that godlike power, latent in every human being, which in every age has enabled man to perform the 'impossible.'"[63]

Such commercial approaches to "self-help" are less complicated than those that recognize contextual factors in people's outcomes. Among the twentieth century's most unabashedly individualist and simplistic boosters was Dale Carnegie (1888–1955), who followed in the wake of cheerleaders like Conwell, Haddock, and Marden. Like the other "positive thinkers," Carnegie urged aspirants to seek individual worldly success, even if at others' expense. He applied his own experiences in sales to promote strategies in the positive thinking tradition by which everyone could move ahead profitably, and thereby sell anything to anyone, to succeed in any situation, regardless of origins. Accordingly, his iconic and perennially best-selling book, *How to Win Friends and Influence People*, has promised a key to *self*-help since 1936. Its sensational debut during the Great Depression reflected how Americans sought ways to pull themselves up by their personalities: within three weeks, it sold 70,000 copies, and one million in three years.[64] With the arrival of prosperity after World War II, Carnegie's promises of self-making continued to promote belief in and hopes for self-agency, by then in a growth context in which people actually had good chances to improve their circumstances.

SELF-MAKING IN THE ROARING TWENTIES

Although the phrase "self-made" turned up in many venues and for many purposes within the 1920s' common parlance, the meanings consistently referred to climbing an economic ladder. On the surface, economic growth in the 1920s apparently vindicated material ambition and assured success for the worthy. Yet, despite popular stereotypes of the Roaring Twenties with their Flappers, moving pictures, gangsters, sensational speakeasies, radios, and other novel consumer products for the middle and upper classes, below the surface, multitudes struggled, especially in rural areas and urban slums that crushed the promise of self-improvement for many.[65]

In the 1920s, "self-made" appeared in books, newspapers, and other popular venues conveying a focus on individualist economic gain that would have been objectionable a century earlier. This worldly meaning was so pervasive and casual that no one bothered to explain it, even those who rejected the notion as out of date. For example, in 1924 publisher Richard J. Walsh predicted the imminent "doom of the self-made man" in the elite literary and current events journal, *The Century Magazine*. He projected that "The inexorable hand of competition will thrust him away" out of "the delicate organism of industry." A self-made man in business was no longer any more qualified than a self-made – that is, uneducated – doctor or lawyer. This essay saw daylight at least seven more times in the next few months.[66]

As did earlier meanings of self-making, those in the twenties often emphasized a lack of formal education, but in keeping with a narrow, modern ambition of economic climbing. As *Al Capone: The Biography of a Self-Made Man* explained in

1930, the gangster Capone (1899–1947) ended his schooling with the fourth grade "to help his parents in the struggle for existence in the slums." Fortunately for him, an "urbane" mentor had pulled him up and "instructed him in the social graces," thereby "polishing" this "Horatio Alger of prohibition."[67] No less a guide to social "polishing" than Emily Post offered a section of her 1922 bestselling *Etiquette in Society, in Business, in Politics and at Home* to guide "The Self-Made Man and World-Made Manners" for those whose formal education was limited. Assuming, like everyone else, that the measure of self-made success was financial, she augmented her social arguments with the assertion that the "business genius" would find his "authority in business would be even greater" with "polished manners."[68]

Obituaries and other public tributes often praised men whose careers included service, as of old. However, what made these men "self-made" in the 1920s was their economic success, not their civic contributions – no preachers or teachers here.[69] "A Well Made Man" was the title of a 1920 tribute to Judge William D. McHugh that credited him as one of the "very successful self-made men" who were also good citizens, unlike the "commonly ill-made," self-made men. A typical obituary of this genre in January 1930 reported that Vermont State Senator Selden C. Greene had "learned a trade" and "finally became head of a prosperous business." What earned his special praise here was that he "represented a swiftly passing type of self-made men," having "served the public in many capacities." On a much larger scale, by 1923 James Couzens had acquired a fortune of $30,000,000 as an early leader in Ford Motor Company. He earned praise then for his "career and character," having served in multiple administrative roles in Detroit, including as mayor of that city until his appointment to the US Senate in 1922, where he served fourteen years.[70]

Some 1920s references to self-made men questioned the cost of self-making because a hard-hearted focus on money required "self-made millionaires ... to become mechanical calculators." Others found the self-made man concept amusing. Their syndicated column fillers appeared in newspapers everywhere and showed how taken-for-granted the modern meaning had become, if irreverently so. One such observation quipped that "There are a lot of self made men, but you never hear a man who has made a fool of himself claiming the credit for it." In another, a boy asks, "Pa, what's a self-made man?" to which the father replied, "Usually a bore, my son, when he starts talking about it." Poets added their levity: "Of many a self-made man we know/ There can be little doubt;/ In some respects he'd be improved/ Had he given the contract out."[71] "Self-made" could also appear glib when applied to women, as in an article on "self-made eyebrows" that imitated actor Greta Garbo's style "to improve on nature." Or a column syndicated out of New York advising on "New Type of Venus, Self-Made Beauty" that advised women on what *not* to do to be attractive.[72]

The descriptor "self-made man" also found its way into entertainment venues. The popular performer and social commentator Will Rogers wrote *Letters of a Self-Made Diplomat to His President* in 1926. He implied his rough-and-ready roots, but never mentioned them beyond his choice of title, which was all he needed to remind audiences of his country-style persona. A late 1920s newspaper fiction series described "the inferiority complex that is the bugaboo of even the most completely successful of self-made men." *The Golden Bed*, a book, newspaper serial, and Cecil B. DeMille silent film appeared in 1925 to tell the story of a "self-made millionaire" and his "all too human combination of strength and weakness" in affairs of the heart. Other silent films included *A Self-Made Man* in 1922 and a comedy, *A Self-Made Failure*, in 1925.[73] The term was quite fully embedded in popular culture, taken for granted and ripe for the coming decade's rhetorical contests for political authority.

Meanwhile, the related concept of individualism flourished in Roaring Twenties' popular culture venues, reinforcing the modern, self-oriented variant of self-making. The frequency of "individualism" and "individualist" in books and the popular press grew in the 1920s, presaging their even higher incidence in the next decade when they reached their pre-1960 peak.[74] The phrase "rugged American individualism" appeared in newspapers at least by 1903, and in 1909 with a rather dark interpretation as "that characteristic of American civilization, rugged individualism in the pursuit of bank accounts."[75] Occasional appearances (273 in a newspaper archive for that decade) continued through the 1920s until Herbert Hoover (1874–1964) raised its profile in 1928 during his successful presidential campaign (44,018 articles in the same newspaper archive for the 1930s.)[76] One of America's most respected men, he had directed humanitarian relief in Europe during and after World War I, and he served as Secretary of Commerce through the Twenties before becoming president in 1929. He wrote a small book in 1922, *American Individualism*, arguing for an ideal that stimulated initiative but was "tempered with that firm and fixed ideal of American individualism – *an equality of opportunity*" and "sense of service." No reference at all to "*rugged* individualism."[77]

Pitches for individualism and its genre of self-help appeared in every print medium and public forum, sometimes even pulpits – embraced hopefully in the Roaring Twenties and desperately in the Great Depression. Yet, for all their fervent hyping, none of these promotions altered the basic storylines of the myth even as they added urgency and promises. Likewise, as they had for decades, hordes of dime novelists and other popular media adventure writers continued to crank out stories to fill imaginations with heroic tales. All of these entrepreneurs, whether in fiction or coaching, spread and validated the myth of heroic self-agency, but their goals were either commercial or instructive, to raise or exploit others' hopes.[78] More apprehensive storytellers would take the next steps in the myth's evolution after political and cultural crises stirred them to action during the New Deal.

9

Stories Against the New Deal

"The chief business of the American people is business" seemed a fitting slogan to many Americans when President Calvin Coolidge pronounced it in 1925. And until the Crash of 1929, the decade's political leadership at local and national levels agreed with Coolidge.[1] Championing business success and prosperity prevailed in mainstream culture and politics, and in that context the meaning of self-made success seemed settled: merit measured by financial achievement. Boosters such as P. T. Barnum and his successors promoting the *self*-help approach of so-called "positive thinkers," including Dale Carnegie, had hardened belief in self-agency into a mindset that proclaimed individuals' power over their lives, regardless of their circumstances. Together, these storytellers deprived the self-making concept of its older associations with service for the common good.

Such overconfidence and ambitions contributed significantly to the financial Crash of 1929, ensuing economic disaster, and the despair of the Great Depression. Popular attitudes toward business and its practices soured: a critic asked in 1933, "Where Are Those Mighty Self-Made Men" and their "genial if somewhat pompous accounts" of their successes? Nonetheless, business's advocates did not yield the floor. Instead, they turned from the complacent comfort of cultural and political dominance to militant defensiveness, which included underscoring the myth of self-made success. For example, on January 1, 1930, the Newspaper Enterprise Association, a Howard-Scripps syndicate, distributed an "encouraging New Year's message" from Charles M. Schwab (1862–1939). This "outstanding self-made man" had made a fortune as a mutually made man among Pennsylvania's steelmen, pulled up by Andrew Carnegie and his associates. Unchastened by the financial collapse, he assured "the ambitious young men of today" that they had "more great, wide-open opportunities" than "when I was young."[2]

Even at that moment, for some the myth of self-making justified evaluating success and failure as individual matters: a global financial collapse did not excuse either despair or attempts at systemic change. To reinforce that standard and to resist reforms, business advocates invested enormous resources in a contest for cultural authority that included assertions of the myth of self-made success like

Schwab's statement: "I don't know what human limits are."[3] To defend their collapsed political and cultural order against community-based reform, conservatives built a corpus of narratives that accused reformers of threatening Americans' freedom and opportunities.[4] Among their rhetorical tools were stories of self-made success that they *imagined* as the legacy of Horatio Alger, Jr., a prolific nineteenth-century author of books for youth. Their partisan revival of Alger's renown aimed to legitimate their vision for America with an illusion about its past.

"HORATIO ALGER AT THE BRIDGE"

In May 1936, the *Saturday Evening Post* published "Horatio Alger at the Bridge." Boyden Sparkes's six-page, illustrated article surveyed "our successful men" to learn how the work they did in their youth provided "training for the future" while "building character." The title alluded to Lord Macaulay's then popular poem "Horatius at the Bridge," which extols a hero who, according to legend, risked death defending Rome against overwhelming odds.[5] The sense of crisis that inspired the *Post*, one of the nation's most popular magazines and famous for its heartwarming covers, called for militancy in battles won or lost in the political arena but waged with stories in the cultural arena. Thus, the hero called on to avert ruin was not a warrior, but a storyteller – Horatio Alger, Jr., the genteel nineteenth-century author of more than one hundred books read by millions of young people. Such was the sense of danger that conservative storytellers reinvented Alger as a capitalist hero and appropriated his strive-and-succeed theme as if it were about self-made success, a term he never used.

What had provoked the *Saturday Evening Post*'s sense of crisis in 1936? After the 1920s' greed and inequality undid the economy and Franklin D. Roosevelt became president in 1933, community-oriented advocates regained prominence and guided the New Deal's efforts to save capitalism from the capitalists. Widespread expansion of government powers brought new regulations, taxes, social welfare programs, and labor empowerment, challenging the system in which business leaders had generally held the upper hand. Employers had not only controlled the sites of production, they had powerful support among those who controlled civil governance, from police and militia to officials and courts. Previous decades of labor militancy and unionizing had forcefully challenged employers' authority, to be sure, motivating them to activism, including the formation of organizations to advocate on their behalf.[6] However, never had businessmen and their advocates so profoundly lost their influence among government's various levels and branches as during the 1930s, and labor's renewed activism further challenged employers' hegemony.

So deeply had individualism, the credo of American business, lost its cultural authority in the Great Depression that a grassroots, nonpartisan association rejected it outright as a way to address problems. "The philosophy of self-sufficiency ... is a bone-crushing juggernaut whose final achievement is ruin." This affirmation exemplifies Alcoholics Anonymous (AA) and its approaches to inspire self-help and to support those in need. According to its classic 1953 handbook *Twelve Steps and Twelve Traditions*, AA was founded in 1935, when "The struggle for wealth, power, and prestige was tearing humanity apart as never before." As people on other sorts of margins had already discovered, self-help – in the sense of individual and community mutual improvement – could best meet their needs. Against the grain of rugged individualism, AA reckoned with a "paradox": "The group must survive or the individual will not." Therefore, "common welfare comes first." Their self-help approach "cherished" the whole, which, in turn, "lavishes ... devoted care upon its individual members." This reckoning noted that in mid-century America "the word 'dependence'" seemed "distasteful." However, properly directed and balanced with personal responsibility, dependence can be a "chief source of strength." Likewise, "Humility, as a word and as an ideal, has a very bad time of it in our world." Whether or not Alcoholics Anonymous has approached the troubles of alcoholism optimally, its challenges to a harsh bootstraps individualism have reached many tens of millions of people over the last century, helping them swim against the individualist mainstream. On a wider perspective, too many "problems besides alcohol," AA cautioned, "will not yield to a headlong assault powered by the individual alone."[7]

After 1932, the nation's officials and agencies had both a new mandate and a new inclination to alter the balance of cultural and workplace authority. It's no wonder, then, that the New Deal so unnerved businessmen and their allies. Although most reforms infringed less on businesses than conservatives feared, especially in light of contemporary European extremism, many invested in rebuilding public regard for business.[8] Whether high-profile business and financial leaders, with nationally eminent names such as du Pont and Pew, or businessmen whose names carried only local prominence, they were angry, fearful of the progressive state, anxious about the increasingly alienated middle class, and contemptuous of the disheartened poor. Girding for the second presidential election since the Crash, pro-business conservatives insisted that individuals control their own fates and that all who were willing to work – to pull themselves up by their bootstraps – fared just fine in the land of the free. Discounting the systemic problems that the Great Depression had made so apparent to others, they challenged New Deal programs, such as Social Security, that, they believed, dangerously offered workers a free pass. For these partisans, the New Deal and the rejection of traditional deference it reflected were the danger at the nation's bridge.

Conservatives reacted in many ways to what they perceived as dangers on political, intellectual, legal, labor, and economic fronts.[9] They competed for cultural authority with politicized phrases, especially "free enterprise" and "the American Way," clichés that convey a tenet that branches of government should not interfere with how businesses function even though they generally assist businesses at the expense of other citizens and communities.[10] Because cultural authority is the basis for trust, social esteem and political authority require it. Stories reign in that arena.[11]

Thus, with rekindled urgency, twentieth-century business advocates turned to America's imagined past for many of their rhetorical tools. In addition to allusions to Horatio Alger, they revived the term "bootstraps," warping that concept. Back in the day when people actually wore boots with straps, one way to mock a man was to joke that he was "attempting to lift himself by his boot-straps, or, what is much better, is '*sitting in a wheelbarrow trying to wheel himself*,'" as a critic said of a politician's proposals in 1843. Another observer equated "heady and factious" opponents "of the party in power" to the "fabulous individual who undertook to lift himself by his boot-straps [but] might better have been idly sucking his thumbs." Similarly, government policies that did not support "practical education" were in 1836 as "preposterous" as attempting to perform that foolish trick. Such uses emphasized either "being too enterprising" or foolish in imagining that individual efforts could overcome lack of communal supports. It took the better part of a century to reinvent bootstrapping as something admirable, once its physical and logical absurdity was forgotten: in 1928 a newspaper column filler jested that "There are fewer self-made men now... Also, they've stopped putting boot-straps on boots."[12]

BRINGING HORATIO ALGER INTO THE TWENTIETH CENTURY

Decades after his death in 1899, hazy memories of Alger's "strive and succeed" tales inspired storytelling in hopes of shining a favorable light on traditional hierarchies of political, economic, and cultural authority, hierarchies about which the Great Depression had cast widespread doubt. Those defensive tales distilled the "pluck" of success from Alger's "pluck and luck" plots and filtered out the luck that Alger had featured prominently. Since 1933, opponents of the welfare and regulatory state have forged a streamlined, one-dimensional icon out of Alger's narratives, despite his hope that they would "have the effect of enlisting the sympathies of his readers in behalf of the unfortunate children whose life is described ... to ameliorate their condition," as he wrote in the preface to *Ragged Dick* (1868), his most famous tale.[13] Instead, Alger's name has come to symbolize an individualistic and often harsh "bootstraps" mythology.

Horatio Alger, Jr. (1832–1899) was a product of his family's deep Calvinist roots and the Romanticism that had flourished in the New England of his youth, including at Harvard where he trained for the clergy. Like many contemporaries, he struggled to reconcile tensions among those ethical systems and a volatile economy and nation. Through it all, despite his failure as a preacher, he abided by the Puritans' ancient determination to serve both faith and community through self-improvement – work, duty, civility, and betterment.[14] Accordingly, in 1857, one of Alger's first publications excoriated the idle rich. "Nothing to Do: A Tilt at Our Best Society" was a sledgehammer of an epic poem that may have embarrassed his literary sensibilities later, but he never deviated from its derision of the self-serving, oblivious wealthy.[15] Instead, like so many of his contemporaries, Alger championed "character," which referred to a person's ethics and effort and was the subject of definitions and didactic pronouncements too numerous to count. "Good" character was then a touchstone for balancing worldly ambitions and inherited values of service and skepticism toward wealth.[16]

Even though "a Horatio Alger story" became almost synonymous with the myth of rags-to-riches after his death, throughout his life, Alger favored cooperation over competition. This is evident in his stories, where aid to distressed neighbors and fair-minded employers always look better than seeking riches. Virtue, not entrepreneurship, lit the path to success and esteem. Wage cuts, stock and price manipulation, and claims that business success was its own reward never fared well, while cooperation between citizens and workers did. In short, a capitalism propelled by ambitions of rags-to-riches or rugged individualism had no place in Alger's ethos.[17]

There is no better evidence of the striking contrast between Alger's writings and the twentieth-century's iconic Alger myth than his 1872 *Strive and Succeed*, volume 4 in the "Luck and Pluck Series." In this novel, Walter Conrad, the tale's hero, achieved success by striving, to be sure, but his goal was not to make a fortune or to experience adventure. Instead, he sought to recover his family's purloined wealth from an evil businessman, whom he tracked across country and outsmarted. Rather than enter business himself after retrieving his family's assets, Walter returned to boarding school to complete his preparation for college. Moreover, he quickly shared his assets to facilitate a family reconciliation and to send a cousin to school, properly outfitted. He was never in rags and never sought riches as anything more than the means for self-improvement, helping others, and contributing to his community. Hence the book's subtitle, *The Progress of Walter Conrad*, which was reminiscent of the Calvinist classic, *Pilgrim's Progress*.[18]

Beginning in the 1860s and continuing well after his death in 1899, many millions of people, especially boys and the adults who bought books for them, eagerly read his tales. To compete with dime novels in the later decades of his life,

Figure 9.1 Institutions in the mid twentieth century often looked back to two important historical figures, Benjamin Franklin and Horatio Alger, Jr. This 1948 photograph of a window display of Alger's books at the Franklin Society for Building and Saving features a banner reminding passers-by that Alger "taught a valuable lesson in *THRIFT*." This display more accurately depicts Alger's messages than did opponents of the New Deal who imagined that his stories promoted a rough, bootstraps ethos.
(Photo by © Ken O'Brien Collection / CORBIS / Corbis via Getty Images)

Alger lowered the moralistic tone of his books and raised their adventurism but still didn't fare well in the coarsening market. He tried to reach dime novels' audiences with ethical messages and criticized their sensationalism because "they do much harm and are very objectionable," yet he still lost his traditional markets among schools and libraries and faded from view by the 1920s.[19]

Horatio Alger's name reappeared later in some surprising places. In 1936 – the same year as "Horatio Alger at the Bridge" – a panel at Harvard University considered anointing alumnus Alger to a proposed (but apparently not completed) literary hall of fame. Bruce Catton, a future Pulitzer Prize-winning historian who wrote for a Scripps-Howard newspaper syndicate at the time, argued "Why Not?" Although Catton agreed with most well-educated adults that Alger's books lacked artistic sophistication, he declared that none of Harvard's "distinguished alumni" had "influenced the life of his time more profoundly" than had Alger through the extraordinary reach of his stories.[20]

Catton recognized that, by 1936, Alger "had ceased to be anything more than a name." Instead of the long-deceased author's own plotlines, if readers recalled anything, Catton, like most others, recollected the abridged versions that had posthumously replaced Alger's full stories. By the mid 1930s, Catton concluded, Alger was misremembered for taking "the rags-to-riches myth, the log-cabin-to-the-White-House saga, and rivet[ing] it into the brains of whole generations of Americans." Catton explained, the "Horatio Alger story became part of the American credo – in a sense, it was the American credo. It was what we all believed." This "expression of our faith that America was the land of opportunity" contradicted what Catton saw in 1936. As did the notion that individual merit always triumphed over adversity and inequality. "We have made a good deal of trouble for ourselves in the last decade or so by refusing to admit that life isn't quite so simple as Horatio Alger told us it was."[21]

Nonetheless, business advocates who adopted, adapted, and distorted Alger's legacy in the twentieth century promoted that "simple" notion of inequality and its justifications. As Catton surmised, "a good deal of trouble" has resulted.

STORIES ABOUT WORK, CAPITALISM, AND DEMOCRACY

The specific danger that "Horatio Alger at the Bridge" confronted was a proposed Constitutional amendment to ban child labor. Author Sparkes admired successful business leaders and wrote of their triumphs here, as he also did in biographies of Walter P. Chrysler and Alfred P. Sloan, among others. In this 1936 paean to work, he described two dozen successful American businessmen as having "an abundance of experience tending to prove that the surest prescription for starting an American boy toward outstanding success is to let him go to work before he is fully grown." His biographies and testimonials should undercut "so much eagerness among the New Dealers" to legislate away youth's opportunities for work. For instance, Benjamin Franklin Affleck, president of a division of United States Steel Corporation, began the article with this basic message: "my education as a man really began when I got a job as a boy, at a boy's pay, in a machine shop." Frederick H. Ecker, president of the Metropolitan Life Insurance Company, went so far as to say that preventing teenage boys from working before they turned eighteen could result in "a situation where there won't be any work for anybody." Sparkes asked S. S. McClure, the magazine publishing "legend," if he would have been "better off" had the government furnished him "with the means of living." McClure responded adamantly, "No! That would have injured a vital part of my spirit, my self-reliance. Self-reliance is one of the most important things a man can acquire." He emphasized, "There is no possibility of proper development unless you have to depend on yourself. That is basic!"[22]

"Work and chores," it seems, did more for boys than schooling. Yet none of Sparkes's exemplars ever worked in dangerous, dead-end jobs in fields, coal mines, or factories of the sorts that the proposed reform targeted. Nor did Sparkes note that grown men were at that moment desperately seeking work in a job-starved economy.[23] With so much at stake – boys' character, capitalism, and even democracy itself – conservatives competed against daily stories of ruin and struggles in print, radio, photographs by Dorothea Lange and Walker Evans, and theaters' newsreels, which all captured grim dramas in both rural and urban settings. Unemployment had exploded from 3.2 percent in 1929 to 8.7 percent the next year, and 24.9 percent in 1933; over 5,000 banks closed, taking their depositors' savings, and sometimes their homes, with them.[24] Millions of women and men sought work of every sort and in every place, often uprooting their families to continue their search.

In contrast to tales about capitalism's blessings, the damage caused by business practices disillusioned many, including artists, writers, musicians, poets, playwrights, actors, and filmmakers, who applied their talents to build stories from their experiences. Together with Roosevelt's critiques of business-as-usual, they aimed for a popular culture in sympathy with laborers that resonated with widespread fear, anger, poignancy, and grief. For example, the 1936 Hollywood movie *My Man Godfrey* confronted the standard view of self-made failure with lines such as, "The only difference between a derelict and a man is a job."[25]

As the flood of rival stories rose, business elites could no longer assume that the citizenry would accept their leadership out of deference to power and position. They had to shape and broadcast stories that explained why the privileged still deserved esteem as well as the practical and economic benefits of their traditional control over the state and the workplace. Similar stories of triumph argued that responsibility for success and failure fell squarely on individuals alone, regardless of their situations, upholding inequality as a defensible result of merit. As did "Horatio Alger at the Bridge," many of those forays also featured grim warnings that American citizens would soon lose freedom and any hope for prosperity unless they resisted the state's encroachment on both business's prerogatives and workers' incentives. They applied the streamlined Alger icon to claim abundant opportunities. "Horatio Alger at the Bridge" confirmed that symbol's potency in the 1930s: it featured his name in the title but never again mentioned him. Alger's name sufficed to herald intent.

Mobilized against the New Deal but continuing well after national prosperity returned, business advocates relentlessly repeated refrains of "strive and succeed," "self-made success," "rags-to-riches," and "rugged individualism" as upbeat applause for their vision of capitalism. Spotlights on pluck eclipsed luck, which generally remained invisible in business advocates' claims to the moral high ground. Although luck comes in many forms, including access to social and financial capital, education, timing, or raw talents, individual pluck was all that they took from Horatio Alger and his stories. Appeals to Alger's legacy also ignored his antiquarian settings, reminiscent of the preindustrial nation that had already gone out-of-date when he wrote. While fortuitous contacts between shoeshine boys or newsboys and wealthy men never provided reliable career paths, their relevance to the twentieth century was more apt for satire than sermons.[26]

One aspect of Alger's stories that conservatives did not have to reimagine was the apparent absence of the state, set as they were decades before the Depression-era's federal government expansion. Except for the occasional kindly policeman, teacher, or judge, there were no pesky state agencies to step in on behalf of the weak or mistreated. Alger certainly recognized that people suffered at the hands of greedy landlords and wicked employers, yet, in his experience, the arms of the state rarely reached out to struggling or endangered people.[27] Instead, before the New Deal, insofar as the government intervened between employers and employees, it typically did so on behalf of the former, as during the 1892 Homestead Strike. This antique void in Alger's stories suited those who claimed them in the twentieth century. Better that Ragged Dick happened along to save a drowning child, thereby earning the gratitude of a wealthy father, than that regulations should force a ferry's owner to erect safety rails and forestall that dramatic opportunity for a plucky young fellow.

HEROIC STORIES TO IMMUNIZE THE NATION

Widespread tragedies after 1929 unsettled trust and confidence in traditional patterns of political, cultural, and social authority, creating a mandate for state and federal governments to step in between businesses and individuals. Despite the hesitant and incremental nature of the New Deal's reforms, they ran counter to business leaders' expectations of respect and deference and appeared dangerously alien to what they saw as *their* nation. Businesspeople often genuinely believed that they had governed the nation's economics and politics in good faith, and some came to believe that the New Deal's experiments in search of solutions to the Depression's crises revealed a sickness that had to be confronted with every possible weapon.[28] For instance, in 1934, Delaware Senator Daniel O. Hastings declared that "the New Deal is like a dangerous disease." As late as 1945, the president of the Pennsylvania Manufacturers' Association and a Republican national committeeman decried the New Deal's "security" programs as a "disease of national morality" that shriveled the willingness to work.[29]

One prolific storyteller for the capitalist status quo was Berton Braley, a self-described "busy bard of business," who published "verses by the thousands" according to his 1966 *New York Times* obituary. Praising American capitalism and industry while condemning state interference and workers' poor attitudes, Braley prospered selling verses to trade publications, such as *Coal Age* and *American Machinist*, as well as to popular magazines such as the *Saturday Evening Post*. In his 1934 memoir, he compared himself favorably to Horatio Alger's "heroes," who, he asserted, had no more "ambition and industry" than he had. In this self-glorifying light, he denounced New Deal policies that he believed rewarded the least ambitious and least industrious at the expense of diligent workers and taxpayers. This theme ran through his 1936 collection of *New Deal Ditties*, which included the verse "Horatio Alger (Up to Date)." The third stanza explains in rhyme this particular symptom of the New Deal disease:

> "Keep trying," Mr. Alger said, "and seize on every chance
> To use your brains and energy to further your advance;
> Keep trying to improve yourself" – (And what you've laid aside
> Will then be confiscated for the Folks Who Never Tried!)

As a measure of Braley's success in pleasing his patrons, the *New York Times* declared in 1934 that his "verse today is as ubiquitous as a Ford car. And like a Ford car, it gets places."[30]

The appreciative audiences for the *New York Times* and Braley's other business-oriented venues were not the working-class targets of their scorn but, rather, others who shared the values of a business-dominated culture. To reach them and convert others, some advocates for business explicitly invested in publishing and broadcasting in order to spread both capitalism's good news and diatribes against the New Deal. They took up the banner against what William A. Thomson, the director of the American Newspaper Publishers Association's advertising bureau, described in 1937 as "unfair attacks on commercial America, upon profit-making enterprises, upon property rights." Businessmen, Thomson declared, must wage a "war against public ignorance in order to make our country safe for industry" and free of "the cost of social and political experiments." To do so, "the united voice of business must arise … to organize the mighty force of public opinion behind it." A 1937 study published first in *Harper's Magazine* likewise declared that "business" realized that it had to find "its voice."[31]

Joseph N. Pew, Jr. (1886–1963), and his brother, J. Howard Pew (1882–1971), heirs to the Sun Oil Company, considered themselves superpatriots who could do just that. They undertook aggressive propaganda campaigns, diverting some of their vast wealth to anti-New Deal, anti-state, and anti-labor campaigns, generously supporting conservative religious organizations, as well.[32] Hardworking but decidedly not rags-to-riches themselves, the Pew brothers fervently opposed the New Deal lest it encourage and enable sloth in others.

Among the Pews' storytelling strategies was the 1934 purchase of a controlling interest in the Chilton Company, publisher of key trade journals, including *Iron Age* and the *Dry Goods Economist*.[33] Chilton, its journals, and its other publications became conduits for their opposition to the New Deal and Roosevelt. Also in 1936, Joseph Pew purchased the *Farm Journal* and merged it with the *Farmer's Wife* to add their 1.4 million subscribers to his audiences.[34]

As the 1930s ended and the 1940s began, advocates for mainstream business culture continued their vivid but inaccurate appeals to Horatio Alger as a symbol for faith in upward mobility and immunity from the scourge of indolence. For instance, in 1939, A. Graves Williams, president of the Ohio Chamber of Commerce, reminded an audience of Congressmen and businessmen of the "time when businessmen ... were held in rather high esteem" and when "success stories were the order of the day" in popular magazines. And he asked them to "remember the works of Horatio Alger, where a poor boy always had an opportunity to become president of a large corporation or of the United States." Nostalgic, he mourned the day when "incentive ... inspired you" and "we literally raised ourselves by our boot straps from nothing to something." Williams's speech struck a chord and found its way into the *Congressional Record*, although few Horatio Alger heroes ever worked for a corporation, and none came to command one. Williams ended with a call to release "unknown men" from the "strait jacket of Federal legislation" and thereby restore their willingness to work the nation's way "out of the hopeless morass" of the times.[35]

The next year, taking a more optimistic tack, the *Christian Science Monitor* featured the illustrated title page of Alger's *Luck and Pluck*, while recognizing that his once ubiquitous books were gradually fading into "the limbo of unthumbed oblivion." "Yet," they assured readers, "however much the realists may smile at the old-fashioned externals with which Alger garbed his idealism, the success story of 1940 is based on the same essentials of character." Perhaps success stories of modern "resourceful individuals" would encourage belief that "a resourceful nation [could also] turn the problem of 10,000,000 unemployed into a national success story."[36]

The New Deal's contests hardened the lines of debate about appropriate levels of government intervention between businesses, consumers, and laborers. Many businessmen who had previously considered themselves to be reform-minded supporters for progressive changes on issues such as women's suffrage or child labor protections or food and drug regulations could not abide this new era's developments.[37] Despite the ideological diversity that continued among businesspeople, according to the loudest and best-financed voices, the New Deal's "disease" presented an unacceptably harsh and direct threat to business. As World War II began, they hoped that Americans' beliefs in opportunity had survived the Great Depression and the New Deal, and they continued to refashion the Horatio Alger narrative as a useful motif in their efforts to secure cultural authority for their visions of capitalism.

"PAGING HORATIO ALGER" IN WARTIME

Wartime spending brought profits back to business, created jobs, reduced inequality, and rebuilt prosperity. Nonetheless, conservative advocates for business were distressed by centralized spending, even when it profited their own industries. Fair employment policies had given unions advantages and initiated desegregation practices, along with other wartime regulations and policies that challenged business leaders' authority. Legislators, newspapers, and other business advocates were vocal in opposition to what they perceived as an extension of New Deal principles and practices under cover of wartime military necessity.[38] In the preceding decade conservatives had honed both their stories and their access to popular media through the largely sympathetic press and radio venues that their advertisements supported and that carried their stories into the public arena.

References to Horatio Alger from newspapers placed in the *Congressional Record* illustrate the iconic status and appeal of inaccurately recalled rags-to-riches plots. For instance, the title of a *Washington Daily News* newspaper article on December 15, 1942, shouted out "Paging Horatio Alger." Representative Roy O. Woodruff, a Michigan Republican who served in the House from 1921 to 1953, placed the article in the *Record* as one of his many jabs at FDR and the New Deal. This particular article attacked wartime proposals that would cap salaries and pull "the rug from under the so-called big shot." It would embed "in our way of life, because of warfare, a new philosophy that outlaws the incentive which made our country, with all its faults, the most productive, the richest, and the freest in all the wide world." Inequality represented by the wealth of "the Jay Goulds," it seemed, was a reasonable cost for America's greatness. Moreover, according to its fanciful but by now boilerplate accounts, Henry Ford deserved both his wealth and our gratitude. "Starting with less than a shoestring, in 20 years he built himself a personal bankroll of half a billion, the while raising wages, cutting the prices of his product, expanding employment, changing the whole course of our Nation's life." We should glory in his riches, not "envy" them. "Are we dropping the idea of doing it the hard way?" the article asked. "Are we all seeking a featherbed on the Government pay roll, taking in each other's washing being the future limit of our ambitions?" Any effort to lessen inequality, even when wealth resulted from "grafts ... and speculative sprees," risked poverty for all. The remedy was to remember Horatio Alger. "He was the popular expression of the America of his time. . . . His theme was always the same, barefoot boy to big shot." Thankfully, "Horatio's memory lingers on."[39] More accurately, Representative Woodruff reshaped Alger's "memory" to justify inequality and rationalize worker discipline.

A couple of months later, in February 1943, the *Chicago Daily Tribune*'s editors chided Vice President Henry Wallace in "Horatio Alger Rides Again," which also found its way into the *Congressional Record*. They scoffed at Wallace's reiteration of the New Deal's support for business and berated his article, "Horatio Alger is Not Dead," where he confirmed that "private initiative, private capital, [and] private enterprise" were all essential to full employment. With no mention of Alger's content, Wallace, too, used the name alone, confident that readers would get the symbol's significance, to signal and reinforce the "driving force of self-interest" and the "principle that hard work must be rewarded to encourage workers to do their best." He assured readers that Social Security would not relieve anyone of the need to work but would only "provide protection against the contingencies the individual cannot avoid." Wallace lauded "the spirit of free competition" and "incentives to individual effort and progress," concluding that "Horatio Alger is not dead in America and never will be." He did qualify, however, that the nation should "develop a kind of mixed society where both business and government have responsibilities" to "the community and the citizens." Unpersuaded by Wallace's reassurances that he supported free enterprise, the *Tribune*'s editors ridiculed his goal for all Americans to be able to join the middle class. They satirized this goal through "exhilarating" scenarios in which bankers would deliberately make bad decisions until they lost their wealth, and barkeepers would donate drinks to the father "accustomed to blowing his Saturday paycheck in the pub." They saw no benefit in a citizenry "leveled out" to a "frozen" middle class, regardless of merit. Calling one of Alger's titles to mind, the *Tribune's* editors declared that they were "pretty certain . . . that Government [would ensure] that Strong and Steady, or Paddle Your Own Canoe is preempted."[40]

Thus, both New Dealers and their opponents appealed to the historical storyteller's reinvented legacy. For Horatio Alger in his time and the New Dealers in theirs, inequality and poverty were unsettling human problems that called for correction, even though they approached the problems differently. Alger wrote to encourage individual and small-scale community self-help, and the New Deal's progressives called upon the nation as a whole to take responsibility. In contrast, Alger's most prolific latter-day devotees believed that inequality reflected realistic and perfectly acceptable different "circumstances" between the "well-heeled" affluent and the "shiftless" drunks and undeserving "hobo[es] riding the rods," as the *Chicago Daily Tribune* explained in 1943.[41] Because both sets of partisans applied Alger's name quite independently of his notions about inequality and what should be done about it, claims to his legacy could support opposite policies. Yet, businesses advertised, generating most of the revenue for mainstream media. Consequently, their uses of the symbolic Alger prevailed in popular media, crowding out sympathetic interpretations of inequality like the ones Alger himself penned.

As an example, Tom M. Girdler filled his 1943 autobiography, *Boot Straps*, with stories about how "devotion to our work" made solid his family, his business, and his America. Individuals bore the entire responsibility for their lives, including "squalor." "Only shiftless people were dirty," he pronounced, and anyone who complained about slumlords or employers was suspect. The first president of Republic Steel Corporation, Girdler had initially supported some New Deal policies. However, he became an ardent foe in 1935 when the National Labor Relations Act, better known as the Wagner Act, constrained employers' ability to prevent unionization. Like many others who appealed to Alger's legacy, Girdler believed that "the rotten core in all of the New Deal thinking" was that "work being unimportant to them, they never seem to realize why other men so highly prize the right to work." He and other employers were furious about "tyranny disguised as a labor movement" that kept people from being "allowed to work." In contrast, the people he admired worked in "the Horatio Alger pattern," that is, they "found [their] fun working." Even so, Girdler's own claim to pulling himself up by his bootstraps involved what one reviewer called "a little poetic license," given his family's considerable advantages. Nonetheless, Girdler insisted that "we ought to rewrite Horatio Alger, so that those who try to emulate his hardworking, conscientious heroes may realize that in a machine age a boy can't start [working] too soon." Young men should carry "many Horatio Alger books" with them as they go in search of adventure, education, and work.[42] Of course, neither Alger's tales of newsboys-who-made-good nor Girdler's notions of work that was "fun" applied to the steelworkers or coal miners whose unions he scorned.

In this vein, the *Chicago Times* carried a tale, also in 1943, of "A New Deal Alger Boy" who had managed to maintain his "rugged individualism" despite having been raised in a generation of "youngsters who can recall nothing but new deal government." The tale began by bemoaning that "Horatio Alger has had a tough time lately. His success stories read a bit sour during the long depression." To make matters worse, the "boys on the far left of economic thought scoffed heartily at the whole string of Alger rags-to-riches romances."[43] Similarly, the *New York Times* selected July 4th, 1944, to publish "Land of Opportunity" to dispute "the delusion ... that the era of great opportunities for humble people in this country has ended." It featured a "fact-finding" survey by the Bell Telephone System of eighteen top officers, which had discovered that they had all begun "at the bottom" even though "we are gloomily told that the work-and-win, strive-and-succeed days passed beyond recall when the romantic Horatio Alger laid down his pen." Bell's publicists recognized the cultural capital to be gained with this narrative and placed a two-page ad at the front of *Life* magazine to showcase and leverage its "Up from the Ranks" stories of white-collar success.[44]

Eric Johnston, who was elected president of the US Chamber of Commerce in 1942, admitted that "ideologies of despair" from the right and left challenged his "basic beliefs." He published *America Unlimited* in 1944 to express "American attitudes in which we all shared." Chief among these was "the Horatio Alger rags-to-riches tradition ... of little tykes who grow into big tycoons," which he admitted was "true, not in the literal sense but in the symbolic sense." This "tradition," he exulted, "is deeply American" and "as near as anything we have to a body of folklore" that prevents growing "accustomed to looking upon poverty as an insuperable, or even serious, obstacle." Admitting that he was "assuredly no Alger hero" because of his family's "genteel" roots, his life fit the "Alger pattern" anyway. His "work-filled boyhood ... did not stir me to revolt; it only served as a spur to ambition," confident that he would not "remain forever stuck in the mud of poverty." It speaks to how deeply the myth of self-making was embedded in mid-century mainstream thinking that this influential spokesman for the business community could confess to his "genteel" roots and also boast of his youthful ambition to leave behind "the mud of poverty" because "opportunity seemed to us unbounded." Despite his belief that "capitalism must justify itself continually in deeds," Johnston was utterly insensitive to the realities of poverty that truly was "insuperable," rather than "genteel" as his had been. Poor people who "reconcile themselves to it ... lack the moral energy to advance themselves." In turning to Alger-esque stories, Johnston sought to rebuild confidence in business, fulfilling what *Life* magazine called "his destiny ... to rescue a class – the class comprising the American business community – from despair and even from possible suicide."[45]

IN SEARCH OF "A MODERN HORATIO ALGER"

The wartime achievements of American businesses went a long way toward raising public opinion toward them, yet ongoing New Deal policies, wartime government planning, and a national wave of postwar labor strikes alarmed conservatives. As a result, full-scale onslaughts on New Deal policies continued, intently targeting labor unions and federal government expansion.[46] For instance, at the end of 1947, despite a powerful anti-union victory with the Labor Management Relations Act, better known as the Taft-Hartley Act, the Pews' Chilton Company sponsored a two-page spread in *Advertising Age* that called out, "WANTED! ... A MODERN HORATIO ALGER." This advertisement lamented that "today, those who believe in the philosophy of *Strive and Succeed* are all too few." The solution required "an author who can popularize *today's* success stories!" Someone must take on "the task of writing stories that will carry the message to our youth – and their elders." The ad urged "modern *true* stories of success to prove that hard work is the highroad to success," not mentioning that Alger's entirely fictional tales featured heroes who always benefited from luck and community support, and who never had to work or succeed in America's modern economy of large corporate firms. The plea concluded that "lacking a modern Horatio Alger, the job of reviving the belief that hard work pays off for the worker must be done by all those concerned about the future of America."[47]

The Pews and people of like mind might have found reassurance in a 1948 survey that reported "workers" glad to "OK Alger story." A 1948 article in *Modern Industry* began with an allusion to antique abolition lyrics: "Horatio Alger's body may be a'moldering in the grave – but his soul goes marching on." According to a broad survey, the "American working man, the competent, independent, ofttimes difficult individual who makes U.S. capitalism work still believes in opportunity and the success story." Of "these assorted strivers," 78 percent believed that their chances to achieve their ambitions were "very good" or "fair." The "corrosive cynicism of the far left has, to date, failed to win over a majority of the 'industrial proletariat' in this country."[48]

Only in America

Horatio Alger could not have imagined the complex political dynamics that would resuscitate his fame – although as a symbol whose meanings diverged markedly from his own writing. Imagining the future from 1897, he predicted that if he "could come back 50 years from now probably I should feel bewildered in reading the New York *Tribune* of 1947." He wondered about the future's "'strange new world' with many wonderful inventions and discoveries."[49] As it happened, he truly would have been startled because in that very year his legacy received a posthumous tribute, but as an icon of individualist self-making rather than for what he actually wrote. In a major milestone, an Horatio Alger Awards program launched. The previous year, Kenneth J. Beebe (d. 1970) had made two awards on behalf of his American Schools and Colleges Association (ASCA) to spotlight successful businessmen as role models for youth. Those awards hadn't attracted any publicity, however, and Beebe speculated that associating the awards with Alger's "strive and succeed" theme would enhance the awards' public visibility and appeal. The 1947 program awarded a handful of recipients, all highly prominent men whose prestige attracted news media coverage for the award. The *New York Times* grandly announced these new awards: "The traditional

American success story – in the manner of the Horatio Alger heroes – is symbolized best by five business leaders."[50]

The Horatio Alger theme gave the award cultural stature and presented the press with a compelling narrative about American capitalism and its blessings. Beebe later wrote that he believed that each award over the ensuing years served as "freedom's living proof that equality of economic opportunity is still in operation for Americans who apply initiative and hard work."[51] The program highlighted the lives of men and, much later, women – primarily businesspeople – to inspire young people to pursue what the 1948 certificates described as "the American tradition of overcoming handicaps and achieving success through industry, sacrifice and ethics." *New York Times* coverage of the 1948 awards exclaimed that "America still presents the greatest field of opportunity and adventure" and quoted recipient Bernard Baruch's assertion that opportunities remained "as great as ever existed before."[52]

Every year since then, Horatio Alger Award publicity has reaffirmed two related myths very much as Beebe interpreted them – one about Alger's stories and the other about equal opportunity for anyone willing to work.[53] Not only have the *Times* and other popular outlets continued to publicize the Horatio Alger Awards, but boosters in Congress have used their access to the *Congressional Record* to acclaim and preserve memory of their constituents' awards, publicizing them alongside politically appealing stories. For instance, Senator Everett Dirksen noted in 1957 that he was "proud" that his "own career has paralleled this typically American story" of "the rise of men from humble beginnings to positions of great public trust" before summarizing the successes of "two Illinoisans" about to receive the award. Of the 1,038 mentions of the nineteenth-century author in the *Congressional Record* from 1947 to early 2019, at least 152 were placed by representatives and senators to honor awardees from their districts. The rest are mostly "tributes" to upright citizens whose careers, as Dirksen described his own, "paralleled this typically American story."[54]

In 1947, the year before Earl Bunting received his Horatio Alger Award, he made the papers with a speech to the Advertising Club of New York that "declared war" on "economic goldbrickers" in order to protect the "American system." He equated programs that relieved the hardships of inequality with "communism and socialism." President of the National Association of Manufacturers (NAM), he dedicated that organization and its 16,500 members to this ideological "war" and, like Chilton, called on the advertising industry to show "the public that the American individual enterprise system was the only economic system that guaranteed complete freedom to the people."[55] The next year, Bunting received his Alger award and the NAM made good on his pledge, publishing and distributing widely *The Free Enterprise System*. Among its twenty-two pages of aphorisms and statistics, the pamphlet proclaimed that "Communism is content that no man should be rich." In contrast, "Capitalism strives that no man shall be poor." The "greatest paradox of today," it bemoaned, was that "free enterprise, with its unparalleled record of achievement, is under attack and on the defensive all over the globe." Hence, the need for stories to convince all Americans that they had "hit the jackpot" by living here.[56]

In the context of conservatives' postwar worries, 1947 was an auspicious time for Kenneth Beebe's invention of the Horatio Alger Awards' storytelling strategy. An Alger biographer, Edwin P. Hoyt, observed that the simplified Alger-esque icon of rugged individualism rose as memories of the stories themselves faded. Hoyt explained that the "Alger vogue [had] continued until nearly 1910 and then died out; soon Alger was famous only as the name for an American syndrome, the rags to riches story." Accordingly, "Horatio Alger's memory languished until nearly mid-century, when social critics became concerned with the slippage and perversion of the old American dream and began delving into the psyche of capitalism." Capitalism's defenders "discovered then that Horatio had been the high priest of the system," Hoyt inaccurately alleged looking back from his present. As we might expect from an author recruited by the Pews' Chilton Book Company to write Alger's biography, Hoyt identified his subject as "a symbol of a dream" of individualism that Alger himself would have found an uncomfortable fit.[57]

Beebe's great innovation in this context was his strategy to foster and disseminate clusters of stories about "living Americans" who could make a claim to having been self-made by the prevailing meanings of the phrase. The Horatio Alger Award project was so successful that Beebe's group incorporated in 1951 as the Horatio Alger Awards Committee (HAAC) of the Schools & Colleges Association, Inc. Ever since, through decades of struggle then growth, it has stayed true to the "purposes" defined in its "Certificate of Incorporation":

> To promote, advance, support, sponsor, foster, stimulate, cultivate, revive, renew, and otherwise encourage a wholesome interest and regard in and for the maintenance, preservation, and perpetuation of that American tradition of fair play, adventure, industry, equality of opportunity, and the democratic principles of free and competitive enterprise popularly known as the "Horatio Alger" success story.

Despite the modesty of HAAC's initial $5,000 annual budget, often more aspirational than actual during the early years, the founders sought widespread distribution of their message. Beebe and his collaborators were concerned that "things were slipping badly," so they pursued this mission through two mutually reinforcing narratives, one about Horatio Alger and the other about "living" exemplars of "strive and succeed."⁵⁸

The title of the HAAC's first major publication embodied Beebe's strategy: *A Decade of Living Proof of the Opportunities in Our American Way of Life*. That "living proof" included photos and biographies of the seventy award winners from 1947 through 1956, statements of purpose and process, plus a student's "prize-winning Horatio Alger essay" that expounded on "The American Free Enterprise System and the Equality of Opportunity Which It Offers." *Living Proof* began with a dedication "to the American Way as opposed to foreign ideologies." Out of concern for "the trend among young people towards the mind-poisoning belief that equal opportunity was a thing of the past," the HAAC's "new approach to this problem" sought to showcase "living individuals who by their own efforts had pulled themselves up by their bootstraps in the American tradition." A brief essay on "The American Success Story" illustrates the distance traveled in the idea of self-making from mid-nineteenth-century biographical compilations. In a juxtaposition that would have seemed strange a century earlier, it pairs a "rags-to-riches tradition" with the distinctly modern notion of "free enterprise," attributing that pairing to the nation's founding. To "rekindle the American pioneer spirit" of "individual effort, diligence and self-reliance" the awards provide "graphic proof for American youth that opportunity is knocking every minute, but it's up to the individual to open the door." The following year, the HAAC began episodically publishing an expanded version of *Living Proof* with the title *Opportunity Still Knocks*. The most recent edition of *Only in America* was published in 2022, the organization's seventy-fifth anniversary – a much grander and glossier 213-page volume than Beebe and his colleagues could have imagined.⁵⁹

A TRIUMPH OF SELF-AGENCY

One of the nation's most widely published and broadcast public figures within the twentieth century, Norman Vincent Peale (1898–1993), became a dedicated leader of the HAAC, earnestly connecting myths about Alger's stories and material success with patriotism and spirituality. Following in the *self*-help path of the "positive thinkers" of the late nineteenth and early twentieth century, Peale spread a similar faith: people could "make" their own lives regardless of what the world handed them. According to Peale, self-agency was unmoored from Providence and community and, instead, put into service of individuals' well-being. Peale's faith in self-agency and worldly ambitions would have been blasphemous and incomprehensible to the Puritans, except possibly as the work of Satan.

Figure 9.2 The plaque accompanying this statue of Norman Vincent Peale in front of his Marble Collegiate Church in New York City lauds his promotion of the power of "positive thinking." Peale's bestselling books, radio and television shows, and friendships with powerful leaders made him an important proponent of a deeply individualistic ethos that he based in part on nostalgia for Horatio Alger's stories. (Photo taken in 2017 by Bill Tompkins / Michael Ochs Archives via Getty Images)

Peale's autobiography is full of nostalgia for what he remembered as his childhood's simpler time. Among his memories were the deep roots that Alger's stories had in his life.

Born in 1898, he credited both his father and his fifth-grade teacher for educating him with Horatio Alger stories and the McGuffey Reader, both already antiquarian even then. That especially memorable teacher periodically reinforced the "positive thinking" lessons of those classics by writing "CAN'T" on the blackboard, then asking the students "What shall I do now?" The correct answer was to erase the "T" and learn the lesson that "you can if you think you can."[60] Likewise, although Peale spent most of his adult life as pastor of the Marble Collegiate Church in Midtown Manhattan, he always called himself a "country boy" at heart.[61]

Peale received the Horatio Alger Award in 1952, the same year he published *The Power of Positive Thinking*, which, like his full repertoire, linked spirituality, psychology, and material success. *Positive Thinking* stayed on the *New York Times*' bestseller list an astounding 186 weeks and was the number one nonfiction bestseller for forty-eight weeks. Through his own ministry and forty other books, more than five decades of weekly radio broadcasts beginning in 1933, plus his widely distributed magazine, *Guideposts*, the "businessman's preacher" spread a pro-business, anti-progressive, hyper-patriotic, hope-filled message, replete with how-to-succeed guidelines and anecdotes to illustrate them. His abundance of easy charm contributed to that reach, as did his high profile in the religious resurgence of the 1950s and 1960s. He also attracted support from wealthy businessmen, including Fred Trump, Donald J. Trump's father. Cold War anxieties, employer/labor strife, and pressures on adults to meet rising standards as consumers and parents, added to extensive fear-inspiring campaigns by well-funded anti-state, anti-union organizations, and evangelical operations, such as Billy Graham's, roiled the nation, fueling the tensions that Peale promised to soothe through "positive thinking."[62]

Peale spread his messages widely through many organizations and venues, and the HAAC's mission attracted Peale's long-term loyalty and leadership. Moreover, Peale's upbeat, storytelling approach reinforced Beebe's inclinations, and together they set the organization's tone that continues still. So closely did Peale become identified with the HAAC's core that his current biography on the Association's website explains that he "is considered a co-founder of the Association because he was responsible for ensuring the perpetuation of Kenneth Beebe's vision." That attribution appears elsewhere among the HAAC's records and publications as well, testimony to Peale's influence, as is the separate award the HAAC created in his memory in 1996 to honor Horatio Alger Award winners who make extra contributions to the Association's mission.[63]

Just as Horatio Alger's stories could be construed as capitalism's good news from a simpler time, Peale intended his own prolific stories to be the good news of faith, positive thinking, and capitalism. Communities played no role in abating misfortune for Peale, although they did for Alger. Looking back in fulsome nostalgia on his privileged, if not affluent, childhood, Peale claims to "have always resented poverty for myself or for anyone else." He gloried in "a period when the Horatio Alger 'strive and succeed' work ethic was universally believed in." He had always "believed that by my own efforts in a free society, I could move up." Fittingly, Peale's biography on the Horatio Alger Association's website highlights this aphorism: "Empty pockets never held anyone back. Only empty heads and empty hearts can do that."[64] Although Horatio Alger wrote fiction and idealistic fantasy, he had a more realistic understanding of people's struggles and debts than Peale: pluck gained nothing without luck; individuals gained nothing without communities. Whatever Peale's intentions, by placing all responsibility for individuals' fates on their shoulders, he justified inequality.

In 1956, Kenneth Beebe asked the seventy Horatio Alger Award winners from the first decade "to what they attribute their successes." He summed up their responses in two ways: "Work, Faith, and Inspiration," and a maxim, "Work hard and enjoy your work." Beebe explained that they "all agree they worked hard and still enjoy it."[65] What the organization's literature called the "graphic proof" of those seventy heroes revealed the narrow range of who could expect hard work to bootstrap success, with only two women and one African American man among them. Peale, for one, had little sympathy for Americans whose work ground down their bodies and spirits. Instead, all difficulties paled in light of the *Power of Positive Thinking*, for "neither age nor circumstance needs to deprive us of energy and vitality" if one has faith in oneself, religion, and nation. Even a factory worker can find tireless joy if he "will work in harmony with the rhythm of his machine." In preaching, he had learned: "Give your job all you've got" and do so "in a relaxed and easy manner." The world's laborers need not worry. "If you think in positive terms you will achieve positive results." This is "the basis of an astonishing law of prosperity and success. In three words: Believe and succeed."[66] Even the romantic Horatio Alger knew that belief alone did not provide gainful or dignified employment.

Not everyone who shared Peale's notions of Horatio Alger's lessons also shared Peale's eternal optimism about unrestricted capitalism's blessings. For example, in 1950, Massachusetts Congressman Thomas J. Lane described an ongoing conundrum: "How to reconcile the claims of the individual and society is the stand-out problem of our age." Granting that the community, through the government, had to provide a "substitute" during emergencies, he worried that "our present concentration on group security" threatened men's drive. He affirmed that "cases too numerous to mention where a man started at the very bottom without wealth or influence and made his own way to the top" were not "mere" Horatio Alger stories. After all, "the doors of opportunity will open to any average man who makes a real and continuing effort." If only "collective action, through which the strong are assessed to help the weak," did not destroy a man's "ambition to improve himself," the nation's "competitive system which inspires every man to give his best" could continue to do its magic.[67]

A few years later, speakers regaled the National Association of Foremen with similar messages, worried that "we can't have both Government-provided security and individual freedom." Free enterprise was "American idealism in action" in which "the individual is free to make something of himself." Neglect of "responsibilities" and "too much of a craving for excitement . . . leads to moral abuse." The solution? Young people should read "more Horatio Alger and less Superman."[68] Young people have read a whole lot more Superman than Horatio Alger, but in the hands of conservative storytellers the dual myths about Horatio Alger and self-made success kept growing stronger. As the myth of self-made success rose in cultural authority, its storytellers increasingly applied it to influence policymaking.

10

Targeting the Common Good, 1950–2000

During his 1960 presidential bid, Vice President Richard M. Nixon declared that "In this time of challenge to the American economy, taxes designed in an earlier time and still in the law to punish success are now obsolescent." In this, his major economic speech of the campaign, he warned that such taxes "hobble the Nation's advance."[1] Insofar as taxes fulfill a debt to community, statements like Nixon's indicate how thoroughly ideas of self-making had diverged from recognizing communal obligation or gratitude.

Indeed, by this time, Nixon's declaration seemed straightforward and even intuitive to many. His audience at the annual meeting of the Association of Business Economists gave him several standing ovations, and newspapers across the nation commented favorably on the speech.[2] Yet these chapters have shown that the assumptions about individuals' success that underlaid Nixon's logic and prevailing creeds were neither straightforward nor intuitive. According to his assumptions, heroes who are the modern paragons of self-making incur no obligations along their paths. Instead, they might be victims of laws "to punish success." Contrast this idea with those of Boston merchant Robert Keayne three centuries earlier, who in 1653 would have felt that both his eternal soul and any chance for earthly esteem were imperiled if he did not freely acknowledge his debts to God, who "out of His free bounty ... gives us our estates," and to community – "the commonwealth or place where we live and where we have got more or less of that estate."[3] Money was not then enough to save either souls or esteem.

Across the three centuries separating Keayne and Nixon (1913–1994), self-agency had not only found acceptance, but had become a common explanation for success and a measure of worthiness: people determined their own fates as self-made successes or self-made failures. Stories with this simple theme, uncomplicated by historical and social factors, had increasingly promoted elites' esteem and cultural authority since the mid nineteenth century. Sometimes these stories were fanciful, as with distortions of Horatio Alger's tales that left out the luck he emphasized, and sometimes they were biographies of real people that isolated protagonists' outcomes from their advantages. Other stories reproached people who struggle, likewise isolating them from historical and social contexts. Some stories came from boosters – sincere or cynical – through a thriving commerce on self-help topics ranging from spiritual guidance to achieving practical goals for jobs, health, or appearance. As well, arguments for a meritocracy appeared all across the political spectrum, sometimes as a goal, other times to justify success or to condemn failure.

Some of each genre, as highlighted in this chapter, were products of well-funded drives to advance individualist viewpoints and reduce support for community-based concerns, unfortunate people, and progressive state programs. In these storylines, unions, poverty, and public institutions alike were products of an unwillingness to "work hard." Such campaigns aimed to convince Americans that democracy depended on "free enterprise" within a market economy also imagined as free and equal, and which could solve problems if the government stepped aside. In this spirit, the myth of self-made success was recruited into the rhetoric of policymaking.

Each of these types of stories rested in one way or another on the myth of self-made success and failure. Mid-century advocates of the myth did not start from scratch: when they opposed Great Society initiatives of the 1960s, they could draw on the storylines that had opposed the New Deal during the Great Depression. Then, in the 1970s, the mythology of self-making was energized further by new national challenges, and that amplification of the myth has continued since. Organizations such as the US Chamber of Commerce and the Horatio Alger Association of Distinguished Americans (HAADA), along with public figures such as Ronald Reagan, Billy Graham, and Milton Friedman, flourished by telling stories to boost individualism. So did promoters and champions of various forms of self-help that emphasized *self* rather than *help*. Books, seminars, lectures, popular press articles, and other media ready to guide mundane aspects of personal development, such as appearance and health, also exploded. The economic and cultural turbulence of the 1970s increased the appeal of self-employment, with both the promise of entrepreneurship and its uncertainties.[4] With these stories, repeated and amplified across popular culture, avarice no longer required any justification, and individualist ambition required no apology. Conversely, this deluge of advice frustrated and shamed anyone who somehow couldn't find the magic.

MERITOCRACY

From our perspective in the 2020s, the term "meritocracy" seems quite compatible with the virtues of self-made success. And, yet, in 1958 Michael Young (1915–2002) published *The Rise of the Meritocracy, 1870–2033* to critique that very ethos. His narrator looked back from 2033 to warn Young's contemporaries about the dangers of a professional ranking system that replaced arist*ocracy*, a rigid hierarchy based on inheritance, with an equally rigid ranking ostensibly based on *merit*– hence, *meritocracy*. In that dystopian society, batteries of standardized tests and constant workplace surveillance wholly determined people's roles and ranks throughout their lives. Put in place more to maximize efficiency and productivity than fairness, the grim system never looked good to those in the lower ranks, which is why, in the end, they rose up to destroy it.[5]

Young's fictional system and its fraudulent assumption of equal opportunity came down hardest on non-elites. They could no longer comfort themselves by saying: "Had I had a proper chance I would have shown the world." Young's narrator scornfully concluded about the pre-meritocratic past that "inequality of opportunity fostered the myth of human equality." This imagined meritocratic future abandoned that ancient myth, and yet chances in life remained unequal because not everyone was raised in an orphanage and, therefore, "equally unhappy." Truly equal access to equivalent education and social capital would always be impossible because families "desire equal opportunity for everyone else's children, extra for their own." Elite families could always use their privileges, including their connections, to ensure that inequality continued, but under the new guise of merit.[6]

The American edition of *The Rise of the Meritocracy* came out a year later, and the term caught on quickly. Reactions varied, but whatever a reviewer's take on the book and its argument (they usually recognized its critical tones), they disseminated the term "meritocracy."[7] Within months of the book's American edition, educators, public speakers, and other commentators were using the word without even mentioning Young or his book, often marking the term's novelty with quotation marks and dashes. For example, an insurance company's vice president, Louie Throgmorton, traveled through the southern states, boasting to local Chambers of Commerce and Lions Clubs that America "constitutes the only 'meritocracy' in the world." Everyone "can rise to whatever height he sets," a front-page article proclaimed. And, "America is more than a democracy. It is a 'merit-cracy' – we rise and shine by our own merit." Throgmorton's enthusiasm moved him to declare that "businessmen ... are the uncrowned kings of this land."[8] In contrast, educators concerned with inequality, such as Horace Mann Bond of Atlanta University, father of civil rights leader Julian Bond, took to heart the dangers of a "'meritocracy' based on verbalism" that would exacerbate inequality within a grossly unequal educational system.[9]

No one was more surprised than Young at how rapidly "this unpleasant term" spread, especially in the United States, as an ideal rather than a danger. Young had intended it to reinforce negative opinions about inherited privileges disguised as merit-based, and instead it came to connote precisely the opposite:

the illusion of individual self-making. A major policymaker in Britain, Young had previously drafted the Labour Party's goals for a "free, democratic, efficient, public-spirited country with its material resources organized in the service of the British people." Consequently, Young lamented in the 1994 introduction to a new edition of his book that his invented coinage was helping powerful people to avoid "self-doubt." That is, "People of power and privilege were readier than ever to ... congratulate themselves on being like aristocrats but going one better by earning power and privilege on merit." It angered him that the "rich and powerful were encouraged by the general culture to believe that they fully deserved all that they had." If power were no longer "open to criticism," the powerful could be "convinced it was all for the common good," thereby excusing that they are "ruthless in pursuing their own advantage." In 2001, the year before he died, Young put it poignantly and succinctly: "I have been sadly disappointed by my 1958 book."[10] Just as Horatio Alger the author became "the Horatio Alger" icon, Young's "meritocracy" had become a tool to counterfeit equal opportunity.

Young's futuristic satire was so brilliantly subtle that not all of its readers then or since have caught his critique. For example, the conservative Daniel Seligman, an editor at *Fortune*, reviewed the 1994 edition of Young's book for the *National Review*, introducing it as Young's "utopian (or is it dystopian? ...) fantasy." Seligman considered Young's work "eerily prescient" of the "mere reality" that Richard Herrnstein and Charles Murray described that same year in *The Bell Curve*, in which they made their case for elitist and racist IQ-based discrimination. What troubled Young was exactly what Seligman applauded, namely that "many low-IQ workers" would have "to recognize that they have an inferior status ... because they *are* inferior." He winked, "Tough to take, eh?" Seligman was content with a meritocracy that would not "be easy" for "the not-very-smart."[11] Life is, after all, hard for self-made losers.

Young laid out the appeal of a façade of equal educational opportunity whose illusions could legitimate "rule not so much by the people as by the cleverest people; not an aristocracy of birth, not a plutocracy of wealth, but a true meritocracy of talent." In that most efficient and modern of systems, "Intelligence and effort together make up merit $(I+E=M)$." Thanks to the (alleged) objectivity of standardized tests and "work measurement," wages and stature could be assessed precisely.[12] Everyone gets what they deserve, so it seems to some, and in Young's mind that expectation was meritocracy's peril. Anyone, like Seligman, who believes that a meritocracy exists can combine that with the self-making principle and, thereby, readily judge the worth of all people by their worldly successes. There would be no need to equalize opportunity or to aim for equality of outcomes.

Progressives have taken a mix of approaches to the idea of meritocracy. Since the 1980s, some, such as social philosopher Michael Sandel, have advanced Young's critique. They attack the meritocratic ideal as an excuse for perpetuating inequality under cultural rules based on the myth of self-made success and its corollary, self-made failure. In addition to differential impacts on human dignity and esteem, they argue that the belief can alienate sections of the citizenry from the whole.[13] But for many moderate progressives, the notion of meritocracy has been a positive ideal, a goal toward which programs such as Head Start and all levels of public education, including vocational education, should aspire to raise the floor for everyone. In that vein, when Hillary Clinton ran for president in 2016, she declared "I want this to be a true meritocracy. I'm tired of inequality. I want people to feel like they can get ahead if they work for it." Like other progressive leaders, such as former presidents Lyndon B. Johnson, Bill Clinton, and Barack Obama, who all supported policies to equalize opportunities, Hillary Clinton did not think that people can succeed as autonomous individuals. Accordingly, the first sentence in her 1996 book, *It Takes a Village*, is "Children are not rugged individualists."[14] Unlike Seligman and others who accept the self-making myth, none of these progressive advocates for equality applied ideas about meritocracy to reprove disadvantaged people.

Young was surprised by the unwanted track his book's title took. He remarked in 1994 that "the most influential books are always those that are not read," and, in his case, too many readers had "neglected, or not noticed, the fact that the book is satirical."[15] As a result of selective reading and cliché-grabbing, Young joined Adam Smith, Horatio Alger, and Samuel Smiles as authors whose titles or phrases were appropriated for purposes other than their intended balances of individual and community interests. Although Young himself did not acquire the iconic status of Smith, Alger, and Smiles, the word "meritocracy" certainly did. By the end of the twentieth century, "meritocracy" had become a watchword for storytellers who found it useful both for aggrandizing (and ennobling or at least vindicating) the successful as well as by progressives wishing to raise the odds for success among outliers. Across the political spectrum and through the rest of the century, three fantasies – meritocracy, equal opportunity, and self-making – became increasingly entangled. The notions can simultaneously inspire egalitarian reforms and allow elites and their advocates to believe that they have earned their places and the benefits that flow from them.

FANTASIES OF INDIVIDUAL SELF-MAKING VERSUS THE STATE

Wartime spending and expansive infrastructure projects rebuilt the economy after the Great Depression so that the 1950s fostered optimism in many Americans about their opportunities. The economic benefits of federal infrastructure investments – such as President Dwight D. Eisenhower's interstate highway program and support for education, especially after Russia launched Sputnik in 1957 – were apparent to Americans at all levels of society, business, and government, and across political parties. The need to demonstrate superiority relative to Cold War rivals also reinforced bipartisan support for nation building. Therefore within the mainstream's ranks, which now included Euro-Americans previously excluded, the American Dream seemed possible, although still limited by race, gender, and class. To varying degrees, Americans accepted the democratic process as the way to determine a nation's direction collectively. Faith in human agency prevailed over the sovereignty of Providence earlier, totalitarianism then, or markets later.[16]

Much of the postwar business community shared these optimistic views. However, when turmoil resurfaced in the 1960s and 1970s, businesspeople and their advocates faced a renewed crisis of confidence, this time better prepared than in the 1930s. Anti-war protests, stagflation, the energy crisis, student unrest, and youth alienation challenged mainstream traditions, all against the dark backdrop of the Cold War. As was true with the New Deal, President Lyndon Johnson's Great Society measures addressed the nation's problems by increasing the federal government's influence to support consumer, educational, environmental, workplace, and civil rights, as well as an expanded welfare state. For some, these measures seemed to threaten their ideas for how the nation should operate and how individuals should conduct their lives. They distrusted the community's judgment, fearing that it would punish success and eliminate incentives for ambitious, creative individuals. As an alternative to federal regulation and the social safety net, these policy skeptics increasingly promoted reverence for the "market" as the solution to all economic and social problems. The greatly influential economists Rose and Milton Friedman typified this market-oriented ideology in their 1979 bestseller and 1980 television series, *Free to Choose*.[17] They championed an unfettered marketplace even as corporations closed factories across the country and reopened abroad to exploit cheaper labor. Following this free market logic, restrictions on financial institutions were weakened, which contributed to the savings and loan crisis of the 1980s and 1990s, and, likewise, the 2008 economic collapse not too much later.

William E. Simon (1927–2000) illustrates the fears that drove very successful, powerful people toward an adamant faith in the "free market" and those he believed were the self-made and self-determining individuals who operated within it. Simon served as Treasury Secretary under Presidents Nixon and Gerald Ford, and his 1978 memoir, *A Time for Truth*, begins and ends with dread about the nation's course. Milton Friedman authored the preface with high praise for Simon and his attempts in and out of office to halt the nation's "suicidal course."

Another hugely influential economist, Friedrich von Hayek, urgently endorsed Simon's book. He believed that Simon "is not unduly an alarmist." Rather, this jeremiad "still [may help] avert the threatening collapse of our political and economic order," although Hayek could not hold out "much hope." Simon ended with some hope that his book would "inspire ... others" to "battle" against "tyranny" imposed in the name of a "collectivist construct called the People."[18]

As Simon mused about his life's path in *A Time for Truth*, he noted early clues to his success in his "extremely competitive nature" and "capacity for grueling self-discipline." Born in 1927 to a family that had "lost its wealth" to the Depression, Simon nonetheless attended the prestigious Newark Academy in Livingston, New Jersey. He eventually transferred his energies from surfing New Jersey's "great waves" to Wall Street, where he "instantly displayed the signs of the 'workaholic'" and rose quickly. In high government posts, he relished being at odds with "those [Congressional] coconuts on the Hill" as well as his presidential bosses. And he was proud of his tag "William the Terrible." He somehow triumphed despite what he bemoaned as Americans' loss of freedom "to plan, to save, to invest, to build, to produce, to invent, to hire, to fire, to resist coercive unionization, to exchange goods and services, to risk, to profit, to grow." Once out of public service, he pioneered leveraged buyouts, most famously making a $70,000,000 profit buying Gibson Greeting Cards in 1982, almost entirely on debt, then taking it public fourteen months later. The *New York Times*'s 2000 obituary described him as "emblematic of a breed of aggressive investor" for which the free-wheeling 1980s were notorious.[19]

Just as Simon explained his own successes in terms of his personal qualities, he explained away the fates of those who remained poor by the same logic. It wasn't that *all* poor people deserved their plight, but that "the distinction between deserving and undeserving poor is important." He considered it a "virtue to assist those who are in acute need through no fault of their own," which his own foundation continues to do. However, one of his "general principles" was that chronic, rather than acute, poverty was quite another matter because it "may result from sloth, incompetence, and dishonesty." Another of Simon's principles, "which must be communicated forcefully," was that poverty is the inevitable outcome of state intervention in economic affairs. Specifically, Great Society programs were not "*warring* on poverty" as much as they were "*creating* poverty" by depriving some citizens of the incentive to work while punishing others who worked. The welfare system, he asserted, exists "*not* to assist the helpless, but to redistribute the wealth." Thus, "the more one achieves, the more one is punished; the less one achieves, the more one is rewarded." The Founders' "glorious" intent, he declared, was to build "a competitive *meritocracy*" in which "men should share an equal opportunity to face the challenges of life, each free to achieve what he could and rise to the level he could by his own wit, effort, and merit," possibly "from 'rags-to-riches.'" Such "individual achievement" can triumph, however, only if "egalitarians" and their erroneous appeals to American generosity could be kept from using the power of the state to enforce a "mediocrity." By that "lethal pattern," the "nation will be destroyed."[20]

In Simon's dramatic scenarios, the only force that meaningfully constrains individual self-determination is the state – not social or cultural circumstances, not deeply lodged racial and gender inequalities, not the broader forces of globalization and capital, and not access to education and other opportunities. Like the surprised Michael Young who attributed the success of *The Rise of the Meritocracy* to the times, Simon explained his book's long tenure on the *New York Times*'s bestseller lists by saying that "it catches the mood of the moment."[21] Each of these books offered dystopian visions. Young's vision satirized the notion of meritocracy, while Simon's insisted that prioritizing and rewarding individual merit was the only way to avoid doom. Fear fueled competitions for cultural authority then as now, often incentivized as the path to political authority.

To advance the case for self-made Americans in a self-made nation, some storytellers revised national origins tales to fit the mold. For example, US schoolchildren typically learn that the Pilgrims resolutely started building the self-reliant American character in 1620 when they landed at Plymouth Rock. In 1975, the National Federation of Republican Women's magazine, *Challenge*, published a particularly distorted version of this powerful and popular, if misleading, origin myth in "Nobody Helped the Pilgrims":

> They landed in a forbidding wilderness. No Federal Housing, so they went to work and built their own. No Food Stamp program, so they raised what food they ate, and when they didn't raise enough, went without. No Free Schools, so mothers taught their children. ... No Social Security – no security at all, except what each provided for himself. But there were compensations. No rioters demanding something for nothing. ... No wasteful bureaucrats paying themselves out of the workers' production. Nothing really for the Pilgrims but hard work and a lot of it. Did it pay off? Our standard of living proves it.[22]

Reeking of disdain for Great Society programs, this proclamation insisted that the United States was self-made by determined, individualist strivers whose virtue could be measured by the material rewards they wrested from the wilderness. They made themselves while making a nation.

Yet the Pilgrims themselves would not have recognized this description. Neither they nor the larger community of contemporary Puritans understood their survival and eventual prosperity in the New World as a credit to themselves, except – and this is no small thing – insofar as they were God's Elect. Among their earthly sources of aid and sustenance were Native Americans, whose food and guidance helped them to survive. In some cases, they and other European migrants took over Native supplies and villages abandoned because of disease. Moreover, they practiced communal approaches to production, consumption, and property that would have sorely distressed the *Challenge*'s 1975 audience, just as they had frustrated the contemporary entrepreneurial imperialist John Smith. Their preachers and civil leaders alike railed against the dangers of individualist and materialist ambitions that threatened their social order.[23]

Nonetheless, *Challenge* was not alone in refashioning origins stories to support individualistic attitudes in twentieth-century America. That same year William Simon – then Treasury Secretary – asked rhetorically in *Playboy* magazine, "What the hell happened to the American free-enterprise spirit: *Did the Puritans need subsidies?*"[24] And, yet, early Anglo-American colonizers *did* rely on "subsidies." They balanced entrepreneurship with communal values and aid from European patrons and Native Americans, but that complexity was invisible in these twentieth-century tales of early American bootstrapping.

MOVING BUSINESSPEOPLE TO ACTION

Conservatives' sense of crisis in their cultural authority and its implications for political authority inspired many to put their shoulders to the wheel of cultural politics in the 1970s. They invested seemingly limitless dollars and other resources to defend their notion of individualism against publicly based constraints and, thereby, to regain control of the country's political and cultural narratives through publicity, publications, trade associations, think tanks, lobbying, religious movements, and sympathetic organizations.[25] For example, the Business Roundtable, an association of corporate chief executive officers, formed in 1972, and in 1975 it produced an "economic education" program. The Roundtable spent much of its revenues, about $1.2 million (equivalent to almost $7 million in 2024), hoping to teach Americans about big business's perspectives.[26]

The US Chamber of Commerce, which has long called itself "The Voice of Business," also mobilized in the early 1970s to rally businesspeople who were worried about business's reputation. To inspire anyone who wasn't sufficiently worried already, Lewis F. Powell, Jr., in 1971 shortly before he was appointed to the US Supreme Court, crafted a provocative document, "Attack on American Free Enterprise System." The fears highlighted in this thirty-four-page typescript were not unique to him, but he articulated them forcefully and from a position of high respect. He began: "No thoughtful person can question that the American economic system is under broad attack." The Chamber took Powell's ominous warning to heart. The next year, for example, they published "Meeting the Attack against Business" in their *Washington Report* to alert American business that it faced "the test of survival." To dramatize their warning, the article's illustration showed red paint thrown against homes and industries.[27]

Despite such efforts to energize businesspeople, when Richard Lesher became the US Chamber's president in 1975, he did not believe that the organization had done enough to combat business's cultural and political challenges. Determined to "kick-start the Chamber of Commerce into a modern, relevant force," he soon "focused in particular on . . . the Powell Memorandum," which closed with Powell's warning that "business and the enterprise system are in deep trouble, and the hour is late." Knowing that storytelling was key to his mission, Lesher moved quickly, in part by producing a widely disseminated weekly newspaper column, "The Voice of Business." Also early on, he built a television studio in the Chamber's Washington, DC, headquarters, and, in 1979, launched the nationally syndicated weekly show *It's Your Business*. This master communicator understood how to reach his audiences: "we have the news program and tuck in policy issues and stories within that, and we'll get our message out loud and clear."[28] And the Chamber did just that. During Lesher's five years leading the Chamber, its membership nearly doubled from 52,000 to almost 98,000 companies.[29]

Lesher was glad to take credit for the Chamber's expanded reach during his twenty-two years there, calling his 2017 memoir *The Voice of Business*, with the subtitle: *The Man Who Transformed the United States Chamber of Commerce*. The jacket declared the book "a hopeful and uniquely American story, a remarkable testament to personal perseverance and the ever-present opportunities in a free society." Lesher portrayed himself as a self-made hero in "the tale of a bold and independent child who came from meager means and faced many difficult obstacles, with nothing handed to him along the way as he charted the course of his life." His alcoholic father hadn't brought home enough money, sometimes not even enough for the rent. To get along, Richard and his sister took multiple, often harsh, jobs early on, and his "work ethic took root during those formative years. During the Depression, if you wanted something, you had to earn it." He even came to appreciate how his father "made me tenacious and independent" with "his dark, violent, and underachieving legacy."[30]

The contrast between Richard Lesher's background and his accomplishments, plus his high-profile advocacy for free enterprise made him a strong candidate for the Horatio Alger Award Committee (HAAC), and he received that honor five years after rising to lead the Chamber. His pride was still evident in 2017, when his hometown newspaper, *Public Opinion*, interviewed him and featured a photograph of him holding his award with the caption: "Richard

Lesher's life is a story about rising above hardships. He is shown with a 1980 Horatio Alger Award."[31]

"THE HORATIO ALGER DREAM OF AMERICA"

Another recipient of the Horatio Alger Award incidentally testified to the resurgence of interest in the Victorian-era author as a mid-twentieth-century symbol of individualist bootstrapping. Paul Gray Hoffman was a man of extraordinary achievements: CEO of Studebaker Corporation, first president of the Ford Foundation, a leader in international postwar economic planning, and recipient of the Medal of Freedom for implementing the Marshall Plan. Yet a *New Yorker* reporter overheard him say at the 1953 Horatio Alger Awards ceremony that he had "never read Horatio Alger, or even heard of him, until five years ago." As it happened, Hoffman had been a finalist for that first year of the award, which, given the timing of his confession, may well have been his first contact with the iconic Alger. During the ceremony, he admitted to having started life with advantages but, nevertheless, he "heartily" endorsed "hard work," regardless of one's initial circumstances. The Horatio Alger Award Committee's (HAAC) project of spreading "the Horatio Alger dream of America" and its inspiration was making headway.[32]

The HAAC's 1951 mission statement featured their dedication to the "American tradition of fair play, adventure, industry, equality of opportunity, and the democratic principles of free and competitive enterprise popularly known as the 'Horatio Alger' success story." As we saw earlier, misreadings of Alger's legacy rather than the books themselves or Alger's actual beliefs inspired this mission. During a "Special Meeting" in 1970 shortly after the death of founder Kenneth Beebe, board members considered a variety of options to raise public interest and engage youth. Charles E. Wilson wondered "about the original Horatio Alger books" and confessed that he "has never seen a copy and would like to." He suggested that "maybe we could bring them back." Fellow board colleague Frank K. Noll, however, declared that "the original books are not good for the present." Period. More gently, he offered to send a copy "to Mr. Wilson if he wanted to look it over." Actually reading Alger was beside the point.[33]

Alger's symbolism colored decades of board minutes in yet another way. The most common phrase they used among themselves to refer to the organization and its goals was "Horatio Alger," such as in 1975 when the board deliberated "the future of Horatio Alger."[34] In their conversations and board minutes, they transformed "Horatio Alger" from a person and author to their institution and its cause. For them, the antiquated author had been reduced to a symbol – their symbol.

RAGS-TO-RICHES FOR "THE HORATIO ALGER"

From its origins in 1947 through the 1970s, the HAAC struggled. Dedicated board members tried to figure out how best to select awardees and also how to define and fulfill "a purpose to the youth of the nation," as Arthur Rubloff urged in 1976. Rubloff had received the Horatio Alger Award in 1955 as a real estate "mogul," "colossus," and "czar" who was prominent in the redevelopment of Chicago's downtown. Dedicated to the "Horatio Alger" cause, he pressed the board to make "an organized effort to collect money" and to recruit awardees "who are interested in supporting this organization." Through all their discussions, a growing sense of urgency became apparent in the mid 1970s, not only about the organization's prospects, but about the nation's. Most agreed that the awards event should include "a short speech on Americanism," perhaps even by Ronald Reagan, who had accepted the award in 1969 while governor of California. Board leader Norman Vincent Peale noted that promoting the HAAC's version of Horatio Alger's legacy "to its greatest potential [would] let the youth of America be aware of our country's great free enterprise system that is still very much alive today."[35]

Despite all of these deliberations and efforts, as late as 1979, the HAAC was still "operating on a shoe string budget," its board worried. They resolved to strengthen HAAC's ability to "spread the Free Enterprise philosophy of the organization and expand the awards program across the nation" but were unsure how to do that. The old business model by which the organization received most of its revenues through the sale of books full of "living proof" stories on successes in free enterprise and testimonials from its award winners could not support grander visions. Soliciting contributions from individuals yielded little, and support from awardees' employers or foundations wasn't forthcoming, especially under that decade's stagflation burdens. The HAAC had to offer more. Even its tax-exempt status could be at risk, one board member noted, if they didn't do more, such as offer scholarships large enough to make a difference in students' circumstances. In 1975, a board member pointed out "that the Committee has done nothing in the area of benevolence during the thirty years of its existence and that this must be changed immediately" in order to justify its calls for support.[36] Yet the numbers of that "shoe string budget" were daunting: in 1975, total assets were $112,754.60 although projected expenses for the next year added up to about $150,000.[37]

In this context, the dramatic expansion of the US Chamber of Commerce's outreach and membership, and the public exposure that Richard Lesher built along the way, offered a useful model for the HAAC as it continued to search for its path into the 1980s. Abraham Ellis expressed his sense of urgency when board members met in 1976 to discuss fundraising: "HAAC must convince the companies and foundations that the free enterprise system is on the line." He had served actively on the HAAC board since 1951, and now he joined others to urge that the organization amplify support to meet broad national threats by recruiting corporate support. He predicted "That is where the money will come from, not from the individuals." As part of that same conversation, Rubloff agreed that award winners should open doors to their corporations, foundations, and acquaintances, as well as contribute themselves.[38]

About the same time that the HAAC was worrying about both its finances and the free enterprise system, President Jimmy Carter warned of a "crisis of confidence" in the country.[39] (Only the press and Carter's rivals used the term "malaise" in reference to this speech.) As those concerns, especially about America's youth, spread through the press and the promotions of organizations such as the Chamber and Business Roundtable, the HAAC's mission rang true to many able to invest in it. Thus, the HAAC rose on the same tide of pro-business advocacy that fostered the Chamber's numbers and Reagan's election. Total HAAC assets in March of 1980 were higher than its 1979 "shoe string budget," at $291,858.78. Soon, they made more dramatic progress: the 1983 awards event in Pittsburgh hosted 700 guests following a massive outreach campaign to corporations and business leaders, posting a substantial profit despite the current recession. That year's first quarter balance was $779,844. And in 1986, Executive Director Love Smith announced that HAAC held assets of $1,205,728 as of September 30, more than three times that for the same time in 1983. Large gifts, some in six figures, started to appear.[40] Fittingly for an organization named for Horatio Alger, pluck and luck came together at long last.

During the 1980s Horatio Alger's fame spread. People of wealth and power became persuaded that the HAAC's message to the nation's youth was vital. The HAAC renamed itself the Horatio Alger Association of Distinguished Americans (HAADA) in 1981. In 1982 the United States Postal Service issued a commemorative stamp to honor Alger picturing four of his heroes. On the Postal Service's companion postcard, Alger appears stern, with the steadfast visage of a captain of industry, and three vignettes portray scenes of boys scrapping and striving.[41] Nothing reflects Alger's mild demeanor or that *his* heroes always reached their modest successes through wise mentors who rewarded the boys' good character. The postcard's text admitted that Alger's name had become "a colloquialism... widely used to describe a self-made individual who has achieved dramatic economic and social success." That storyline was just fine for his new fans. In 1986, the *New York Times* quoted an HAADA representative as saying that "Horatio Alger is very 'in' these days."[42] Since 1984, the organization has administered a generous college scholarship program, and by 1988, it had built extensive outreach to high schools and the public. Alger had been refashioned and customized into an idiom of individualism and self-making earlier in the century, which harmonized with the neo-individualist character of the century's last decades. And "the Horatio Alger's" coffers were filling fast.

Horatio Alger
His uplifting rags-to-riches stories
inspired young boys to strive for success.

Figure 10.1 Opponents of the New Deal reimagined the stories of the nineteenth-century author Horatio Alger, Jr. Conservatives ever since have remolded his strive-and-succeed themes into individualist "self-made" success stories. This 1982 commemorative stamp and first day of issue envelope from the US Postal Service honored Alger's 150th birthday, but his stern expression on the specially printed envelope belies his gentle nature. Its reference to "rags-to-riches" is also misleading as Alger's heroes got "respectable," never rich. (In author's possession; gift of Terri Lonier)

In the twenty-first century, about 1,000 people typically attend the Horatio Alger Awards ceremonies – elegant affairs complete with black tie and gowns.[43] In 1989, the HAADA moved from New York City to new quarters in Alexandria, Virginia, to be closer to the seat of government. No longer operating on a shoestring, the HAADA ended 2021 with assets of $378,285,688.[44] Scholarships have totaled $245 million since 1984. Alger would surely have rejoiced in these aids to young people, but he would likely have been less content with a new criterion for the HAADA awards: over the last two decades nominations for the award have required a $200,000 pledge on a nominee's behalf.[45] Personal wealth or connections to wealth had not been a formal part of the association's early criteria, and this change reflects how accepting the reality of inequality grew, even within "the Horatio Alger."[46]

STORIES OF SELF-MAKING AND THE POLITICS OF INEQUALITY

President Ronald Reagan confirmed the HAADA's dramatic ascent when he presented Horatio Alger Awards to ten recipients at a huge gala in 1988 that far exceeded founder Kenneth Beebe's most extravagant dreams. During the ceremony, Reagan declared, "I've been fortunate to have won many awards, but I'm most proud of being named recipient of the Horatio Alger Award. I will treasure it all my life." The HAADA exulted in this high-profile endorsement as well as in record-breaking pledges and national media coverage, applauding the awardees and thirty college scholarship recipients.[47]

Reagan had entered the White House in 1981 as a lifelong Horatio Alger fan. Some saw him as a model of Alger-esque success, as did an article that year syndicated by the Newhouse News Service: "Reagan Followed Horatio Alger Path to White House."[48] In 1977, he had proclaimed his Horatio Alger credentials in response to the Mobile [Alabama] Public Library's request to 100 famous Americans to name five books that had influenced them as youths. While most respondents listed what they *ought* to have read, Reagan's letter charmingly confessed to having walked to the library for adventure books such as *Tarzan*. Among the favorites he listed were tales from Horatio Alger and Mark Twain. He concluded that "all my reading left an abiding belief in the triumph of good over evil." The fictions reassured him that "There were heroes who lived by standards of morality and fair play."[49] The adult Ronald Reagan was notable for just that genial manner that the letter to an obscure librarian conveyed.

Yet Reagan (1911–2004) was no more "self-made" than anyone else. A not-really-rags-to-not-quite-riches media star, his movie career was flagging in 1954 when General Electric's management pulled him up by their bootstraps. They hired him to persuade workers and the public to reject the New Deal aspiration to balance business and community interests. Despite his previous union leadership and support for the New Deal, Reagan accepted GE's generous salary, adopted its aggressive free enterprise, anti-union, anti-regulation stance, and took it on the road and over the airwaves.[50] A splendid storyteller who always added a dash of charm and nostalgia to his stories, he made his career and, finally, his fame and fortune telling stories about self-making, both success and failure. Others, including the HAADA, have used his story to make their case for the triumph of ambition and goodness.

As the 1981 "Horatio Alger Path to the White House" article explained, "Both his father and the Horatio Alger books told Ronald that he could accomplish anything if he just had enough ambition." To augment the morality tale and justify his politics, the article continued: "He sincerely believed that the path to success through hard work is still open to all but a fraction of Americans today, poor people and minorities included." Years later, just after Reagan's death in 2004, "The Reagan Example," syndicated by the Scripps Howard News Service, remembered him to be "like one of those honest, hardworking heroes in a Horatio Alger tale." The lesson from that rise was clear – and misleading – that personal responsibility (while necessary) was sufficient on its own: "Ours was and is a land of very nearly endless opportunity." Success, however, required "the inner resources to seek it out and take advantage" of those opportunities. On the other hand, "Convince people of their helplessness, and you diminish the chances that they will ever grasp the values that will rescue them from their plight." They must "hold themselves accountable for themselves ... and apply themselves."[51]

The promoter of a hyperinflated worldview of self-agency, George Gilder ranked high among the influences on Reagan's approach to policymaking. He loathes the progressive state and, like William Simon, blames it for modern poverty. Born in 1939 into Yankee gentry and educated at the very elite and very expensive Exeter Academy and Harvard University thanks to Rockefeller family largesse, Gilder identified, nonetheless, with the troubles of the unfortunate because he lost his father as a child. In middle age, he explained to the *Washington Post*, "When I read Thomas Pettigrew's book dealing with the fatherless black boy, I said 'Hey, that's me.'" Gilder has made his mark on the conservative repertoire with his shrill defenses of inequality, most notably in 1981 with *Wealth and Poverty*, which instantly became canonical for conservatives. His advocacy for "trickle-down economics," also known as "supply-side economics," brought cheers from such powerful storytellers as Reagan and became foundational to his economic policy.[52]

Most relevant here are Gilder's stories about self-made success and self-made failure that blame the poor and the progressive state for America's poverty amid affluence. The preface to *Wealth and Poverty* proclaims it "a great historic irony" that leading figures on "the 'New Right' have become the best friends of the poor in America, while Liberalism administers new forms of bondage and new fashions of moral corruption to poor families." He argues that poor people, lured by the siren songs of welfare programs, cannot find a path to "upward mobility" because "any welfare system will eventually extend and perpetuate poverty" and, thereby, eliminate the incentives "that prompted previous generations of poor people to escape poverty through the invariable routes of work, family, and faith." Although himself the beneficiary of Rockefeller benevolence, he contended that a "subsidy" can "dissolve ... the disciplines of work." He recommended that "generous and seductive programs" should be replaced by "relatively unpalatable in-kind supports."[53]

Likewise, Gilder blamed the progressive state and its taxes for reducing ambition among the wealthy because "demagogic politicians impose" taxes "to punish" the rich. If allowed free rein, the rich would fulfill their "function," namely to create "opportunities for the classes below." In his chapter "The War Against Wealth" Gilder lamented "society's hostility to its greatest benefactors, the producers of wealth." To his regret, "what causes poverty is the widespread belief that wealth does." Black people, he judged, are especially victims of this "false and crippling view of society" which can "incapacitate all of the poor who believe it," making impossible their "upward admiration" and mobility.[54]

Gilder decried the "moral hazards" of the welfare state that, he believed, "promote the value of being 'poor.'" The social safety net generates perverse incentives, he believed, that encourage welfare recipients to maximize their benefits and lower their "motivation and self-reliance." He assumed that everyone's situation was self-made and that poor people have no internal motivation for self-improvement, instead imposing "a rising burden of taxation on working families." In doing so, he reinforced the myth of self-made success – and failure. In a chapter with the title "The Myths of Discrimination," he denied that racial discrimination affected poverty because it was "hard to find . . . anywhere."[55]

A cluster of news stories reinforced diatribes like Gilder's to aggravate public concerns and racial prejudices. One theme featured so-called "welfare queens" and blamed the Great Society and safety net programs. In 1974 the *Chicago Tribune* drew attention to this theme with an article about Linda Taylor, a disturbingly accomplished cheater. This article and those that followed described her as living luxuriously using a clutch of aliases to defraud welfare programs, pension plans in several states, and insurance companies. Chicago's *Daily Herald* called Taylor a "ripoff artist" and quoted a former Illinois Public Aid Director who described Taylor's as "the most massive case of welfare fraud ever perpetrated in the 50 states."[56] Widespread attention to her notoriously successful swindling colored welfare cheating as Black and female.

Just as stories of exceptional rises like Andrew Carnegie's or Henry Ford's have justified capitalist enterprise, exceptional stories of welfare abuse have vilified public programs. These opposite storylines apply the same logic, namely that exceptional lives can be generalized to judge an entire socioeconomic system or a portion of its citizenry, in these cases to endorse inequality. Whether the narratives are accurate, exaggerated, or entirely fictional matters less than if a constituency accepts them. Ronald Reagan, a master storyteller, built an anti-welfare litany that included his boast about having "lopped 400,000 off the welfare rolls" while California governor. One of his narrative tools then was a form letter that his office sent out in response to complaints about fraud: "We receive hundreds of letters daily from overburdened taxpayers citing news accounts of welfare fraud." Reagan's tales were both notorious and well-wrought but not at all unique among parables about "deadbeat dads" and "welfare queens" who cheated "hard-working," over-taxed citizens because of an indulgent social safety net that reduced everyone's potential for self-making.[57]

Reagan had added a critique of welfare abuse to his anti-welfare repertoire as he bid for the Republican presidential nomination in 1976. Although he seems not to have used the term "welfare queen" in stump speeches, he did use it in a radio broadcast that year, and he alluded to it often. More to the point, he repeatedly told audiences about an unnamed Chicago woman's welfare swindles as an indicator of allegedly widespread misuse of public funds. In a typical speech in New Hampshire, he described this person as having "80 names, 30 addresses, 12 Social Security cards and is collecting veterans benefits on four nonexisting deceased husbands." Her "tax-free cash income alone is over $150,000," he alleged. Elsewhere, he described her as having stolen a million dollars, used more than fifty addresses, driven several new cars, and so on. However, all that could be proven against her in a court case that sent her to prison in 1977 was a stolen $8,000.[58] The "welfare queen" as a straw woman in anti-welfare, anti-government rhetoric mattered vastly more than the facts of the case. Stories, whether fictional or merely exaggerated, about heroes and villains play better than stories about government agencies that benefit faceless multitudes, especially if those multitudes can be unjustly vilified as unworthy slackers.

Reagan's presidential administration ended or curtailed several federal programs and offices, and imposed eligibility rules that made it difficult for beneficiaries of assistance to build savings from wage work or to own a car for commuting. Similarly, a reduction in childcare subsidies made wage work more difficult to secure.[59] Program cuts in Reagan's first two years, combined with heightened eligibility restrictions, pushed 35 percent of working parents out of Aid to Families with Dependent Children (AFDC), and reduced by 28 percent child nutrition programs, among other cuts. Overall, despite the administration's emphasis on the morality of work, many of its cuts raised the barriers to holding jobs, increasing poverty not independence. As inequality widened between 1980 and 1988, average real incomes among the lowest fifth of families fell by about 2 percent.[60] Thus, President Reagan could report in his first State of the Union Address that his proposals to slash budgets for social programs would cut $44 billion "because available resources are going not to the needy, but to the greedy."[61]

Despite Reagan's constant cheerleading for entrepreneurship, as president he approached citizens' attempts at starting and operating small businesses from the same perspective as welfare benefits, namely denying even small amounts of aid to people striving at the lower end of the economy. In that spirit, the Reagan administration immediately attacked the Small Business Administration (SBA). David Stockman, Reagan's Director of the Office of Management and Budget, lumped the SBA into his deep "social pork barrel," in part because of its support for minority-owned businesses.[62]

That a convivial and genial leader waged harsh attacks against the country's poor and less fortunate seems inconsistent. But his belief in the myth of

Figure 10.2 In 1981, early in his first term, President Ronald Reagan signed the Economic Recovery Tax Act while at his California ranch. This law reflected his policy goals to minimize taxes on the affluent and reduce government functions for everyone else. (Bettmann via Getty Images)

self-making and his abiding belief in that possibility for others demonstrates how a myth can smooth the rough edges of contradiction. After all, if one person can rise above his origins with enough determination, then he needn't have patience for those who did not.

SELF-MADE FAILURE IN THE 1990S

The tall tale of the "welfare queen" continued prominently in the public imagination to justify policy "reforms," and this momentum extended into Democrat Bill Clinton's White House.[63] Polls in the 1990s indicated that while most Americans believed that genuinely needful people should receive public assistance, they objected to welfare programs out of concern for widespread fraud.[64] The phantasm of the "welfare queen," which also evoked Americans' anti-aristocratic traditions, supported a critique that went beyond concerns about fraud. It conjured a general impression that recipients of aid were lazy, idle, and entitled – the very antithesis of the self-made hero of modern life. Tacit appeals to the myth of self-made success and failure through lurid and humiliating stories excused reductions in public support and, thereby, hopes for individual and cross-generational improvement among Americans with the hardest lives.

These myths about welfare programs became so ingrained so quickly because they built on the vibrant myth of self-making, timeless prejudices of caste, and regressive stories that discredit the progressive state. The so-called "undeserving poor" offered a ready explanation to citizens distressed by the nation's economic troubles after 1970, alongside what they saw as other signs of moral and cultural decay. This view became so prevalent in the 1980s that Bill Clinton (b. 1946) successfully campaigned in 1992 on a platform that included promises to "end welfare as we know it." From July 1992 when he accepted the Democratic Party's nomination to the end of 2000, Clinton used the phrase "end welfare as we know it" on hundreds of public occasions, reflecting and reinforcing the triumphs of storytellers on cultural and political stages. With broad bipartisan, if not at all universal, support, Clinton then shepherded the Personal Responsibility and Work Opportunity Reconciliation Act (PRWORA) into law. He highlighted what had become a slogan when he signed the PRWORA on August 22, 1996, "an historic opportunity to end welfare as we know it ... by promoting the fundamental values of work, responsibility, and family." The term "Personal Responsibility" in the Act's title had become a modern equivalent of "self-making" and "self-improvement." The implication was clear that people within the welfare system lacked America's "fundamental values." Only a new "system of incentives which reinforce work and family and independence" could "change what is wrong."[65]

PRWORA did not by any means head off further attacks on Great Society and even New Deal programs. A prominent source of attacks was Republican Congressional Representative Newt Gingrich, who in 1994 had co-authored the "Contract with America." Clinton incorporated many of its recommendations into PRWORA and hoped, in vain, that "now welfare is no longer a political football to be kicked around." Although Clinton insisted that "It's a personal responsibility of every American who ever criticized the welfare system to help the poor people now to move from welfare to work," critics, including Gingrich, did not take up the call to "help." Instead, they only intensified their insistence that people had only themselves to blame, despite significant reductions in public resources. Near the end of his tenure in December of 2000, Clinton attributed to PRWORA's success "a renewed sense of responsibility [for] millions of former welfare recipients [who] now know the dignity of work." He boasted that "we've cut welfare caseloads by more than 8 million people," including "1.2 million parents ... determined to build better lives."[66] This boast implicitly denied that those people might have been doing their best all along "to build better lives" as they scraped by.

Clinton saw himself as a progressive who had risen from circumstances arguably more dire than Reagan's (although Clinton never received the HAADC's consecration). That he could believe and promote the logic of meritocracy – that work and personal responsibility sufficed for success – proves the pervasiveness of the myth of self-made failure, the flip side of the myth of self-made success. Decades of stories that had been pounded out to condemn allegedly derelict people who gamed public assistance had done their damage and reinforced age-old class and racial prejudices about a pathological culture of poverty. The practical outcomes of less-is-more policies have included cuts to education, food stamps, Medicaid, and other programs for survival and self-improvement on the margins. Racist undertones have also obscured the realities of White poverty. Ignoring White people in need condemned them as outliers who should have been self-sufficient rather than self-made failures.[67]

TAXES, COMMUNITY, AND SELF-MADE SUCCESS

Because tax codes enact political decisions about government actions, debates about taxes are always arenas for contests over cultural as well as political authority. Applying the myth of self-made success to such debates was unimaginable back when it referred to self-made drunks, generals, and preachers, but once the myth applied to material conditions, it became useful as a rhetorical tool to shape tax codes.

"Taxation has always been intimately related to democracy" begins economic historian Sidney Ratner's 1942 classic, *American Taxation: Its History as a Social Force in Democracy*. Taxation, he continued, "has always been a major source of conflict" because some try to use it "for concentrating wealth and income," while others believe it should facilitate "a society free of glaring inequalities." A tax system should, Ratner believed, "be measured in terms of all its human consequences," and his measure was whether it "enable[d] most individuals within a society to maintain their sense of independence."[68] Ratner's description of taxes calls to mind earlier forms of community obligation and service that were once integral to versions of self-making as self-improvement to serve. In contrast, ideas of self-making have come to support the self-made success myth that has facilitated avoiding obligations to a shared community. Advocates for regressive tax codes use language and stories that help frame progressive taxation as unfairly punishing the successes of hard-working citizens rather than as advancing the common good.

The concept that taxation "punishes" success has arisen episodically. In 1894, for example, the Wilson-Gorman Act imposed a modest income tax as a partial substitute for reduced tariffs – partially replacing a regressive tax with a progressive one. Less than 1 percent of the population would have paid this 2 percent tax, but objectors claimed to express widespread distress. Newspapers warned that "The income tax may be defined as a penal affair, intended to punish men for being successful in business."[69] Thirty years later, the idea of self-making was summoned to justify a tax policy when none other than the exceedingly rich Treasury Secretary Andrew Mellon insisted that no fiscal policy should be "a means of punishing wealth." Because "equality of opportunity" was a founding principle of the nation, he asserted, "monetary success is not a crime." Taxing it, even if "in some way for the social good of our civilization," violated national principles. Although few citizens read Mellon's detailed analysis of tax policies, in 1931 newspapers nationwide picked up on a key passage: "Taxation should not be used as a field for socialistic experiment, or as a club to punish success, but as a means of raising revenue to support the Government."[70] This sentence appeared widely as a column filler, apparently requiring no commentary or explanation.[71]

Thus, Richard Nixon's 1960 campaign speech to the Association of Business Economists joined a long tradition when it decried taxes as unduly punitive and burdensome on the successful. Mid-century assertions that taxation penalized success grew more forceful as a way to oppose progressive social programs. Senator Barry Goldwater blended those arguments in his widely influential 1960 book, *The Conscience of a Conservative*. "I do not believe in punishing success," he declared regarding the graduated income tax. It was "immoral – to deny the man whose labor has produced more abundant fruit ... the opportunity of enjoying the abundance he has created." In this view, "he" – a single individual – "has created" this abundance alone and without incurring debts to the community. Goldwater worried that taxes that support "the Welfare State," as "the currently favored instrument of collectivization," could destroy free enterprise and freedom if citizens vote to become "wards and dependents" of the state. A presumption of individualist self-making was fundamental to Goldwater's notion of freedom: "if we take from a man the personal responsibility for caring for his material needs, we take from him also the will and the opportunity to be free."[72] Again, "personal responsibility" replaced the older duty for "self-improvement" but here as a means to pursue individual freedom and not as an obligation to advance the common good.

A Harris Survey the month before the 1964 presidential election between Barry Goldwater and Lyndon B. Johnson similarly linked the myth of self-made success and opposition to progressive social policies. The poll asked "a carefully drawn cross-section of the electorate" about their beliefs regarding the "welfare state." Setting the tone in self-making terms, the first statement to rank was "Self-reliance is a trait of the strong." Overall 84 percent of respondents agreed, with slightly more among Goldwater voters than among Johnson voters. The other dozen statements elicited greater divergences. For example, 82 percent of Goldwater supporters believed that "Welfare and relief make people lazy," compared to 59 percent of Johnson's. Asked if "The New Deal has outlived its usefulness," the proportions were 75 percent and 44 percent, respectively. On the idea that the "Federal tax system is used to punish success," Goldwater supporters agreed exactly twice as frequently as Johnson supporters, 48 percent and 24 percent. Although Louis Harris concluded that there was no "mandate to undo the last 30 years of welfare measures," bringing together questions about self-reliance, taxing the successful, and "lazy" welfare recipients showed that they had all become elements of the same political debate, and all colored by the cultural authority self-making's advocates had achieved.[73]

In this same spirit, President Ronald Reagan complemented his regressive social policies with opposition to progressive tax policies. Speaking in 1984 to the Conservative Political Action Conference, he rejoiced in America's "opportunity society" while "others run down America and seek to punish success." It was okay, he assured his audience, to be called "greedy for not wanting government to take more and more of your earnings" and, also, to reject calls for "shared sacrifices." Casting welfare recipients as freeloaders, pushing them into self-reliant independence was for their own good and not just for taxpayers' relief: "mediocrity and despair" would result from "treating [adults] as helpless children to be forever dependent."[74]

All in all, by the end of the twentieth century, a corrosive and powerful paradox had emerged that has continued to gain momentum: even as resources were cut that could assist those who were not affluent to improve themselves, the individualist mythology of self-making grew stronger and limited traditional obligations to assist. Whereas revering wealth and taking credit for success were once sins against God, the poor, and the community, the myth of self-made success had evolved to make reverence for self-agency admirable and wealth the measure of self-improvement. The historical burdens of class, race, and gender inequalities have no place in this rhetoric. The presidential election of 2000 reinforced this specter of self-made success and showed how people with rare advantages could claim its blessings. Since then, the arrogant notion of self-made success has increasingly fed the hubris of individualist capitalism to justify replacing communities' goals and means for improvement with individuals' goals and means, subsidized by regressive tax codes.

11

The Myth's Twenty-First-Century Victories

A newspaper advertisement for Jack Welch's 2001 autobiography, *Jack: Straight from the Gut*, proclaims it to be "the story of a self-made man and a self-described rebel." Another ad promises that "the self-made business mogul provides guidance for attaining your goals." Yet in his "Author's Note" Welch ardently rejected the notion of succeeding alone, insisting instead that "Nearly everything I've done in my life has been accomplished with other people." It's not that he was averse to the term "self-made," but he used it only to refer to his predecessor CEO at General Electric, Reg Jones, who also grew up in modest circumstances. Whatever Welch's actual thoughts on self-making, marketing his story in the new millennium required connecting it unambiguously to the myth. Such was the myth's cultural authority.[1]

In the years since, the strength of the myth of self-made success has survived any number of challenges, including national calamities fostered by self-interest and business hubris. Welch, for example, dedicated *Jack* "To the hundreds of thousands of GE employees whose ideas and efforts made this book possible," but he treated underlings as expendable, as if GE needed only him. And this despite decades of encouraging horizontal, team-oriented management methods. Thus, beginning in 1981 he aggressively eliminated jobs and moved others to Asia. Among managers, he gave top performers bonuses and fired the bottom 10 percent annually as a matter of policy; when he retired, he still admonished managers that it was "a sin to keep the bottom 10 percent." Non-managerial employees were also cut, sometimes whole units at a time. Over his first five years, he proudly noted, "81,000 people – or 1 in every 5 in our industrial businesses – lost their jobs for productivity reasons." Hence his nickname "Neutron Jack," evoking the terror of a weapon designed to destroy people but leave buildings undamaged. Nonetheless, it became apparent not long after his retirement that Welch's relentless drive for profits regardless of means had, in fact, damaged GE's structures. Without a $139 billion bailout from the federal government, the onetime industrial giant would have collapsed in 2008, and it eventually had to be dismantled in 2021.[2] Yet, in one of many, many instances of celebrity more manufactured than earned by merit, popular culture still perpetuates the story of

Welch's mythical CEO heroism and the broader myth of self-made heroism that accepted his persona of rugged individualism.[3]

With the turn into this millennium, the four-century evolution of the myth of self-made success – and its corollary, self-made failure – had etched itself deeply into American culture. No longer blasphemous or in violation of cultural norms, self-made success seemed not only possible; it had become an expected assessment, independent of individuals' circumstances. Storytellers can now take for granted the myth's explanation for everyone's fates as they construct tales on behalf of their personal, cultural, social, or political agendas. To be sure, challenges to its use continue, coming to the fore when claimants overstep their credibility, exceed their ability to control their own fates and others', or the consequences of their ambitions are obviously dire. Yet even when challenged, it is clear that the myth has solidified into a hard individualism, and the original reason to praise self-making – to reward self-improvement in service of the common good – has slipped away, unnoticed.

To help gauge how deeply the self-made myth permeates twenty-first-century American values and policies, we can place its uses into three broad and often overlapping clusters of stories. These clusters vary according to how obviously their narratives depend on the myth, but they are alike in the ideological work that the myth does to legitimate worldly ambitions and rapidly rising inequality.[4] The most flagrant uses fall into the first cluster, "Illusions about Self-Made Success," in which advocates seek cultural or political authority based on claims to self-made success and its esteem despite their abundant advantages. These stories highlight how their protagonists overcame headwinds but ignore their beneficial tailwinds.

A second cluster, "Stories and Effects," includes more subtle appeals to the myth that underlie assumptions shaping public attitudes and policymaking. Into this cluster fall beliefs about the nation as a pure meritocracy in which self-making reigns; these beliefs can lead to despair as much as they can inspire ambition. Also into this cluster falls policymaking where the shadow of the self-made myth prevails, such as in "reforms" of welfare and tax policies like those we saw under Presidents Ronald Reagan and Bill Clinton; the second President Bush added to that genre. Arguments for rolling back regulations in the name of free enterprise and individualist opportunities appear in this second cluster, as well, with consequences that included the scandals and financial crashes that initiated the Great Recession in 2008. Yet tolerance continues for what brilliant, if ethically challenged, businesspeople do to seek their fortunes.

The third cluster encompasses a variety of cultural presumptions and policies regarding philanthropy. "Giving Back But Holding On" looks through the lens of self-made success and reveals a paradox that seems benign on its surface, but that, like most everything else related to the modern myth of self-making, undercuts the community and excuses withdrawing from it – even while "giving back." Donors at any level can do a lot of good, of course, so it's not that their activities are necessarily harmful in themselves. It's that their freedom to do whatever they wish with large accumulations of wealth assumes that none of the people, communities, or institutions that make wealth generation possible have any right or usefulness in determining its allocation. That assumption, of course, stems directly from the myth of self-made success: if tycoons make their fortunes on their own, they should be able to dispense them on their own, gleaning a veneer of respectability and loads of flattery along the way.

It was not always so. Before the myth of self-made success gained its modern cultural authority, individuals' wealth was embedded in webs of obligation. Boston's seventeenth-century merchant Robert Keayne was an unpleasant, self-righteous man, but he gave back to God's community through taxes and bequest out of recognition that his material success depended on forces beyond himself.[5] He was neither kind nor generous, but a century of hard sell about self-made success had not dulled his grasp of the limits of his own self-agency.

ILLUSIONS ABOUT SELF-MADE SUCCESS

Claimants to self-made success can display remarkable self-righteousness, regardless of how illusory their own claims are to that honorific. Three prominent twenty-first-century cases illustrate how deeply ingrained the myth has become in American culture, impervious to people's actual situations: George W. Bush, Donald J. Trump, and Kylie Jenner. Each of these people began their lives in great wealth – both financial and social – yet they all believed they were self-made, with a range of effects. For each of the former presidents, the consequences included tax codes and cutbacks to social programs that have worked against people whose beginnings are truly difficult. The impact of Jenner's story came from the story itself, which got wide distribution within popular culture and, as some critics pointed out, implied that there was no reason why anyone couldn't do so well. Each of these cases, and others that this chapter will report, suggests that anyone who hadn't become rich wasn't really trying and, perhaps, hadn't deserved to do better, after all.

Former President George W. Bush inherited a vast estate of social, political, and financial capital from both parents, with prominent family roots since the seventeenth century that have included senators, judges, governors, and, notably, his father, former President George H. W. Bush. Nonetheless, when Oprah Winfrey interviewed him during the 2000 presidential campaign, he wistfully denied any benefit from those riches and privileges, not even from his

Figure 11.1 During the 2000 presidential campaign, Oprah Winfrey interviewed both major party candidates. George W. Bush presented himself as a self-made success, denying that he had received any advantages from his wealthy and high-powered family other than the "great gift of unconditional love." (Photo by TANNEN MAURY / AFP via Getty Images)

"daddy's name." Somehow he imagined that his only advantage had been his parents' "great gift of unconditional love."[6] He must have forgotten his access to powerful networks, legacy admissions to elite schools, and the $15 million profit from his 1989 purchase of a tiny piece of the Texas Rangers baseball team with money borrowed from a bank on whose board he sat. A consortium of family and friends had funded the other 99.4 percent purchase price, glad to include the son of a sitting president. The next year he profited from selling stock in the floundering Harken Energy Corporation while he sat on its board, which had been supported for several years by outsized investments from the Harvard Management Company – investments that began in 1986 while his father was vice president and were incomprehensible from a strictly financial view. The Securities and Exchange Commission investigated what seemed like insider trading, but as president, Bush denied full disclosure of the SEC's report. The myth of self-made success enabled Bush's selective memory about these and other episodes. It always exacerbates the human penchant to underestimate – or even be oblivious to – the tailwinds that push us forward, while the headwinds that challenge us are ever visible, typically inflated relative to others' challenges.[7]

THE MYTH'S TWENTY-FIRST-CENTURY VICTORIES

Bolstered by his faith in having made his own way in the world, when Bush announced his presidential campaign in 1999, he said that his "first goal is to usher in the responsibility era." The next year, during his interview with Winfrey, he again emphasized the importance of personal "accountability" and objected to what he saw as a widespread "culture of irresponsibility." In keeping with standard individualist platitudes, he explained that when "government" stepped in to assist people, it reduced their "individual responsibility" and "freedom" to make "decisions in their own lives." Yet, accepting responsibility for one's actions can play out differently according to one's circumstances. For example, in 1976 when Bush was thirty years old, he was arrested for drunken driving in Maine near his family's Kennebunkport estate. He spent ninety minutes in custody and paid a $150 fine (almost $850 in 2024) – neither of which was burdensome for this son of privilege. Years later, in 1993, his parents thanked the arresting officer for how he "handled" the situation, which they said was "part of the learning process" for their adult son.[8]

When that story went public during Bush's 2000 presidential campaign, he admitted that "I've oftentimes said that years ago I made some mistakes." Yet this and other "mistakes" had no significant consequences for him, in contrast to the likely outcomes for those less privileged, whose youthful mistakes can upend their lives, put them in debt or prison, cost them future employment and bank credit. Associated Press editor Gary Fields recently listed "family, education, jobs, friends, neighborhoods, adult interventions, hard work and good luck" among "the things you need to go right to lift the weight of your birth circumstances" for "children born poor regardless of race."[9] In other words, poor children have precious few buffers to protect them from mistakes.

Soon after this patrician politician became president in 2001, his illusions about self-making carried real-world consequences that worsened inequality and made it harder for many to improve their lots, however hard they tried. One month after he entered the White House, Bush proposed a budget that would keep "the American Dream in everyone's reach" so that citizens could "move up the economic ladder of success." The reformed tax code would "not penalize hard work" or "block the way for hard-working people" into the middle class. His plan would "erase inequities" and reduce "the struggles of American families" through "tax relief for everybody who pays taxes." Nonetheless, despite this rosy pledge, the "Bush tax cuts" in 2001 and 2003, like Reagan's two decades earlier, had dire impacts, exacerbating inequality and massively increasing the national debt. According to a 2010 analysis, 38 percent of the reduction went to the tiny top 1 percent of tax filers, and 55 percent to the top 10 percent. The lowest 20 percent of tax filers received 1 percent of the cuts. Put another way, taxable income between $17,000 and $68,000 received no rate reduction at all, while rates for incomes above $374,000 dropped 4.6 percent. Bush pledged that the national debt would fall, but financiers were the only people who benefited when it increased $2.6 trillion by 2010 because federal revenue losses exceeded 2 percent of GDP, which raised everyone's costs of borrowing and thereby the national debt's costs to taxpayers, house buyers, and small business owners.[10]

To make their case, Bush and his anti-tax partners continued the earlier self-making theme that "high income tax rates punish success." Other leading Republicans who supported tax cuts, including on capital gains, reinforced that rhetoric. Senator Sam Brownback of Kansas insisted in 2001 that the "American people should not be taxed on success, but that is exactly what we are doing when we impose high rates of taxation, particularly on capital gains. We punish people for innovation, thrift, and hard work, and we penalize them for being successful." Representative Steve King of Iowa called taxes on capital gains "this blight on America's economy" as he and others pushed Bush to cut them in 2003.[11] Rhetorical flourishes about protecting small businesses and farmers notwithstanding, capital gains come from asset sales, not from inventing, producing, or selling goods. The effect was to shelter financial profits, not assist people of moderate assets and incomes.[12]

The well-funded anti-tax drumbeat of individualist rhetoric aims to justify and enable retreat from community-based goals and decisions.[13] Nonetheless, while public opinion polls at the time indicated that voters agreed that tax "relief" was a fine idea (as voters generally do), they also expressed even stronger support for other priorities, especially education, health, infrastructure, and reducing the national debt. Since 1973, the National Opinion Research Center at the University of Chicago has conducted polls showing that there never had been a time across those five decades when Americans wanted to cut taxes more than they wanted to add to programs they valued. Even in 2000, despite three decades of aggressive anti-tax campaigning, overall net support for domestic social spending (support for *more* spending minus support for less) was a whopping 35.5 percent, with health and education at the top of preferences.[14] According to these and other polls, Bush's tax "relief" overrode public opinion about priorities, taking on enormous and expensive debt to compensate for lost government revenues. Tax codes based on his actual, not rhetorical, ethos minimize what the affluent owe to the whole and, therefore, what the whole – including its unfortunate members – can ask of its most affluent.

"You can spend your money better than the Government can." American individuals and families "deserve to keep more of their own money." No government should "tell families how to spend their money."[15] "*Your* money" – constantly repeating this phrase pushed hard against trust in the wisdom of the community and its roles to enhance individual lives. In contrast, Boston's seventeenth-century merchant Robert Keayne and his fellow Puritans understood, as we saw earlier, that no one's money comes out of a vacuum. Making money requires markets and exchange mechanisms. As well, making money requires infrastructure such as transportation and communication systems, plus, at a minimum, monetary, legal, and policing systems to protect property and transactions. Keayne reluctantly accepted that "the commonwealth or place where we live and where we have got more or less of that estate is also to be considered."[16] As Benjamin Franklin put it in 1783, "All Property, indeed, ... seems to me to be the Creature of publick Convention."[17]

There was a time when two-term President Donald J. Trump presented himself to the world as a self-made man whose extraordinary entrepreneurship had made billions. Certainly, no one else could muster more conceit to tell wannabe businesspeople that "You're fired!" as he did on the "reality" television show *The Apprentice* from 2004 to 2015.[18] That was also a time when journalists and scholars used his sometimes bizarre self-aggrandizement for easy target practice. They pointed, for example, to the fortune with which his father, Fred C. Trump, capitalized and often bailed out Donald's business ventures, as well as the millions Fred distributed to his children in ways that avoided taxes. Researchers also brought to the surface ways that Donald Trump used bankruptcy laws to avoid paying contractors, investors, and workers when his projects failed. Education in his father's circles taught him lucrative skills for applying loopholes in zoning laws and tax codes, and for exploiting workers. It was never difficult to dispute his claims of self-making as a businessman. Instead, it was TV stardom that brought Trump celebrity.[19]

It's easy to see how Trump came to prize the notion of self-made success. As a youth, he and his family had attended Norman Vincent Peale's Marble Collegiate Church in New York City, where the good reverend preached the gospel of positive thinking and money making. Peale wrote admiringly in his own autobiography of the Trumps, father and son. About Donald: "Surely he is one of America's top positive thinkers and positive doers." Trump reciprocated this admiration. He credited Peale as an inspiration, for example in 2009, after he had climbed out of almost a billion dollars of debt, he explicitly attributed his success to Peale, who taught him to be "a firm believer in the power of being positive."[20] Reinforcing Peale's earnest preaching, Trump's father received the Horatio Alger Award in 1985, despite his own inherited advantages. Pictures of Donald at the ceremony include one of him holding his father's trophy.

When Trump's ambitions turned to politics, he sought to be a hero in the Andrew Jackson cast. Jackson was an early victor in nineteenth-century anti-aristocratic electoral campaigns in which "self-making" became acceptable, beginning its movement toward modern meanings. Trump and Jackson share

Figure 11.2 In 1985, Fred Trump, left, Donald J. Trump's father, received the Horatio Alger Award from the Horatio Alger Association of Distinguished Americans. Both men have regarded themselves as self-made despite their substantial inherited social and financial advantages. (Photo by Ron Galella / Ron Galella Collection via Getty Images)

racism and provocative appeals to White populations that feel threatened, as well as claims to self-made success and allegations of having been denied a presidential election. (Jackson won a plurality among four candidates in 1824 but lost in the Electoral College; Trump alleges that he won the 2020 election.) Other commonalities include their intense vindictiveness and rhetorical attacks on elites – from their own positions of wealth and power. Pleased by whatever he knew of the comparisons, Trump spent his time in the Oval Office with a portrait of Andrew Jackson just over his shoulder, prominent in every photo opportunity.[21]

When Ronald Reagan and George W. Bush made their cases for what they called tax "reforms," they argued for "personal responsibility" and against "punishing success," clichés sheltered under the rhetorical umbrella of the myth of self-made success. In contrast, Donald Trump explicitly rejected talk about "reforms," saying that "people don't know what reform is, neither do I. People want tax cuts." Therefore, he only half-jokingly called the draconian 2017 tax bill "the tax cut, cut, cut bill." His stated justification, nonetheless, for the Tax Cut and Jobs Bill came down to mere individualist property ownership, in line with the title of a chapter in his 2011 book, *Time to Get Tough: Making America #1 Again*: "It's Your Money – You Should Keep More of It." In the chapter's first paragraph, he pronounced that "the government confiscates ... your hard-earned money." In 2016, he announced that "I hate what they do with my tax money."[22]

Living in a self-made fantasy breeds arrogance, especially when no real-world accountability bursts the bubble protected by teams of accountants and lawyers. Taxation is a cost of building a community's infrastructure and human resources, but someone who is "self-made" needn't recognize any benefit from a community, so why pay that cost? In the 2016 presidential debates, Hillary Clinton challenged Trump's breach of the four-decade practice of candidates making public their tax returns. She pointed out that the only returns he had ever revealed showed no federal income tax payments. His unhesitating rejoinder: "That makes me smart." Smarter than anyone else, and also more deserving than the citizenry. The commonwealth would have "squandered" what he considered "his money," unlike his spending on gold-plated household fixtures, sundry improprieties, and lawyers to avoid accountability.[23]

Believing himself self-made, Trump's rhetoric has approached the messianic – he alone can save the nation. For example, he told the Conservative Political Action Conference in March 2023 that he was their "voice," their "warrior," their "justice," and most provocatively, "for those who have been wronged and betrayed, I am your retribution." Early in the 2024 presidential campaign, he proclaimed to an audience in New Hampshire that "2024 is our final battle." At a New Hampshire rally following the January primary, he said that winning was the only hope for the country, which otherwise "would be finished." In a melodramatic speech on Super Tuesday, March 5, 2024, he declared that "We're going to win this election, because we have no choice." He told his loyalists, "If we lose this election, we're not going to have a country left," because, he contended, "our country is dying." His hyperbolic attacks against immigrants escalated to include theatrical oaths that "I will stop this invasion. I'm going to do it. . . . I will end the agony of our people ... and the conquest of our country."[24] This heroic rhetoric is grandiose and dangerously divisive as it draws from and reinforces the individualist myth of self-making, as we saw during the 2024 campaign and since the election.

When *Forbes* magazine anointed Kylie Jenner as the "youngest-ever self-made billionaire" in 2019, it raised a firestorm. Could someone with her enormous advantages truly be considered self-made? Although *Forbes* does not represent the nation, it has a high-profile standing among those who are either affluent or have ambitions to become so. In promoting entrepreneurs, *Forbes* began reporting on and ranking what it considered to be self-made billionaires in 2014. Other publications that aim at the ambitious, such as *Business Insider* and *Fortune*, similarly confer the self-made label generously. In short, like *Forbes*, other cheerleaders for the American version of capitalism consider people to be self-made who did not inherit their business or the bulk of their wealth. They rarely take into account unequally distributed non-financial advantages, nor the maxim that it takes some money to make more money.[25]

In defending the *Forbes* accolade, Kim Kardashian, Kylie Jenner's older half-sister, quite rightly noted that many celebrity offspring with similar advantages turn out badly. She reported that she and her sisters are "all 'self-made'" as they never "depended on our parents for anything besides advice." *Forbes* agreed and rated Jenner as a "7" (problematically close to Oprah Winfrey's "10") because this child of a rich celebrity clan did not inherit her wealth, strictly speaking. Her parents "cut her off at the age of 15," she said, and she received no money from them thereafter. Nevertheless, she lived in her mother's mansion until she was almost 18 and benefited from rare social capital and family-based stardom that brought in large sums from modeling and performing.[26] Not wasting inherited social and financial capital can, it seems, count as self-making among the privileged according to those who share a limited appreciation for the advantages *and disadvantages* that affect people's prospects.[27]

Not everyone who participated in the Internet commotion that followed Jenner's coronation agreed that she had earned the tribute. Yes, she had made a lot of money, but, no, her origins were hardly obscure or disadvantaged. How could *Forbes*'s editors have ignored Jenner's advantages? One contributor to that Twitterstorm poignantly expressed the most important point of all, namely that "Calling Kylie Jenner self-made without acknowledging anywhere the incredible head start she had is what allows people to turn around and look at poor people and ask them why they haven't become billionaires yet." In other words, touting self-made success implies self-made failure for everyone else. Aditi Juneja, whom *Forbes* placed on its 2018 "30 under 30" list, explained that such lists "often gloss over the role intergenerational wealth and access plays in success," including that "privilege and access [can] allow some of us to take career risks and be entrepreneurial in ways others can't." Juneja put it succinctly: *Forbes*'s lists fuel "the myth that if you just work hard enough, you can pull yourself up by your own bootstraps. They ignore that some people have neither boots nor straps."[28]

MASTERS AND SHARKS

The arrogance that accompanies belief in one's own self-made success has bestowed recent American popular culture and reality with abundant misfortunes, both personal and national. The Wall Street protagonist of Tom Wolfe's 1987 bestseller novel and 1990 movie *Bonfire of the Vanities* thought of himself as a "Master of the Universe," more than half seriously comparing himself to the hyper-masculine toy figures, which Wolfe describes as "lurid, rapacious plastic dolls." There was "no limit whatsoever" to the money that this Master and his Wall Street colleagues could make with their dealings. Wolfe's portrait of "well-educated young white men baying for money on the bond market" mocked their presumption that they were meritocrats, a "new breed ... of Wall Street egalitarian, a Master of the Universe who was a respecter only of performance." Idleness in "the greed storm" was "a sin not against the self or against God but against Mammon."[29] Yet, in the end, this self-made "Master" came undone because he resolutely disregarded the possibility that the rest of the world could bring him down, which it did.

In that same decade, other fictional Masters were brought low, such as Gordon Gekko in the film *Wall Street* (also 1987), who proclaimed the famously misquoted statement, "The point is, ladies and gentlemen, that greed – for lack of a better word – is good. Greed is right. Greed works." ("Greed is good" is how popular culture boiled down that lengthy passage.) In the real world, people who imagined themselves Masters of the Universe also went down, including Ivan Boesky, who actually said "Greed is all right" in a 1986 university commencement speech and two years later went to prison for insider trading. Boesky's testimony brought down other Masters, most notably Michael Milken, whose prison sentence began in 1990.[30]

Yet the just deserts that undid both fictional and nonfictional "self-made men" as the nation headed toward the new millennium did not shake loose the myth's hold on American culture. Even the 2001 Enron collapse, the nation's largest bankruptcy until that time, did not seriously challenge the cultural or regulatory systems that encouraged the pursuit of evermore profits with little regard for norms – or, in Enron's case, using flagrantly illegal and unregulated financial maneuverings that destroyed employees' pensions and investors' funds.[31]

The cost of Enron's collapse was slight compared to the national and global costs of the Great Recession that began in 2007 and officially ended as 2009 closed, although the harms have continued.[32] This devastating economic downturn, the nation's worst since the Great Depression, resulted in between six and ten million households losing their homes and a rise in unemployment to over 10 percent. The multitude of causes included a housing bubble and a speculation spree fostered by experiments with risky, often incomprehensible, banking practices. In fact, the origins were so complicated that it has taken years to analyze them.[33] What is clear, however, is that entrepreneurs' hubris and brilliance energized the crisis because their unconventional and poorly understood banking instruments, structures, and operations destabilized the economy. In the spirit of the failed Enron, fearless entrepreneurs invented novel financial instruments even they couldn't understand or control.

The myth of self-made success animated the hubris that allowed these entrepreneurs to believe in their own brilliance and efficacy. One of those entrepreneurs was Sanford I. Weill, who rose from modest origins to become a titan of American finance. Like Jack Welch before him, Weill co-authored a memoir marketed as that of a "self-made billionaire." According to newspaper ads, *The Real Deal: My Life in Business and Philanthropy* "shares his path to success in a brutally honest portrayal of his astounding life and career trajectory."[34] At that point, 2006, Weill thought that his titanic creation, Citigroup, was "impregnable." In 2007, the *New York Times* included him in a fawning article that featured several of "The Richest of the Rich, Proud of a New Gilded Age." It described a display of tributes to Weill's achievements in the hallway to his office, especially a collection of framed magazine covers that "heralds Mr. Weill's genius in assembling Citigroup into the most powerful financial institution since the House of Morgan a century ago." Also adorning this hallway was one of the pens with which President Bill Clinton had signed the repeal of what the *Times* described as "stultifying constraints" from the New Deal. Under those regulations, Weill's anticipated megamerger to create Citigroup would have been illegal, but Clinton handed him the trophy pen for successfully lobbying for their repeal. Among the tributes to Weill's success that decorated his walls was a picture of his "humble childhood home in Brooklyn," lest anyone deny the glory of his climb.[35]

Weill drew broad lessons from his successes. In a self-congratulatory, individualist tone suggestive of Milton Friedman or George W. Bush, Weill boasted in 2007 that "We didn't rely on somebody else to build what we built and," he insisted, "we shouldn't rely on somebody else to provide all the services our society needs." He acknowledged his good luck that tax cuts and deregulation had made his fortune possible, and he also defended his wealth, declaring that his company's stock prices "justified what I got." Not everyone agreed. Two days after this laudatory article, the *Times* published a set of letters to the editor gathered under the title "The Richest Owe a Debt to the Rest." They pointed out the tycoons' debt to the citizenry's "social investments" and called for "outrage" against such overweening pride and self-righteous defense of unequal power and wealth, while also reminding the moguls of their dependence on employees and other taxpaying citizens.[36]

Soon, Weill and other self-satisfied tycoons indeed found themselves the targets of widespread outrage that they could no longer ignore. In 2008, as the whole economy sank, a writer for Bloomberg News disdainfully labeled Citigroup "a ward of the government." Its stock had fallen 87 percent over the course of the year, from $55.12 to the neighborhood of one dollar, and massive bailouts demolished the reputations for "genius" and self-reliance to which Weill and his peers had felt justified not long before. Overall, the federal government invested $9.7 *trillion* to shore up the nation's financial and insurance sectors that Citigroup had once led.[37] It had been a very long year since Weill had admonished others for relying on "somebody else."

As the fallout of the economic crisis continued, Weill's reputation took a good measure of hits, but his fortune did not. As Robert Scheer, an award-winning journalist, pointed out, in 2010 Weill added a $31 million California vineyard to his real estate holdings that already included a 14-acre Greenwich, Connecticut, manor, a 120-acre Adirondack park, and a New York City penthouse, purchased in 2007 as the housing bubble burst but still valued at $42 million in 2010. Even the *New York Times*, which had not so long before lauded him and his efforts at successfully dismantling New Deal "constraints," by 2010 regretfully admitted its own errors and pronounced that "Mr. Weill's legacy has taken on a darker hue." According to "some critics" he was "the architect of a shoddily constructed, unmanageable financial supermarket whose troubles have sideswiped investors, employees and average citizens nationwide." And, yet, "He remains baronially wealthy." In keeping with his individualism, Weill blamed the people who managed Citigroup after he stepped down, not the system that made both the firm's collapse and his fortune possible.[38]

Despite the anger citizens expressed about bailing out overreaching and profit-mad businesses, the Great Recession did not turn mainstream opinion against the system that had given so much leeway to brash, self-serving entrepreneurs. True, public opinion turned against some of the most visible villains in the crisis, and also against the politicians who didn't put perpetrators in jail and instead bailed out institutions "too big to fail." Even Forbes.com's 2023 summary of the collapse concluded that, "What started as a classic tale of greed and deregulation ended in a global crisis." Nonetheless, few challenged the system's individualist foundations. One high-profile exception, the Occupy Wall Street movement in the last months of 2011, did raise questions about the system and pointed to the ills of inequality symbolized in its slogan, "We're the 99%." But individualist entrepreneurship's cultural authority retained its hegemony. Only one banker went to jail, unlike the hundreds who were imprisoned after the savings and loan crisis of the 1980s.[39] Instead, the crisis seemed to put the myth on steroids. Moving into this cultural opportunity in 2009, as the Great Recession's crisis began to wind down, a "reality" television show put adventures in entrepreneurial self-making on a new, high-profile stage.

Myths, like conspiracy theories, work their most potent magic when people's lives seem out of their control and their fears most haunt them. Coming hard on the heels of the extravagant 1980s and 1990s, the Great Recession generated just such an environment, one in which some took the fantasies of individualism that caused the crash as the key to their own fortunes. This irony pumped energy into *Shark Tank*, a reality television show that became a megahit quickly after its opening episodes in 2009. Even as millions of Americans struggled, its promoters offered ambitious entrepreneurs success to reward their individual personalities, business acumen, and products.[40] In many ways, *Shark Tank* combines P. T. Barnum-esque showmanship with that master's promotion of capitalist ambitions.

By 2009 Mark Burnett had already created and produced several pathbreaking reality shows, most notably *Survivor* in 2000, followed in 2004 by *The Apprentice*, which famously gave Donald Trump a platform for building his national reputation as a tough businessman. Like these, *Shark Tank* draws in and entertains audiences with high drama and skilled production. These shows also project a foundational presumption of self-making – one that reflects their creator's attitude, which intensified as his shows prospered. According to the memoir of Dianne Burnett, his second wife, the greater Mark Burnett succeeded, the more he replaced "'we' and 'our'" with "'I' and 'my,'" even while relying on personal and business networks and organizations.[41] His perspective pervades the production, and viewers cannot avoid the constant drumbeat of self-made success and failure. As the show's website declares, the Sharks are "tough, self-made, multimillionaire and billionaire tycoons" on the hunt for America's best opportunities for money making. The show's competitions and confrontations "give budding entrepreneurs the chance to secure business deals that could make them millionaires."[42] If, that is, they and their innovations perform well in this competition styled as a survival of the fittest.

Shark Tank's successful appeal to the myth of self-making echoes through its press coverage. Articles around the country routinely identify the Sharks as self-made, and that seems to be the only credential they need to hold authority. Most of the references are somewhat neutral, taking the term for granted as a qualification for judging others, such as in this typical description: "the reality show in which budding entrepreneurs pitch to self-made millionaires in search of fresh investment deals." Even observers who find the show cruel accept the myth on which it is based: these "five ruthless self-made multi-millionaires" remind us that a shark is a "teeth bearing, flesh tearing sea animal."[43] Most comment admiringly, as in "From Rags to Race Car," a 2012 interview with one of the Sharks, Robert Herjavec. As usual, the interview introduced the Sharks as "five self-made millionaire entrepreneurs." When asked if their experience qualified them for judging others, Herjavec gave a soliloquy right out of the entrepreneurial gospel: "The beauty of America is that we have the highest percentage of self-made millionaires in the world. I think what the show tells people is if you want to do it and you have the skill to do, you can do it." To tie this to the Sharks themselves, he continued: "And you have five people who have done it. We didn't inherit this money; nobody gave it to us. We did it." This crystal-clear synopsis of the myth of self-made success ignored the ongoing impact of the Great Recession – US unemployment at 8.2 percent – dismissing all those 12.7 million unemployed people as not trying to "do it."[44]

Shark Robert Herjavec credited "perseverance" for his success. He was proud of never lacking for confidence or hope: "when I get knocked down, I just get up again." To be sure, entrepreneurship, like self-improvement, requires hope. Enough hope to fuel the effort to pull together everything else – all the forms of human, social, and financial capital – that a successful foray into the marketplace involves. A supposed meritocracy demands hope against all odds; it insists that, as Herjavec put it, "The difference between success and failure is just getting up one more time."[45] This doesn't leave much room for maneuver, however, when tenacity alone cannot overcome life's conditions or obstacles. Nor does the faddish notion that "failing fast" lights the road to success. As *Forbes* explained in 2014, this "silliness" is "mostly hype" among people who actually "scramble hysterically to avoid failure." Within the current entrepreneurial culture, failure may not carry its traditional stigma; climbing out of it can make for good press, and there is a lot to gain from its lessons. But "just getting up one more time" doesn't work magic without resources.[46] Claiming otherwise is just another self-making boast. When hope gets beaten down in this climate, despair may take its place, and people may turn to perverse means to relieve their despair.

STORIES AND EFFECTS – MERITOCRACY AND DESPAIR

For anyone who accepts the myth of self-made success, self-made failure is a corollary that obscures evidence about context and other variables, such as the reality that poverty begets unwed teens' pregnancies, not the converse, as President George W. Bush asserted. This pair of blinders makes it easy to tell simple stories that enable refusing children and their families education and medical resources, as did Bush's tax cuts in the name of "ushering in the responsibility era." The blinders rationalized policies that contributed to, among other problems, raising childhood poverty rates from 16 percent in 2000 to 28 percent in 2005; and that was before the 2008 crash.[47] With the two myths so deeply embedded, crediting or blaming individuals for their lives' outcomes seemed reasonable to policymakers on both sides of the legislative aisle. Although abundant scientific evidence shows the developmental problems of children who suffer from poor nutrition, limited medical access, subpar education, and unsafe levels of pollution, policymakers, like Bush, can freely accuse children and their parents of bad choices and willful irresponsibility.[48]

Accusations of laziness and irresponsibility – self-made failure – disregard the amount of work under stress that scraping by requires, such as multiple jobs with irregular hours, low pay, and no health benefits. But in a society that envisions itself as a meritocracy and possesses a strong presumption of fundamentally equal opportunity, such accusations make sense: the idea of a meritocracy rewards elites with esteem for allegedly earning success's practical benefits while also implying others' inferiority. The resulting assaults on the self-respect of not-so-successful people exacerbate their practical burdens and frustrations – ignoring very real contingencies, such as current and historical discrimination by gender, race, and class, or regional economic decline. As we saw in the previous chapter, Michael Young's 1958 satirical novel, *The Rise of the Meritocracy, 1870–2033*, introduced the term "meritocracy" and warned about the dangers of an ideology that promoted the notion that rewards accrued according to merit, an offshoot of the myth of self-made success.[49]

In *Meritocracy*'s dystopia, the working-class victims of disrespect rise up and overturn their nation's hierarchy and its fraudulent assertions of equal opportunity. In America's dystopia, the victims of disrespect, instead, harm themselves. Physical and emotional pain dominates the lives of people whose hopes and self-esteem strain under a toxic mix of concrete hardships and cultural disparagement in the guise of moralizing about self-reliance for those "left behind" in rural or urban settings. In the years since the Great Recession that began in 2008, what have come to be known as "deaths of despair" have climbed steeply among midlife Americans who lead the most precarious and disheartening lives. The concept originally focused on White working-class people whose grief and anger followed economic decline with the decay of US industry and unions, deepened by a sense of relative loss of cultural status following civil-rights era changes. Their plight prompted reports of disturbing increases in deaths associated with suicide, drug overdose, and alcoholism between 1999 and 2013, especially for middle-aged White Americans without a college degree. Comparisons in 2017 between White Americans with and without college degrees revealed the class-based roots of the problem: from the early 1990s until 2017, death rates of people with degrees declined by 40 percent while the mortality of others increased by 25 percent. In the decade between 2013 and 2022, overall despair mortality among White Americans rose from 72.15 per 100,000 to 102.63.[50]

Although people of color have always experienced grave problems that include disproportionally high mortality from all causes, their midlife deaths of despair used to be lower than for Whites. They have, however, now increased even more rapidly. Among Black Americans, the rates almost tripled between

2013 and 2022, from 36.24 to 103.81 per 100,000, rising severely since 2015. Meanwhile, Native American and Alaska Native populations suffered deaths of despair at 241.7 per 100,000 in 2022, 2.36 times those among White Americans.[51] Statistics on this scale do not reflect individual failings as much as broad conditions that challenge whole populations' survival.

In any casualty calculation, such as about automobile accidents or warfare, fatalities are usually a small fraction of those who suffer but survive in some fashion. It is, therefore, not enough to mourn the departed if we don't attend to the ongoing needs of survivors and whatever hopes they may still hold. Yet if policymakers perceive disadvantaged people's struggles as problems of individuals – self-made failures caused by bad decisions and irresponsibility – rather than problems of the whole, there is little likelihood of improvement. Thus, in early 2024 during debates about expanding Medicaid, Speaker of the Kansas House Dan Hawkins contended that doing so would remove too many people's "reason to work." Instead, he favored enforcing "an individual responsibility." Hawkins dismissed a 2024 bill's work requirement as too weak, "a joke," although 69 percent of the people who would be covered already hold at least one job or have chronic conditions that render them unable to work.[52]

Accusing people among the working poor of looking for excuses not to work is a symptom of the cultural dysfunction that flourishes among those who accept the myth of self-made success. Speaker Hawkins, for example, somehow imagines that receiving Medicaid would reduce the incentive to work, as if that benefit could generate a livelihood. Two powerful chronicles argue for the contrary: Barbara Ehrenreich's renowned *Nickle and Dimed: On (Not) Getting By in America* (2001) and Linda Tirado's *Hand to Mouth: Living in Bootstrap America* (2015). Although each woman's experience among the working poor was temporary – journalist Ehrenreich's was voluntary, and Tirado's was exacerbated by what she confessed to be "terrible decisions" – they lived their own struggles and witnessed those of hard-working others as they strained to manage within poverty. Each of them emphasizes that the working poor are not necessarily unskilled or unemployed, although both their skills and their jobs tend to be undervalued by the affluent. They saw that instability and spending on cigarettes and other chemistry for relief are more the products than the causes of their problems. Moreover, the working poor are subject to continuous humiliations, such as body and purse searches, insults from employers and customers, evictions, and other reminders of their inferior status. The dread of capricious firings is constant. Holding two jobs with irregular hours inevitably reduces availability for one and increases the chances of getting fired from one or both. And, of course, poor health care compounds every other problem when employers are strongly incentivized to hold hours below the lower limits for eligibility for health insurance.

Scarcity can itself generate a cycle of instability and hopelessness from which escape can seem – and often be – impossible.[53] Systemic dysfunctions create the contexts for what can look like individual dysfunctions, self-made failures.

Judgment, though, is often more attractive and easier than digging into the complicated ways in which individual lives are shaped by national-scale politics. J.D. Vance's melancholic ode to self-made failure, *Hillbilly Elegy: A Memoir of a Family and Culture in Crisis*, reached the *New York Times* bestseller list in the summer of 2016 and stayed there for twenty-four weeks. This engaging narrative of Vance's rise out of poverty recounts how he made his way to the Marines, then college and Yale Law School. After those earnest efforts at self-improvement, he moved into high finance and acquired the patronage of libertarian billionaire Peter Thiel, who contributed $15 million to help fund Vance's successful 2022 senatorial campaign in Ohio and who recruited other libertarian billionaires in the cause of Vance's successful vice presidential run in 2024.[54] Vance's story is, at the core, about how he came to recognize and act on his own self-agency in profound contrast to neighbors' and kinfolks' "lack of agency – a feeling that you have little control over your life and a willingness to blame everyone but yourself." In this manner, he embeds his own story within criticism of those he left behind: "Nearly every person … is deeply flawed."[55] Vance includes himself among the flawed, but admitting to that only increases his fascination with his success in contrast to others' failures. No Puritan preacher ever had a greater proclivity for judgment.

Instead of exploring whether the dysfunctions he sees are rooted in policies that have closed off avenues of advancement or broader vistas for people, Vance finds congenial the language of personal responsibility – self-agency – with little faith in anything else. In this, he reflects the late twentieth-century language of self-making, such as that in President Bill Clinton's Personal Responsibility and Work Opportunity Reconciliation Act of 1996. Self-agency is certainly important, but it is *all* that Vance sees. A childhood of abuse, for instance, did not in his view give one "a perpetual moral get-out-of-jail-free card." Would a young friend learn "a sense that he can control his own destiny" or "take refuge in resentment at forces beyond his control"?[56]

For Vance, "the community" is fundamentally local, and he doesn't acknowledge the relevance of broader contexts. He is effusively grateful to the Marines for teaching him how to become an adult and to The Ohio State University for his college education, but he ignores that they are national and state institutions supported by taxpayers beyond his hometown's meager capabilities. Wearing his individualist blinders, he concludes, "Public policy can help, but there is no government that can fix these problems for us."[57] Looking only at ground level, that may be true enough. But Vance's dichotomy misses how context and individual choices interact; or how, for instance, health and educational policies and offshoring corporate jobs can improve or harm individual and community lives. Moreover, whatever nuance his mid-life memoir holds has evaporated in the heat of political ambition.

In this fashion, Vance illustrates how the myth of self-made success does ideological work against social programs from opposite directions. People who see themselves as reasonably self-reliant benefit from programs that are almost invisible as government programs – like mortgage tax deductions, medical research, road construction, and all levels of education. Because of what Suzanne Mettler calls "the submerged state," people can take advantage of such programs but still pride themselves on their independence.[58] At the same time, they can look askance at people who need Medicaid, unemployment benefits, or welfare, and resent having to support those programs, which operate by direct interaction with government agencies and are, therefore, visible. The myth's implications for self-made failure in turn impose on recipients the burden of reproach, both their own and of others'. To make it all more dysfunctional, the century-long assault on social programs that began against the New Deal has used the language of self-reliance to weaken social programs in a self-fulfilling cycle that reduces effectiveness and increases frustrations from every angle.

GIVING BACK BUT HOLDING ON

Back in the so-called Robber Baron days, some prominent figures such as Andrew Carnegie and John D. Rockefeller gave away enormous sums of money, while others, such as Jay Gould and Russell Sage did not. (Russell Sage is only associated with philanthropy because his widow, Olivia Sage, donated her inheritance in her husband's name.) Philanthropic aims and practices still vary widely, and their striking diversity presents a conundrum precisely because these decisions *can* be entirely idiosyncratic.[59] Abetted by the myth of self-made success, the wealthy have acquired license to decide for themselves whether and how to "give back" to their communities. The submerged state adds weight to this individualist license by minimizing both the credibility of collective actions and the resources for them.[60]

Andrew Carnegie earnestly took a leadership role in self-making's hard sell. As the Enlightenment moralist Adam Smith noted in *The Theory of Moral Sentiments* in 1759, people wish "not only praise, but praiseworthiness," and Carnegie wanted to be seen as kind and wise as well as self-made, rich, and hard-driving.[61] However, he insisted that the right to decide how best to employ his wealth was his alone. To justify this, he forged what became the definitive rationale for wealth makers' philanthropic autonomy in his well-known 1889 essay on "Wealth," republished in 1900 as "The Gospel of Wealth." In short, he declared that "the law of competition ... insures the survival of the fittest," and in the modern business world, the necessary "talent ... invariably secures for its possessor enormous rewards." The blessings of this "intense Individualism," Carnegie assured everyone, include prosperity and "separating the drones from the bees." Rather than distribute those "enormous rewards" either solely to family or to "public uses" after death, he insisted that the best chance to promote "the reconciliation of the rich and the poor – a reign of harmony" was to follow "the most intense individualism." Applying the logic of self-made success accordingly, "it requires the exercise of not less ability than that which acquired the wealth to use it so as to be really beneficial to the community."[62]

Those whose labor made Carnegie's fortunes saw his obligations differently. For example, an 1899 editorial in a labor newspaper began: "After having robbed the American workingman of a cool $150,000,000, Mr. Andrew Carnegie is going to turn over a new leaf and be good." The tycoon "is going to retire to his lordly castle in Scotland and dole out charity with a lavish hand." This scathing commentary predicted – wrongly, as it happened – that "when he merely retires like some philanthropical feudal baron of the middle ages, he ... will gain no more gratitude from posterity than they did." In 1900, another observer objected to Carnegie's "Vesuvius of gold pieces" flowing toward libraries, galleries, and parks because "real philanthropy" would "enable the aspiring poor to also have homes and food and health for their young." The core injustice was the "shameful thing that from the toil of others a man should be permitted to wring and cling to as much as he has" while self-righteously indulging in the "stately praise of poverty." The inequities of Carnegie's colleague, Henry Clay Frick, did not escape notice either, such as that of a 1905 observer who declared: "To rob the people, shoot some of them and then get back your credit by making them presents is a neat trick."[63]

People's reasons for giving are complex, but prior to 1917, US tax codes were not part of the mix because they had no relevant provisions. A few years before, in 1913, Congress had initiated the modern income tax system mainly to relieve the burdens on low- and mid-income households from excise taxes that were the federal government's main revenue source. As the costs of the Great War loomed, however, Congress targeted the income tax as a way to meet those costs. The resulting War Revenue Act of 1917 expanded the income tax obligation from affecting less than 2 percent to applying to 5 percent of the population and raised the maximum rate from 15 percent of income to 67 percent. Out of concern that wealthy taxpayers would react to their new tax burden by curtailing their charitable contributions, Congress unanimously agreed to a deduction of 15 percent of income for appropriate gifts, complicating the array of motivations for philanthropy ever since.[64]

The cultural authority of individualist self-making promotes regressive tax codes that facilitate dramatic, voluntary contributions that are widely greeted as fortuitous manna from a free market heaven. In 1960, Senator Barry Goldwater complained in his highly influential *Conscience of a Conservative* that people who vote for and pay taxes "trying to care for the needs of their fellow citizens" cannot "be commended and rewarded, at some moment in eternity, for their 'charity.'" Each person should, "instead, contribute what he regards as his just share of human welfare to a private charity." That is, praise and esteem can only come from voluntary contributions. Likewise, Ronald Reagan favored voluntarism rather than government aid. He wanted people to take up again the good deeds that "we once considered were really ours to do voluntarily, out of the goodness of our hearts and a sense of community pride and neighborliness," rather than delegate to government representatives. As Rose and Milton Friedman insisted in *Free to Choose* in 1979, "Few of us believe in a moral code that justifies forcing people to give up much of what they produce to finance payments to persons they do not know for purposes they may not approve of." Policies "enacted in the name of a noble ideal such as equality" were no better in this regard than those enacted out of "naked interest." The Friedmans exorcised wealthy people of wrongdoing with vague references to philanthropy. (Curiously, their one specific example of philanthropic assistance to "the poor... in their daily problems" looks to the decidedly progressive activists at Chicago's Hull House with their modest budget.)[65]

Bolstered by the free market ideology of self-making, donors can also claim the right to feel good about what they do. During its sixtieth anniversary in 2007, the Horatio Alger Association of Distinguished Americans celebrated "Why We Give." This once struggling organization was by then "invest[ing] in America's future" to the tune of more than $8.5 million each year in need-based scholarships. Although "American free enterprise provides an equal track for all who wish to run the race," they admitted that there are "youth who are hard working but in great need." However, rather than support community-based programs to prevent "great need" where it starts, the targets of their funding were "individual students in need."[66] And, as a plus, they could feel good about it when they met those students. That pleasure is much more satisfying than supporting public programs that serve anonymous people and can't credit anonymous taxpayers, as Goldwater and the Friedmans noted. Surplus wealth can purchase abundant good feelings when distributed in such personal and direct ways, as in the current fashion for distributing cash at college graduations, unlike the grudging feelings that come with paying taxes that contribute to the commonweal anonymously and at a distance.

Carnegie composed his "Gospel of Wealth" in part to persuade other affluent people to take seriously their duties to donate "for public ends [that] would work good to the community." To discourage "hoarding great sums," he favored a graduated tax on estates as "the wisest" form of taxation because "the community, in the form of the state, cannot thus be deprived of its proper share." If rich people did not properly use their wealth, taxing "more and more heavily large estates at death" was a justified penance by which "the state marks its condemnation of the selfish millionaire's unworthy life."[67] Many of the audiences for his moralizing accept this obligation, but current tax codes, including the minimalist estate tax of recent decades, do not enforce Carnegie's "condemnation" of those who do not. As a result, in 2021, 156 billionaires on the *Forbes* list of the 400 richest Americans donated less than 1 percent of their wealth, including Jeff Bezos and Elon Musk, even as their wealth skyrocketed during the COVID19 pandemic.[68]

Whether philanthropists see their projects as challenges, burdens on their time and ingenuity, or sources of esteem and gratification, the individualist culture that the myth of self-making has contributed to gives them autonomy within an inequitable tax environment. Even traditional oversight of charitable organizations by the Internal Revenue Service is increasingly impossible because private foundations and donor-advised funds are not subject to public scrutiny. These entities can hold "donations" in perpetuity, removing funds from tax rolls and keeping them under donors' control without ever sending money "out-the-door," as *Forbes* explains, which is why it excludes those wealth transfers when it calculates billionaires' philanthropy.[69] There is neither accountability nor guidance from the community and its representatives.

For example, upon the birth of their first child Priscilla Chan and Mark Zuckerberg set up the Chan Zuckerberg Initiative (CZI) at the end of 2015 as a limited liability corporation into which they are pouring billions of dollars of Facebook assets. While there is no tax write-off for the transfer, as there would have been for a traditional charity gift, the assets remain under their control and are not subject to any transparency requirements, or even requirements to spend investment income on aid, as with standard charities. This is not to say that CZI won't disperse funds usefully, but it has already and could continue to spend on political lobbying, as well as continue to make profits. The tax benefits of placing up to 99 percent of their vast fortune in this corporation include avoiding capital gains and estate taxes altogether.[70] Without challenging Chan and Zuckerberg's intentions, it is easy to see that US legal and cultural systems presume that individuals who make money have the sole right to disperse that money. Only a society that accepts wealthmakers as "self-made" can accept this disregard of the public investments on which their successes depend.

Without the help of tax policies that slow down ballooning fortunes, disposing of vast wealth isn't automatic. Writing for *Forbes* in 2000, Quentin Hardy explained that the newly "superrich" often consider it a "copout" to turn their billions over to traditional foundations or to donate carelessly. As eBay's inventor Pierre Omidyar explained to Hardy, he was concerned about efficiency and didn't consider existing charities a "decent delivery mechanism." How to decide among "too many good causes"? Hardy reported that others among the superrich worry that existing charities can't handle the fortunes coming to them over the coming decades. Omidyar even fretted about the loss of an "idea of a community ... and common responsibility," and yet nowhere in an eight-page article does he or anyone mention the efficiencies that would come from proactively preventing a host of problems by building public infrastructure such as schools, housing, and medical access, or providing gainful employment as in the New Deal. Instead, Omidyar hired a financial manager to help him avoid the pitfalls of what he called "ridiculous" wealth. This professional offered to "give it all away" for him, but said "I have to know what you want."[71] The question presumed Omidyar's right to control.

In this same line of thinking, and in order to encourage and facilitate philanthropy among their wealthy fellows, Melinda French Gates, Bill Gates, and Warren Buffett recruited forty ultra-wealthy Americans to form the Giving Pledge in 2010. Their mission is to "help tackle the world's most pressing problems" through philanthropy, through committing "to give the majority of their wealth to charitable causes, either during their lifetimes or in their wills."[72] Each of the founders has made extensive public and private arguments in support of this project, noble in its sentiments, but all assuming that the world's problems rest on the shoulders of "self-made" fortunes to remedy.

Before this century and its explosion of extreme fortunes, a frequent argument against raising taxes on the very rich calculated that spreading their wealth around could not solve major problems. Similar arguments against reducing the tax benefit to the rich for their deductions worry about losses to receiving institutions. However, if those funds were available to relieve rather than aggravate inequality, then their distribution could more efficiently address the ills that philanthropy often aims to ease. Cultural institutions could, likewise, apply more of their funds directly to their missions rather than to wooing wealthy donors. All of these arguments ignore questions of fairness, but fairness doesn't go far in an ideological debate. Now, however, when 0.1 percent of Americans possess more net worth than half of the rest of the population, all these older arguments have lost their credibility.[73]

The cultural seeds that Andrew Carnegie planted during the Gilded Age ripened as individualism deepened. The language of "your money" and "my money" reinforces beliefs that accomplished and often well-intentioned people are the best judges for how to spend "their money." Philanthropists, like everyone else, are embedded in a powerful culture that brings great rewards of esteem and gratification to those who take wealth and then "give back." Yet the essential infrastructural, financial, and legal supports that make their accumulations possible and secure are community resources that undergird everything, and it should therefore be a community affair to distribute some significant portion of the riches. If we could see past the myth of self-made success, we would question, not endorse, a system that makes the choices theirs alone.

* * *

How much responsibility and, therefore, credit can human beings take for their fates? Are our lives the results of forces outside of our control? Or are we completely our own creations? On practical matters, neither extreme is a good guide. On ideological matters, however, stories have covered the entire spectrum at one time and place or another. Across the span of American history, storytellers with the loudest voices have increasingly endorsed the notion of self-making, originally as praise reserved for preachers and public servants. Once the idea slipped out of that realm to promote ambitious politicians, it soon bestowed its esteem for economic success and, conversely, to penalize failure. Now, as we begin 2025, a cohort of crass individualists who accept an extreme version of the myth of self-made success threaten to engulf America's resources and governance. They and their storytellers blithely intend to accelerate inequality along their way, sure of their right to do as they please as self-made men.

Yet there *is* another vision, an alternate storyline kept alive by people who are not blind to their own advantages or others' disadvantages. This book has uncovered from America's long and entangled history stories of people mostly outside the mainstream who have emphasized the "help" in self-*help*. Frederick Douglass and Booker T. Washington, for example, firmly agreed that every individual is responsible for self-improvement *and*, in turn, community-improvement. Others who also urged collective self-help, such as reformer Dorothea Dix and labor leader Robert D. Layton, lived and worked by the principle that Mary Church Terrell advanced for the National Association of Colored Women, "Lifting as We Climb." The mainstream has also harbored voices calling for a balance of individual and communal responsibility for improvement, such as the Patriotic Millionaires, founded in 2010, "a group of millionaires demanding a political economy that works for everyone in America, not just wealthy people like us."[74] America's past has plenty of stories to help us balance our lives and our polity, and this history brings them to light.

"Yes, we must indeed all hang together, or most assuredly we shall all hang separately." An oft-told tale of the American Revolution tells us that Benjamin

Franklin offered this adage when John Hancock called for a unanimous vote on the Declaration of Independence. Although no record survives documenting this story from 1776, it has flourished ever since as an immensely popular Franklin-esque parable.[75] Uncertainties and certain dangers loomed then – as they do now. We could do no better than to heed this advice, whether or not it actually came from Franklin, because it reflects the dedication to self-improvement and service to community with which the idea of self-making began centuries ago.

Acknowledgments

Nothing reveals the impossibility of self-made success more than writing a book. That is especially true for one that, like this, takes more than twenty years. Over those years, I and this project have benefited beyond measure from the encouragement, guidance, and input of dozens and dozens of strangers, acquaintances, colleagues, and friends. So many good people have helped that I have long worried about the impossibility of adequately thanking any of them, much less all of them. Please know that I am grateful to you all.

In many ways, everyone who helped and encouraged me with my second book project, *Pull: Networking and Success Since Benjamin Franklin*, deserves appreciation here, as well, because both books tie into the theme of self-made success but from different angles. Some of those good people who have stayed with me to offer their encouragement and advice include Myra Rich and Daniel Horowitz, who read this manuscript generously and astutely.

Since 1989 many University of Colorado Denver colleagues have graciously talked with me about the history and impact of the myth of self-making, including Chris Agee, Peter Anthamatten, Sasha Breger-Bush, Maria Buszek, Ryan Crewe, Dennis DeBay, Karen Fennell, Tabitha Fitzpatrick, Lisa Forbes, Rachel Gross, Peter Kopp, Betsy Metzger, Elizabeth Pugliano, Dale Stahl, Christine Sundberg, and William Wagner. Jarett Zuboy's contributions to this project began as the best-ever research assistant before becoming a friend and astute reader. Kayla Gabehart also entered my life as an extraordinary student. It has been a profound pleasure to become friends and to watch her mature into a scholar in her own right.

The Business History Conference has provided another home to me for many decades. It is the oldest and largest international organization dedicated to the scholarship of business history and its contexts. Sharing interests, discussions, intellectual explorations with other participants has brought me enormous pleasure and a never-ending wealth of encouragement and ideas. Among the many, many historians whose work and conversations have contributed to my thinking on this project are Edward Balleisen, Jennifer Black, Christy Chapin, Jennifer Delton, Colleen Dunlavy, Justene Hill Edwards, Walter Friedman, Per

ACKNOWLEDGMENTS

Hansen, Roger Horowitz, Richard R. John, Maggie Levenstein, Susan Ingalls Lewis, Sharon Murphy, Susie Pak, Chad Pearson, Kim Phillips-Fein, Laura Phillips-Sawyer, Mark Rose, and Jocelyn Wills.

No friend or colleague has joined in this project more than Vilja Hulden. I have benefited beyond measure from her shared interests, cheerful reassurances, and detailed reading of every chapter. So careful, insightful, and detailed were her observations and suggestions that I can't imagine pulling this project into reality without her! Pamela Haag read almost all of the manuscript and provided a rich array of detailed recommendations. David Farber commented on a very early conference paper and urged me to avoid writing yet another history of the ideas about self-made success, but, instead, to learn about the people whose stories shaped and shared their ideas – goals that have guided me ever since.

The Auraria Library is the only library in the United States that serves three different institutions of higher education, including the University of Colorado Denver. Over decades, I have admired and appreciated the dedication and creativity of those who have made that work, especially including my intrepid friend, Eric Baker, as well as all those at the circulation desk and interlibrary loan who found materials for me from around the country.

Other institutions that have made my research possible are the Internet Archive, which I discovered during the COVID-19 pandemic, desperate for access to libraries but unable to enter them. It is also a boon to scholars seeking books unavailable locally – or anywhere – instantly and in the middle of the night.

I am grateful to the Horatio Alger Association of Distinguished Americans for permission to use the wonderful materials in their archive at the Gotlieb Archive Center at Boston University. Their publications, public events, and internal meetings have made clear how truly dedicated the organization and its participants have long been to providing support to young people. I also appreciate the help of the Gotlieb Archive Center for making access possible.

Per Hansen and Mads Mordhorst of the Copenhagen Business School have long encouraged my explorations of the myth of self-made success. They invited me to Denmark for an early presentation on this project, where they and colleagues helped me with questions and suggestions. Mads and Stefan Schwarzkopf then co-edited a 2017 special issue of *Business History* on "The Narrative Turn in Business History." The article that resulted, "How Business Historians Can Save the World – From the Fallacy of Self-made Success," sent some of my ideas out into the world.

I am so very fortunate that Michael Watson, Head of Trade Publishing & Executive Publisher, History, Cambridge University Press, was among the people who saw that article. He has nurtured this book and guided me with patience and insight, for which I am immensely grateful. Also at the Press, Rosa Martin,

ACKNOWLEDGMENTS

Editorial Assistant, and Lisa Carter, Senior Content Manager, have capably and graciously helped me bring the book to life. Additionally, I am grateful to the Press's anonymous readers who offered thoughtful and helpful suggestions to improve the work. Outside of the Press, I very much appreciate the timely and professional work of indexer Belle Tuten and copyeditor Kay McKechnie to improve the book.

Many other treasured friends and family have cheered me on over the years. These include Lori Breslow, Diana Craig, Marlea and Richard Fulchiron, Peter Laird, Carole Levin, and Susan Bonsall Rosenberry, as well as Jeanne M. Johnson, Susan and Jon Hokama, Dolores Leal Owens, and their families. They will all be glad to be relieved of patiently asking "how is the book coming?"

In keeping with academic protocol, the first in my mind and heart appears last in this essay of gratitude. Frank N. Laird has been my partner in every sense, in every part of my life. He has made me whole in ways that I never imagined before knowing him. Early in our life together, we made our watchword "Grow old with me/The best is yet to be," John Lennon's adaptation of Robert Browning's line. Every day brings another opportunity to be grateful for our life together – as we grow old together.

Notes

ABBREVIATIONS

APP — The American Presidency Project, www.presidency.ucsb.edu
HAAC — The Horatio Alger Association Collection, archived at the Howard Gotlieb Archival Research Center at Boston University, Boston, MA
HAADA — The Horatio Alger Association of Distinguished Americans, archived at the Howard Gotlieb Archival Research Center at Boston University, Boston, MA
KJV — King James Version, 1611
NYT — *The New York Times*

INTRODUCTION

1 Natalie Robehmed, "At 21, Kylie Jenner Becomes the Youngest Self-Made Billionaire Ever," *Forbes*, Mar. 5, 2019; Kerry A. Dolan, "Here's What Forbes Means by Self-Made: From Bootstrappers to Silver Spoons," Forbes.com, Jul. 13, 2018; "America's Women Billionaires," *Forbes*, Aug. 31, 2018, front cover. Lisa Respers France, "Backlash over *Forbes* Dubbing Kylie Jenner 'Self-Made,'" CNN.com, Jul. 12, 2018.
2 Emily Chubbuck Judson, *Allen Lucas: The Self-Made Man* (New York: Sheldon & Company, 1871); Harriet Beecher Stowe, *The Lives and Deeds of Our Self-Made Men* (Hartford, CT: Worthington, Dustin & Co., 1872), v, vii–viii.
3 Robehmed, "At 21." Greg Swales, "'Money Always Matters': The Kardashians Tell All About Their New Reality TV Reign," variety.com, Mar. 9, 2022.
4 Wilbur Cortez Abbott, *Writings and Speeches of Oliver Cromwell*, 4 vols. (Cambridge, MA: Harvard University Press, 1945), vol. 3, 451–453, 460.
5 T. B., *Logoi apologetikoi* (London, no pub., 1649), title page. University of Michigan Library, name.umdl.umich.edu/A76378.0001.001.
6 Blair Worden, "Providence and Politics in Cromwellian England," *Past & Present* 11 (Nov. 1985): 55–99; Christopher Hill, *God's Englishman: Oliver Cromwell and the English Revolution* (London, UK: Penguin Books, 2019; first ed. 1970), 110–111, 204–206. On Cromwell's historiographical legacy, see J. C. Davis, *Oliver Cromwell* (New York: Oxford University Press, 2001), chap. 3, quote 87.

7 Davis, *Oliver Cromwell*, chap. 4; Abbott, *Writings and Speeches of Oliver Cromwell*, 452. Note that "gentleman" referred then to a man of high social rank rather than to a man who behaves properly.
8 Daniel T. Rodgers, *The Work Ethic in Industrial America, 1850–1920* (Chicago: University of Chicago Press, 1974), xi–xii. Raymond Williams describes how words, meanings, and the values they represent can dominate at times, while others go dormant or fade, *Marxism and Literature* (Oxford, UK: Oxford University Press, 1977), chap. 8. On the value of not untangling complex historical threads, see Pamela Walker Laird, "Entangled: Civil Rights in Corporate America since 1964," in Richard R. John and Kim Phillips-Fein, eds., *Capital Gains: Business and Politics in Twentieth-Century America* (Philadelphia: University of Pennsylvania Press, 2016), 217–234.
9 Stories reside at the "heart" of politics because they address "the problem of collective action." See Frederick W. Mayer, *Narrative Politics: Stories and Collective Action* (New York: Oxford University Press, 2014), 3. For comparison of political leanings and use of stories, see David M. Ricci, *Politics without Stories: The Liberal Predicament* (New York: Cambridge University Press, 2016); and Ricci, *Why Conservatives Tell Stories and Liberals Don't* (Boulder, CO: Paradigm Publishers, 2011). See also Joseph R. Gusfield, *The Culture of Public Problems: Drinking Driving and the Symbolic Order* (Chicago: University of Chicago Press, 1981); Deborah A. Stone, *Policy Paradox and Political Reason* (Glenview, IL, 1988), chap. 6; Peter L. Berger and Thomas Luckman, *The Social Construction of Reality: A Treatise in the Sociology of Knowledge* (Garden City, NY: Doubleday & Co., 1966), chap. 2. For a description of how business advocates learned to tell their stories, see Roland Marchand, *Creating the Corporate Soul: The Rise of Public Relations and Corporate Imagery in American Big Business* (Berkeley: California University Press, 1998), esp. chap. 6.
10 Steve Fraser and Gary Gerstle, eds., *Ruling America: A History of Wealth and Power in a Democracy*, argues for the importance of examining all levels of power to understand America's history (Cambridge, MA: Harvard University Press, 2005).
11 Pamela Walker Laird, *Pull: Networking and Success since Benjamin Franklin* (Cambridge, MA: Harvard University Press, 2006), esp. chap. 1.
12 For example, see Peter E. Gordon, "Bookworms and Fieldworkers: How Did Marxism Become Marxism?" *The Nation* (Dec. 25, 2023 – Jan. 1, 2024): 56–58, 60. On the workings of myths, see Alex Zakaras, *The Roots of American Individualism: Political Myth in the Age of Jackson* (Princeton, NJ: Princeton University Press, 2022).
13 For example, "On the Ruinous Effects of Ardent Spirits," *Vermont Watchman and State Journal* (Montpelier, VT), Sept. 19, 1815. Other editorials, as in *Lancaster Intelligencer and Journal* (PA), Sept. 5, 1812, repeated the "bloated patriots" phrase from *National Intelligencer*. *Virginia Argus* (Richmond), Aug. 24, 1812.
14 "The Christian Chart" and untitled filler, *Weekly Statement* (Raleigh, NC), Jun. 14, 1843. The correct spelling is McMannen.
15 "President Jackson," *North Carolina Sentinel* (New Bern, NC), Aug. 29, 1829; reprinted from *Eastern Argus*.

16 Shai Davidai and Thomas Gilovich, "The Headwinds/Tailwinds Asymmetry: An Availability Bias in Assessments of Barriers and Blessings," *Journal of Personality and Social Psychology*, 111, no. 6 (2016): 835–851.
17 Judith A. McGaw, *Most Wonderful Machine: Mechanization and Social Change in Berkshire Paper Making, 1801–1885* (Princeton, NJ: Princeton University Press, 1987), 127, 157. For a sterling example of finely balanced life stories, see James M. Durant III and Jeffrey M. Allen, eds., *My Story... From Humble Beginnings to Professional Success: A Young Professional's Guide* (New York: Routledge, 2023).
18 For example, see, Anne Case and Angus Deaton, *Deaths of Despair and the Future of Capitalism* (Princeton, NJ: Princeton University Press, 2021); Robert H. Frank, *Success and Luck: Good Fortune and the Myth of Meritocracy* (Princeton, NJ: Princeton University Press, 2016); Daniel Horowitz, *Entertaining Entrepreneurs: Reality TV's Shark Tank and the American Dream in Uncertain Times* (Chapel Hill: University of North Carolina Press, 2020); Pamela Walker Laird, "How Business Historians Can Save the World – from the Fallacy of Self-Made Success," *Business History*, 59, no. 8 (2017): 1201–1217; Brian Miller and Mike Lapham, *The Self-Made Myth: And the Truth about how Government Helps Individuals and Businesses Succeed* (San Francisco: Berrett-Koehler Publishers, 2012); Alissa Quart, *Bootstrapped: Liberating Ourselves from the American Dream* (New York: HarperCollins, 2023); and Michael J. Sandel, *The Tyranny of Merit: What's Become of the Common Good?* (New York: Farrar, Straus and Giroux, 2020). The canon on the American history of the idea of self-made success includes: John G. Cawelti, *Apostles of the Self-Made Man* (Chicago: University of Chicago Press, 1965); Richard M. Huber, *The American Idea of Success* (New York: McGraw-Hill Book Company, 1971); Edward Chase Kirkland, *Dream and Thought in the Business Community, 1860–1900* (Ithaca, NY: Cornell University Press, 1956); Richard Weiss, *The American Myth of Success: From Horatio Alger to Norman Vincent Peale* (New York: Basic Books, 1969); Irvin G. Wyllie, *The Self-Made Man in America: The Myth of Rags to Riches* (New Brunswick, NJ: Rutgers University Press, 1954).

CHAPTER 1

1 Stephen Greenblatt, *Renaissance Self-Fashioning: From More to Shakespeare* (Chicago: Chicago University Press, 1980), 1–3, 9, 256.
2 Frank Whigham, *Ambition and Privilege: The Social Tropes of Elizabethan Courtesy Theory* (Berkeley: University of California Press, 1984), 147–148; Lawrence Stone, "Social Mobility in England, 1500–1700," *Past & Present*, 33 (Apr. 1966): 16–55.
3 There were six editions the first year alone and four more editions in the seventeenth century. Edwin Haviland Miller, "Introduction" to Robert Greene, *Ciceronis Amor: Tullies Love (1589) and A Quip for an Upstart Courtier (1592)* (Gainesville, FL: Scholars' Facsimiles & Reprints, 1954), 5–9.
4 Stone, "Social Mobility in England"; William Casey King, *Ambition, A History: From Vice to Virtue* (New Haven, CT: Yale University Press, 2013), esp. chap. 4.

5 For a discussion of the concept of agency, see James E. Block, *A Nation of Agents: The American Path to a Modern Self and Society* (Cambridge, MA: Harvard University Press, 2002), esp. 22–23; and Stephen Carl Arch, *After Franklin: The Emergence of Autobiography in Post-Revolutionary America, 1780–1830* (Hanover, NH: University Press of New England, 2001), esp. 6–8.

6 In troubled times, in times of transition or threat, people make explicit the values and needs that they generally leave unspoken, taken for granted as valid and valued. Peter Berger and Thomas Luckmann, *The Social Construction of Reality: A Treatise in the Sociology of Knowledge* (Garden City, NY: Doubleday & Co., 1966).

7 John Smith, *Captain John Smith: A Select Edition of His Writings*, ed. Karen Ordahl Kupperman (Chapel Hill, NC: University of North Carolina Press, 1988), 1–5, 36, 41; Warner F. Gookin, "Who Was Bartholomew Gosnold?" *William and Mary Quarterly*, 6, no. 3 (Jul. 1949): 398–415, esp. 403–406. See Philip L. Barbour, *The Three Worlds of Captain John Smith* (Boston: Houghton Mifflin Company, 1964).

8 Stephen Alford, *London's Triumph: Merchants, Adventurers, Money in Shakespeare's City* (New York: Bloomsbury USA, 2017); John Butman and Simon Targett, *New World, Inc.: The Making of America by England's Merchant Adventurers* (New York: Little, Brown and Company, 2018); Gookin, "Who Was Bartholomew Gosnold?" 403; Smith, *Captain John Smith*, 281. For the era's distinction between "present profit" and "honest gain," see Stephen Innes, *Creating the Commonwealth: The Economic Culture of Puritan New England* (New York: W. W. Norton & Company, 1995), 75–76.

9 Smith, *Captain John Smith*, 282–283.

10 For a classic rendition of English colonizing efforts before 1620, see David Beers Quinn, *England and the Discovery of America, 1481–1620* (New York: Alfred A. Knopf, 1974). Karen Ordahl Kupperman, "Apathy and Death in Early Jamestown," *Journal of American History*, 66, no. 1 (Jun. 1979): 24–40.

11 For this era, the modern term "middle class" is inappropriate for designating people between upper and lower ranks. Instead, the historical term "middling sorts" is appropriate, and it also carries fewer connotations of rigidity and judgment than "ranks." Burton J. Bledstein and Robert D. Johnston, eds., *The Middling Sorts: Explorations in the History of the American Middle Class* (New York: Routledge, 2001).

12 Barbour, *Three Worlds*; Innes, *Creating the Commonwealth*, chaps. 2 and 3; quotes 391, 488.

13 Smith, *Captain John Smith*, 246.

14 John Smith, *The Complete Works of Captain John Smith, 1580–1631*, ed. Philip L. Barbour, 3 vols. (Chapel Hill, NC: University of North Carolina Press, 1986), vol. 1, 346; Smith, *Captain John Smith*, 241, 267, 272.

15 Smith, *The Complete Works*, 2:41–42; Smith, *Captain John Smith*, 35, 286.

16 Although there was no single Puritanism to which all conformed, there was enough consistency regarding the variables related to this project that I will stick with the term and use the traditional upper case.

17 John Cotton, "Christ the Fountain of Life, Sermon VIII," c. 1628, in Alan Heimert and Andrew Delbanco, eds., *The Puritans in America: A Narrative Anthology* (Cambridge, MA: Harvard University Press, 1985), 30–31.

18 See especially Bernard Bailyn, *The New England Merchants in the Seventeenth Century* (Cambridge, MA: Harvard University Press, 1955); Christine Leigh Heyrman, *Commerce and Culture: The Maritime Communities of Colonial Massachusetts, 1690–1750* (New York: W. W. Norton & Company, 1984); Stephen Innes, *Labor in a New Land: Economy and Society in Seventeenth-Century Springfield* (Princeton, NJ: Princeton University Press, 1983); Innes, *Creating the Commonwealth*; and Walter W. Woodward, *Prospero's America: John Winthrop, Jr., Alchemy, and the Creation of New England Culture, 1606–1676* (Chapel Hill: University of North Carolina Press, 2010). For an in-depth study of this "palpable" "tension between self-interest and the general good" in early New England, see David D. Hall, *A Reforming People: Puritanism and the Transformation of Public Life in New England* (New York: Alfred A. Knopf, 2011), quote 195. The links between Calvinism and capitalism are too complicated to address here, or even to list the analysts who have explored the question.

19 Bernard Bailyn, "The *Apologia* of Robert Keayne," *William and Mary Quarterly*, 7, no. 4 (October 1950): 568–587, especially 570–571; Mark Valeri, *Heavenly Merchandize: How Religion Shaped Commerce in Puritan America* (Princeton, NJ: Princeton University Press, 2010), 14, 27–29; Robert Keayne, *The Apologia of Robert Keayne: The Self Portrait of a Puritan Merchant*, ed. Bernard Bailyn (Gloucester, MA: Peter Smith, 1970), 41.

20 Valeri, *Heavenly Merchandize*, 14–15, 22; Winthrop quoted in Bailyn, "*Apologia*," 571.

21 Bailyn, "*Apologia*"; Bailyn, introduction to *Apologia* by Keayne, vii-xii.

22 John Winthrop, "The Case of Robert Keayne," in *Winthrop's Journal: History of New England, 1630–1649*, vol. 1, ed. James Kendall Hosmer (New York: 1908), 315–318. According to Stephen Innes, these were Cotton's words, transcribed by Winthrop (*Creating the Commonwealth*, 169). For details of this oft-told tale, see Valeri, *Heavenly Merchandize*, chaps. 1, 2; Bailyn, "*Apologia*"; and Innes, *Creating the Commonwealth*, chap. 4.

23 Keayne, *Apologia*, 5–6.

24 Margaret C. Jacob and Catherine Secretan, eds., *The Self-Perception of Early Modern Capitalists* (New York: Palgrave Macmillan, 2008), esp. 1–2; Innes, *Creating the Commonwealth*, 160–175, 359–360n10.

25 Keayne, *Apologia*, 1; Valeri, *Heavenly Merchandize*, 15–20. As Richard L. Bushman explained, using Keayne as his example, "The people could not distinguish respectable industry from covetousness: their ambitions drove them on year after year, while self-doubts were never far below the surface." *From Puritan to Yankee: Character and the Social Order in Connecticut, 1690–1765* (New York: W. W. Norton & Company, 1967), 189.

26 Bailyn, *New England Merchants*, 20–21, 44; Keayne, *Apologia*, 50; Valeri, *Heavenly Merchandize*, 26–39; Innes, *Creating the Commonwealth*, chap. 4 and 118–120.

27 Daniel T. Rodgers, *As a City on a Hill: The Story of America's Most Famous Lay Sermon* (Princeton, NJ: Princeton University Press, 2018), 306–308.

28 Keayne, *Apologia*, 26, 29, 45, 73, 75–76, 82, 84; Valeri, *Heavenly Merchandize*, 11.

29 Keayne, *Apologia*, 50, 84–85.

30 Keayne, *Apologia*, 82.

31 See Innes, *Creating the Commonwealth*, chap. 1, esp., 39–42, and 131, 349–351n64 on the work ethic in early Euro-America. On gendered criteria for worth, see E. Anthony

Rotundo, *American Manhood: Transformations in Masculinity from the Revolution to the Modern Era* (New York: Basic Books, 1993), chap. 1.

32 Blair Worden, "Providence and Politics in Cromwellian England," *Past & Present*, 11 (Nov. 1985): 55–99; Christopher Hill, *God's Englishman: Oliver Cromwell and the English Revolution* (London, UK: Penguin Books, 2019; first ed. 1970), 190–192. Although scholars have debated the impact of ideas about predestination on the modern West for a century or more, the perplexing logic with which early modern intellectuals and some preachers wrestled did not loom over most people's lives then or since. As David D. Hall recently noted, at "informal events where I am asked to describe Puritan theology, someone *always* asks about predestination, and in far too many monographs it turns up as the centerpiece of Puritanism," *Puritans*, 5. In contrast, the seeming immediacy of God's influence over their lives and souls in the absence of other explanations was compelling, hence the power of providentialism.

33 Smith, *Captain John Smith*, 286; Francis Bacon, *The Works of Francis Bacon*, ed. James Spedding, Robert Leslie Ellis, and Douglas Denon Heath, 15 vols. (London: Longman and Co, 1857), 3:432.

34 Innes, *Creating the Commonwealth*, 6, 9, 12–15, 310, and chap. 3.

35 Cotton, "The way of Life" (1641) in Perry Miller and Thomas H. Johnson, eds., *The Puritans: A Sourcebook of Their Writings* (Mineola, NY: Dover Publications, 2001, first pub. 1963), 320–324; and Cotton, "Christ the Fountain of Life," 31.

36 Richard Sibbes, "The Soul's Conflict With Itself, and Victory over Itself by Faith," in *The Complete Works of Richard Sibbes*, ed. Alexander Balloch Grosart (Edinburgh: James Nichol, 1862), 1:182.

37 Keayne, *Apologia*, 28, 29, 68–74.

38 Bailyn, "Apologia," 585; Innes, *Creating the Commonwealth*, 111; Jan de Vries, *The Industrious Revolution: Consumer Behavior and the Household Economy, 1650 to the Present* (Cambridge, UK: Cambridge University Press, 2008), 40–43; William Caferro, "Premodern European Capitalism, Christianity, and Florence," *Business History Review*, 94 (Spring 2020): 39–72.

39 Innes addresses the Weberian paradox directly and succinctly, explaining that "While it was not possible to prove one's election by exhibiting diligence, conscientiousness, and moral seriousness, the failure to display these qualities, all agreed, signified reprobation." For a concise and compelling overview of the standard arguments about capitalism and the so-called Protestant ethic, see Innes, *Creating the Commonwealth*, 131, 349–351n64.

40 On the value of not untangling complex historical threads, see Caferro, "Premodern European Capitalism," 72; Pamela Walker Laird, "Entangled: Civil Rights in Corporate America since 1964," in Richard R. John and Kim Phillips-Fein, eds., *Capital Gains: Business and Politics in Twentieth-Century America* (Philadelphia: University of Pennsylvania Press, 2016), 217–234.

41 Genesis 3:17; 2 Thessalonians 3:10; Ephesians 4:28; 1 Corinthians 16:14; Matthew 6:24–29 and 11:28; Luke 10:38–42; Matthew 6:9–13, King James Version (KJV). The KJV was completed in 1611; approximately 90 percent of it was copied from the John

Calvin-inspired and Puritan-generated Geneva Bible, published in 1557, which was the first scholarly English translation.

42 Kate Crassons, *The Claims of Poverty: Literature, Culture, and Ideology in Late Medieval England* (Notre Dame, IN: Notre Dame University Press, 2010), 1–4; Jamie Kreiner, *The Social Life of Hagiography in the Merovingian Kingdom* (Cambridge, UK: Cambridge University Press, 2014), 189, 214, 226; Peter Brown, *Through the Eye of a Needle: Wealth, the Fall of Rome, and the Making of Christianity in the West, 350–550 AD* (Princeton, NJ: Princeton University Press, 2012).

43 Crassons, *Claims of Poverty*, 7–8; Butman and Targett, *New World, Inc.*, xxiv-xxv, 9–13; Hill, *God's Englishman*, 40, 44, 217; Edmund S. Morgan, *American Slavery, American Freedom: The Ordeal of Colonial Virginia* (New York: W. W. Norton & Company, 1975), 62–65.

44 Richard Hakluyt, *A Discourse Concerning Western Planting*, ed. Charles Deane (Cambridge, MA: Press of John Wilson and Son, 1877), 3, 36–37. See Nancy Isenberg, *White Trash: The 400-Year Untold History of Class in America* (New York: Viking, 2016), esp. chap. 1.

45 John Winthrop, "Reasons to be Considered for Justifying the Undertakers of the intended Plantation in New England," in Charles Deane, ed., *Proceedings of the Massachusetts Historical Society, 1872* (Boston: The Society, 1873), 237–245, quote 240.

46 On insensitivity to working poor, see Crassons, *Claims of Poverty*, 11, and epilogue. For the early US Republic, see Seth Rockman, *Scraping By: Wage Labor, Slavery, and Survival in Early Baltimore* (Baltimore, MD: Johns Hopkins University Press, 2009); for a longer view, see Isenberg, *White Trash*.

47 Hill, *God's Englishman*, 184–185; Keayne, *Apologia*, 19, 45.

48 Rodgers, *As a City on a Hill*, chap. 8, esp. 109; Edmund S. Morgan, "The Labor Problem at Jamestown, 1607–18," *American Historical Review*, 76, no. 3 (Jun., 1971): 595–611; Morgan, *American Slavery, American Freedom*, 62–70; Crassons, *Claims of Poverty*, 5–8, 268; Innes, *Creating the Commonwealth*, 116–118.

49 As quoted in Hill, *God's Englishman*, 186–187.

50 2 Thessalonians 3:10–11 (KJV); Smith, *Captain John Smith*, 108–109; Barbour, *Three Worlds*, 239; Raymond F. Dolle, "Captain John Smith's Satire of Sir Walter Raleigh," in Kathryn Zabelle Derounian-Stodola, ed., *Early American Literature and Culture: Essays Honoring Harrison T. Meserole* (Newark, DE: University of Delaware Press, 1992), 73–83.

51 Morgan, "Labor Problem at Jamestown," 595; Kupperman, "Apathy and Death in Early Jamestown," 25–26; Smith, *Captain John Smith*, 130, 283.

52 Kupperman effectively makes this comparison in "Apathy and Death in Early Jamestown."

53 Smith, *Captain John Smith*, 227–229.

54 John Winthrop, "Reasons to Be Considered for Justifying … the Plantation in New England" (1629), in Peter C. Mancall, ed., *Envisioning America: English Plans for the Colonization of North America, 1580–1640* (Boston: Bedford Books, 1995), 138; Hall, *A Reforming People*, 37–38, 131; Innes, *Creating the Commonwealth*, 88; Smith, *Captain John Smith*, 278.

55 For English colonists' cultural closed-mindedness, see William Cronon, *Changes in the Land: Indians, Colonists, and the Ecology of New England* (New York: Hill & Wang, 1983),

esp. chap. 4. Quotes from Thomas Morton, *New English Canaan*, ed. Charles Francis Adams, Jr. (Boston: Prince Society, 1883 [1632]), 175–176.
56 Koji Yamamoto, *Taming Capitalism before its Triumph: Public Service, Distrust, and 'Projecting' in Early Modern England* (Oxford, UK: Oxford University Press, 2018), 18, 271.
57 "Culture" here refers to cultivation. Smith, *Captain John Smith*, 285; John Cotton, "Gods Promise to His Plantations," *Old South Leaflets*, 12th series, no. 6 (Boston, 1894), 5–6, 8; Winthrop et al., "Reasons to be Considered."
58 Brown, *Through the Eye of a Needle*. On the synergies between colonization and European ambition, see King, *Ambition*, chap. 4; Butman and Targett, *New World, Inc.*
59 Edward Cahill, "The English Origins of American Upward Mobility; or, the Invention of Benjamin Franklin," *ELH*, 83, no. 2 (Summer 2016): 543–571; quote 559.
60 Alan Hunt, *Governance of the Consuming Passions: A History of Sumptuary Law* (New York: St. Martin's Press, 1996), 18, 22, 25, 29, 38–39, 214, 253–254; Gary North, "The Puritan Experiment with Sumptuary Legislation," *The Freeman*, 6 (1974): 341–355; quote 345; Jenny Hale Pulsipher, "'The Widow Ranter' and Royalist Culture in Colonial Virginia," *Early American Literature*, 39, no. 1 (2004): 41–66; Innes, *Creating the Commonwealth*, esp. 102–106.
61 Rodgers, *As a City on a Hill*, 291–292; Innes, *Creating the Commonwealth*, 25–26, chap. 2; Valeri, *Heavenly Merchandize*, esp. chap. 3.
62 On attempts to discipline the market, see Valeri, *Heavenly Merchandize*, 57–73; Innes, *Creating the Commonwealth*, esp. the conclusion; Rodgers, *As a City on a Hill*, chap. 7.
63 Winthrop, "A Model of Christian Charity," quoted in Rodgers, *As a City on a Hill*, 301, 305; Smith, *Captain John Smith*, 286. For one of countless warnings about the evils of self-love, see Robert Cushman's *The Sin and Danger of Self-love Described, in a Sermon Preached at Plymouth in New-England, 1621* (Boston: Charles Ewer, 1846).
64 Josiah Henry Benton, *Warning Out in New England, 1656–1817* (Boston: W. B. Clarke Company, 1911), 4–10, 114–120; Rodgers, *As a City on a Hill*, 116.
65 Winthrop et al., "Reasons to be Considered."
66 Benedict Anderson, *Imagined Communities: Reflections on the Origin and Spread of Nationalism* (London: Verso Editions, 1983); Richard Hollinger, "How Wide the Circle of the 'We'? American Intellectuals and the Problem of the Ethnos since World War II," *American Historical Review*, 98, no. 2 (Apr. 1993): 317–337.
67 Brodie Waddell, *God, Duty and Community in English Economic Life, 1660–1720* (Woodbridge, UK: Boydell Press, 2012).
68 Augustine, sermon 189, in Greenblatt, *Renaissance Self-Fashioning*, 1–3; Joost Hengstmengel, *Divine Providence in Early Modern Economic Thought* (London: Routledge, 2019), 134–135; Block, *Nation of Agents*, esp. 191.

CHAPTER 2

1 Strictly speaking, "improvement" is a relative term that refers to a process of positive change. In the 1400s, it often referred to reaping profits from an asset, but it came to

refer to betterment more broadly, encompassing social institutions as well as individuals. *Oxford English Dictionary Online*, s.v. "Improvement."

2 Frank Lambert, *Inventing the "Great Awakening"* (Princeton, NJ: Princeton University Press, 1999); Caroline Winterer, *American Enlightenments: Pursuing Happiness in the Age of Reason* (New Haven, CT: Yale University Press, 2016). Contemporaries used the terms "awakening" and "enlightenment," but without grand adjectives.

3 William Huntting Howell, *Against Self-Reliance: The Arts of Dependence in the Early United States* (Philadelphia: University of Pennsylvania Press, 2015).

4 Jonathan Lyons, *Society for Useful Knowledge: How Benjamin Franklin and Friends Brought the Enlightenment to America* (New York: Bloomsbury Press, 2013), 1–8, 46–47, 54–55; Alan Houston, *Benjamin Franklin and the Politics of Improvement* (New Haven, CT: Yale University Press, 2008).

5 Christopher Marlowe, *The Tragical History of Doctor Faustus*, 1604 quarto, in *The Works of Christopher Marlowe*, ed. Alexander Dyce (London: George Routledge and Sons, 1876), 79, 81, 112. For other literary treatments of ambition in this time period, see William Casey King, *Ambition, A History: From Vice to Virtue* (New Haven, CT: Yale University Press, 2013), chap. 2.

6 Walter W. Woodward, *Prospero's America: John Winthrop, Jr., Alchemy, and the Creation of New England Culture, 1606–1676* (Chapel Hill: University of North Carolina Press, 2010), 1–4, 12–13, 38, 55, 92, 263–264, 306.

7 Keith Thomas, *Religion and the Decline of Magic: Studies in Popular Beliefs in Sixteenth and Seventeenth Century England* (New York: Oxford University Press, 1997 [1971]), 641, 645–649, 668; David D. Hall, *Worlds of Wonder, Days of Judgment: Popular Religious Beliefs in Early New England* (Cambridge, MA: Harvard University Press, 1989), 7, 99–100, 196–203, 238; Woodward, *Prospero's America*, 164–165.

8 Woodward, *Prospero's America*, chap. 7.

9 Louise A. Breen, "Cotton Mather, the 'Angelical Ministry,' and Inoculation," *Journal of the History of Medicine*, 46, no. 3 (Jul. 1991): 333–357; quotes 334, 351. For a detailed study, see Philippa Koch, *The Course of God's Providence: Religion, Health, and the Body in Early America* (New York: New York University Press, 2021).

10 Hall, *Worlds of Wonder*, 194–196; Cotton Mather, *The Wonders of the Invisible World* (London: John Russell Smith, 1862; reprint of 1693 edition), xii, 4, 79–81, 101–106.

11 Lawrence Stone showed that English elites deliberately slowed mobility there by the late seventeenth century, which may have strengthened Mather's boosterism for American exceptionalism. "Social Mobility in England, 1500–1700," *Past & Present*, 33 (Apr. 1966): 16–55.

12 Interpretations of *Pietas in Patriam* abound. See Philip F. Gura, "Cotton Mather's Life of Phips: 'A Vice with the Vizard of Virtue upon It,'" *New England Quarterly*, 50, no. 3 (Sept. 1977): 440–457; David H. Watters, "The Spectral Identity of Sir William Phips," *Early American Literature*, 18, no. 3 (Winter, 1983/1984): 219–232; and Mark Valeri, *Heavenly Merchandize: How Religion Shaped Commerce in Puritan America* (Princeton, NJ: Princeton University Press, 2010), 128–130.

13 Mather, *Pietas in Patriam*, 1:150–156, 192, 203–208; Gura, "Cotton Mather's Life of Phips." Cotton Mather, *Magnalia Christi Americana, or, The Ecclesiastical History of New-England*, 2 vols. (Hartford, CT: Silas Andrus, 1820; first American edition based on original 1702 London edition), 1:145, 147.
14 John Cotton, "Christ the Fountain of Life, Sermon VIII," c. 1628, in Alan Heimert and Andrew Delbanco, eds., *The Puritans in America: A Narrative Anthology* (Cambridge, MA: Harvard University Press, 1985), 30–31. On the impact of Calvinist theocracy on economic growth, see Valeri, *Heavenly Merchandize*, 2–6, 9–10; Richard L. Bushman, *From Puritan to Yankee: Character and the Social Order in Connecticut, 1690–1765* (Cambridge, MA: Harvard University Press, 1967), esp. 22–26; Stephen Innes, *Creating the Commonwealth: The Economic Culture of Puritan New England* (New York: W. W. Norton & Company, 1995), 33–36, 308–309. See chap. 1 for Robert Keayne's story.
15 Mather, *Pietas in Patriam*, 1:151–153.
16 Mather, *Pietas in Patriam: The Life of His Excellency Sir William Phips, Knt.*, (1697), reprinted in *Magnalia Christi Americana*, 1:149–209; quotes 151, 153, 191–192, 196, 199, 206. Gura, "Cotton Mather's Life of Phips"; Watters, "The Spectral Identity of Sir William Phips."
17 Mather, *Pietas in Patriam*, 1:151–153, 196.
18 Mather, *Pietas in Patriam*, 1:205–206; Mather, *Magnalia Christi Americana*, 1:424.
19 Based on a word search in Mather's *Magnalia Christi Americana*.
20 Cotton Mather, "A Christian at His Calling" (1701), in Moses Rischin, ed., *The American Gospel of Success: Individualism and Beyond* (Chicago: Quadrangle Books, 1965), 23–30, quotes 23–26, 29–30.
21 Mather, "A Christian at His Calling," 23.
22 H. W. Brands, *The First American: The Life and Times of Benjamin Franklin* (New York: Doubleday, 2000), 26–29; Benjamin Franklin, *Papers of Benjamin Franklin*, 43 vols. (New Haven, CT: Yale University Library), 1:8–43, retrieved from franklinpapers.org.
23 Franklin, *Papers*, 1:8–43; Cotton Mather, *Essays to Do Good* (Johnstown, NY: Asa Child, 1815; originally published in Boston, 1710), x–xi, 45, 78–84, 178; Brands, *First American*, 92; The most authoritative rendering of Franklin's *Autobiography* is based on the sole surviving version in Franklin's handwriting, painstakingly edited. All quotations here include everything Franklin wrote except what he deleted. Benjamin Franklin, *The Autobiography of Benjamin Franklin: A Genetic Text*, ed. J. A. Leo Lemay and P. M. Zall (Knoxville: University of Tennessee Press, 1981), 26. Franklin also referred to Mather's book as *An Essay on the Good*. Franklin praised Mather's message many times, including to Mather's son. Franklin, *Autobiography*, 196. See also Houston, *Benjamin Franklin*, 8, 38. Brands, *First American*, 92. For the many similarities between Franklin and Mather, see Phyllis Franklin, *Show Thyself a Man: A Comparison of Benjamin Franklin and Cotton Mather* (The Hague: Mouton, 1969).
24 Franklin, *Autobiography*, 10–11; Houston, *Benjamin Franklin*, 108; John Bunyan, *The Pilgrim's Progress*, ed. David Hawkes (New York: Barnes & Noble Classics, 2005), 93.
25 Lyons, *Society for Useful Knowledge*, 73–77; I. Bernard Cohen, *Science and the Founding Fathers: Science in the Political Thought of Jefferson, Franklin, Adams, and Madison* (New York: W. W. Norton & Company, 1995), 54.

26 Franklin to Peter Collinson, Jul. 29, 1750, in Benjamin Franklin, *Papers of Benjamin Franklin*, 43 vols. (New Haven, CT: Yale University Library; retrieved from franklinpapers.org), 4:9–33; to Collinson, May 25, 1747, Franklin, *Papers*, 3:126–134; to Collinson, Aug. 14, 1747, Franklin, *Papers*, 3:171; to Collinson, Apr. 29, 1749, Franklin, *Papers*, 3:352. Lyons, *Society for Useful Knowledge*, 1–5, 74–80; Cohen, *Science and the Founding Fathers*, 142–147.

27 Franklin to John Mitchell, Apr. 29, 1749, Franklin, *Papers*, 3:365–376; Franklin to Collinson, Jul. 29, 1750, Franklin, *Papers*, 4:9–33.

28 J. A. L. Lemay, "Franklin and Kinnersley," *Isis*, 52, no. 4 (Dec. 1961): 575–581; Lyons, *Society for Useful Knowledge*, 76.

29 Franklin to John Perkins, Aug. 13, 1752, Franklin, *Papers*, 4:340; Franklin to Peter Collinson, Sept. 1753, Franklin, *Papers*, 5:68–78. Brands, *First American*, 202.

30 *Poor Richard improved: Being an Almanack and Ephemeris ... for the Year of our Lord 1753*, Franklin, *Papers*, 4:403–8; Franklin, *Autobiography*, 153–154. Regarding Franklin's free distribution of guidelines for lightning rods as well as his other inventions, patenting was very difficult prior to the US patent law of 1790 and subsequent legislation. Before that, inventors had to apply for patents in each colony, then each state after 1776. Nonetheless, he could have easily filed for patents in two or three of the most populous colonies or, later, states, had he sought revenues from his inventions.

31 Franklin, *Autobiography*, 153; Trent A. Mitchell, "The Politics of Experiment in the Eighteenth Century: The Pursuit of Audience and the Manipulation of Consensus in the Debate over Lightning Rods," *Eighteenth-Century Studies*, 31, no. 3 (Spring 1998): 307–331.

32 Emerson W. Baker, *A Storm of Witchcraft: The Salem Trials and the American Experiment* (Oxford, UK: Oxford University Press, 2015), 3–4; Brands, *First American*, 12.

33 *Poor Richard improved: Being an Almanack and Ephemeris ... for the Year of our Lord 1753*, Franklin, *Papers*, 4:403–8.

34 Lyons, *Society for Useful Knowledge*, 50–51, 74–86; Lemay, "Franklin and Kinnersley," 575; Mitchell, "The Politics of Experiment in the Eighteenth Century"; Cohen, *Science and the Founding Fathers*, 164–171, 212–215. Cohen points out that some people feared diverting lightning's effects on earthquakes for physical reasons.

35 Robert Wuthnow, "Religious Movements and Counter-Movements in North America," in James A. Beckford, ed., *New Religious Movements and Rapid Social Change* (Beverly Hills, CA: SAGE Publications/UNESCO, 1986), 1–28; Jon Butler, "Magic, Astrology, and the Early American Religious Heritage, 1600–1760," *American Historical Review*, 84, no. 2 (Apr. 1979): 317–346. For the Great Awakening's transatlantic breadth, see Susan O'Brien, "A Transatlantic Community of Saints: The Great Awakening and the First Evangelical Network, 1735–1755," *American Historical Review*, 91, no. 4 (Oct. 1986): 811–832.

36 Michael H. Shute, "A Little Great Awakening: An Episode in the American Enlightenment," *Journal of the History of Ideas*, 37, no. 4 (Oct.–Dec. 1976): 589–602; Koch, *The Course of God's Providence*.

37 Jonathan Edwards, *Selected Writings of Jonathan Edwards*, ed. Harold P. Simonson (New York: Frederick Ungar Publishing Co., 1970), 18–19, 96, 106; Cedric B. Cowing, "Sex

and Preaching in the Great Awakening," *American Quarterly*, 20, no. 3 (Autumn 1968): 624–644.
38 Edwards, *Selected Writings*, 106–107, 109–110; "*left behind*" quoted in Frank Lambert, *Inventing the "Great Awakening"* (Princeton, NJ: Princeton University Press, 1999), 66–67.
39 Edwards as quoted in Lambert, *Inventing the "Great Awakening,"* 67.
40 Frank Lambert, "'Pedlar in Divinity': George Whitefield and the Great Awakening, 1737–1745," *Journal of American History*, 77, no. 3 (Dec. 1990): 812–837. On the burgeoning consumer culture, see J. E. Crowley, *This Sheba, Self: The Conceptualization of Economic Life in Eighteenth-Century America* (Baltimore, MD: Johns Hopkins University Press, 1974); John E. Crowley, "The Sensibility of Comfort," *American Historical Review*, 104, no. 3 (Jun. 1999): 749–782; Paul G. E. Clemens, "The Consumer Culture of the Middle Atlantic, 1760–1820," *William and Mary Quarterly*, 3rd series, 62, no. 4 (Oct. 2005): 577–624; T. H. Breen, *The Marketplace of Revolution: How Consumer Politics Shaped American Independence* (New York: Oxford University Press, 2004).
41 Jonathan Edwards, *A careful and strict Enquiry into the modern prevailing Notions of that Freedom of Will* (Boston: S. Kneeland, 1754), 27–29, 98, 220, 226, 291.
42 Daniel Walker Howe, *Making the American Self: Jonathan Edwards to Abraham Lincoln* (New York: Oxford University Press, 2009; first pub.1997), 38–41; Edwards, *Selected Writings*, 11–21; O'Brien, "A Transatlantic Community of Saints," 822, 832; Lambert, "'Pedlar in Divinity,'" 823.
43 William S. Simmons, "Red Yankees: Narragansett Conversion in the Great Awakening," *American Ethnologist*, 10, no. 2 (May 1983): 253–271; Jane T. Merritt, "Dreaming of the Savior's Blood: Moravians and the Indian Great Awakening in Pennsylvania," *William and Mary Quarterly*, 54, no. 4 (Oct. 1997): 723–746; Frank Lambert, "'I Saw the Book Talk': Slave Readings of the First Great Awakening," *Journal of African American History*, 87, no. 1 (Winter 2002): 12–25; Lambert, *Inventing the Great Awakening*, 255; John Howard Smith, *The First Great Awakening: Redefining Religion in British America, 1725–1775* (Lanham, MD: Fairleigh Dickinson University Press, 2014); Nell Irvin Painter, *Creating Black Americans: African-American History and Its Meanings, 1619 to the Present* (New York: Oxford University Press, 2006), 45, 47.
44 Lambert, "Pedlar in Divinity," 832; Jon Butler, "Enthusiasm Described and Decried: The Great Awakening as Interpretative Fiction," *Journal of American History*, 69, no. 2 (Sept. 1982): 305–325, esp. 318–319; Phillis Wheatley, *Poems of Phillis Wheatley: A Native African and a Slave* (Bedford, MA: Applewood Books, 1969; first pub. 1773), 12, 16; Lambert, "'I Saw the Book Talk',"12–17; Lambert, *Inventing the Great Awakening*, 141–142, 168, 199–200. Although Whitefield made some efforts to improve the worldly conditions of enslaved people, he did not argue against slavery, which he actually considered as a reasonable way to lower the costs of his Georgia orphanage.
45 Charles Chauncy, *Enthusiasm described and caution'd against* (Boston: J. Draper, 1742; Ann Arbor: Text Creation Partnership; quod.lib.umich.edu/e/evans/N03978.0001.001/1:4)13–16; Cowing, "Sex and Preaching in the Great Awakening," 625, 628–629, 632–641, 644. The beginning of Chauncy's demand for women's silence came from 1 Corinthians 14:34.

46 Chauncy, *Enthusiasm described*, 13–16; Harry S. Stout, "Religion, Communications, and the Ideological Origins of the American Revolution," *William and Mary Quarterly*, 3rd series, 34, no. 4 (Oct. 1977): 519–541, esp. 527, 530–533, 539.

47 For sampling and reviews of historical arguments on the Great Awakening's impacts, see Butler, "Enthusiasm Described and Decried"; on the rising consumer culture's impacts, see Breen, *The Marketplace of Revolution*; on the Enlightenment's impact, Gordon S. Wood, *The Radicalism of the American Revolution* (New York: Alfred A. Knopf, 1992). On the value of not untangling complex historical threads, see Pamela Walker Laird, "Entangled: Civil Rights in Corporate America since 1964," in Richard R. John and Kim Phillips-Fein, eds., *Capital Gains: Business and Politics in Twentieth-Century America* (Philadelphia: University of Pennsylvania Press, 2016), 217–234.

CHAPTER 3

1 Nestor [Benjamin Rush], "To the People of the United States," *Independent Gazetteer, or, The Chronicle of Freedom* (Philadelphia), Jun. 3, 1786. Eric Foner, *Tom Paine and Revolutionary America* (New York: Oxford University Press, 1976), 136–138. According to the *Oxford English Dictionary* online, there was no relevant use of "mobility" prior to 1900.

2 Adam Smith, *The Theory of Moral Sentiments* (Washington, DC: Regnery Publishing, 1997; based on an 1817 Boston edition of Smith's sixth and final edition), III.ii, 152.

3 On the use of self-fulfilling logic to disadvantage "out-groups," see Robert K. Merton, "The Self-Fulfilling Prophecy," in *Social Theory and Social Structure: Toward the Codification of Theory and Research* (Glencoe, Il: The Free Press, 1949), 179–195.

4 For interpretations of the Revolution and its impacts, see Gordon S. Wood, *The Radicalism of the American Revolution* (New York: Alfred A. Knopf, 1992); and Alan Taylor, *American Revolutions: A Continental History, 1750–1804* (New York: W.W. Norton & Company, 2016). See also Douglas Bradburn, "The Problem of Citizenship in the American Revolution," *History Compass* 8/9 (2010): 1093–1113; T. H. Breen, *The Marketplace of Revolution: How Consumer Politics Shaped American Independence* (New York: Oxford University Press, 2004).

5 Paul D. Ellenbogan, "Political Inequality in a Democratic Society: Adams, Jefferson and the Natural Aristocracy" (PhD dissertation, Duke University, 1993), 165.

6 John Smith quote in *Captain John Smith: A Select Edition of His Writings*, ed. Karen Ordahl Kupperman (Chapel Hill: University of North Carolina Press, 1988), 278. See Chapter 1 for more on John Smith and work as a measure of merit.

7 See Chapter 1 for more on early colonizers' hostility to anyone they interpreted as not working in earnest.

8 The costs of mercantilist constraints on colonial manufacturing were actually quite small. John J. McCusker and Russell R. Menard, *The Economy of British America, 1607–1789* (Chapel Hill: University of North Carolina Press, 1985), 309–310, 354–355.

9 Even so, the immediate stimulus for this action had actually reduced tea prices to Americans from this monopoly, in effect allowing the British East India Company to

put its overstock of tea on sale. This undercut enterprising colonial smugglers and merchants but still demanded the authority to set taxes without colonists' input. Richard D. Brown, *Revolutionary Politics in Massachusetts: The Boston Committee of Correspondence and the Towns, 1772–1774* (Cambridge, MA: Harvard University Press, 1970), 159.

10 McCusker and Menard, *Economy of British America*, 354–355.

11 See Chapters 1 and 2.

12 For a review of historical works on republican virtue, see Daniel T. Rodgers, "Republicanism: The Career of a Concept," *Journal of American History*, 79, no. 1 (Jun. 1992): 11–38. See also Bradburn, "The Problem of Citizenship in the American Revolution."

The assault on idle aristocracies did not arise anew from the American frustrations and self-righteousness that heated and applied it. A long intellectual foundation had Renaissance precursors, most notably Niccolò Machiavelli (1467–1527) and Francis Bacon (1561–1626), who developed early visions of the modern state and the roles of individuals within them, including the notion that states and individuals constructed themselves. America's intellectual elites were well aware of these and others, especially John Locke (1632–1704).

13 Foner, *Tom Paine and Revolutionary America*; Alfred F. Young, *The Shoemaker and the Tea Party: Memory and the American Revolution* (Boston: Beacon Press, 1999).

14 Saul Cornell, "Aristocracy Assailed: The Ideology of Backcountry Anti-Federalism" *Journal of American History*, 76, no. 4 (Mar. 1990): 1148–1172; quotes 1149, 1152, 1156–1157; Samuel Eliot Morison, ed., "William Manning's The Key of Libberty," *William and Mary Quarterly*, 13, no. 2 (Apr. 1956): 202–254, quotes 211–212.

15 James P. Walsh, "'Mechanics and Citizens': The Connecticut Artisan Protest of 1792" *William and Mary Quarterly*, 42, no. 1 (Jan. 1985): 66–89; quotes 69, 76, 87–88.

16 Sean Wilentz, *Chants Democratic: New York City & the Rise of the American Working Class, 1788–1850* (New York: Oxford University Press, 1984), 69, 71.

17 For a long view of elites' challenges in the political sphere, see Steve Fraser and Gary Gerstle, eds., *Ruling America: A History of Wealth and Power in a Democracy* (Cambridge, MA: Harvard University Press, 2005). For the early period, see Gary J. Kornblith and John M. Murrin, "The Dilemmas of Ruling Elites in Revolutionary America," in Fraser and Gerstle, eds., *Ruling America*, 17–63; and Wood, *Radicalism of the American Revolution*, 261–265, 267.

18 Edmund S. Morgan, *Inventing the People: The Rise of Popular Sovereignty in England and America* (New York: W. W. Norton & Company, 1988), 292–293, 305–306.

19 John P. Kaminski, *George Clinton: Yeoman Politician of the New Republic* (Madison, WI: Madison House Publishers, Inc., 1993), 1–2, 24–26, 185–186.

20 Kaminski, *George Clinton*, 1–2, 12–13, 16, 24–26; quote 25.

21 Kaminski, *George Clinton*, 26; Charles Carroll quoted in Taylor, *American Revolutions*, 355.

22 Daniel T. Rodgers, *As a City on a Hill: The Story of America's Most Famous Lay Sermon* (Princeton, NJ: Princeton University Press, 2018), 117–119; Christine Leigh Heyrman, "The Fashion Among More Superior People: Charity and Social Change in Provincial

New England, 1700–1740," *American Quarterly*, 34, no. 2 (Summer 1982): 107–124, quote 110; Heli Meltsner, *The Poorhouses of Massachusetts: A Cultural and Architectural History* (Jefferson, NC: McFarland & Company, 2012).

23 Merton, "The Self-Fulfilling Prophecy." On slavery's "world of perpetual exploitation and incessant degradation," see Peter H. Wood, "Slave Labor Camps in Early America: Overcoming Denial and Discovering the Gulag," in Carla Gardina Pestana and Sharon V. Salinger, eds., *Inequality in Early America* (Hanover, NH: University Press of New England, 1999), 222–238, quote 234.

24 James Edward Oglethorpe, *A New and Accurate Account of the Provinces of South-Carolina and Georgia* (London: J. Worrall, 1732), retrieved from docsouth.unc.edu/southlit/oglethorpe/oglethorpe.html, 35; Betty Wood, *Slavery in Colonial Georgia, 1730–1775* (Athens, GA: University of Georgia Press, 1984), esp. chaps. 1, 6, quote 3; Betty Wood, "James Edward Oglethorpe, Race, and Slavery: A Reassessment," in Phinizy Spaulding and Harvey H. Jackson, eds., *Oglethorpe in Perspective: Georgia's Founder after Two Hundred Years* (Tuscaloosa, AL: University of Alabama Press, 1989), 66–79, quote 71.

25 For a history of slavery in South Carolina including its impacts on White workers, see Justene Hill Edwards, *Unfree Markets: The Slaves' Economy and the Rise of Capitalism in South Carolina* (New York: Columbia University Press, 2021).

26 Oglethorpe also recognized that "a Gentleman, or Merchant" would find even a day thus spent to be "severe." Oglethorpe, *A New and Accurate Account*, 32, 39; Wood, *Slavery in Colonial Georgia*, esp. chaps. 2, 6.

27 Judith Ann Carney, *Black Rice: The African Origins of Rice Cultivation in the Americas* (Cambridge, MA: Harvard University Press, 2001), 109–111; 1936 quote 160–161; for another egregious example, see 98–99. See also Michael Adas, *Machines as the Measure of Men: Science, Technology, and Ideologies of Western Dominance* (Ithaca, NY: Cornell University Press, 1989).

28 It is worth noting that even under enslavement's constraints, people were sometimes able to participate in market economies for wages, profit, and a measure of self-agency. See Edwards, *Unfree Markets*; and Juliet E. K. Walker, *The History of Black Business in America: Capitalism, Race, Entrepreneurship* (New York: Twayne Publishers, 1998), 52–82.

29 Mary V. Thompson, *"The Only Unavoidable Subject of Regret": George Washington, Slavery, and the Enslaved Community at Mount Vernon* (Charlottesville: University of Virginia Press, 2019), 20–22.

30 Among Washington's peers, treating enslaved people as objects and assets was common. For example, in 1792, Thomas Jefferson indicated to Washington that he had had a 4 percent profit from their reproduction the year before. He later referred to this as a "silent profit." Caitlin Rosenthal, *Accounting for Slavery: Masters and Management* (Cambridge, MA: Harvard University Press, 2018), 130–131; Thompson, *"The Only Unavoidable Subject of Regret"*, chap. 4; 28, 192–199, 213; Gordon S. Wood, *Revolutionary Characters: What Made the Founders Different* (New York: Penguin Books, 2006), 37–41; Ira Berlin, *Many Thousands Gone: The First Two Centuries of Slavery in North America* (Cambridge, MA: Harvard University Press, 1998), 220–222, 257–259, 278.

31 Berlin, *Many Thousands Gone*; Edmund S. Morgan, *American Slavery, American Freedom: The Ordeal of Colonial Virginia* (New York: W.W. Norton & Company, 1975); Rosenthal, *Accounting for Slavery*.
32 Thompson, *"Only Unavoidable Subject of Regret"*, 109, 165–167, 172–180; Kenneth Morgan, "George Washington and the Problem of Slavery," *Journal of American Studies*, 34, no. 2 (Aug. 2000): 279–301; Rosenthal, *Accounting for Slavery*.
33 On Washington's determined self-improvement, see Adrienne M. Harrison, *A Powerful Mind: The Self-Education of George Washington* (Dulles, VA: Potomac Books, 2015).
34 Thompson, *"Only Unavoidable Subject of Regret"*, 38, 42, 77, 190–191; Berlin, *Many Thousands Gone*, 136–140, 164, 277, 347–348; Kelly Kean Sharp, "Planters' Plots to Backlot Stewpots: Food, Race, and Labor in Charleston, South Carolina, 1780–1850" (PhD dissertation, University of California, Davis, 2018), 26, 32; Edwards, *Unfree Markets*; Berlin, *Many Thousands Gone*, 119, 268–270, 277, 319–320.
35 Thompson, *"Only Unavoidable Subject of Regret"*, 180.
36 George Washington, "George Washington's Last Will and Testament, 9 July 1799," *Founders Online*, National Archives. The 1782 Virginia law permitted manumission without state approval but required provision for the support of people too young, old, or infirm to work. "An act to authorize the manumission of slaves," *Encyclopedia Virginia*, Virginia Humanities. Washington also forbade removing from Virginia "any Slave I may die possessed of, under any pretence whatsoever" as a precaution against the horrors of plantations farther south. For a detailed historical treatment of the evolution of Washington's thinking, see Morgan, "George Washington and the Problem of Slavery."
37 Henry Wiencek, *An Imperfect God: George Washington, His Slaves, and the Creation of America* (New York: Farrar, Straus and Giroux, 2003), 55, 272–274, 278; Rosemarie Zagarri, ed., *David Humphreys' "Life of General Washington" with George Washington's "Remarks"* (Athens: University of Georgia Press, 1991), xxvii, xxxvi, liv, 78.
38 J. A. Leo Lemay and P. M. Zall, introduction and "The Text," in Benjamin Franklin, *The Autobiography of Benjamin Franklin: A Genetic Text*, ed. J. A. Leo Lemay and P. M. Zall (Knoxville: University of Tennessee Press, 1981), xvii, xx–xxi, liii–lviii; quotes lvi, 1.
39 Lemay and Zall in Franklin, *Autobiography*, lvi–lvii, 68.
40 Lemay and Zall in Franklin, *Autobiography*, lvi–lvii, 68. For historical studies of reputation's importance, see Joanne B. Freeman, *Affairs of Honor: National Politics in the New Republic* (New Haven, CT: Yale University Press, 2001), 282–284; Alan Houston, *Benjamin Franklin and the Politics of Improvement* (New Haven, CT: Yale University Press, 2008), 47–52; Toby L. Ditz, "Shipwrecked; or, Masculinity Imperiled: Mercantile Representations of Failure and the Gendered Self in Eighteenth-Century Philadelphia," *Journal of American History*, 81, no. 1 (Jun. 1994): 51–80; John Smail, "Credit, Risk, and Honor in Eighteenth-Century Commerce," *Journal of British Studies*, 44, no. 3 (Jul. 2005): 439–456; Pamela Walker Laird, "Putting Social Capital to Work," *Business History*, 50, no. 6 (Nov. 2008): 685–694.
41 Franklin, *Autobiography*, lvi, 1–2. Judith A. McGaw coined a more apt expression that Franklin would have accepted and understood: "mutually-made men." *Most Wonderful*

Machine: Mechanization and Social Change in Berkshire Paper Making, 1801–1885 (Princeton, NJ: Princeton University Press, 1987), 127, 131, 137–146.

42 Franklin, *Autobiography*, 8, 28; Gordon S. Wood, *The Americanization of Benjamin Franklin* (New York: Penguin Press, 2004), 25–27; Henry Steele Commager, Introduction, *Autobiography of Benjamin Franklin* (New York: Random House, 1944), xi.

43 Franklin, *Autobiography*, 57–58, 60; Wood, *Americanization of Benjamin Franklin*, 25–27. On the necessity of patronage for education and mobility, see Joseph F. Kett, *The Pursuit of Knowledge Under Difficulties: From Self-Improvement to Adult Education in America, 1750–1990* (Stanford: Stanford University Press, 1994), 12–13, 22–24, 36–37.

44 Thomas L. Purvis, *Colonial America to 1763* (New York: Facts on File, Inc., 1999), 136, 222, 227–229; Purvis, *Revolutionary America: 1763–1800* (New York: Facts on File, Inc., 1995), 138, 158–159, 260–261. The census data defined male adulthood at sixteen years and older; race and gender approximations based on comparative census proportions.

45 For example, see Paul E. Johnson, *A Shopkeeper's Millennium: Society and revivals in Rochester, New York, 1815–1837* (New York: Hill and Wang, 1978), 48–55, 139–141. Sam B. Warner, Jr., documents this phenomenon for later in the century in *Streetcar Suburbs: The Process of Growth in Boston, 1870–1900* (Cambridge, MA: Harvard University Press, 1962), 18–19, 53–58, 65–66, 164–166.

46 John Demos, *Circles and Lines: The Shape of Life in Early America* (Cambridge, MA: Harvard University Press, 2004), 80; Stephen Innes, *Creating the Commonwealth: The Economic Culture of Puritan New England* (New York: W.W. Norton & Company, 1995), 17–27; Mark Valeri, *Heavenly Merchandize: How Religion Shaped Commerce in Puritan America* (Princeton, NJ: Princeton University Press, 2010), 234–249.

47 Franklin, *Autobiography*, 24–25, 79–89; Houston, *Benjamin Franklin*, 13–18, 26–27, 51, 108.

48 Innes, *Creating the Commonwealth*, 17–27; Valeri, *Heavenly Merchandize*, 234–249.

49 Franklin made this pledge as part of the Silence Dogood essays he wrote at sixteen, Franklin, *Papers*, 1:8–43. See chap. 2. See also Wood, *Radicalism of the American Revolution*, 22, 38, 85–86, 118–119; Wood, *Americanization of Benjamin Franklin*, 51, 54–59; Kett, *Pursuit of Knowledge Under Difficulties*, chap. 1. Houston persuasively refutes Max Weber's depiction of Franklin as a narrow-minded capitalist in the appendix to *Benjamin Franklin*, 225–229.

50 Scholarly works on the history of attitudes toward self-interest include J. E. Crowley, *This Sheba, Self: The Conceptualization of Economic Life in Eighteenth-Century America* (Baltimore, MD: Johns Hopkins University Press, 1974); Daniel Walker Howe, *Making the American Self: Jonathan Edwards to Abraham Lincoln* (Cambridge, MA: Harvard University Press, 1997); Albert O. Hirschman, *The Passions and the Interests: Political Arguments for Capitalism before its Triumph* (Princeton, NJ: Princeton University Press, 1977); Jane J. Mansbridge, ed., *Beyond Self-Interest* (Chicago: University of Chicago Press, 1990); Steven G. Medema, *The Hesitant Hand: Taming Self-Interest in the History of Economic Ideas* (Princeton, NJ: Princeton University Press, 2009); Steve Pincus, "Neither Machiavellian Moment nor Possessive Individualism: Commercial Society and the Defenders of the English Commonwealth," *American Historical Review*, 103, no. 3 (Jun. 1998): 705–736; Andrew S. Trees, *The Founding Fathers and the Politics of Character* (Princeton, NJ: Princeton University Press, 2004).

51 William Casey King, *Ambition, A History: From Vice to Virtue* (New Haven, CT: Yale University Press, 2013); Koji Yamamoto, *Taming Capitalism before Its Triumph: Public Service, Distrust, and "Projecting" in Early Modern England* (Oxford, UK: Oxford University Press, 2018).

52 *Independent Gazetteer* (Philadelphia, PA), Apr. 24, 1790; *Massachusetts Centinel* [sic] (Boston, MA), Apr. 28, 1790; *Federal Gazette and Philadelphia Daily Advertiser* (Philadelphia, PA), Apr. 19, 1790.

53 *Pennsylvania Mercury, and Universal Advertiser* (Philadelphia, PA), Apr. 22, 1790. This text appeared, often verbatim, elsewhere, including: *New-York Packet*, Apr. 22, 1790; *New-York Daily Gazette*, Apr. 22, 1790; *Gazette of the United States* (New York, NY), Apr. 24, 1790; *New-Jersey Journal, and Political Intelligencer* (Elizabethtown, NJ), Apr. 28, 1790; *Newport Herald* (Newport, RI), Apr. 29, 1790.

54 William Smith, *Eulogium on Benjamin Franklin, L.L.D* (Philadelphia, PA: Benjamin Franklin Bache, 1792), errata page not numbered, 1, 11–12, 25. Wood, *Americanization of Benjamin Franklin*, 233–234. Elsewhere Smith mistakenly accused Franklin of taking credit for work done by Ebenezer Kinnersley, see J. A. L. Lemay, "Franklin and Kinnersley," *Isis*, 52, no. 4 (Dec. 1961): 575–581, esp. 578–579.

55 Foner, *Tom Paine*, 34, 36; Lemay and Zall, *Autobiography of Benjamin Franklin*, xlvii-liii; Carla Mulford, "Figuring Benjamin Franklin in American Cultural Memory," *New England Quarterly*, 72, no. 3 (Sept. 1999): 415–443; Wood, *Revolutionary Characters*, 263–266; Edward Cahill, "The English Origins of American Upward Mobility; or, the Invention of Benjamin Franklin," *ELH*, 83, no. 2 (Summer 2016): 543–571.

56 Richard Saunders [Franklin], *Poor Richard improved: Being an Almanack and Ephemeris . . . for the Year of our Lord 1758* (Philadelphia, PA: Printed and Sold by B. Franklin, and D. Hall, 1758), Benjamin Franklin, *Papers of Benjamin Franklin*, 43 vols. (New Haven, CT: Yale University Library) 1:8–43, retrieved from franklinpapers.org, 7:326–355. Franklin, *Autobiography*, 93–94. For a careful and appreciative study of how Father Abraham's "Harangue" found fame as "The Way of Wealth" and its "afterlives," see the beautifully produced homage to the arts of writing and printing by James N. Green and Peter Stallybrass, *Benjamin Franklin: Writer and Printer* (New Castle, DE: Oak Knoll Press; and Philadelphia, PA: Library Company of Philadelphia, 2006), 127–143.

57 Franklin to Robert Morris, Dec. 25, 1783; *Benjamin Franklin Papers*, listed as unpublished at franklinpapers.org.

CHAPTER 4

1 On the cultural roles of heroes, see Marshall W. Fishwick, *American Heroes: Myth and Reality* (Westport, CT: Greenwood Press, 1954), 4–8, 230–231; Peter Karsten, *Patriot-Heroes in England and America: Political Symbolism and Changing Values over Three Centuries* (Madison, WI: University of Wisconsin Press, 1978), 1–3, 11. On the intellectual history of individualism in this period, see Alex Zakaras, *The Roots of American Individualism: Political Myth in the Age of Jackson* (Princeton, NJ: Princeton University Press, 2022). On the purposes and

purposefulness of storytelling, see Frederick W. Mayer, *Narrative Politics: Stories and Collective Action* (New York: Oxford University Press, 2014).

2 D'Anville (Nancy [Anne] Kingsbury Wollstonecraft), *Boston Monthly Magazine*, 1, no. 6 (Nov. 1825): 305, 309–312. Alan M. S. J. Coffee, "Nancy Kingsbury Wollstonecraft and the Logic of Freedom as Independence," *Journal of the History of Philosophy*, 61. no. 2 (Apr. 2023): 257–282.

3 For overviews, see John Lauritz Larson, *The Market Revolution in America: Liberty, Ambition, and the Eclipse of the Common Good* (New York: Cambridge University Press, 2010); Charles Sellers, *The Market Revolution: Jacksonian America, 1815–1846* (New York: Oxford University Press, 1991).

4 See Chapters 1–2 for more on Euro-Americans fighting self-righteous battles against people living in ways they deemed strange on lands that they coveted. For an example of how nineteenth-century European immigrants observed Native Americans and their removal but still considered the land "empty," see Gunlög Fur, "Indians and Immigrants – Entangled Histories," *Journal of American Ethnic History*, 33, no. 3 (Spring 2014): 55–76.

5 Walt Whitman, *Leaves of Grass*, ed. Harold W. Blodgett and Sculley Bradley (New York: New York University Press, 1965), 729.

6 Patricia Kelly Hall and Steven Ruggles, "'Restless in the Midst of Their Prosperity': New Englanders on the Internal Migration of Americans, 1850–2000," *Journal of American History*, 91, no. 3 (Dec. 2004): 829–846; Ariell Zimran, "Internal Migration in the United States: Rates, Selection, and Destination Choice, 1850–1940," National Bureau of Economic Research Working Paper 30384 (Cambridge, MA, 2022).

7 Joyce Appleby describes America's "perpetual-motion society" in *Inheriting the Revolution: The First Generation of Americans* (Cambridge, MA: Harvard University Press, 2000), 6. On economic growth, see also George Rogers Taylor's *The Transportation Revolution, 1815–1860* (New York: Harper Torchbooks, 1951). On motivations to migrate, see J. M. Opal, *Beyond the Farm: National Ambitions in Rural New England* (Philadelphia, PA: University of Pennsylvania Press, 2013); Brian P. Luskey, *On the Make: Clerks and the Quest for Capital in Nineteenth-Century America* (New York: New York University Press, 2010).

8 "On the Ruinous Effects of Ardent Spirits," *Vermont Watchman and State Journal* (Montpelier, VT), Sept. 19, 1815; "On Drunkenness," *Weekly Raleigh Register* (Raleigh, NC), Nov. 29, 1822. This usage continued, for example: "Report to the Sandusky Washingtonian Society," *The Sandusky Clarion* (OH), Nov. 30, 1844; "Hē Mikra Mania Esti," *Morganton Star* (NC), Jan. 6, 1888; "Sentiment vs. Justice," *El Paso Times* (TX), Apr. 27, 1892.

9 "Air Balloon Exhibition, the 4th July 1806, on Woodstock Green," *Post-Boy* (Windsor, VT), Jul. 8, 1806. At least two untitled editorials repeated the "bloated patriots" diatribe from *National Intelligencer*: *Virginia Argus* (Richmond, VA), Aug. 24, 1812; and *Lancaster Intelligencer and Journal* (PA), Sept. 5, 1812. "The Pedigree and Residence of Happiness: A Vision," reprinted in *The Christian Monitor and Religious Intelligencer* from *The Evangelical Magazine*, Apr. 3, 1813. George Hall, "To Captain John Allen," *The Long-Island Star* (Brooklyn, NY), Jul. 19, 1820. "News of the Week," *New York Daily Herald*,

May 22, 1837, from the *Weekly Herald*, May 20, 1837. "Wreath, or Independence Day," *Balance* (Jun. 28, 1808): 104; "The Warrior," *Pittsburgh Weekly Gazette* (Pittsburgh, PA), Jun. 25, 1813.

10 Christopher Harris, "Mason Locke Weems's Life of Washington: The Making of a Bestseller," *Southern Literary Journal*, 19, no. 2 (Spring 1987): 92–101.

11 M. L. Weems, *The Life of Benjamin Franklin: With Many Choice Anecdotes* (Philadelphia, PA: Uriah Hunt & Son, 1815), 13, 23, 39, 86, 164, 190. Weems's one positive use of "self" described Washington's "self-possession" in a 1755 battle, 188. See Chapter 3 regarding William Temple Franklin's rewrite of his grandfather's autobiography.

12 Paul D. Ellenhogan, "Political Inequality in a Democratic Society: Adams, Jefferson, and the Natural Aristocracy" (PhD dissertation, Duke University, 1993).

13 "Biography: Sketch of the Life of Samuel Miller, Esq." *Advisor: or, Vermont Evangelical Magazine*, Jun. 1810, reprinted in *Panoplist and Missionary Magazine*, Aug. 1810, and *Religion Instructor*, Apr. 11, 1811. David Mitchell Stameshkin, "The Town's College: Middlebury College, 1800–1915" (PhD dissertation, University of Michigan, 1978), 5, 26–28, 35, 83. Searches in 2012 and 2021 of Newspapers.com, American Periodicals, 18th and 19th Century Newspapers & Periodicals Accessible Archives, and 19th Century U.S. Newspapers revealed no reference to "self-made" in a positive sense earlier than this 1810 biography of Samuel Miller. Searches on Google Ngrams or similar digital resources are not useful for this question because they cannot disaggregate positive and negative uses.

14 "Life of Andrew Fuller," *Theological Review and General Repository*, Oct. 1, 1822. A journal in Vermont had already published an admiring biography of Fuller in 1818: *Christian Chronicle*, Sept. 19, 1818, as had others. A search of Newspapers.com on Jan. 16, 2022, revealed 674 citations.

15 Alney McLean, speaking in the House of Representatives on "Compensation Law," *History of Congress* (Jan. 1817), column 656; "Biographical Directory of the United States Congress," bioguide.congress.gov/search/bio/M000544

16 Richard L. Bushman, *From Puritan to Yankee: Character and the Social Order in Connecticut, 1690–1765* (New York: W. W. Norton & Company, 1970; first edition 1967), 287.

17 See Michael A. Lofaro, ed., *Boone, Black Hawk, and Crockett in 1833: Unsettling the Mythic West* (Knoxville: University of Tennessee Press, 2019), esp. vii–x, xxiv, xxxiv–ix; Richard Slotkin, *Regeneration Through Violence: The Mythology of the American Frontier, 1600-1860* (Middletown, CT: Wesleyan University Press, 1973), esp. chaps. X, XI, XII; M. J. Heale, "The Role of the Frontier in Jacksonian Politics: David Crockett and the Myth of the Self-Made Man," *Western Historical Quarterly*, 4, no. 4 (Oct. 1973): 405-423.

18 John Filson, *The Adventures of Col. Daniel Boon: Containing a Narrative of the Wars of Kentucke* (Wilmington, DE: John Adams, 1784), 49–50, 80–82.

19 Lord Byron, *Don Juan* (Halifax: Milner and Sowerby, 1837; incomplete version pub. 1819; retrieved from www.gutenberg.org). For an analysis of frontier literature back to earlier centuries' captivity and Indian war narratives, see Slotkin, *Regeneration Through Violence*.

20 "A Crockett Chronology," in Michael A. Lofaro and Joe Cummings, eds., *Crockett at Two Hundred: New Perspectives on the Man and the Myth* (Knoxville: University of Tennessee Press, 1989), xxi–xxvi.
21 "A Crockett Chronology," Lofaro and Cummings, eds., *Crockett at Two Hundred*, xxi-xxvi.
22 James Parton, "David Crockett," *Massachusetts Ploughman and New England Journal of Agriculture*, 29, no. 48 (Aug. 27, 1870): 4.
23 "David Crockett," *North Star* (Danville, VT), Jul. 12 1831, reprinted from *Winchester Republican* (Winchester, VA). This item appeared verbatim in multiple other papers, as was common at the time, including *Brattleboro Messenger* (Brattleboro, VT), May 14, 1831; *Natchez Weekly Courier* (Natchez, MI), Jul. 29, 1831.
24 Richard Boyd Hauck, "The Man in the Buckskin Hunting Shirt: Fact and Fiction in the Crockett Story," in Michael A. Lofaro, ed., *Davy Crockett: The Man, the Legend, the Legacy, 1786–1986* (Knoxville: University of Tennessee Press, 1985), 3–20; Melvin Rosser Mason, "'The Lion of the West': Satire on Davy Crockett and Frances Trollope," *South Central Bulletin*, 29, no. 4 (Winter 1969): 143–145.
25 Michael Montgomery, "David Crockett and the Rhetoric of Tennessee Politics," and Joe Cummings, "Celebrating Crockett in Tennessee," in Lofaro and Cummings, eds., *Crockett at Two Hundred*, 50, 68–69; Walter Blair, "Six Davy Crocketts," *Southwest Review*, 25, no. 4 (Jul. 1940): 443–462; Heale, "The Role of the Frontier in Jacksonian Politics"; Richard Boyd Hauck, "The Man in the Buckskin Hunting Shirt," *Register of Debates in Congress*, 788 (Feb. 24, 1831).
26 "David Crockett," *North Star* (Danville, VT), Jul. 12, 1831. Blair, "Six Davy Crocketts"; Heale, "The Role of the Frontier in Jacksonian Politics."
27 On the evolution of versions of Crockett imagery and uncertainties about the authorship and veracity of biographies, see Lofaro and Cummings, *Crockett at Two Hundred*, and Blair, "Six Davy Crocketts." See also Davy Crockett and Richard Penn Smith, *Davy Crockett's Own Story: As Written by Himself* (New York: Citadel Press, 1955; first pub. 1834). For his speeches, *Register of Debates in Congress*, 717 (Mar. 30, 1830); 480 (Dec. 23, 1829); 583 (Feb. 25, 1830); 200 (Jan. 12, 1829).
28 *Register of Debates in Congress*, 717 (Mar. 30, 1830); 480 (Dec. 23, 1829); 583 (Feb. 25, 1830); 200 (Jan. 12, 1829).
29 Bertram Wyatt-Brown, "Andrew Jackson's Honor," *Journal of the Early American Republic*, 17, no. 1 (Spring, 1997): 1–36, see 29; Marquis James, *The Life of Andrew Jackson* (Indianapolis and New York: Bobbs-Merrill Company, 1938), 5–7, 10, 31, 34–35; Eric W. Nye, *Pounds Sterling to Dollars: Historical Conversion of Currency*, www.uwyo.edu/numimage/currency.htm
30 Jon Meacham, *American Lion: Andrew Jackson in the White House* (New York: Random House, 2008); Steven Watts, *The Republic Reborn: War and the Making of Liberal America, 1790–1820* (Baltimore, MD: Johns Hopkins University Press, 1987), 294–296. S[amuel] Putnam Waldo, *Memoirs of Andrew Jackson*, 5th ed. (Hartford, CT: J. & W. Russell, 1819; 1st ed. 1818), 18, 35, 334.
31 Waldo, *Memoirs of Andrew Jackson*, 18, 35, 334.

32 David S. Heidler and Jeanne T. Heidler, *The Rise of Andrew Jackson: Myth, Manipulation, and the Making of Modern Politics* (New York: Basic Books, 2018). For a detailed study of the roles of key newspapermen in that decade, see Donald B. Cole, *Vindicating Andrew Jackson: The 1828 Election and the Rise of the Two-Party System* (Lawrence: University Press of Kansas, 2009). On the early history of newspapers, see Gerald J. Baldasty, *The Commercialization of News in the Nineteenth Century* (Madison: University of Wisconsin Press, 1992). By 1810, the US had more newspapers circulating than any other nation per capita in history, much of that growth driven by partisanship; Joseph F. Kett, *The Pursuit of Knowledge Under Difficulties: From Self-Improvement to Adult Education, 1750–1990* (Stanford, CA: Stanford University Press, 1994), 67.

33 Thomas H. Hall, "To the Freemen" and "Candidates," *North-Carolina Free Press* (Halifax, NC), Jul. 30, 1824; *History, Art & Archives, U.S. House of Representatives*, history.house.gov/People/Listing/H/HALL,-Thomas-H–(H000072)/

34 "Desultory Sketches No. III," *Natchez Gazette* (Natchez, MS), Nov. 19, 1825.

35 "Remarks of Mr. Le Compte," Mar. 21, 1826, *Daily National Journal*, Apr. 4, 1826; *History, Art & Archives, U.S. House of Representatives*, "LECOMPTE, Joseph," history.house.gov/People/Listing/L/LECOMPTE,-Joseph-(L000186)/. The speaker's spellings differ in the two records.

36 "Biographical Directory of the United States Congress," bioguide.congress.gov/search/bio/S000349.

37 "Professor Newman's Address: A Self-Made Man," *Youth's Companion* (Boston), vol. 1, no. 42 (Mar. 14, 1828): 167.

38 B[ela] B[ates] Edwards, *Biography of Self-Taught Men* (Boston: Perkins & Marvin, 1832), iv-vii, xv, xx, xxxii-xxxiii, 3, 5, 12, 68. "Edwards, Bela Bates," in *Marquis Who Was Who in America 1607–1984* (New York: Marquis Who's Who LLC, 2009). A search on Newspapers.com, Jan. 27, 2022, turned up more than fifty references to Sherman between 1828 and 1860.

39 See Chapter 3.

40 George Washington, "Farewell Address," *American Daily Advertiser* (Philadelphia, PA): Sept. 19, 1796; American Presidency Project, www.presidency.ucsb.edu/node/200675.

41 "SELF MADE MEN," *Quarterly Register and journal of the American Education Society*, 2, no. 2 (Nov. 1829): 104.

42 "SELF-MADE MEN," *Daily National Journal* (Washington, DC), Dec. 14, 1829, vol. 6, no. 1879.

CHAPTER 5

1 See Chapter 4 on geographical mobility. See also Mary P. Ryan, *Cradle of the Middle Class: The Family in Oneida County, New York, 1790–1865* (Cambridge, UK: Cambridge University Press, 1981); Paul E. Johnson, *A Shopkeeper's Millennium: Society and Revival in Rochester, New York, 1815–1837* (New York: Hill & Wang, 1978); Michael Zakim,

Accounting for Capitalism: The World the Clerk Made (Chicago: University of Chicago Press, 2018).
2 Joel Hawes, *Lectures to Young Men on the Formation of Character, &c.* (Hartford, CT: Cooke and Co., 1832), 168, 52, 135, 141–142.
3 Hawes, *Lectures to Young Men*, 44–45, 55, 60.
4 Hawes, *Lectures to Young Men*, 3, 94–95, 100–102, 169.
5 Edward A. Lawrence, *The Life of Rev. Joel Hawes, D.D.*, 2nd ed. (Boston, MA: [s.n.], 1881; 1st ed. 1871), 117–118, 135. Search of Newspapers.com Mar. 12, 2022, 1820–1880: 1,147; references continued after his death in 1867. Gale Nineteenth-Century U.S. Newspapers yielded 157 before 1900 without ads; ProQuest Periodicals yielded 218 without ads. A cursory review showed very little overlap between databases. "Reply" to *Webster's American Dictionary* request, *National Intelligencer* (Washington, DC), 24, issue 7359, Sept. 13, 1836; *Charleston Mercury* (SC), Nov. 19, 1828.
6 "Hawes' Lectures to Young Men," *Western Luminary* (Lexington, KY), Feb. 24, 1830, vol. 6, p. 33.
7 Hawes, *Lectures to Young Men*, 168–169.
8 Lawrence, *Life of Rev. Joel Hawes*, 110, 135. Charles G[randison] Finney, *Lectures on Revivals of Religion* (New York: Fleming H. Revell Company, 1868; first pub. 1835), 12–13, 45, 167, 186, 358, 396, 413. Timothy L. Smith, *Revivalism and Social Reform: American Protestantism on the Eve of the Civil War* (New York: Harper Torchbooks, 1957), 104–113.
9 Nathan O. Hatch, *The Democratization of American Christianity* (New Haven, CT: Yale University Press, 1989), esp. 10–11, 101; Joseph Conforti, "The Invention of the Great Awakening, 1795–1842," *Early American Literature*, 26, no. 2 (1991): 99–118.
10 Keith J. Hardman, *Charles Grandison Finney, 1792–1875: Revivalist and Reformer* (Syracuse, NY: Syracuse University Press, 1987), 2, 10. Finney, *Lectures on Revivals of Religion*, 288, 398, 407, 415–416. Hawes, *Lectures to Young Men*, 10, 29, 142.
11 Charles C. Cole, Jr., "The New Lebanon Convention," *New York History*, 31, no. 4 (Oct. 1960): 385–397; Hardman, *Charles Grandison Finney*, 100–103. Glenna Matthews, *The Rise of Public Woman: Woman's Power and Woman's Place in the United States, 1630–1970* (New York: Oxford University Press, 1992), 103–106; Lois W. Banner, "Religion and Reform in the Early Republic: The Role of Youth," *American Quarterly*, 23, no. 5 (Dec. 1971): 677–695; R. Claire Snyder, "Radical Civic Virtue: Women in 19th-Century Civil Society," *New Political Science*, 26, no. 1 (Mar. 2004): 52–69; Donald G. Mathews, "The Second Great Awakening as an Organizing Process, 1780–1830: An Hypothesis," *American Quarterly*, 21, no. 1 (Spring 1969): 23–43; Ryan, *Cradle of the Middle Class*.
12 Survey of Newspapers.com for "self-reliance," May 6, 2022: 7 in 1820s, 82 in 1830s, 780 in 1840s, 3,057 in 1850s, 417 in 1860s. Google Books Ngrams searched for "self-reliance" and "self reliance," Dec. 20, 2023.
13 "President Jackson," *North Carolina Sentinel* (New Bern), Aug. 29, 1829; reprinted from *Eastern Argus*. *York Gazette* (York, PA), May 3, 1825; *Evening Post* (New York), Jan. 27, 1834; *New York Tribune*, Feb. 6, 1846.
14 Figuring out the new Republic's identity and that of its denizens occupied any number of commentators during its first half century. Among the most famous were two French

aristocrats: John Hector St. John, born in 1735 as Michel Guillaume Jean de Crèvecœur, who became an American citizen but moved across the Atlantic frequently, published *Letters from an American Farmer* in London in 1782, and died in France in 1813. Alexis de Tocqueville (1805–1859), authored *Democracy in America* (1835 and 1840). These and others sought to distinguish the new society and culture from Europe's, sometimes breathlessly praising the range of opportunities and openness to religious and ethnic diversity, at least among Euro-Americans.

15 Mary Kupiec Cayton, "The Making of an American Prophet: Emerson, His Audiences, and the Rise of the Culture Industry in Nineteenth-Century America," *American Historical Review*, 92, no. 3 (Jun. 1987): 597–620. Numbers of articles in American Periodicals database for Emerson "anywhere"; this reflects not absolute numbers but relative frequencies. 1830–1840, 180; 1841–1850, 1,169; 1851–1860, 649; 1861–1870, 220; total, 2,218 (Jul. 11, 2013). Britain's Thomas Carlyle had a strong influence on this trend, including on Emerson's thinking.

16 Robert E. Spiller and Alfred R. Ferguson, eds., *The Collected Works of Ralph Waldo Emerson* (Cambridge, MA: Harvard University Press, 1971), 1: 217–219, 222–225, 242.

17 Emerson, *Collected Works*, 1: 69–70; R. W. Emerson, "Self-Reliance," *The Tennessean* (Nashville, TN), May 13, 1841. This snippet appeared in dozens of papers that year, according to Newspapers.com, checked on Mar. 18, 2022.

18 Zakim, *Accounting for Capitalism*, esp. chap. 3; Brian P. Luskey, *On the Make: Clerks and the Quest for Capital in Nineteenth-Century America* (New York: New York University Press, 2010); Cayton, "The Making of an American Prophet," 604–608.

19 Emerson, "Self-Reliance," *The Tennessean*.

20 Jeffrey Sklansky, *The Soul's Economy: Market Society and Selfhood in American Thought, 1820–1920* (Chapel Hill: University of North Carolina Press, 2002), 41.

21 In addition to Emerson's lectures and free-standing publications with that title, that was the second entry in his bestselling 1841 book *Essays*. The "bestselling" designation required 175,000 sales in the 1840s, 1 percent of the nation's population then. Frank Luther Mott, *Golden Multitudes: The Story of Best Sellers in the United States* (New York: Macmillan Company, 1947), 303, 307.

22 Cayton, "The Making of an American Prophet," 613–615, 619. Ralph Waldo Emerson, *Journals and Miscellaneous Notebooks*, vol. 5: *1835–1838*, ed. Merton L. Sealts, Jr. (Cambridge, MA: Harvard University Press, 1965), 334; Emerson, *Journals and Miscellaneous Notebooks*, vol. 8: *1841–1843*, ed. William H. Gilman and J. E. Parsons (Cambridge, MA: Harvard University Press, 1970), 295; Emerson, *The Conduct of Life* (Boston: Houghton, Mifflin and Company, 1904; first pub. 1860), 100.

23 "Self-Reliance," *New Orleans Crescent* (New Orleans, LA), Apr. 12, 1848.

24 Among the many historical analyses of these constraints, including the coverture laws that permitted only unmarried women to own property in their names, see for cultural constraints, Ryan, *Cradle of the Middle-Class*, 186–191. For women as managers of businesses in their husbands' or fathers' names, see Susan Ingalls Lewis, *Unexceptional Women: Female Proprietors in Mid-Nineteenth-Century Albany, New York, 1830–1885* (Columbus: The Ohio State University Press, 2009).

25 Joel Hawes, *"A Looking-glass for Ladies," or the Formation and Excellence of the Female Character* (Boston, MA: William D. Ticknor and Company, 1845), 5. See Linda K. Kerber, "Women and Individualism in American History," *Massachusetts Review*, 30, no. 4 (Winter 1989): 589–609.

26 Margaret A. Oppenheimer, *Remarkable Rise of Eliza Jumel: A Story of Marriage and Money in the Early Republic* (Chicago: Chicago Review Press, 2016), 1–11; quote 10. For recent studies of women's last resort, see Katie M. Hemphill, *Bawdy City: Commercial Sex and Regulation in Baltimore, 1790–1915* (New York: Cambridge University Press, 2020), esp. 55–56; and Barbara Meil Hobson, *Uneasy Virtue: The Politics of Prostitution and the American Reform Traditon* (Chicago: University of Chicago Press, 1987), esp. 74–109.

27 The two classic works on this subject are Karen Halttunen, *Confidence Men and Painted Women: A Study of Middle-Class Culture in America, 1830–1870* (New Haven, CT: Yale University Press, 1982); and John F. Kasson, *Rudeness and Civility: Manners in Nineteenth-Century Urban America* (New York: Hill and Wang, 1990).

28 Oppenheimer, *Remarkable Rise*, 29–32.

29 Oppenheimer, *Remarkable Rise*, 34–38, 41–42, 49–50, 63–66; sources vary between 229 and over 240 paintings according to Oppenheimer, 78, 85–87. That some were reproductions did not diminish their cultural value in the days before chromolithography. Dianne Sachko Macleod, "Eliza Bowen Jumel: Collecting and Cultural Politics in Early America," *Journal of the History of Collections*, 13, no. 1 (2001): 57–75;

30 Oppenheimer, *Remarkable Rise*, 59–60, 142–144, 150–152, 156–157, 170–171.

31 Oppenheimer, *Remarkable Rise*, 96–97, 109–111, 113, 117–118, 126, 141, 175, 186–187, 194, 215, 238, 259.

32 "The Widow of Aaron Burr," *New York Observer*, Jul. 20, 1865; "Obituary. Madame Eliza B. Jumel," *New York Times (NYT)*, Jul. 18, 1865. Oppenheimer, *Remarkable Rise*, 220–255.

33 "The Jumel Case," *NYT*, Jan. 14, 1873; "Jumel Will Case," *Rutland Weekly Herald* (Rutland, VT), Mar. 6, 1873. It is highly likely that the *Herald* duplicated this article from another newspaper, although there is no indication of the source. In that century, newspapers copied freely from one another.

34 William Cary Duncan, *The Amazing Madame Jumel* (New York: Frederick A. Stokes Company, 1935), x.

35 Among the many death notices using this or related phrases: "Dorothea Dix," *Daily American* (Nashville, TN), Jul 20, 1887; "Died in One of Her Asylums," *Boston Globe* (Boston, MA), Jul. 19, 1887.

36 David Gollaher, *Voice for the Mad: The Life of Dorothea Dix* (New York: The Free Press, 1995), 2, 8, 19–21, 27, 32, 40–41, 49, 54, 103,

37 Francis B. Tiffany, *Life of Dorothea Lynde Dix* (Boston: Houghton, Mifflin and Company, 1890), 2–3, 26, 91.

38 John Gorham Palfrey, "Brother and Sister," *The National Gazette* (Philadelphia, PA), Jul. 22, 1834; Tiffany, *Life of Dorothea Dix*, 85, 90.

39 Gollaher, *Voice for the Mad*, 47, 196, 443–444; L. M. Child, "The Missionary of Prisons," *Vermont Union Whig* (Rutland, VT), Jan. 18. 1844.

40 For an example of ambitious frontier men who became elites only to find themselves on the wrong side of the "Revolution's legacy to legitimate upstarts," see Alan Taylor, "From Fathers to Friends of the People: Political Personas in the Early Republic," *Journal of the Early Republic*, 11, no. 4 (Winter, 1991): 465–491; quote 491.

41 Robert Gray Gunderson, *The Log Cabin Campaign* (Westport, CT: Greenwood Press, 1957), 74–77, 212–216.

42 Richard Smith Elliott, *Notes Taken in Sixty Years* (St. Louis, MO: R. P. Studley & Co., 1883), 120–121; Gunderson, *The Log Cabin Campaign*, 6, 74–77, 212–216.

43 "Who is Martin Van Buren" and "The Ignorance of the People," *Lancaster Intelligencer and Journal* (Lancaster, PA), Aug. 4, 1840; "Noble Birth," *The Comet* (Raymond, MS), Aug. 7, 1840.

44 Elliott, *Notes Taken in Sixty Years*, 121–126, 128; Gunderson, *Log Cabin Campaign*, 100–107, 109, 201–218. For the long view, see Edward Pessen, *The Log Cabin Myth: The Social Backgrounds of the Presidents* (New Haven, CT: Yale University Press, 1984).

45 Robert Remini, *Henry Clay: Statesman for the Union* (New York: W. W. Norton & Company, 1991), chap. 1 and p. 126; Fischer, *Revolution*, 19–20, 29–49, 179–80. *Annals of Congress*, 18th Cong., 1 sess., 1824, 1313–1314.

46 David S. Heidler and Jeanne T. Heidler, *Henry Clay: The Essential American* (New York: Random House, 2010), 4–15, 28–31, 38–42, 229; Glyndon G. Van Deusen, *The Life of Henry Clay* (Westport, CT: Greenwood Press, 1979), 6–7, 23–24. Remini, *Henry Clay*, 2–6; Clay quotes 2.

47 Search of Newspapers.com, May 29, 2022.

48 Clay, "Valedictory Address to the Senate," Mar. 31, 1842, *The Works of Henry Clay*, 6 vols. (New York: Barnes & Burr, 1863), 6:565.

49 *Raleigh Register* (Raleigh, NC), Jun. 17, 1842; copied from *Alexandria Gazette*. *Louisville Daily Journal* (Louisville, KY), Jun. 21, 1842; reprinted from *Lynchburg Virginian*. *Alexandria Gazette* (Alexandria, VA), Jun. 27, 1842; reprinted from *Richmond Enquirer*. *Raleigh Register*, Jul. 15, 1842; reprinted from *Alexandria Gazette*.

50 "The Mill Boy of the Slashes," *Tennessean* (Nashville, TN), Aug. 10, 1842.

51 George Pope Morris and Henry Russell, "A Song for the Man: A Henry Clay Ballad" (New York: Firth & Hall, 1844).

52 Clay quoted in Heidler and Heidler, *Henry Clay*, 372. For an analysis of the innovative political biographies of this era, see Scott E. Casper, *Constructing American Lives: Biography and Culture in Nineteenth-Century America* (Chapel Hill: University of North Carolina Press, 1999), esp. 94–106.

53 Junius (Calvin Colton), *Life of Henry Clay*, in *The Junius Tracts No. IV* (New York: Greeley & McElrath, Sept. 1844), 50; "Tennessee," *York Gazette* (York, PA), Jul. 23, 1844; reprinted from *Nashville Union*.

54 *Register of Debates in Congress*, 277 (Feb. 2, 1832). On internal improvements, see John Lauritz Larson, *Internal Improvements: National Public Works and the Promise of Popular Government in the Early United States* (Chapel Hill: University of North Carolina Press, 2001); the 1824 quote on 147. See also Stephen Minicucci, "Internal Improvements and the Union, 1790–1860," *Studies in American Political Development*, 18 (Fall 2004): 160–185.

55 "Tennessee," *York Gazette* (York, PA), Jul. 23, 1844; reprinted from *Nashville Union*.
56 "How He Rose – A True Sketch" and "Great Wealth," *Camden Weekly Journal* (Camden, SC), Mar. 8, 1848. See also "The Christian Chart" and untitled, *Weekly Statement* (Raleigh, NC), Jun. 14, 1843, for a similar example. Casper, *Constructing American Lives*, shows that biographies of the era typically were didactic.
57 "John Jacob Astor," *Charleston Mercury* (Charleston, SC), Aug. 20, 1844; originally published in the *Boston Post* and including paragraphs excerpted from *Hunt's Merchant's Magazine*, the era's leading business periodical.

CHAPTER 6

1 Wendy Woloson, *Crap: A History of Cheap Stuff in America* (Chicago: University of Chicago Press, 2020), esp. chap. 1; Pamela Walker Laird, *Advertising Progress: The Rise of Consumer Marketing* (Baltimore, MD: Johns Hopkins University Press, 1998); David Jaffee, *A New Nation of Goods: The Material Culture of Early America* (Philadelphia: University of Pennsylvania Press, 2010); Daniel Horowitz, *Morality in Spending: Attitudes toward the Consumer Society in America, 1875–1940* (Baltimore, MD: Johns Hopkins University Press, 1985), esp. intro., chap. 1.
2 Thomas P[oage] Hunt, *Book of Wealth: In Which It Is Proved from the Bible, that It Is the Duty of Every Man, to Become Rich* (New York: Ezra Collier, 1836), 1, 6, 1, 9–10, 37, 111, 113, 118; S. C. Hunt, ed., *Life and Thoughts of Rev. Thomas P. Hunt: An Autobiography* (Wilkes-Barre, PA: Robt. Baur & Son, Printers, 1901).
3 Mrs. C. H. Butler, "Looking Up," *Commercial* (Wilmington, NC), Feb. 12, 1847.
4 "Death of William Price, Esq. – Tribute of Respect," *The Sun* (Baltimore, MD), Nov. 28, 1868; J. Thomas Scharf, *History of Western Maryland ... Including Biographical Sketches of their Representative Men*, vol. 2 (Philadelphia, PA: Louis H. Everts, 1882), 1118–1120. William Price, *Clement Falconer: or, the Memoirs of a Young Whig*. 2 vols. (Baltimore, MD: N. Hickman, 1838). Thirty-two unique references to self-making and *Clement Falconer* were found in three databases: Nineteenth Century U.S. Newspapers, American Periodicals, and Google, Sept. 24, 2012.
5 "CLEMENT FALCONER: or, the Memoirs of a Young Whig," *Daily National Intelligencer* (Washington, DC) issue 7961, Aug. 20, 1838; "Review of New Books," *The Gentleman's Magazine*, 3, no. 3, Sept. 1838.
6 "Variety: Self-made Men," *Boston Investigator*, issue 6 (Jun. 15, 1842). The original passage in *Clement Falconer* appears on pp. 71–72.
7 For an overview of statistical studies on mobility, see Walter A. Friedman and Richard S. Tedlow, "Statistical Portraits of American Business Elites: A Review Essay," *Business History*, 45, no. 4 (Oct. 2003): 89–113. See also Edward Pessen, ed., *Three Centuries of Social Mobility in America* (Lexington, MA: Heath, 1974); Pessen, "Social Mobility in American History: Some Brief Reflections," *Journal of Southern History*, 45, no. 2 (May 1979): 165–184; Kevin Phillips, *Wealth and Democracy: A Political History of the American Rich* (New York: Broadway Books/Random House, 2002), esp. chap. 1.

8 "Art of Doing Good," *Boston Investigator*, issue 6, Jun. 15, 1842. I use Christopher Lasch's expression, *Haven in a Heartless World: The Family Besieged* (New York: Basic Books, 1978).
9 Price, *Clement Falconer*, 77–78.
10 "Valuable Religious Books," *Tennessee Baptist* (Nashville, TN), Jul. 31, 1847, p. 3; Emily Chubbuck (Judson), *Allen Lucas; The Self-Made Man* (New York: Lewis Colby & Co., 1874; first pub. 1843), 142, 154–155, 157–159. Ann D. Wood, "The 'Scribbling Women' and Fanny Fern: Why Women Wrote," *American Quarterly*, 23, no. 1 (Spring 1971): 3–24; quote 11. Chubbuck also published as "Fanny Forrester" and under her married name, Emily Judson.
11 John Frost, *Self-Made Men of America* (New York: W. H. Graham, 1848), iii–iv; *Lives of American Merchants: Eminent for Integrity, Enterprise and Public Spirit* (New York: Saxton and Miles, 1846). Julius W. Pratt, "The Origin of 'Manifest Destiny,'" *American Historical Review*, 32, no. 4 (July 1927): 795–798. Bibliographic information from WorldCat Identities, OCLC, Sept. 2, 2021.
12 Frost, *Self-Made Men*, 53, 59–60.
13 Frost, *Self-Made Men*, 205–218.
14 Prospectus for *Young American's Magazine of Self-Improvement* (Boston, nd), np.
15 *Young American's Magazine*, Jan. and Dec. 1847. Details of the 1846 edition of *Biography of Self-Taught Men* are not given in the review, but it is likely to have been vol. 2, compiled by Stephen Greenleaf Bulfinch (Boston: Benjamin Perkins & Co., 1846). Vol. 1, compiled by B. B. Edwards, appeared in 1832; see Chapter 4, note 39 above.
16 "The Pauper Lad of Woodend: Or, a Will and a Way: A Tale of Real Life," *Young American's Magazine*, 1, Jan. 1847.
17 Leonard Withington, "Keeping up Appearances," *Young American's Magazine*, 1, Mar. 1847.
18 George S. Hillard, "A Patch on Both Knees and Gloves On: In Imitation of Dr. Franklin," reprinted from the *Boston Courier in Young American's Magazine*, 1, Jan. 1847.
19 T(imothy). S(hay). Arthur, *Who Is Greatest? And Other Stories* (Philadelphia: Lippincott, Granbo & Co., 1852), 50–53.
20 Frank Luther Mott, *Golden Multitudes: The Story of Best Sellers in the United States* (New York: Macmillan Company, 1947), 129–130; bibliographic information from WorldCat Identities, OCLC, Sept. 2, 2021.
21 Arthur, *Who Is Greatest?*, 9. See Judy Hilkey, *Character is Capital: Success Manuals and Manhood in Gilded Age America* (Chapel Hill: University of North Carolina Press, 1997).
22 T. S. Arthur, *Ten Nights in a Bar-Room and What I Saw There* (Boston, MA: L. P. Crown & Company; Philadelphia, PA: J. Bradley, 1854). *Ten Nights* set sales records for decades, and various editions of it remained in print through the 1920s, Mott, *Golden Multitudes*, 129–130. On the rise and decline of alcohol consumption, see W. J. Rorabaugh, *The Alcoholic Republic: An American Tradition* (Oxford: Oxford University Press, 1979), 6–21, 120–146, 178–182, 189–203, 210–213; Michele Rotunda, *A Drunkard's Defense: Alcohol, Murder, and Medical Jurisprudence in Nineteenth-Century America* (Amherst, MA: University of Massachusetts Press, 2021); Paul Johnson, "Drinking, Temperance, and the

Construction of Identity in Nineteenth-Century America," *Social Science Information*, 25, no. 2 (1986): 521–530; David S. Reynolds, "Black Cats and Delirium Tremens: Temperance and the American Renaissance," in Reynolds and Debra J. Rosenthal, eds., *The Serpent in the Cup: Temperance in American Literature* (Amherst, MA: University of Massachusetts Press, 1997), 22, 31.

23 Madeleine B. Stern, *Heads & Headlines: The Phrenological Fowlers* (Norman: University of Oklahoma Press, 1971); Stephen Tomlinson, *Head Masters: Phrenology, Secular Education, and Nineteenth-Century Social Thought* (Tuscaloosa: University of Alabama Press, 2005); Carla Bittel, "Woman, Know Thyself: Producing and Using Phrenological Knowledge in 19th-Century America," *Centaurus*, 55, no. 2 (May 2013): 104–130; Cynthia Eagle Russett, *Sexual Science: The Victorian Construction of Womanhood* (Cambridge, MA: Harvard University Press, 1989); Rachel E. Walker, *Beauty and the Brain: The Science of Human Nature in Early America* (Chicago: University of Chicago Press, 2022).

24 "Self-Made or Never Made," *Detroit Free Press*, Oct. 7, 1847; "Good Books by Mail, Published by Fowlers & Wells," *Anti-Slavery Bugle* (Lisbon, OH), Dec. 2, 1854. The ad credited this sentence to the *Commercial School Advocate*.

25 O[rson]. S[quire]. Fowler, *Self-Culture, and Perfection of Character, Including the Management of Youth* (New York: Fowlers and Wells, Publishers, 7th ed., 1853; first ed. 1842); William E[llery]. Channing, *Self-Culture* (Boston, MA: James Munroe & Co., 1839), 5.

26 Fowler, *Self-Culture*, i-v, 312.

27 Fowler, *Self-Culture*, 34–41. On faculties and their centrality to nineteenth-century Americans' understandings of human psychology, see Daniel Walker Howe, *Making the American Self: Jonathan Edwards to Abraham Lincoln* (Oxford, UK: Oxford University Press, 2009).

28 Fowler, *Self-Culture*, 56, 64–65, 88–81, 208–209.

29 Fowler, *Self-Culture*, iii, 133, 138–140; O. S. Fowler and L. N. Fowler, *Self-Instructor in Phrenology and Physiology* (New York: Fowler and Wells, Publishers, 1859), 67, 73, 83–84.

30 *Self-Culture*, 138; post–Civil War quoted in Stern, *Heads & Headlines*, 20.

31 On prison reform, for example, see Davies, *Phrenology Fad and Science*, 101–105. On critiques, see Stern, *Heads & Headlines*, 82–84, 130–134; Davies, esp. chap. 5; and Susan Branson, "Phrenology and the Science of Race in Antebellum America," *Early American Studies*, 15, no. 1 (Winter 2017): 164–193. Fowler, *Self-Culture*, 138.

32 Davies, *Phrenology Fad and Science*, 31–32, 86, 108–109, 120–125, 163; Bittel, "Woman, Know Thyself"; R. J. Cooter, "Phrenology: The Provocation of Progress," *History of Science*, 14, no. 4 (Dec. 1976): 211–234.

33 Quoted in Stern, *Heads & Headlines*, 244.

34 Bittel, "Woman, Know Thyself," 14, 16–17.

35 Quoted in Branson, "Phrenology and the Science of Race," 192.

36 Fowler and Fowler, *Illustrated Self-Instructor*, 41.

37 P[hineas]. T[aylor]. Barnum, *The Life of P. T. Barnum, Written by Himself* (New York: Redfield, 1855), 39, 190, 360–362, 395; Edwin T. Freedley, *A Practical Treatise on Business: Or How to Get, Save, Spend, Give, Lend, and Bequeath Money* (Philadelphia, PA: Lippincott, Grambo, & Co., 1853), 303; Barnum, *The Art of Money Getting, Or Golden*

Rules for Making Money (first pub.: Philadelphia, PA: Bell & Co., 1880) accessed through the Gutenberg Project; np. See Neil Harris, *Humbug: The Art of P. T. Barnum* (Chicago: University of Chicago Press, 1973); A. H. Saxon, *P. T. Barnum: The Legend and the Man* (New York: Columbia University Press, 1989); Steven Belletto, "Drink Versus Printer's Ink: Temperance and the Management of Financial Speculation in *The Life of P. T. Barnum*," American Studies, 46, no. 1 (Spring 2005): 45–65; Bluford Adams, *E Pluribus Barnum: The Great Showman & the Making of U.S. Popular Culture* (Minneapolis: University of Minnesota Press, 1997), 90–97; M. R. Werner, *Barnum* (Garden City, NY: Garden City Publishing Company,1926; first pub. 1923), 107–113, 288–289.

38 Barnum, *Life of P. T. Barnum*, ii; Barnum, *Art of Money Getting*, np; Saxon, *P. T. Barnum*, 216–224.
39 Saxon, *P. T. Barnum*, 52–58, 205, quote 224.
40 Barnum, broadside for lectures in Springfield and Westfield, MA, "The Art of Money Getting," 1863 (Library of Congress: www.loc.gov/item/rbpe.0700070a/)
41 Charity quotes in Barnum, *Art of Money Getting*, np, and Saxon, *P. T. Barnum*, 252.
42 Barnum, *Life of P. T. Barnum*, 398.
43 Barnum, *Art of Money Getting*, np.
44 Barnum, *Art of Money Getting*, np; Saxon, *P. T. Barnum*, 83–85, 205, 220–221. On that era's attitudes about failure, see Edward J. Balleisen, *Navigating Failure: Bankruptcy and Commercial Society in Antebellum America* (Chapel Hill: University of North Carolina Press, 2001.)
45 Luke xxii, 42; quote from Werner, *Barnum*, 371.
46 "Barnum's Autobiography," *New York Times* (*NYT*), Dec. 12, 1854; "The Lesson of Barnum's Life," *NYT*, Dec. 16, 1854.
47 Charles C. B. Seymour, *Self-Made Men* (New York: Harper and Bros., 1868, first pub. 1858), v; "Funeral of the Late Charles C. B. Seymour," *New York Herald*, May 6, 1869, p. 4; "Editor's Table," *Russell's Magazine* (Charleston, SC), 1858, p. 283; "Self-Made Men," *National Era* (Washington, DC), Nov. 11, 1858, p. 179; information from WorldCat Identities, Sept. 19, 2022.
48 Joyce Appleby, *Inheriting the Revolution: The First Generation of Americans* (Cambridge, MA: Belknap Press of Harvard University Press, 2000). However, of 488 autobiographies, Appleby "rejected" 300 because they were "irrelevant to my questions." These authors were mostly clergymen, whose stories were very relevant to the history of self-made success. Appleby, "New Cultural Heroes in the Early National Period," in Thomas L. Haskell and Richard F. Teichgraeber III, eds., *The Culture of the Market: Historical Essays* (Cambridge, UK: Cambridge University Press, 1996), 171n11.
49 Harriet Beecher Stowe, *The Lives and Deeds of Our Self-Made Men* (Hartford, CT: Worthington, Dustin & Co., 1872), vii–viii, 265–266, 349. Not that Colfax hadn't tried to get rich, as the exposure shortly thereafter of his marginal involvement in the Crédit Mobilier scandal showed.
50 Harriet Beecher Stowe, *Men of Our Times; or Leading Patriots of the Day* (Hartford, CT: Hartford Publishing Co., 1868), vii, 214.
51 Stowe, *Lives and Deeds of Our Self-Made Men*, 579, 601.

52 James D. McCabe, Jr., *Great Fortunes, and How They Were Made: or, The Struggles and Triumphs of Our Self-Made Men* (Philadelphia, New York, and Boston: George MacLean, 1871). Stowe's brother, the renowned Henry Ward Beecher, is the only man treated in both compilations. Publication information on McCabe's *Great Fortunes* retrieved Sept. 2, 2021, from WorldCat Identities, OCLC; on Stowe's *Lives and Deeds of Our Self-Made Men*, WorldCat Identities, OCLC.
53 Stowe, *Lives and Deeds*, vi–vii; McCabe, *Great Fortunes*, 6–7; "Agents Wanted," *Semi-Weekly Clarion* (Jackson, MS), Oct. 31, 1871.
54 A widely quoted book repeats McCabe's volume verbatim, but without authorial credit to McCabe or contributors. Walter R. Houghton, ed., *Kings of Fortune, or the Triumphs and Achievements of Noble, Self-Made Men* (Chicago: Loomis National Library Association, 1888), this paragraph p. 5.
55 McCabe, *Great Fortunes*, 5, 6. Scott E. Casper, *Constructing American Lives: Biography and Culture in Nineteenth-Century America* (Chapel Hill: University of North Carolina Press, 1999).

CHAPTER 7

1 Thomas Mellon, *Thomas Mellon and His Times*, ed. Mary Louis Briscoe, 2nd ed. (Pittsburgh: University of Pittsburgh Press, 1994), 33; James Mellon, *The Judge: A Life of Thomas Mellon, Founder of a Fortune* (New Haven, CT: Yale University Press, 2011), 225–226. Mellon heirs ranked as America's twenty-eighth richest family in 2020 according to Forbes.com: www.forbes.com/profile/mellon/?sh=4073eaf26c8b. A century earlier, they ranked in the top handful largely because Thomas's sons, especially Andrew, took the initial fortune and grew it beyond even their father's dreams. William Larimer Mellon and Boyden Sparkes (collaborator), *Judge Mellon's Sons* (privately printed 1948), 22.
2 George W. Ogden, "Pittsburgh in 1821," in Roy Lubove, ed., *Pittsburgh* (New York: New Viewpoints, 1976), 5–7. "Pittsburgh, Pennsylvania Population History," www.biggestuscities.com/city/pittsburgh-pennsylvania. Mellon, *The Judge*, 208–209, 223.
3 See Steve Fraser and Gary Gerstle, eds., *Ruling America: A History of Wealth and Power in a Democracy* (Cambridge, MA: Harvard University Press, 2005).
4 Mellon, *Thomas Mellon*, 74.
5 Google Books Ngram Viewer search, Dec. 24, 2023. Mellon, *Thomas Mellon*, 98, 233, 425, 382; Mellon, *The Judge*, 166–167.
6 United States Congress, Senate, Committee on Education and Labor, *Report upon the Relations Between Labor and Capital* (Washington, DC: Government Printing Office, 1885), 1088–1089.
7 Mellon, *Thomas Mellon*, 33, 63, 47–79. Mellon's charity was of a private sort, assisting people with whom he had personal contacts or relationships. Typical of many philanthropists then and now, he objected to taxes and state-based institutions.
8 Mellon, *Thomas Mellon*, 33, 240, 382.

9 Mellon, *Thomas Mellon*, 34, 59–62, 419.
10 Mellon, *Thomas Mellon*, 126–128.
11 "The Mellons Celebrate: Pittsburg Capitalist and Wife Both Over Ninety Years Old," *New-York Tribune*, Feb. 14, 1907; "Judge and Mrs. Thomas Mellon Reach Ripe Old Age: His Life a Real Romance," *Pittsburgh Gazette Times*, Feb. 3, 1907.
12 "Judge Thomas Mellon Dies," *New York Times (NYT)*, Feb. 4, 1908; Mellon, *Thomas Mellon*, 45–51, 91, 461.
13 Mellon, *Thomas Mellon*, 154, 169, 180–181.
14 Frank G. Carpenter, "Self-Made Millionaires: A Score of Rich Men and Their Fight for Fortunes," *Chicago Daily Tribune* (Dec. 11, 1887), 26.
15 For an analytical overview of statistical studies on mobility, see Walter A. Friedman and Richard S. Tedlow, "Statistical Portraits of American Business Elites: A Review Essay," *Business History*, 45, no. 4 (Oct. 2003): 89–113. See also Alan B. Krueger, "The Apple Falls Close to the Tree, Even in the Land of Opportunity," *New York Times* (Nov. 14, 2002), C2; Edward Pessen, ed., *Three Centuries of Social Mobility in America* (Lexington, MA: Heath, 1974); Pessen, "Social Mobility in American History: Some Brief Reflections," *Journal of Southern History*, 45, no. 2 (May 1979): 165–184; Kevin Phillips, *Wealth and Democracy: A Political History of the American Rich* (New York: Broadway Books/Random House, 2002), esp. chap. 1.
16 This biblical exhortation (Proverbs 22:29) appeared widely. Examples include: Seymour Eaton, *One Hundred Lessons in Business* (Boston, MA: Seymour Eaton, 1887), np; William M. Thayer, *Onward to Fame and Fortune, Or, Climbing Life's Ladder* (New York: The Christian Herald, 1893), front cover; Thomas H. Jones, "The Hardwareman's Influence in the Development of the Country," speech before the Ohio Hardware Association, published in *The Iron Age*, 57 (Jan. 30, 1896): 499–500. On the cultural shift, see Clark Davis, *Company Men: White-Collar Life and Corporate Cultures in Los Angeles, 1892–1941* (Baltimore, MD: Johns Hopkins University Press, 2000); Judy Hilkey, *Character is Capital: Success Manuals and Manhood in Gilded Age America* (Chapel Hill: University of North Carolina Press, 1997); Brian P. Luskey, *On the Make: Clerks and the Quest for Capital in Nineteenth-Century America* (New York: New York University Press, 2010); Michael Zakim, *Accounting for Capitalism: The World the Clerk Made* (Chicago: Chicago University Press, 2018). Regarding consumer culture, see Thorstein Veblen, *The Theory of the Leisure Class: An Economic Study of Institutions* (New York: Vanguard Press, 1926, first pub. 1899), 74, 77, 81–83.
17 Pamela Walker Laird, *Advertising Progress: American Business and the Rise of Consumer Marketing* (Baltimore, MD: Johns Hopkins University Press, 1998), esp. 101–118. Susan Ingalls Lewis shows that women functioned successfully in business, and in large numbers, stereotypes notwithstanding. *Unexceptional Women: Female Proprietors in Mid-Nineteenth-Century Albany, New York, 1830–1885* (Columbus: The Ohio State University Press, 2009).
18 Ralph Waldo Emerson, *Self-Reliance and Other Essays* (New York: Dover Publications, 1993), 27. Carnegie quoted in Alfred L. Thimm, *Business Ideologies in the Reform-Progressive Era, 1880–1914* (Tuscaloosa: University of Alabama Press, 1976), 205; Laird, *Advertising*

Progress, 105–108. Only rarely did women's names reach the public as founders and heads of enterprises, such as Lydia Pinkham. Although female entrepreneurs built reputations beyond their localities, many women operated businesses under the names of male family members. Lewis, *Unexceptional Women*.

19 So important to businesspeople was this naming tradition that they resisted the transition in the late nineteenth and early twentieth century toward other tradenames that corporate mergers and modern marketing imposed on them. Laird, *Advertising Progress*, 185–191, 203–206, 269–271, 377, chap. 4. Joseph Addison, *The Tatler* (London), 224 (Sept. 12–14, 1710).

20 Gerald J. Baldasty, *The Commercialization of News in the Nineteenth Century* (Madison: University of Wisconsin Press, 1992), 52–53, 81, 112, 115–134, 139–144.

21 Pamela Walker Laird, *Pull: Networking and Success Since Benjamin Franklin* (Cambridge, MA: Harvard University Press, 2006), 2, 94–95, 100–103, 124–136. This phenomenon is well documented in science and politics as well as in business.

22 Mellon, *The Judge*, 229–233, 275. Dollar calculation on Oct. 23, 2024, at "CPI Inflation Calculator," www.officialdata.org/us/inflation/1871?amount = 10000

23 Kenneth Warren, *Triumphant Capitalism: Henry Clay Frick and the Industrial Transformation of America* (Pittsburgh: University of Pittsburgh Press, 1996), 12–13, 369.

24 "Henry Clay Frick," *NYT*, Dec. 3, 1919; "The Passing of Frick – and His Era," *Literary Digest*, 6, no. 12 (Dec. 20, 1919): 44, 47, 48.

25 "Henry Clay Frick," *NYT*, Dec. 3, 1919; "Henry C. Frick Dies; Leaves Art to City," *NYT*, Dec. 3, 1919; George Harvey, "Henry Clay Frick: Builder and Individualist," *North American Review*, 240, no. 771 (Feb. 1920): 145–149; "Frick the Silent," *World's Work*, 14 (1907): 8849–8858, quote 8858.

26 Judith A. McGaw, *Most Wonderful Machine: Mechanization and Social Change in Berkshire Paper Making, 1801–1885* (Princeton, NJ: Princeton University Press, 1987), 127, 157; Laird, *Pull*, esp. chap. 1. For a detailed analysis of iron and steel networks, see John N. Ingham, *The Iron Barons: A Social Analysis of an American Urban Elite, 1874–1965* (Westport, CT: Greenwood Press, 1978).

27 On the advantages of first movers, see Herbert G. Gutman, "The Reality of the Rags-to-Riches 'Myth,'" in *Work, Culture, and Society in Industrializing America* (New York: Vintage Books, 1977), 211–33.

28 Richard White devastates the reputations of that era's railroad builders, who built their fortunes despite gross ineptness and poorly disguised corruption in *Railroaded: The Transcontinentals and the Making of Modern America* (New York: W.W. Norton & Company, 2011). Others have challenged the notion of superiority as central to business success; see note 18 in the Introduction.

29 Susie J. Pak, *Gentlemen Bankers: The World of J. P. Morgan* (Cambridge, MA: Harvard University Press, 2013), esp. Introduction; Ingham, *The Iron Barons*, 114, 118–127.

30 Ingham, *The Iron Barons*, 114, 118–127; Laird, *Pull*, 83–85, 168–173, 303–310; Pak, *Gentlemen Bankers*, 68–69.

31 Vilja Hulden, *The Bosses' Union: How Employers Organized to Fight Labor before the New Deal* (Urbana: University of Illinois Press, 2023), esp. chap. 5; Ingham, *The Iron Barons*, 114,

118–127; Pak, *Gentlemen Bankers*, 68–69. On the Senate, see "Frick the Silent"; David J. Rothman, *Politics and Power: The United States Senate, 1869–1901* (Cambridge, MA: Harvard University Press, 1966), regarding Senators who moved between business and office holding, 115, 121–31.

32 Louis Galambos, *Competition and Cooperation: The Emergence of a National Trade Association* (Baltimore, MD: Johns Hopkins Press, 1966), 4–10.

33 Naomi R. Lamoreaux, *The Great Merger Movement in American Business, 1895–1904* (Cambridge, UK: Cambridge University Press, 1985), 1–2; Ralph L. Nelson, *Merger Movements in American Industry, 1895–1956* (Princeton, NJ: Princeton University Press, 1959), 5, 6, 34.

34 Edward Sherwood Mead, *Trust Finance: A Study of the Genesis, Organization, and Management of Industrial Organizations* (New York: D. Appleton and Company, 1909), 23, 71–76. NB: the title page incorrectly spells the author's name as Meade. See also William Letwin, *Law and Economic Policy in America: The Evolution of the Sherman Antitrust Act* (Chicago: University of Chicago Press, 1965), 8–11.

35 Warren, *Triumphant Capitalism*, 55, 297–299; Mead, *Trust Finance*, 211.

36 Mead, *Trust Finance*, 213–217.

37 S. J. Kleinberg, *The Shadow of the Mills: Working-class Families in Pittsburgh, 1870–1907* (Pittsburgh, PA: University of Pittsburgh Press, 1989); Paul Krause, *The Battle for Homestead, 1880–1892: Politics, Culture, and Steel* (Pittsburgh, PA: University of Pittsburgh Press, 1992), 228–231; Carnegie quote 231.

38 Kim Voss, *The Making of American Exceptionalism: The Knights of Labor and Class Formation in the Nineteenth Century* (Ithaca, NY: Cornell University Press, 1993), esp. 32; Paul G. Faler, *Mechanics and Manufacturers in the Early Industrial Revolution: Lynn, Massachusetts, 1780–1860* (Albany, NY: State University of New York Press, 1981), esp. 183; Mead, *Trust Finance*, 288; David Montgomery, *The Fall of the House of Labor: The Workplace, the State, and American Labor Activism, 1865–1925* (Cambridge, UK: Cambridge University Press, 1987), 18, 32, 41–43; Kleinberg, *Shadow of the Mills*, 238–239.

39 Warren, *Triumphant Capitalism*, 333; a slightly different phrasing in "The Passing of Frick," 44. See Daniel T. Rodgers, *The Work Ethic in Industrial America, 1850–1920* (Chicago: Chicago University Press, 1974).

40 Hubbard's obfuscations and falsehoods include that Carnegie never speculated nor "bought a share of stock on margin." Elbert Hubbard, *Andrew Carnegie: Eminent Business Man and Philanthropist* (New York: The Hartford Lunch Co., 1919; first pub. East Aurora, NY: Roycrofters, 1909), 9–10, 16. Mellon, *Thomas Mellon*, 233, 413.

41 Robert V. Bruce, *1877: Year of Violence* (New York: Ivan R. Dee., 1989; first pub. 1959) 312–314; Debby Applegate, *The Most Famous Man in America: The Biography of Henry Ward Beecher* (New York: Doubleday, 2006), 265. Dollar calculation on Oct. 23, 2024, at "CPI Inflation Calculator," www.officialdata.org/us/inflation/1877?

42 Phineas T. Barnum, *Dollars and Sense: Or How to Get On* (New York: Henry S. Allen, 1890), 77–79; Laird, *Pull*, 39–43. Mellon, *Thomas Mellon*, 28–29, 233.

43 Hilkey estimates that by 1900, several million copies of advice books were in circulation; *Character is Capital*, 21–22. "The Rich Man's Son – How He Is Being Trained to Succeed His Father," *NYT*, Jan. 14, 1906.

44 See the classic work of E. Anthony Rotundo, *American Manhood: Transformations in Masculinity from the Revolution to the Modern Era* (New York: Basic Books, 1993).

45 Theodore Roosevelt, "The Strenuous Life," Apr. 10, 1899, *The Strenuous Life: Essays and Addresses* (New York: The Century Co., 1902), 1, 2, 3, 8; "Fact Sheet," *History of the BSA* (Irving, TX: Boy Scouts of America, nd), 8.

46 John T. Faris, *Men Who Made Good* (New York: Fleming H. Revell Company, 1912), 6. Sigmund Diamond, *The Reputation of the American Businessman* (Cambridge, MA: Harvard University Press, 1955), chap. 4, quote 82. See also "Sons of Millionaires Who Have Made Successes," *NYT*, Apr. 10, 1910; "The Rich Man's Son – How He Is Being Trained to Succeed His Father," *NYT*, Jan. 14, 1906.

47 According to Google's Ngrams, the post-Civil War peak for the percentage of appearances of the bigram (two-word pair) "self made" in books and magazines (case insensitive and hyphen insensitive) came just before 1900. In Newspapers.com, the peak came shortly after 1900. Earlier peaks appeared during the heavy uses of the term in political and religious contests. Keeping in mind that these are measures of percentages, it is worth noting that the earlier percentages were actually higher than later ones, reflecting the dominance of religious and political publishing before the Civil War. The most recent peak came just after 2010 in Ngrams but around 1990 in Newspapers.com. Searches Sept. 2022.

48 William Dean Howells, *The Rise of Silas Lapham* (Boston, MA: Ticknor and Company, 1885); Laird, *Business History Review*, 81, no. 1 (Spring 2007): 125–128.

49 "A Covert Insinuation," *Daily Intelligencer* (Mexico, MO), Sept. 12, 1900, reprinted from *Baltimore American*.

50 William Larremore, "The Personal Equation in American Politics," *Overland Monthly and Out West Magazine*, 15, no. 86, (San Francisco, CA), Feb. 1890, 134.

51 Jan Cohn, *Creating America: George Horace Lorimer and the Saturday Evening Post* (Pittsburgh, PA: University of Pittsburgh Press, 1989), 33–39. Charles Eustace Merriman, *Letters from a Son to His Self-Made Father* (Boston, MA: The Robinson, Luce Company, 1904), 11–15, 29, 54, 153. Maurice Switzer, *Letters from a Self-Made Failure* (Boston, MA: Small, Maynard and Company Publishers, 1914) x–xi, 38–41, 63, 102.

52 Kleinberg, *Shadow of the Mills*, 21, 303 305. See also Seth Rockman, *Scraping By: Wage Labor, Slavery, and Survival in Early America* (Baltimore, MD: Johns Hopkins University Press, 2009); Nancy Isenberg, *White Trash: The 400-Year Untold History of Class in America* (New York: Viking, 2016); Kristin O'Brassill-Kulfan, *Vagrants and Vagabonds: Poverty and Mobility in the Early American Republic* (New York: New York University Press, 2019); and Keri Leigh Merritt, *Masterless Men: Poor Whites and Slavery in the Antebellum South* (Cambridge, UK: Cambridge University Press, 2017).

53 "Two Kinds of Workingmen," *St. Louis Globe-Democrat* (St. Louis, MO), Aug. 27, 1877.

54 "A Solid Sermon," *The Moulton Advertiser* (Moulton, AL), Nov. 24, 1887; G. W. Southwick, "The Use of Firearms," *Inter Ocean* (Chicago), May 2, 1885; "Our Weakness," *Industrialist* (Manhattan, KS), Apr. 23, 1887; reprinted from *Western Rural*. "The Bondage of Land-Owners," *Chicago Tribune*, Sept. 4, 1887.

55 "The Self-Made Man," *The Labor World* (Duluth, MN), Apr. 30, 1898.

56 "Self-Made or Made for Self," *The Labor World* (Duluth, MN), Nov. 29, 1902.

57 "Would Socialism Destroy Individualism?" *The Labor World* (Duluth, MN), Sept. 1, 1906; "The First Labor Novel," *Labor World* (Duluth, MN), May 9, 1908.
58 Samuel Gompers, "Gompers Flays Young Rockefeller's Attitude," *Labor World* (Duluth, MN), June 6, 1914.
59 Grover Cleveland, *The Self-Made Man in American Life* (New York: Thomas Y. Crowell & Company, 1897), 8–12.

CHAPTER 8

1 Published versions of this speech differ over the years. Frederick Douglass, "Self-Made Men," as published following delivery at the Indian Industrial School, Carlisle, PA, March 1893, in Nicholas Buccola, ed., *The Essential Douglass: Selected Writings & Speeches* (Indianapolis: Hackett Publishing Company, 2016), 332–349. The wording seems identical to that published in 1872 and available at monadnock.net/douglass/self-made-men.html. The "absurdity" quotation comes from "Frederick Douglass in Easton," *Easton Gazette* (Easton, MD), Nov. 30, 1878, where his delivery reflected the location's significance. See David W. Blight, *Frederick Douglass: Prophet of Freedom* (New York: Simon & Schuster, 2018), 470, 564–568.
2 Douglass, "Self-Made Men," 349.
3 Douglass, "Self-Made Men," 348–349.
4 Gary J. Kornblith, "Self-Made Men: The Development of Middling-Class Consciousness in New England," *Massachusetts Review*, 26, no. 2/3 (Summer–Autumn 1985): 461–474, esp. 462–463; David Brundage, "The producing classes and the saloon: Denver in the 1880s," *Labor History*, 86, no. 1 (1985): 29–52; David Montgomery, *The Fall of the House of Labor: The Workplace, the State, and American Labor Activism, 1865–1925* (Cambridge, UK: Cambridge University Press, 1987), 146, 295; Richard T. Ely, *The Labor Movement in America* (New York: Macmillan Company, 1905), 128–130. S. J. Kleinberg, *The Shadow of the Mills: Working-class Families in Pittsburgh, 1870–1907* (Pittsburgh, PA: University of Pittsburgh Press, 1989); Paul Krause, *The Battle for Homestead, 1880–1892: Politics, Culture, and Steel* (Pittsburgh, PA: University of Pittsburgh Press, 1992); H. Roger Grant, *Self-Help in the 1890s Depression* (Ames: Iowa State University Press, 1983).
5 Douglass, "Self-Made Men," 340. David T. Beito, *From Mutual Aid to the Welfare State: Fraternal Societies and Social Services, 1890–1967* (Chapel Hill: University of North Carolina Press, 2000), esp. chap. 1; Grant, *Self-Help in the 1890s Depression*.
6 Harriet Beecher Stowe, *The Lives and Deeds of Our Self-Made Men* (Hartford, CT: Worthington, Dustin & Co., 1872), 382.
7 Douglass, "The Trials and Triumphs of Self-Made Men," in John Stauffer and Henry Louis Gates, Jr., eds., *The Portable Frederick Douglass* (New York: Penguin Books, 2016), 302.
8 John Stauffer, Zoe Trodd, and Celeste-Marie Bernier, *Picturing Frederick Douglass: An Illustrated Biography of the Nineteenth Century's Most Photographed American* (New York: Liveright Publishing Corporation, 2015), ix–xvii.

9 Douglass, "Self-Made Men," 340, 346–347.
10 Douglass, "Self-Made Men," 336, 340–341.
11 "Frederick Douglass in Easton."
12 Gabor S. Boritt, *Lincoln and the Economics of the American Dream* (Urbana: University of Illinois Press, 1978), 174–177, 220–222. Allen Thorndike Rice, ed., *Reminiscences of Abraham Lincoln by Distinguished Men of His Time* (New York: North American Publishing Company, 1886), 185–195.
13 Boritt, *Lincoln and the Economics of the American Dream*, 133, 182–185.
14 United States Congress, Senate, Committee on Education and Labor, *Report upon the Relations Between Labor and Capital* (Washington, DC: Government Printing Office, 1885), 1, 23, 39.
15 Education and Labor, *Report*, 90–91, 323–324, 562–564. Gompers reported this as part of a conversation with business leaders in the home of Charles R. Flint, a master of business combinations. Flint was instrumental in forming U.S. Rubber in 1892 and Computing-Tabulating-Recording Company in 1911, precursor to IBM, among others. Samuel Gompers, *Seventy Years of Life and Labor: An Autobiography*, vol. 2 (New York: E. P. Dutton, 1925) 111–112; *IBM Archives*, www.ibm.com/ibm/history/exhibits/builders/builders_flint.html.
16 William Letwin, *Law and Economic Policy in America: The Evolution of the Sherman Antitrust Act* (New York: Random House, 1965), 122–128, 155–161; "Conspiring against Commerce," *New York Times (NYT)*, Dec. 10, 1892.
17 Education and Labor, *Report*, 317, 651–652, 811. See Chad E. Pearson, *Capital's Terrorists: Klansmen, Lawmen and Employers in the Long Nineteenth Century* (Chapel Hill: University of North Carolina Press, 2022), 3, 81–85. On the use and consequences of blacklisting by Carnegie Steel, Krause, *Battle for Homestead*, 4, 87, 236, 299, 329–330.
18 Pearson, *Capital's Terrorists*, esp.13–14, and *Reform or Repression*, 3–12; Vilja Hulden, *The Bosses' Union: How Employers Organized to Fight Labor before the New Deal* (Urbana: University of Illinois Press, 2023), esp. 4–6.
19 Harvey, "Henry Clay Frick," 145–148.
20 Kenneth Warren, *Triumphant Capitalism: Henry Clay Frick and the Industrial Transformation of America* (Pittsburgh, PA: University of Pittsburgh Press, 1996), 77–78; Krause, *Battle for Homestead*, 141–142, 209–210, 241–242, 246.
21 Calculation from www.in2013dollars.com/us/inflation/1892?endYear=2024&amount=500000.
22 Warren, *Triumphant Capitalism*, 79–82, 85–89, 92; Krause, *Battle for Homestead*, esp. 330, 334–339. See Nell Irvin Painter, *Standing at Armageddon: The United States, 1877–1919* (New York: W. W. Norton & Company, 1987), 110–114, for a summary of the Homestead Strike in the context of turmoil between labor and employers before World War I.
23 Warren, *Triumphant Capitalism*, 79–82, 85–89, 92. "Mr. Frick's Business Career," *NYT*, Jul. 24, 1892.
24 Jennifer A. Delton, *The Industrialists: How the National Association of Manufacturers Shaped American Capitalism* (Princeton, NJ: Princeton University Press, 2020). For other organizations with similar goals, see Chad Pearson, "'Free Shops for Free Men'?: The

Challenges of Strikebreaking and Union-Busting in the Progressive Era," in Rosemary Feurer and Pearson, eds., *Against Labor: How U.S. Employers Organized to Defeat Union Activism* (Urbana: University of Illinois Press, 2017), 53–54. For an overview of "Collective Action for Employers' Rights," see Hulden, *Bosses' Union*, 20–24.

25 John Kirby, Jr., "Address of Mr. John Kirby, Jr., in Accepting the Presidency of the National Association of Manufacturers, May 19, 1909," *American Industries*, 9, no. 8 (1909): 5–10.

26 "The Indians and the Dawes Bill," *Boston Evening Transcript* (Boston, MA), Jun. 10, 1887.

27 Robert W. Hanning, "The Dawes Act of 1887: A Dream of 'Civilizing the Savages' that Became a Nightmare for Native Americans," in Nancy van Deusen, ed., *Dreams and Visions: An Interdisciplinary Enquiry* (Leiden, The Netherlands: Brill, 2010), 353.

28 Loring Benson Priest, *Uncle Sam's Stepchildren: The Reformation of United States Indian Policy, 1865–1887* (New Brunswick, NJ: Rutgers University Press, 1942), esp. 233–247.

29 Senate Report no. 283, 48 Cong, 1st sess. (Mar. 7, 1884), 81.

30 *Report of the Board of Indian Commissioners* (Washington, DC: H.R. Exec. Doc. no. 1, 48 Cong. 1 sess., 1883), 715. William T. Hagan, "Private Property, the Indian's Door to Civilization," *Ethnohistory*, 3, no. 2 (Spring 1956): 126–137, quote 128. Carl Schurz, *Report of the Secretary of the Interior* (Washington, DC, 1879), 4.

31 Hagan, "Private Property," 126–137.

32 "The Indians and the Dawes Bill," *Boston Evening Transcript* (Boston, MA), Jun. 10, 1887.

33 "The Indian Land Question," *St. Louis Globe-Democrat* (St. Louis, MS), Jun. 28, 1887. Schurz, *Report*, 6, 12. Quoted in Priest, *Uncle Sam's Stepchildren*, 246–247. "An Act to provide for the allotment of lands in severalty to Indians on the various reservations, and to extend the protection of the laws of the United States and the Territories over the Indians, and for other purposes," Pub. L. 49–119.

34 Hagan, "Private Property," 133, 137.

35 Henry Davenport Northrop, Joseph R. Gay, and I. Garland Penn, *The College of Life, or Practical Self-Educator: A Manual of Self-Improvement for the Colored Race* (Chicago: Chicago Publication and Lithograph Co., 1895), iv, 71. W. E. B. DuBois, ed., *The Negro in Business: A Report of a Social Study Made Under the Direction of Atlanta University; Together with the Proceedings of the Fourth Conference for the Study of the Negro Problems, Held at Atlanta University, May 30–31, 1899* (Atlanta, GA: Atlanta University, 1899), 5, 50. Marcus Garvey, *Philosophy and Opinions of Marcus Garvey*, ed. Amy Jacques-Garvey, vol. 2 (New York: Atheneum, 1977; first pub. 1925), 23.

36 On differences and similarities between Washington, DuBois, and Garvey, see Jacqueline M. Moore, *Booker T. Washington, W. E. B. DuBois, and the Struggle for Racial Uplift* (Wilmington, DE: Scholarly Resources, 2003). For an historical overview, see Walter A. Friedman, "The African American Gospel of Business Success," in Peter Eisenstadt, ed., *Black Conservatism: Essays in Intellectual and Political History* (New York: Garland Publishing, 1999), chap. 6.

37 Elizabeth Lindsay Davis, *Lifting as They Climb* (New York: G. K. Hall & Co., 1996; first published 1933), xv–xxxiii, 3, 5–6; Mark Whitaker, *Smoketown: The Untold Story of the Other Great Black Renaissance* (New York: Simon & Schuster, 2018), 48–49.

38 Mary Church Terrell, *The Progress of Women* (Washington, DC: Smith Brothers, 1898). Alison M. Parker, *Unceasing Militant: The Life of Mary Church Terrell* (Chapel Hill: University of North Carolina Press, 2020); Sharon Warren Cook, "Mary Church Terrell and Her Mission: Giving Decades of Quiet Service," in Iris B. Carlton-LaNey, ed., *African American Leadership: An Empowerment Tradition in Social Welfare History* (Washington, DC: National Association of Social Workers, 2001).

39 Warren Eugene Milteer, Jr., *Beyond Slavery's Shadow: Free People of Color in the South* (Chapel Hill: University of North Carolina Press, 2021), 253–254.

40 Eric Foner, *Reconstruction: America's Unfinished Revolution, 1863–1877* (New York: Harper & Row, 1988), 96–101.

41 Anne Meis Knupfer, *Toward a Tenderer Humanity and a Nobler Womanhood: African American Women's Clubs in Turn-of-the-Century Chicago* (New York: New York University Press, 1996), 7, 12; Evelyn Brooks Higginbotham, *Righteous Discontent: The Women's Movement in the Black Baptist Church, 1880–1920* (Cambridge, MA: Harvard University Press, 1993), esp. chap. 7, "The Politics of Respectability." See also Fannie Barrier Williams, "Club Movement Among Negro Women," in J. W. Gibson and W. H. Crogman, *Progress of a Race: The Remarkable Advancement of the Colored American* (Naperville, IL: J. L. Nichols & Company, 1912; first pub. 1902), chap. 9.

42 Wilma Peebles-Wilkins and Beverly Koerin, "Moral Goodness and Black Women: Late Nineteenth Century Community Caregivers," in P. Nelson Reid and Philip R. Popple, eds, *The Moral Purposes of Social Work: The Character and Intentions of a Profession* (Chicago: Nelson-Hall Publishers, 1992), 155–172, quote 168. See also Carlton-LaNey, *African American Leadership*, 92, 112–113, 133, 153–155; Joyce Ann Hanson, *Mary McLeod Bethune & Black Women's Political Activism* (Columbia: University of Missouri Press, 2003).

43 Knupfer, *Toward a Tenderer Humanity*, 21–29; Parker, *Unceasing Militant*, 71, 79, 90; 17–22, 165–171.

44 Gibson and Crogman, *Progress of a Race*, 79. Northrop, Gay, and Penn, *College of Life*, 114; part 2, 136.

45 Northrop, Gay, and Penn, *College of Life*, 111, 122–127, 143–144, 149.

46 Booker T. Washington, "Negro Self-Help," *The Independent*, 59, no. 2973 (Nov. 23, 1905): 1207–1208; reprinted in, for example, *New York Age* (New York), Nov. 30, 1905.

47 *Proceedings of the National Negro Business League* (Boston, MA: J. R. Hamm, Publisher, 1901); *New York Age* (New York), Aug. 17, 1905, 4, 54–58. For the NNBL's history, see Michael B. Boston, *The Business Strategy of Booker T. Washington: Its Development and Implementation* (Gainesville: University Press of Florida, 2010), chap. 5.

48 Tiffany M. Gill, *Beauty Shop Politics: African American Women's Activism in the Beauty Industry* (Urbana: University of Illinois Press, 2010), 8, 11–18, 43–48; A'Lelia Bundles, *On Her Own Ground: The Life and Times of Madam C. J. Walker* (New York: Scribner, 2001), 34–35, 44–47. See also Pamela Walker Laird, *Pull: Networking and Success since Benjamin Franklin* (Cambridge, MA: Harvard University Press, 2006), 68–72, 357–358n29.

49 Tyrone McKinley Freeman, *Madam C.J. Walker's Gospel of Giving: Black Women's Philanthropy During Jim Crow* (Urbana: University of Illinois Press, 2020), 37–53; Bundles, *On Her Own Ground*, 49, 64–68, 74, 81–86.

50 Bundles, *On Her Own Ground*, 92–93, 100–101, 133–136, 148–150, 227, 231; Gill, *Beauty Shop Politics*, 23, 31, 35–36, 45, 47.
51 Bundles, *On Her Own Ground*, 135; Freeman, *Madam C. J. Walker's Gospel of Giving*, 8, 22–23, 35–38, 49–50, 57–59.
52 "Wealthiest Negro Woman's Suburban Mansion," *New York Times Magazine*, Nov. 4, 1917, 6; "A Remarkable Woman," *New York Age* (New York), May 31, 1919.
53 *Self-Made: Inspired by the Life of Madam C. J. Walker* (Netflix, 2020); Mike Hale, "In Netflix's 'Self-Made,' an Unlikely Entrepreneur," nytimes.com, Mar. 19, 2020; Nadra Nittle, "Netflix's 'Self-Made' Isn't Inspired Enough by Madame C. J. Walker to Avoid Black Stereotypes," nbcnews.com, Mar. 19, 2020.

Two years later, the toy company Mattel added the "Self-Made and Exceptional" Madam Walker to its Barbie Doll collection to honor "her exceptional business acumen and unflinching determination." Unlike the Netflix drama, Mattel's description highlights her as "a dedicated philanthropist and advocate" and, then, as "the first documented self-made female millionaire in the U.S." Madam C. J. Walker Barbie® Doll, Mattel, shop.mattel.com/products/madam-cj-walker-barbie-inspiring-women-doll-hlm19.
54 Gibson and Crogman, *Progress of a Race*, 4; Allison Dorsey, *To Build Our Lives Together: Community Formation in Black Atlanta, 1875–1906* (Athens, GA: University of Georgia Press, 2004), 8, 147, 166–169; Chris M. Messer, Thomas E. Shriver, and Alison E. Adams, "The Destruction of Black Wall Street: Tulsa's 1921 Riot and the Eradication of Accumulated Wealth," *American Journal of Economics and Sociology*, 77, nos. 3–4 (May–Sept. 2018): 789–819; John Sibley Butler, *Entrepreneurship and Self-Help Among Black Americans: A Reconsideration of Race and Economics* (Albany, NY: State University of New York Press, 1991), chap. 6.
55 Abram L. Harris, *The Negro as Capitalist: A Study of Banking and Business Among American Negroes* (Philadelphia, PA: American Academy of Political and Social Science, 1936), ix–xi, 24, 46–55, 103. See also Robert Higgs, *Competition and Coercion: Blacks in the American Economy, 1865–1914* (Cambridge, UK: Cambridge University Press, 1977), 13, 90–92; Owen James Hyman, "Jim Crow's Cut: White Supremacy and the Destruction of Black Capital in the Forests of the Deep South," in Kenneth Lipartito and Lisa Jacobson, eds., *Capitalism's Hidden Worlds* (Philadelphia: University of Pennsylvania Press, 2020), 81–98.
56 Shennette Garrett-Scott, *Banking on Freedom: Black Women in U.S. Finance Before the New Deal* (New York: Columbia University Press, 2019); Dorsey, *To Build Our Lives Together*; Laird, *Pull*, 79–80.
57 J[ohn]. H[enry]. Harmon, Jr., "The Negro as a Local Business Man," in Harmon, Arnett G. Lindsay, Carter G. Woodson, eds., *The Negro as a Business Man* (College Park, MD: McGrath Publishing Company, 1920), 13–16, 32–33.
58 For a new sample of life stories that convey Douglass's sense of self-help, see James M. Durant III and Jeffrey M. Allen, eds., *My Story... From Humble Beginnings to Professional Success: A Young Professional's Guide* (New York: Routledge, 2023).
59 Donald Meyer, *The Positive Thinkers: A Study of the American Quest for Health, Wealth and Personal Power from Mary Baker Eddy to Norman Vincent Peale* (Garden City, NY: Doubleday

& Company, 1965), 37–41, 104. Walter A. Friedman, *Birth of a Salesman: The Transformation of Selling in America* (Cambridge, MA: Harvard University Press, 2004), 206–207.

60 Russell H. Conwell, *Acres of Diamonds* (New York: Harper & Row, 1915), 21, 30–32; Judy Hilkey, *Character Is Capital: Success Manuals and Manhood in Gilded Age America* (Chapel Hill: University of North Carolina Press, 1997), 58, 92–93, 102–104.

61 Frank Channing Haddock, *Power of Will*, 255th ed. (Meriden, CT: The Pelton Publishing Company, 1918; 1st ed. 1907), x–xiii, 3, 243, 324, 337; Hilkey, *Character Is Capital*, 173–174, n. 4; Meyer, *The Positive Thinkers*, 164–166.

62 Samuel Smiles, *Self-Help with Illustrations of Conduct and Perseverance*, 2nd ed. (Chicago: Belford, Clarke & Co., 1883; first pub. 1866), v–vi, xi. Smiles also wrote *Character* (1871), *Thrift* (1875), *Duty* (1880), and assorted other inspirational volumes. Karen Boiko, "Samuel Smiles, Radical: A Critical Biography" (PhD dissertation, New York University, 2001), 296–313, 316–317.

63 Margaret Connolly, *The Life Story of Orison Swett Marden: A Man Who Benefited Men* (New York: Thomas Y. Crowell Company, 1925), viii, 201.

64 See Meyer, *The Positive Thinkers*, esp. chap. 14; Steven Watts, *Self-Help Messiah: Dale Carnegie and Success in Modern America* (New York: Other Press, 2013), 261–264. Friedman, *Birth of a Salesman*, 157–158, 180, 232–233.

65 For provocative interpretations of that decade, see Maury Klein, *Rainbow's End: The Crash of 1929* (New York: Oxford University Press, 2001); and Frederick Lewis Allen's classic, *Only Yesterday: An Informal History of the Nineteen Twenties* (New York: Harper & Row, 1931).

66 Richard J. Walsh, "The Doom of the Self-Made Man," *Century Magazine*, 109 (1924): 253–258. Search of Newspapers.com, Sept. 23, 2023.

67 Fred D. Pasley, *Al Capone: The Biography of a Self-Made Man* (Garden City, NY: Garden City Publishing Co., 1930), 17–19, 355; Dominic J. Capeci, "Al Capone: Symbol of a Ballyhoo Society," *Journal of Ethnic Studies*, 2, no. 4 (Winter 1975): 33–46.

68 Emily Post, *Etiquette in Society, in Business, in Politics and at Home* (New York: Funk & Wagnalls Company, 1922), chap. 32, quotes 30–32.

69 Stephen L. Rencken, "Fitting-In: The Redefinition of Success in the 1930s," *Journal of Popular Culture*, 27, no. 3 (Winter 1993): 205–222.

70 "A Well Made Man," *Morning World-Herald* (Omaha, NE), Jan. 2 1920; *Rutland Daily Herald* (Rutland, VT), Jan. 1, 1930; "Quit Ford Factory for Seat in U.S. Senate," *Altoona Tribune* (Altoona, PA), Jan. 1, 1923.

71 "Some 'Best Wishes,'" *Marshfield Mail* (Marshfield, MS), Jan. 1, 1920; *Locust Grove Times* (Locust Grove, OK), Jan. 1, 1925; "Correct," *Montana Record-Herald* (Helena, MT), Jan. 1, 1923, from the *Boston Transcript*; "Imperfect Job," *Bloomfield Monitor* (Bloomfield, NE), Jan 1, 1925.

72 "New Type of Venus, Self-Made Beauty," *Norman Transcript* (Norman, OK), Jan. 4, 1928; Alicia Hart, "Glorifying Yourself," *Wilkes-Barre Times Leader* (Wilkes-Barre, PA), Jan. 2, 1933.

73 Will Rogers, *Letters of a Self-Made Diplomat to His President* (New York: Albert and Charles Boni, 1926); William Almon Wolff, "Her Husband's Secretary," chap. 35, *Morning News*

(Wilmington, DE), Jan. 2, 1928; "Our New Serial Story," *Bartlesville Daily Enterprise* (Bartlesville, OK), Jan. 1, 1925; "Picture Shows Today," *Havre Daily Promoter* (Havre, MN), Jan. 1, 1925.

74 Based on searches in Newspapers.com, *NYT*, and Google Books Ngrams for "individualism" and "individualist," Jan. 20, 2024.

75 "Father Thos. Sherman: Distinguished Jesuit Priest Speaks at Cathedral," *Fort Wayne News* (Fort Wayne, IN), Jan. 26, 1903, 7; "Touching the Touchiness of Cadiz," *New-York Tribune*, Nov. 20, 1909.

76 Newspapers.com, Feb. 2, 2024.

77 Herbert Hoover, *American Individualism* (Garden City, NY: Doubleday, Page & Company, 1922), 8–9. "Keep Individuality, Hoover's Final Word of Advice to Nation's Voters," *Los Angeles Times*, Nov. 6, 1928.

78 Rencken, "Fitting-In"; Michael Denning, *Mechanic Accents: Dime Novels and Working-Class Culture in America* (London and New York: Verso, 1987).

CHAPTER 9

1 Calvin Coolidge, "Address to the American Society of Newspaper Editors," Washington, DC (Jan. 17, 1925) APP, www.presidency.ucsb.edu/node/269410. Note that Coolidge did not say that "the business of America is business," although the sentiment is the same. Lawrence Glickman, *Free Enterprise: An American History* (New Haven, CT: Yale University Press, 2019), 65–67.

2 "Where Are Those Mighty Self-Made Men?" *Tulsa Daily World* (Tulsa, OK), Jan. 1, 1933; "Schwab Says Opportunities for Youth Are Greater Now," *The News* (Lynchburg, VA), Jan. 1, 1930.

3 "Schwab Says Opportunities for Youth Are Greater Now."

4 I use the term "conservative" following Kim Phillips-Fein's portrayal of "business activists" who used it to describe themselves and their efforts toward "turning back the New Deal." Kim Phillips-Fein, *Invisible Hands: The Making of the Conservative Movement from the New Deal to Reagan* (New York: W. W. Norton, 2009), 321–22. However, I don't believe that most people who have claimed that term for the last half century deserve its dignity.

5 Boyden Sparkes, "Horatio Alger at the Bridge," *Saturday Evening Post*, May 2, 1936.

6 Chad Pearson, *Reform or Repression?: Organizing America's Anti-Union Movement* (Philadelphia: University of Pennsylvania Press, 2016); Vilja Hulden, *The Bosses' Union: How Employers Organized to Fight Labor before the New Deal* (Urbana: University of Illinois Press, 2023); Jennifer A. Delton, *The Industrialists: How the National Association of Manufacturers Shaped American Capitalism* (Princeton, NJ: Princeton University Press, 2020); Eric Rauchway, *The Great Depression and the New Deal: A Very Short Introduction* (Oxford, UK: Oxford University Press, 2008).

7 [William Griffith Wilson and Robert Holbrook Smith], *Twelve Steps and Twelve Traditions* (New York: Alcoholics Anonymous, 2007; first pub. 1953), 9, 14, 37–40, 70–71, 101, 129–130, 189.

8 Roger Biles, *A New Deal for the American People* (DeKalb: Northern Illinois University Press, 1991), 152–153, 225–233.
9 On reactions to the New Deal, see Jefferson Cowie, *The Great Exception: The New Deal & the Limits of American Politics* (Princeton, NJ: Princeton University Press, 2016), esp. Introduction; Hulden, *The Bosses' Union*, 16–17, 230, 234; Kim Phillips-Fein, "Conservatism: A State of the Field," *Journal of American History*, 98 (Dec. 2011), 723–43. For an overview of businessmen's fears, see Phillips-Fein, *Invisible Hands*, esp. chap. 1.
10 Glickman, *Free Enterprise*; Wendy L. Wall, *Inventing the "American Way": The Politics of Consensus from the New Deal to the Civil Rights Movement* (New York: Oxford University Press, 2008).
11 David M. Ricci, *Politics without Stories: The Liberal Predicament* (New York: Cambridge University Press, 2016); Frederick W. Mayer, *Narrative Politics: Stories and Collective Action* (New York: Oxford University Press, 2014).
12 "Gov. Doty's Proclamation," *Wisconsin Express* (Madison), Feb. 2, 1843; see also "The Self-Acting Pumps at the Linden Lead Works," *Mineral Point Tribune* (Mineral Point, WI), Oct. 9, 1855; "Not a Bad Resolution," *Louisville Daily Journal* (Louisville, KY, from the *New York Tribune*), Nov. 20, 1857; *Vermont Watchman and State Journal* (Montpelier, VT), Dec. 20, 1836; *Clarion-Ledger* (Jackson, MI), Jan. 1, 1928. For a review of mid-nineteenth-century uses, see Benjamin Zimmer, "Figurative 'bootstraps' (1834)," listserv.linguistlist.org/pipermail/ads-l/2005-August/052756.html.
13 Horatio Alger, Jr., *Ragged Dick, or Street Life in New York with the Boot-Blacks* (Philadelphia: A. K. Loring, 1868), Preface, accessed from www.gutenberg.org/files/5348/5348-h/5348-h.htm#link2H_PREF.
14 For excellent biographies, see Carol Nackenoff, *The Fictional Republic: Horatio Alger and American Political Discourse* (New York: Oxford University Press, 1994); and Gary Scharnhorst with Jack Bales, *The Lost Life of Horatio Alger, Jr.* (Bloomington: Indiana University Press, 1985).
15 [Horatio Alger, Jr.], *Nothing to Do: A Tilt at Our Best Society* (Boston, MA: James French & Co., 1857).
16 Judy Hilkey, *Character is Capital: Success Manuals and Manhood in Gilded Age America* (Chapel Hill: University of North Carolina Press, 1997).
17 Scharnhorst with Bales, *Horatio Alger, Jr.*; Nackenoff, *The Fictional Republic*.
18 Horatio Alger, *Strive and Succeed: The Progress of Walter Conrad* (Boston: A. K. Loring, 1872).
19 Denning, *Mechanic Accents*, 60–61, 202–203, 235; Scharnhorst with Bales, *Horatio Alger, Jr.*, 117–120; Martin Woodside, "The Nineteenth-Century Dime Western, Boyhood, and Empowered Adolescence," *Boyhood Studies*, 9, no. 2 (Autumn 2016): 5–24, see 12.
20 Bruce Catton, "Horatio Alger in Hall of Fame? Why Not?" *Sandusky Star*, Sept. 19, 1936, 2.
21 Catton, "Horatio Alger in Hall of Fame?"
22 Sparkes, "Horatio Alger at the Bridge."
23 Sparkes, "Horatio Alger at the Bridge," 74.

24 Bureau of Labor Statistics, *Historical Statistics of the United States Colonial Times to the 1970s, Part I* (Washington, DC: US Government Printing Office, 1975), Series D 85–86 Unemployment: 1890–1970, 135; Cowie, *The Great Exception*, 98.

25 Michael Denning, *The Cultural Front: The Laboring of American Culture in the Twentieth Century* (London and New York: Verso, 1996). *My Man Godfrey* was based on *1101 Park Avenue*, a short novel by Eric S. Hatch. It received six Oscar nominations and a Library of Congress designation in 1999 as "culturally significant"; other adaptations included *Lux Radio Theater*, May 9, 1938.

26 Robert H. Frank, *Success and Luck: Good Fortune and the Myth of Meritocracy* (Princeton, NJ: Princeton University Press, 2016). For one of many scholarly refutations about clichéd notions of Alger's stories and intentions, see Michael Zuckerman, "The Nursery Tales of Horatio Alger," *American Quarterly*, 24, no. 2 (May 1972): 191–209. Perhaps the most popular satire on this topic is Shepherd Mead, *How to Succeed in Business without Really Trying: The Dastard's Guide to Fame and Fortune* (New York: Simon & Schuster,1952); *How to Succeed in Business Without Really Trying*, script by Abe Burrows, Jack Weinstock, and Willie Gilbert; music and lyrics by Frank Loesser (play 1961; film 1967).

27 See Nackenoff, *The Fictional Republic*, on Alger's approach to politics, chap. 7.

28 Pearson, *Reform or Repression?*; Mary Sennholz, *Faith and Freedom: The Journal of a Great American, J. Howard Pew* (Grove City, PA: Grove City College, 1985); Phillips-Fein, *Invisible Hands*, 71; Biles, *A New Deal for the American People*; Rauchway, *The Great Depression and the New Deal*.

29 "Editorial of the Day: When Doctors Disagree," *Bryan Eagle*, Nov. 14, 1934; reprinted from *Christian Science Monitor*. Similar Associated Press stories include "New Dealers Make Sweep in the Nation," *Hagerstown Morning Herald* (MD), Nov. 8, 1934; "Security Is Man's Own Creation," *Somerset American* (PA), Sept. 18, 1945. Other examples include "What Other Editors Think: A New Deal Disease," *Havre Daily News* (MT), Feb. 21, 1936; "New Deal Disease," *Oshkosh Northwestern* (WI), Dec. 2, 1935; Frank R. Kent, "The Great Game of Politics," *Titusville Herald* (PA), Oct. 6, 1938, reprinted from *Baltimore Sun*.

30 Berton Braley, *Pegasus Pulls a Hack: Memoirs of a Modern Minstrel* (New York: Minton, Balch & Company, 1934), 52–4, 165; Berton Braley, *New Deal Ditties: Or Running in the Red with Roosevelt* (New York: Greenberg Publishers, 1936), 10. Rose C. Feld, "Berton Braley's Memoirs of a Modern Minstrel," *New York Times* (*NYT*), Sept. 16, 1934; "Berton Braley, Poet, Dies at 83," *NYT*, Jan. 27, 1966.

31 "Business is Urged to Educate Public," *NYT*, Sept. 16, 1937. S. H. Walker and Paul Sklar, *Business Finds Its Voice: Management's Efforts to Sell the Business Idea to the Public* (New York: Harper & Brothers, 1938), esp. chap. 9.

32 Potomacus, "Pew of Pennsylvania," *New Republic*, May 8, 1944, pp. 625–627; "Mr. Pew at Valley Forge," *Time*, May 6, 1940, pp. 17–23. Carol V. R. George, *God's Salesman: Norman Vincent Peale and the Power of Positive Thinking* (New York: Oxford University Press, 1993), 108, 149, 173; Phillips-Fein, *Invisible Hands*, 70–71, 76–77; Matthew Avery Sutton, *American Apocalypse: A History of Modern Evangelism* (Cambridge, MA: Harvard

University Press, 2014), 320–22; Elizabeth A. Fones-Wolf, *Selling Free Enterprise: The Business Assault on Labor and Liberalism, 1945–60* (Urbana: University of Illinois Press, 1994), 24, 223, 236–43; Kevin M. Kruse, *One Nation Under God: How Corporate America Invented Christian America* (New York: Basic Books, 2015), 17, 20–22, 46, 264. See also Sennholz, *Faith and Freedom.*

33 R. Hindes, "J. Howard Pew Personal Papers," finding aid, Jul. 1981, Accession 1634, p. 263 (Hagley Museum and Library, Wilmington, DE).

34 Potomacus, "Pew of Pennsylvania"; Michael C. Jensen, "The Pews of Philadelphia," *NYT*, Oct. 10, 1971.

35 *Appendix to the Congressional Record*, 76 Cong., 1 sess., Apr. 12, 1939, pp. 1432–1435.

36 "Horatio Alger: Meet Today's Young Men," *Christian Science Monitor*, Mar. 16, 1940.

37 Pearson, *Reform or Repression?*

38 Mark R. Wilson, *Destructive Creation: American Business and the Winning of World War II* (Philadelphia: University of Pennsylvania Press, 2016).

39 *Appendix to the Congressional Record*, 77 Cong., 2 sess., Dec. 1942, p. A4345.

40 *Appendix to the Congressional Record*, 78 Cong., 1 sess., Feb. 8, 1943, p. A482; Henry A. Wallace, "Horatio Alger is Not Dead," in *The Century of the Common Man* (New York: Reynal & Hitchcock, 1943), 56–57.

41 "Horatio Alger Rides Again"; Wallace, "Horatio Alger is Not Dead."

42 Tom M. Girdler, *Boot Straps: The Autobiography of Tom M. Girdler* (New York: Charles Scribner's Sons, 1943), 4, 5, 105, 355–57, 385, 420, 450, 458. "Tom Girdler Reached Top by Easy Way: Career Devoid of Horatio Alger Twist," syndicated by International News Service, *Hammond Times* (IN), Jul. 1, 1937, p. 5; Russell B. Porter, "Tom Girdler, Individualist," *New York Times Book Review*, Oct. 3, 1943, p. 28.

43 "A New Deal Alger Boy," *Twin Falls Times-News*, reprinted from *Chicago Times*, Dec. 21, 1943, p. 4.

44 "Land of Opportunity," *NYT*, Jul. 4, 1944; Bell Telephone, "Up From the Ranks," *Life*, May 22, 1944. Regarding Bell Telephone's astute construction of its public image, see Roland Marchand's magisterial *Creating the Corporate Soul: The Rise of Public Relations and Corporate Imagery in American Big Business* (Berkeley: University of California Press, 1998), esp. chap. 2.

45 Eric Johnston, *America Unlimited* (Garden City, NY: Doubleday, Doran and Company, 1944), 3, 5–8, 14, 242; John Chamberlain, "Eric Johnston," *Life*, Jun. 19, 1944, pp. 96–108, esp. 108.

46 Phillips-Fein, *Invisible Hands*, 31–34.

47 Chilton Company, "Wanted! . . . A Modern Horatio Alger," *Advertising Age*, Dec. 1947, pp. 18–19.

48 "Workers OK Alger story," *Modern Industry*, 16 (Aug. 15, 1948): 35.

49 Quoted in Edwin P. Hoyt, *Horatio's Boys: The Life and Works of Horatio Alger, Jr.* (Radnor, PA: Chilton Book Company, 1974), 230.

50 The *New York Times* lists five recipients, but the *New York Herald Tribune* lists and pictures four. "Business Leaders Receive Awards," *New York Herald Tribune*, Jul. 10, 1947; "Success Poll Won by 5 Business Men," *NYT*, Jul. 3, 1947.

51 Love Smith, *Only in America: Opportunity Still Knocks* (New York: Horatio Alger Association of Distinguished Americans, 1988), 7.
52 "Horatio Alger Prize Awarded to Baruch," *NYT*, May 13, 1948.
53 Horatio Alger Association, "Who We Are," horatioalger.org/about-us/history-of-horatio-alger-association/ (accessed Jun. 15, 2022).
54 *Congressional Record-Senate*, 85 Cong., 1 sess., May 1957, pp. 6274–75.
55 "NAM Set to Fight 'ISMs' Here: Bunting Calls on Advertising Men to Help Industry to 'Sell' Our System," *NYT*, Oct. 9, 1947.
56 Phelps Adams, *The Free Enterprise System: What It Is, How It Works, What It Has Done* (New York: National Association of Manufacturers, 1948), 3, 7, 14, 18. Richard S. Tedlow, "The National Association of Manufacturers and Public Relations during the New Deal," *Business History Review*, 50, no. 1 (Spring 1976): 25–45.
57 Hoyt, *Horatio's Boys*, 232–35, 250. See Scharnhorst with Bales, *Horatio Alger, Jr.*, for a scholarly evaluation of this topic, 149–156.
58 Horatio Alger Association, *Minutes from Meetings* "1951–1979," vol. 1, p. 2, box 3. In contrast, in 2015, the HAA Endowment Fund held $147,376,652 in assets. *Report of Association Activities* (Sept. 2015), p. 32, box 9. Horatio Alger Association Collection #1761 (Howard Gotlieb Archival Research Center at Boston University, Boston, MA; hereafter HAAC). "Slipping" quotation by Margaret Beebe, Kenneth's wife, in Smith, *Only in America*, 8.
59 Horatio Alger Awards Committee, *A Decade of Living Proof of the Opportunities in Our American Way of Life* (New York, 1956), iii, 6, 60; Horatio Alger Association of Distinguished Americans, *Only in America* (Alexandria, VA, 2022).
60 George, *God's Salesman*, 21, 32; Norman Vincent Peale, *The True Joy of Positive Living: An Autobiography* (New York: William Morrow and Company, 1984), 31.
61 *Decade of Living Proof*, 55; Peale, *True Joy of Positive Living*, chap. 1, p. 13.
62 George Vecsey, "Norman Vincent Peale, Preacher of Gospel Optimism, Dies at 95," *NYT*, Dec. 26, 1993; Ron Alexander, "Chronicle," *NYT*, May 31, 1994; George, *God's Salesman*; Kruse, *One Nation Under God*; Sarah Forbes Orwig, "Business Ethics and the Protestant Spirit: How Norman Vincent Peale Shaped the Religious Values of American Business Leaders," *Journal of Business Ethics*, 38 (Jun. 2002): 81–89; Douglas T. Miller, "Popular Religion of the 1950's: Norman Vincent Peale and Billy Graham," *Journal of Popular Culture*, 9, no. 1 (1975): 66–76; Christopher Lane, *Surge of Piety: Norman Vincent Peale and the Remaking of American Religious Life* (New Haven, CT: Yale University Press, 2016).
63 "Norman Vincent Peale," Horatio Alger Association of Distinguished Americans, Inc., horatioalger.org/members/member-detail/norman-vincent-peale/; "Norman Vincent Peale Award," Horatio Alger Association of Distinguished Americans, Inc., horatioalger.org/horatio-alger-award/norman-vincent-peale-award/.
64 Peale, *True Joy of Positive Living*, 36. "Norman Vincent Peale," Horatio Alger Association of Distinguished Americans, Inc.
65 Horatio Alger Association of Distinguished Americans, *Decade of Living Proof*, 55.
66 Norman Vincent Peale, *The Power of Positive Thinking* (New York: Prentice Hall, 1952) 34–36, 176, 227. Daniel Horowitz, *Happier? The History of a Cultural Movement that Aspired to Transform America* (New York: Oxford University Press, 2018), esp. 32–34.

67 *Appendix to the Congressional Record*, 81 Cong., 2 sess., Jan. 17, 1950, pp. A345–46.
68 William M. Freeman, "Deficit Financing Assailed as Peril," *NYT*, Sept. 25, 1953.

CHAPTER 10

1 Richard M. Nixon, "Speech by the Vice President Before the Association of Business Economists," Oct. 20, 1960, American Presidency Project (APP), www.presidency.ucsb.edu/node/274054.
2 Estimate of newspapers based on search of Newspapers.com from October 20 to 30, 1960, on Jun. 13, 2023. For instance, Howard Norton, "Nixon Offers Economic Program," *Baltimore Sun* (Baltimore, MD), Oct. 21, 1960; and Thomas W. Ottenad, "Nixon Presents New Program to Build Economy," *St. Louis Post-Dispatch* (St. Louis, MO), Oct. 20, 1960.
3 Robert Keayne, *The Apologia of Robert Keayne: The Self Portrait of a Puritan Merchant*, ed. Bernard Bailyn (Gloucester, MA: Peter Smith, 1970), 75–76. See Chapter 1 for a fuller discussion of Keayne and his era.
4 See Micki McGee, *Self-Help, Inc.: Makeover Culture in American Life* (New York: Oxford University Press, 2005); Benjamin C. Waterhouse, *One Day I'll Work for Myself: The Dream and Delusion that Conquered America* (New York: W. W. Norton & Company, 2024).
5 Michael Young, *The Rise of the Meritocracy, 1870–2033* (New York: Random House, 1959; first pub. 1958 in the UK); Young, *The Rise of the Meritocracy* (London, UK: Transaction Publishers, 1994), xii. Young's ideas and drafts had circulated widely for years, so the word and the concerns had already appeared in a few obscure places. Ben Jackson, *Equality and the British Left: A Study in Progressive Political Thought, 1900–64* (Manchester, UK: Manchester University Press, 2007), 172; Stephen Meredith, "A 'Society … Divisible into the Blessed and Unblessed': Michael Young and Meritocracy in Postwar Britain," *Political Quarterly*, 91, no. 2 (Apr.– Jun. 2020): 379–387.
6 Young, *Rise of the Meritocracy* (1958 ed.), 18–19, 24–25, 85. "Looking Backward, Sourly," *Time Magazine*, 72, no. 20 (Nov. 17, 1958): 94–96.
7 For example, Harry Jones, Jr., "Life Under 'Meritocracy' Brings Satirical Shafts from a Briton," *Kansas City Star* (Kansas City, MO), Jul. 25, 1959; Michael Holmberg, "Book Tells of 'Utopia' in 2034," *Pittsburgh Press* (Pittsburgh, PA), Jul. 18, 1959.
8 "U.S. Molds Differences into Harmony – Speaker," *West Carroll Gazette* (Oak Grove, LA), Jun. 25, 1959; Betty Jean Clay, "'Get into Orbit,'" *Corsicana Semi-Weekly Light* (Corsicana, TX), Jan. 13, 1959.
9 "Calls for Equalitarian Education," *Daily Defender* (Atlanta, GA), Jul. 28, 1959.
10 Young, *Rise of the Meritocracy* (1958 ed.), 153n2. "Michael Young, 86, Scholar; Coined, Mocked 'Meritocracy'," *New York Times* (*NYT*), Jan. 25, 2002. Young, *Rise of Meritocracy* (1994 ed.), xii-xiii, xv-xvi; Young, "Down with Meritocracy," *Guardian*, Jun. 28, 2001 (available at theguardian.com).
11 Daniel Seligman, "Foretelling *The Bell Curve*," *National Review*, Dec. 19, 1994: 55–56.
12 Young, *Rise of the Meritocracy* (1958 ed.), 18–19, 24–25, 74.

13 Recent critics include Michael J. Sandel, *The Tyranny of Merit: What's Become of the Common Good?* (New York: Farrar, Straus and Giroux, 2020); Jo Littler, *Against Meritocracy: Culture, Power and Myths of Mobility* (London, UK: Routledge, 2018); Daniel Markovits, *The Meritocracy Trap: How America's Foundational Myth Feeds Inequality, Dismantles the Middle-Class, and Devours the Elite* (New York: Penguin Press, 2019).

14 Hillary Clinton, "Remarks at Ohio State University in Columbus," Oct. 10, 2016, APP, www.presidency.ucsb.edu/node/319580. Hillary Rodham Clinton, *It Takes a Village: And Other Lessons Children Teach Us* (New York: Simon and Schuster, 1996), 7.

15 Young, *Rise of Meritocracy* (1994 ed.), xv.

16 Jennifer A. Delton, *Rethinking the 1950s: How Anticommunism and the Cold War Made America Liberal* (New York: Cambridge University Press, 2013).

17 Milton Friedman and Rose D. Friedman, *Free to Choose: A Personal Statement* (New York: Harcourt Brace Jovanovich, 1979). For critiques of this perspective, see Harvey Cox, *The Market as God* (Cambridge, MA: Harvard University Press, 2016); Lawrence B. Glickman, *Free Enterprise: An American History* (New Haven, CT: Yale University Press, 2019); Suzanne Mettler, *The Government-Citizen Disconnect* (New York: Russell Sage Foundation, 2018), chap. 2.

18 William E. Simon, *A Time for Truth* (New York: Reader's Digest Press, 1978), xii, xvi, 12, 239–240.

19 Simon, *A Time for Truth*, 2–6, 234; Richard W. Stevenson, "William E. Simon, Ex-Treasury Secretary and High-Profile Investor, Is Dead at 72," *NYT*, Jun. 5, 2000.

20 Simon, *A Time for Truth*, 199–201, 212, 217, 220.

21 Herbert Mitgang, "Behind the Best Sellers," *NYT*, Nov. 18, 1978; as of Jul. 23, 1978, *A Time for Truth* had already been on the list for four weeks.

22 *Challenge* (Dec.1975): 6; reprinted from East San Gabriel Valley RWC [sic] newsletter.

23 Joseph A. Conforti, *Saints and Strangers: New England in British North America* (Baltimore, MD: Johns Hopkins University Press, 2006), 38–40; Barry Alan Shain, *The Myth of American Individualism: The Protestant Origins of American Political Thought* (Princeton, NJ: Princeton University Press, 1994); Richard L. Bushman, *From Puritan to Yankee: Character and the Social Order in Connecticut, 1690–1765* (New York: W. W. Norton & Company, 1970; first pub. 1967), 3–21, 190.

24 Quoted in Kim Phillips-Fein, *Fear City: New York's Fiscal Crisis and the Rise of Austerity Politics* (New York: Metropolitan Books, 2017), 96, 337.

25 See Kim Phillips-Fein, *Invisible Hands: The Making of the Conservative Movement from the New Deal to Reagan* (New York: W. W. Norton, 2009), esp. chaps. 7–9; Benjamin C. Waterhouse, *Lobbying America: The Politics of Business from Nixon to NAFTA* (Princeton, NJ: Princeton University Press, 2014); Glickman, *Free Enterprise*.

26 Waterhouse, *Lobbying America*, 94–96; Dollar value per *US Inflation Calculator*, www.usinflationcalculator.com.

27 *The Chamber: The Voice of Business* (Hagley Museum and Library, Acc. 1960, box 93, vol. 1973); Lewis F. Powell, Jr., "Confidential Memorandum: Attack on American Free Enterprise System," Aug. 23, 1971, available through Washington and Lee University

School of Law Scholarly Commons, 1, 10, 34; "Meeting the Attack against Business" (Hagley Museum and Library, Acc. 1960, box 93, vol. 1972).

28 Richard Lesher with David Scheiber, *Voice of Business* (Bloomington: Indiana University Press, 2017), 55–57, 69, 103, 107, 109; Powell, "Memo," 8, 34; Waterhouse, *Lobbying America*, 58–71; Phillips-Fein, *Invisible Hands*, 156–160, 200–206; Glickman, *Free Enterprise*, chap. 1.

29 "Lesher Receives Award for Leadership Ability," *Public Opinion* (Chambersburg, PA), May 22, 1980.

30 Lesher, *Voice of Business*, xi, 9–20, back jacket.

31 Jim Hook, "Local man spent 22 years lobbying presidents and countries for American business," *Public Opinion* (Chambersburg, PA), Dec. 15, 2017.

32 Alden Whitman, "Paul G. Hoffman is Dead at 83; Led Marshall Plan and U.N. Aid," *NYT*, October 9, 1974; "Talk of the Town," *New Yorker*, 29 (May 16, 1953): 23–24.

33 Horatio Alger Association, "Minutes from Meetings, 1951–1979," vol. 1: 2, 270–272, 294, 307; Horatio Alger Association Collection #1761 (hereafter HAAC), box 3.

34 HAAC, "Minutes from Meetings, 1951–1979," vol. 1: 2, 270–272, 294, 307; HAAC, #1761, box 3.

35 HAAC, "Minutes from Meetings, 1951–1979," vol. 1: 294–298, 312. "Arthur Rubloff Is Dead at 83," *NYT*, May 24, 1986; "Arthur Rubloff, 83, colossus of real estate development," *Chicago Tribune*, May 25, 1986; "Arthur Rubloff," *Tampa Tribune*, May 25, 1986.

36 HAAC, "Minutes from Meetings, 1980–2004," vol. 2: 117, 302, 313.

37 HAAC, "Minutes from Meetings, 1951–1979," vol. 1: 271, 297, 300–301, 312–313, 336, 338.

38 HAAC, "Minutes from Meetings, 1980–2004," vol. 2: 117, 302, 313.

39 Jimmy Carter, "Address to the Nation on Energy and National Goals," Jul. 15, 1979, APP, www.presidency.ucsb.edu/node/249458.

40 HAAC, "Minutes from Meetings, 1980–2004," vol. 2: 41–44, 58–62, 79–80. *Decade of Living Proof*, v; *Opportunity Still Knocks* (New York: Horatio Alger Awards Committee, 1957), v.

41 Many thanks to Terri Lonier for her gift of the stamp on its "first day of issue" postcard. The Alger boys on the stamp are Ragged Dick, a bootblack; Ben, a luggage boy; Rufus, a newsboy; and Mark, a match boy.

42 Kathleen Teltsch, "Spreading the Spirit of Horatio Alger," *NYT*, Aug. 31, 1986.

43 Horatio Alger Association of Distinguished Americans (HAADA), "About Us," horatioalger.org.

44 HAADA, "Consolidated Financial Report December 31, 2021," 3.

45 "Who We Are," horatioalger.org; HAAC, box 3, V. II, "Minutes from Meetings, 1980–2004," 454–455.

46 Peter H. Lindert and Jeffrey G. Williamson, *Unequal Gains: American Growth and Inequality Since 1700* (Princeton, NJ: Princeton University Press, 2016), chap. 9; Emmanuel Saez and Gabriel Zucman, "Wealth Inequality in the United States Since 1913," *Quarterly Journal of Economics*, 131, no. 2 (May 2016): 519–578.

47 HAAC, "Awards Banquet Achieves Record Success" and "Awards Capture National Coverage," *Executive Forum*, 1, no. 1 (Fall 1988): 2–4.
48 Love Miller, "Reagan Followed Horatio Alger Path to White House," *Syracuse Herald-American*, Jan. 18, 1981.
49 "Reagan's Letter to a Library," *American Libraries*, 12, no. 2 (Feb. 1981): 61; Jerry Griswold, "Young Reagan's Reading: 'I'm a sucker for hero worship,'" *NYT*, Aug. 30, 1981.
50 Phillips-Fein, *Invisible Hands*, 111–114.
51 Miller, "Reagan Followed Horatio Alger Path to White House"; Jay Ambrose, "The Reagan Example," *Gettysburg Times* (Gettysburg, PA), Jun. 11, 2004.
52 Henry Allen, "George Gilder and the Capitalists' Creed," *Washington Post*, Feb. 17, 1981; Michael B. Katz, *The Undeserving Poor: America's Enduring Confrontation with Poverty*, 2nd ed. (New York: Oxford University Press, 2013), 170–173. Pettigrew studied racial discrimination and race-based inequality.
53 George F. Gilder, *Wealth and Poverty* (New York: Basic Books, 1981), xi–xii, 122–123.
54 Gilder, *Wealth and Poverty*, 59–63, 96, 99.
55 Gilder, *Wealth and Poverty*, 111–112, 138.
56 "'Welfare Queen' – a ripoff artist," *Daily Herald* (Chicago) Nov. 17, 1974.
57 Julilly Kohler-Hausmann, "Welfare Crises, Penal Solutions, and the Origins of the 'Welfare Queen,'" *Journal of Urban History*, 4, no. 5 (2015): 756–771, 765; Lisa R. Pruitt, "Welfare Queens and White Trash," *Southern California Interdisciplinary Law Journal*, 25, no. 2 (Spring 2016): 289–312; John A. Gardiner and Theodore R. Lyman, *The Fraud Control Game: State Responses to Fraud and Abuse in AFDC and Medicaid Programs* (Bloomington, IN: Indiana University Press, 1984), 1–2, 10–12, 70–71.
58 George Bliss, "'Welfare queen' jailed in Tucson," *Chicago Tribune*, Oct. 12, 1974; "'Welfare Queen' Becomes Issue in Reagan Campaign," *NYT*, Feb. 15, 1976; John Levin, "The Welfare Queen," *Slate*, Dec. 19, 2013.
59 Katz, *The Undeserving Poor*, 88, 145, 164, 198–199.
60 James Midgley, "Society, Social Policy and the Ideology of Reaganism," *Journal of Sociology and Social Welfare*, 19, no. 1 (Mar. 1992): 13–28; Robert D. Plotnick, "Changes in Poverty, Income Inequality and the Standard of Living during the Reagan Years," *Journal of Sociology and Social Welfare*, 19, no. 1 (Mar. 1992): 29–44.
61 Reagan, "Address ... Reporting on the State of the Union," Jan. 26, 1982, APP, www.presidency.ucsb.edu/node/245636.
62 Waterhouse, *One Day I'll Work for Myself*, 82–84.
63 John Blake, "Return of the 'Welfare Queen'," CNN.com, Jan. 23, 2012; Kaaryn Gustafson, *Cheating Welfare: Public Assistance and the Criminalization of Poverty* (New York: NYU Press, 2011).
64 Martin Gilens, *Why Americans Hate Welfare: Race, Media, and the Politics of Antipoverty Policy* (Chicago: University of Chicago Press, 1999), 64.
65 Of Clinton's documents on the *American Presidency Project*, 134 included this phrase. William J. Clinton, "Statement on Signing the Personal Responsibility and Work Opportunity Reconciliation Act of 1996" and "Remarks on Signing ... and an

Exchange with Reporters," Aug. 22, 1996, APP, www.presidency.ucsb.edu/node/222686 and www.presidency.ucsb.edu/node/222681. See William Graebner, "The End of Liberalism: Narrating Welfare's Decline, from the Moynihan Report (1965) to the Personal Responsibility and Work Opportunity Act (1996)," *Journal of Policy History*, 14, no. 2 (2002): 170–190; Kohler-Hausmann, "Welfare Crises."

66 Clinton, "Remarks on Signing . . . and an Exchange with Reporters"; "The President's Radio Address," Dec. 16, 2020, www.presidency.ucsb.edu/node/220077. Katz, *Undeserving Poor*, 199–202.

67 Pruitt, "Welfare Queens and White Trash."

68 Sidney Ratner, *American Taxation: Its History as a Social Force in Democracy* (New York: W. W. Norton & Company, 1942), 13–15. In *The Government-Citizen Disconnect*, Suzanne Mettler points to the anti-democratic consequences of "the submerged state" that obscures to most Americans the extent to which they benefit from public policies and institutions, thereby fueling resentment against what seems like a government that absorbs taxes mercilessly.

69 "Punishing Success," *Democrat and Chronicle* (Rochester, NY), May 21, 1894; reprinted from *St. Louis Globe-Dispatch*.

70 Andrew W. Mellon, *Taxation: The People's Business* (New York: The Macmillan Company, 1924), 123. Newspapers.com yielded seventy-four hits on "punish success" for 1931, seventy of which repeated Mellon's quotation, Aug. 14, 2023.

71 "What They Say," *Evansville Press* (Evansville, IN), Apr. 18, 1931.

72 Barry Goldwater, *The Conscience of a Conservative* (Shepherdsville, KY: Victor Publishing Co., 1960), 61–62, 69–72, 75.

73 Louis Harris, "Opposition Is Found to Welfare Extension," *Fort Worth Star-Telegram* (Fort Worth, TX), Oct. 5, 1964. Newspapers.com found this article in thirty-eight newspapers, Sept. 18, 2023.

74 Reagan, "Remarks at the Annual Conservative Political Action Conference," Mar. 2, 1984, APP, www.presidency.ucsb.edu/node/260562.

CHAPTER 11

1 Jack Welch and John A. Byrne, *Jack: Straight from the Gut* (New York: Warner Business Books, 2001), ix, 80–81.

2 "Jack Welch signs *Jack: Straight from the Gut*," *Cincinnati Enquirer* (Cincinnati, OH), Oct. 21, 2001; "Meet the Author, Jack Welch," *Boston Globe* (Boston, MA), Oct. 17, 2001; Welch and Byrne, *Jack*, 125–127. David Gelles, *The Man Who Broke Capitalism: How Jack Welch Gutted the Heartland and Crushed the Soul of Corporate America – and How to Undo His Legacy* (New York: Simon & Schuster, 2022), 97.

3 On the nature of celebrity, see Joshua Gamson, *Claims to Fame: Celebrity in Contemporary America* (Berkeley: University of California Press, 1994), esp. chap. 7.

4 Among the many studies of rising inequality, see Thomas Piketty, trans. Arthur Goldhammer, *Capital in the Twenty-First Century* (Cambridge, MA: Harvard University

Press, 2014); Joseph E. Stiglitz, *The Price of Inequality: How Today's Divided Society Endangers Our Future* (New York: W.W. Norton & Company, 2012); Raj Chetty, Nathaniel Hendren, Margaret Jones, and Sonya Porter, "Race and Economic Opportunity in the United States: An Intergenerational Perspective," *Quarterly Journal of Economics*, 135, no. 2 (2020): 711–783.

5 See Chapter 1 for more about Keayne and his era.

6 George W. Bush, "Interview by Oprah Winfrey," *Oprah*, ABC, Sept. 19, 2000. Bush's opponent that year, Al Gore, also came from an old, elite, and wealthy family, but he didn't try to deny those advantages.

7 Craig Calcaterra, "Today in Baseball History: George W. Bush 'buys' the Texas Rangers," NBC Sports (nbcsports.com), Apr. 21, 2020; Michael Kranish, "Harvard fund poured millions into Bush-connected oil firm," *Boston Globe*, Jul. 18, 2002; Mike Allen, "Files: Bush Knew Firm's Plight before Stock Sale," *Washington Post*, Jul. 20, 2002. Shai Davidai and Thomas Gilovich, "The Headwinds/Tailwinds Asymmetry: An Availability Bias in Assessments of Barriers and Blessings," *Journal of Personality and Social Psychology*, 111, no. 6 (2016): 835–851.

8 George W. Bush, "Remarks Announcing Candidacy for the Republican Presidential Nomination," Jun. 12, 1999, American Presidency Project (APP), www.presidency.ucsb.edu/node/278521. Bush, "Interview by Oprah Winfrey." "Bush admits old DUI; Cheney then reveals two," Associated Press at archive.seattletimes.com, Nov. 3, 2000. Calculation from www.in2013dollars.com/us/inflation/1976?amount = 150.

9 Gary Fields, "Children born poor have little margin for mistakes regardless of race," Associated Press News, Dec. 29, 2023.

10 *Revenue Proposals and Tax Cuts in the President's Budget*, Hearing Before the Committee on Finance, United States Senate, Feb. 28, 2001, 36; Bush, "Remarks Announcing the Tax Relief Plan and an Exchange with Reporters," Feb. 5, 2001, APP, www.presidency.ucsb.edu/node/215296. Andrew Fieldhouse and Ethan Pollack, "Tenth Anniversary of the Bush-Era Tax Cuts," *Policy Memorandum*, no. 184 (Jun. 1, 2011); Emily Horton, "The Legacy of the 2001 and 2003 'Bush' Tax Cuts," Center on Budget and Policy Priorities, Oct. 23, 2017. Bush's war made the debt balloon because he was loathe to raise taxes for war, funding it with debt, instead.

11 *Revenue Proposals*, 36; Bush, "Remarks Announcing the Tax Relief Plan." Sam Brownback, "America Needs a Tax Cut," Senate, Jan. 31, 2001, *Congressional Record* (107th Congress); Steve King, "Jobs and Growth Reconciliation Tax Act of 2003," House, May 9, 2003, *Congressional Record* (108th Congress).

12 Jacob S. Hacker and Paul Pierson, "Abandoning the Middle: The Bush Tax Cuts and the Limits of Democratic Control," *Perspectives on Politics*, 3, no. 1 (Mar. 2005): 33–53.

13 Two especially prominent groups pressured legislators hard and advertised broadly: the Club for Growth spent $10 million in 2002 to elect anti-tax lawmakers, and since 1986 – begun at President Ronald Reagan's bidding – Grover Norquist's Americans for Tax Reform has attacked candidates who resisted signing his "Taxpayer Protections Pledge." Hacker and Pierson, "Abandoning the Middle," 40–41; Michael J. Graetz, *The Power to Destroy: How the Antitax Movement Hijacked America* (Princeton, NJ: Princeton

University Press, 2024), esp. chap. 12. On the cultural politics of taxation since 1970, see also my review of Graetz, *The Power to Destroy*, Pamela Walker Laird, "The Beast is Us," *Reviews in American History*, 53, no. 1 (March 2025).

14 Tom W. Smith, "Trends in National Spending Priorities, 1973–2000," General Social Survey, National Opinion Research Center, University of Chicago (Jan. 2001).

15 Bush, "Remarks Announcing the Tax Relief Plan"; Bush, "Remarks at an Iowa Victory 2006 Rally"; Bush, "Remarks at a Georgia Victory 2006 Rally," Oct. 31, 2006, APP, www.presidency.ucsb.edu/node/270807.

16 Robert Keayne, *The Apologia of Robert Keayne: The Self Portrait of a Puritan Merchant*, ed. Bernard Bailyn (Gloucester, MA: Peter Smith, 1970) 75–76; Robert F. Dalzell, Jr., *The Good Rich and What They Cost Us* (New Haven, CT: Yale University Press, 2013), chap. 2. On the broad question of success in isolation, see Brian Miller and Mike Lapham, *The Self-Made Myth: And the Truth About How Government Helps Individuals and Businesses Succeed* (San Francisco: Berrett-Koehler Publishers, 2012).

17 Franklin to Robert Morris, December 25, 1783; *Benjamin Franklin Papers*, listed as unpublished at franklinpapers.org.

18 Daniel Horowitz, *Entertaining Entrepreneurs: Reality TV's Shark Tank and the American Dream in Uncertain Times* (Chapel Hill: University of North Carolina Press, 2020), 28–33, 199–200n6.

19 For example, Dominique Mosbergen, "8 Times Donald Trump Claimed He Was a Self-Made Man," *Huffpost*, Oct. 3, 2018; David Barstow, Susanne Craig, and Russ Buettner, "Trump Engaged in Suspect Tax Schemes as He Reaped Riches from His Father," *New York Times* (*NYT*), Oct. 2, 2018. See also Wayne Barrett, *Trump: The Deals and the Downfall* (New York: HarperCollins, 1992); Miller and Lapham, *The Self-Made Myth*, 28–30; Graetz, *The Power to Destroy*, 217–219, 321n10.

20 Norman Vincent Peale, *The True Joy of Positive Living: An Autobiography* (New York: William Morrow and Company, 1984), 230–231; Jeremy B. White, "How Norman Vincent Peale Taught Donald Trump to Worship Himself," *Politico* (politico.com), Oct. 2015; Michael Kruse, "The Power of Trump's Positive Thinking," *Politico* (politico.com), Oct. 13, 2017; Marilyn Bender, "The Empire and Ego of Donald Trump," *NYT*, Aug. 7, 1983.

21 J. M. Opal, "Populism from Above: Donald Trump, Andrew Jackson, and the Politics of White Vengeance," in Michael Harvey, ed., *Donald Trump in Historical Perspective: Dead Precedents* (New York: Routledge, 2022), 68–80; Daniel Feller, "The Historical Presidency: Andrew Jackson in the Age of Trump," *Presidential Studies Quarterly*, 51, no. 3 (Sept. 2021): 667–681. Samples from the news media: "Johal Engel Bromwich, "The Wild Inauguration of Andrew Jackson, Trump's Populist Predecessor," *NYT* (newyorktimes.com), Jan. 20, 2017; Ed Kilgore, "The Heirs of Andrew Jackson," *New York* (nymag.com), Jun. 4, 2019; Timothy Egan, "A Tyrant's Ghost Guides Trump," *NYT* (nytimes.com), Feb. 3, 2017.

22 Donald J. Trump, "Remarks at a 'Make America Great Again Rally' in Moon Township, Pennsylvania," Mar. 10, 2018, APP, www.presidency.ucsb.edu/node/332443; Donald J. Trump, *Time to Get Tough: Making America #1 Again* (Washington, DC: Regnery Publishing Company, 2011), 49. Graetz, *The Power to Destroy*, 221.

23 Dan Mangan, "Trump brags about not paying taxes: 'That makes me smart,'" *CNBC*, Sept. 26, 2016. In 2024, IRS audits revealed repeated filing violations that point to $100 million in illegally unpaid taxes. Russ Buettner and Paul Kiel, "Trump May Owe $100 Million From Double-Dip Tax Breaks, Audit Shows," *NYT* (nytimes.com), May 11, 2024.

24 Donald J. Trump, "Remarks Following the New Hampshire Primary Election in Nashua, New Hampshire," Jan. 23, 2024, APP, www.presidency.ucsb.edu/node/369407; Interview, *Fox and Friends*, Dec. 2, 2021, APP, www.presidency.ucsb.edu/node/370716; Charles Homans, "Donald Trump Has Never Sounded Like This," *NYT* (nytimes.com), Apr. 27, 2024.

25 Augustino Fontevecchia, "The New Forbes 400 Self-Made Score: From Silver Spooners to Bootstrappers," Forbes.com, Oct. 2, 2014; Kerry A. Dolan, "Here's What Forbes Means by Self-Made: From Bootstrappers to Silver Spoons," Forbes.com, Jul. 13, 2018.

26 Natalie Robehmed, "At 21, Kylie Jenner Becomes the Youngest Self-Made Billionaire Ever," *Forbes*, Mar. 5, 2019; "America's Women Billionaires," *Forbes*, Aug. 31, 2018, front cover; Katherine Gillespie, "Kylie Jenner: Get Rich or Die Following," *Paper*, Feb. 18, 2019.

27 Robehmed, "At 21"; Dolan, "Here's What Forbes Means by Self-Made; "America's Women Billionaires," *Forbes*, Aug. 31, 2018, front cover; Katherine Gillespie, "Kylie Jenner: Get Rich or Die Following," *Paper*, Feb. 18, 2019; "Kylie Jenner, 17, Moves into her $2.7 Million Mansion – How Did She Pay for It?" People.com, Jun. 30, 2015. Given the poverty and hardships from which Winfrey rose, some questioned how Jenner could rank at seven compared to her ten, but that is another matter.

28 Lisa Respers France, "Backlash over Forbes Dubbing Kylie Jenner 'self-made,'" CNN.com, Jul. 12, 2018; Katherine Gillespie, "Kylie Jenner: Get Rich or Die Following," *Paper* (papermag.com), Feb. 18, 2019; Aditi Juneja, "I Was on a Forbes 30 under 30 list. Here Are the Hidden Privileges that Made Me a 'Success,'" Vox.com/first-person, Jul. 14, 2018; updated Nov. 13, 2018.

29 Tom Wolfe, *Bonfire of the Vanities* (New York: Farrar, Straus, Giroux, 1987), 12, 52, 62–65.

30 Leslie Wayne, "Ivan F. Boesky, Rogue Trader in 1980s Wall Street Scandal, Dies at 87," *NYT* (nytimes.com), May 20, 2024.

31 Gavin Benke, *Risk and Ruin: Enron and the Culture of American Capitalism* (Philadelphia: University of Pennsylvania Press, 2018), esp. 5–8, 172–173, 178–179.

32 Wayne Duggan, "A Short History of the Great Recession," Forbes.com, Jun. 21, 2023.

33 See Mark H. Rose, *Market Rules: Bankers, Presidents, and the Origins of the Great Recession* (Philadelphia: University of Pennsylvania Press, 2019).

34 Advertisement, *Palm Beach Post* (West Palm Beach, FL), Nov. 23, 2006; Advertisement, *Roanoke Times* (Roanoke, VA), Nov. 23, 2006; Sanford I. Weill and Judah Kraushaar, *The Real Deal: My Life in Business and Philanthropy* (New York: Hachette Book Group USA, 2006).

35 Louis Uchitelle, "The Richest of the Rich, Proud of a New Gilded Age," *NYT*, Jul. 15, 2007; Katrina Brooker, "Citi's Creator, Alone with His Regrets," *NYT*, Jan. 1, 2010;

Rose, *Market Rules*, 122–124, 129. Robert Scheer, "Root of Meltdown Doing Just Fine," *Columbia Daily Tribune*, Nov. 19, 2010; Brooker, "Citi's Creator, Alone with His Regrets."

36 Uchitelle, "The Richest of the Rich"; "The Richest Owe a Debt to the Rest," *NYT*, Jul. 17, 2007.

37 David Pauly, "Citigroup Shows Folly of Empire-Building," *News Journal* (Wilmington, DE), Nov. 26, 2008; Rose, *Market Rules*, 157.

38 Scheer, "Root of Meltdown Doing Just Fine"; Brooker, "Citi's Creator, Alone with His Regrets."

39 Duggan, "A Short History"; Jesse Eisinger, "Why Only One Top Banker Went to Jail for the Financial Crisis," *NYT* (nytimes.com), Apr. 5, 2014; William H. Cohan, "How Wall Streets' Bankers Stayed out of Jail," *The Atlantic* (www.theatlantic.com), Sept. 2015.

40 Horowitz, *Entertaining Entrepreneurs*, 15–16, 31–33, 160, 184, 190, 227–228, 239n1, 239n2.

41 Horowitz, *Entertaining Entrepreneurs*, 5–6, 26–29, 31–33, 199–200n6.

42 *ABC Shark Tank*, abc.com/show/535e2b07-18a9-4d94-9803-9ed8257b9d23 (2024).

43 Corilyn Shropshire, "Talbott Proves to be Jamba's Cup of Tea," *Chicago Tribune* (Chicago), Feb. 22, 2012. Erin Patricia Griffiths, "Shop Owners Undeterred by 'Shark' Bite," *Gazette* (Hawthorne, NJ), Feb. 4, 2010.

44 Elizabeth Behrman, "From Rags to Race Car," *Tampa Bay Times* (Tampa, FL), Mar. 24, 2023; *The Economics Daily*, Bureau of Labor Statistics, bls.gov/opub/ted/2012/ted_20120710.htm.

45 Behrman, "From Rags to Race Car."

46 Rob Asghar, "Why Silicon Valley's 'Fail Fast' Mantra is Just Hype," Forbes.com, Jul. 14, 2014. See Scott A. Sandage, *Born Losers: A History of Failure in America* (Cambridge, MA: Harvard University Press, 2005); and Edward J. Balleisen, *Navigating Failure: Bankruptcy and Commercial Society in Antebellum America* (Chapel Hill: University of North Carolina Press, 2001).

47 Bush, "Remarks Announcing Candidacy"; Bush, "Remarks at a Republican National Committee Gala." Gail Sahar Zucker and Bernard Weiner, "Conservatism and Perceptions of Poverty: An Attributional Analysis," *Journal of Applied Social Psychology*, 23 (1993): 925–943; Frank F. Furstenberg, *Destinies of the Disadvantaged: The Politics of Teenage Childbearing* (New York: Russell Sage Foundation, 2007), 53–59, 76, 161–164.

48 For example, Samuel Bowles, "A (Science-Based) Poor Kids' Manifesto," *Science*, 340 (May 31, 2013): 1044–1045; Kimberly G. Noble, "Brain Trust," *Scientific American*, 316, no. 3 (Mar. 2017): 45–49.

49 For historical background, see Nancy Isenberg, *White Trash: The 400-Year Untold History of Class in America* (New York: Viking, 2016); Seth Rockman, *Scraping By: Work, Labor, Slavery, and Survival in Early Baltimore* (Baltimore, MD: Johns Hopkins University Press, 2009).

50 Ann Case and Angus Deaton, *Deaths of Despair and the Future of Capitalism* (Princeton, NJ: Princeton University Press, 2020), 57, esp. chaps. 4, 7; Robert Wuthnow, *The Left*

Behind: Decline and Rage in Small-Town America (Princeton, NJ: Princeton University Press, 2016); Jefferson Cowie, *Stayin' Alive: The 1970s and the Last Days of the Working Class* (New York: The New Press, 2010).

51 Joseph Friedman and Helena Hansen, "Trends in Deaths of Despair by Race and Ethnicity from 1999 to 2022," *JAMA Psychiatry*, 81, no. 7 (2024): 731–732.

52 Dale Hogg, "Kansas House Speaker Meets Opposition as He Makes Case against Medicaid Expansion," *Kansas Reflector*, Apr. 18, 2024; Rose Conlon, "Most Kansans Support Expanding Medicaid, Abortion Rights, New Survey Finds," KMUW.org, Oct. 24, 2023.

53 Barbara Ehrenreich, *Nickle and Dimed: On (Not) Getting By in America* (New York: Henry Holt and Company, 2001); Linda Tirado, *Hand to Mouth: Living in Bootstrap America* (New York: Berkeley Books, 2015; first pub. 2014); Matthew Desmond, *Evicted: Poverty and Profit in the American City* (New York: Broadway Books, 2016); Sendhil Mullainathan and Eldar Shafir, *Scarcity: Why Having too Little Means so Much* (New York: Times Books, 2013), chap. 7.

54 Greg Sargent, "Why a Secretive Tech Billionaire Is Bankrolling J.D. Vance," *Washington Post* (washingtonpost.com), May 5, 2022.

55 J.D. Vance, *Hillbilly Elegy: A Memoir of a Family and Culture in Crisis* (New York: HarperCollins, 2016), 7, 9.

56 Vance, *Hillbilly Elegy*, 232, 255.

57 Vance, *Hillbilly Elegy*, 255.

58 Suzanne Mettler, *The Submerged State: How Invisible Government Policies Undermine American Democracy* (Chicago: University of Chicago Press, 2011).

59 There is no point here in trying anew to assess or even list motives, which is difficult enough to attempt for any single donor, much less across the mix. See René Bekkers and Pamala Wiepking, "A Literature Review of Empirical Studies of Philanthropy: Eight Mechanisms that Drive Charitable Giving," *Nonprofit and Voluntary Sector Quarterly*, 40, no. 5 (2011): 924–973.

60 Mettler, *The Submerged State*.

61 Adam Smith, *The Theory of Moral Sentiments* (Washington, DC: Regnery Publishing, 1997; based on an 1817 Boston edition of Smith's sixth and final edition), III.ii, 152.

62 Andrew Carnegie, "Wealth," *North American Review*, 148, no. 391 (1889): 682–689; *The Gospel of Wealth and Other Timely Essays* (New York: Century, 1900).

63 *Labor World* (Duluth, MN), May 20, 1899; Edgar Saltus, "Gospel of Wealth," *Labor World* (Duluth, MN), Nov. 10, 1900; originally published in the *San Francisco Examiner*. *Labor World* (Duluth, MN), May 6, 1905.

64 Nicolas J. Duquette, "Founders' Fortunes and Philanthropy: A History of the U.S. Charitable-Contribution Deduction," *Business History Review*, 93 (Autumn 2019): 553–584; Dalzell, *The Good Rich*; Linda McQuaig and Neil Brooks, *Billionaires' Ball: Gluttony and Hubris in an Age of Epic Inequality* (Boston, MA: Beacon Press, 2012), 227–228.

65 Barry Goldwater, *The Conscience of a Conservative* (Shepherdsville, KY: Victor Publishing Co., 1960), 72, 74. Reagan, "Address to the Nation on the Program for Economic Recovery," Sept. 24, 1981, APP, www.presidency.ucsb.edu/node/247669. Milton

Friedman and Rose D. Friedman, *Free to Choose: A Personal Statement* (New York: Harcourt Brace Jovanovich, 1979), 36–37, 136, 139–140.
66 Horatio Alger Association of Distinguished Americans, *Sixty-Year History* (Alexandria, VA: Horatio Alger Association, 2007), 125.
67 Carnegie, "Wealth," 659.
68 Hank Tucker, "The Forbes Philanthropy Score 2021: How We Ranked Each Forbes 400 Billionaire Based on Their Giving," Forbes.com, Apr. 21, 2022; Helen Flannery, Chuck Collins, and Bella DeVaan, "The True Cost of Billionaire Philanthropy," inequality.org (inequality.org/great-divide/).
69 Tucker, "The Forbes Philanthropy Score 2021."
70 Jesse Eisinger, "How Mark Zuckerberg's Altruism Helps Himself," *NYT* (nytimes.com), Dec. 3, 2015.
71 Quentin Hardy, "The Radical Philanthropist," *Forbes*, May 1, 2000, 114–121.
72 "A Commitment to Philanthropy," The Giving Pledge (givingpledge.org); Anand Giridharadas, "Warren Buffett and the Myth of the 'Good Billionaire,'" *NYT* (nytimes.com), Jun. 13, 2021; Theodore Schleifer, "These are the trade-offs we make when we depend on billionaires to save us," vox.com, Apr. 7, 2020.
73 Board of Governors of the Federal Reserve System (US), "Total Assets Held by the Top 0.1%"; FRED Economic Data, Federal Reserve Bank of St. Louis; fred.stlouisfed.org/series/WFRBLTP1246.
74 patrioticmillionaires.org.
75 H. W. Brands, *The First American: The Life and Times of Benjamin Franklin* (New York: Doubleday, 2000), 512. For an example of this adage's eternal usefulness: David R. Preston, "The Role of Interdependence in Strategic Collaboration," *Handbook of Business Strategy*, 4, no. 1 (2003): 48–53.

Index

abolition, 118, 149–150, 195
"Acres of Diamonds," 182, 201
Adams, Henry, 155
Adams, John, 59, 62, 76, 78, 86, 100
Addison, Joseph, 163
advertisements, 163–164, 216, 222
Affleck, Benjamin Franklin, 212
African Americans, 29, 32, 35, 183
   and deaths of despair, 266
   and education, 196
   and enslavement, *see* enslavement
   and group organization, 193
   and poverty, 244
   and self-help, 194, 196
   in business, 196–201
   religious revivals among, 53–54
Aid to Families with Dependent Children (AFDC), 245
Alcoholics Anonymous (AA), 208
alcoholism, 6, 83–84, 136–137, 144, 266
Alger, Horatio Jr., 209, 211, 221, 241–242, *see* Horatio Alger Awards
   and rags-to-riches mythology, 210
   as "self-made man," 7–8
   misunderstanding of, 212–217, 232, 238
   misuse of, 212–221
   postwar, 220–221
   Ragged Dick, 209, 214
   references to, during World War II, 217–220
allies, 169–170
ambition
   and gender, 116
   and self-agency, 54, 63, 87
   and self-made myth, 119, 121, 260
   and the common good, 16, 31, 116, 151

   and wealth, 31, 35–36, 42–43, 126, 128, 166, 229
   and women, 194
   as morally neutral, 141
   criticism of, 4, 11, 16, 20, 29–30, 32, 37–38, 63, 76, 85, 97, 132
   in service to God, 36
American Dream, 42, 233, 255
American Federation of Labor, 180, 187
American Philosophical Society, 44, 78
American Schools and Colleges Association, 221
Anthony, Susan B., 194
Apprentice, The (television series), 257
Aquinas, Thomas, 23
aristocracy, 80
   and cultural authority, 23, 25–27, 56, 213, 229
   and electoral politics, 63–64, 80, 100, 119
   and First Great Awakening, 55–56
   and meritocracy, 231
   and self-made myth, 173
   and sumptuary laws, 30
   criticisms of, 13, 59–60, 62, 93, 97–98, 123–125, 174, 180
   exclusiveness of, 26, 56, 114, 158, 169
   rejection of, 63, 86, 99, 101
Arthur, Timothy Shea, 136
Astor, John Jacob, 98, 126, 161, 179
   and wealth, 7, 98, 126, 160
   as "self-made man," 126, 146, 150
   death mention of, 7
   philanthropy, 134
Augustine of Hippo, 23, 33
Aurora Reading Club, 194

INDEX

authority, cultural, 57–58, 119, 125
  and aristocracy, 59–60
  and capitalism, 132–133, 216–217, 263
  and community, 44
  and economic power, 161, 166
  and patriarchy, 28
  and self-improvement, 36
  and self-made myth, 81, 146, 151–152, 228, 252
  and work, 12, 56
  competition for, 63, 173
  definition of, 6
authority, political, 57–58, 63
  and cultural authority, 36, 56, 60, 144, 252
  competition for, 63, 83, 98, 125, 173

Bacon, Francis, 20
Bailyn, Bernard, 17
Bannecker, Benjamin, 184
Barnum, Phineas Taylor (P. T.), 143–147, 173
  and patriotism, 144–145
  and self-help, 146–147, 206
  and wealth, 144, 160
  autobiography, 147–148
Barton, Clara, 142
Baruch, Bernard, 222
Beebe, Kenneth J., 221–222, 226, 238, 242
Beecher, Henry Ward, 134, 142
  on poverty, 172–173
Beecher, Lyman, 134, 149
Bell Curve, The (book), 231
Bethune, Mary McLeod, 197
Bezos, Jeff, 272
biographical literature as instruction, 73, 99–101, 133–134, 149–150
Boesky, Ivan, 261
Bonaparte, Napoleon, 85, 97
Bond, Horace Mann, 230
Bond, Julian, 230
Boone, Daniel, 89
"bootstraps" cliché, 8, 208–209, 224, 227, 260, 321n12
Boston Massacre, 61
Boston Tea Party, 60–61
Boy Scouts of America, 175
Braley, Berton, 214–215
Breaking Home Ties (painting), 162
Brewster, Walter, 62

British East India Company, 60
Brown, B. Gratz, 150
Brown, John, 50
Brownback, Sam, 256
Buffett, Warren, 273
Bunyan, John, 44, 84
Burnett, Mark, 264
Burr, Aaron, 114–116
Bush, George H. W., 253
Bush, George W., 252–256, 258, 262, 265
Business Roundtable, 236, 240
Butler, Mrs. C. H., 129–130
Byron, George, 6th Baron Byron, 90

Calvinism, 15–16, 18, 20, 43, 52, 106, 108, 117, 149, 210
capitalism, 161, 207–209, 213, 217, 222–223, 250, 260
  growth of, 128, 153, 155
  idealized, 226
Capone, Al, 204
Carnegie, Andrew, 7, 155, 161, 163, 165, 175, 188, 190, 244, 269–271, 273
  as "self-made man," 171
  on philanthropy, 269–271, 273
Carnegie, Dale, 203, 206
Carpenter, Frank G., 161
Carter, Jimmy, 240
Catton, Bruce, 211–212
Chan Zuckerberg Initiative (CZI), 272
Chan, Priscilla, 272
Channing, William Ellery, 134, 139
Charles I, 4
Chase, Salmon P., 149
Chauncy, Charles, 54–55
Chilton Book Company, 216, 223
Christian Science, 201
Chrysler, Walter P., 212
Clay, Henry, 88–89, 103, 119, 124, 130, 177
  1844 campaign, 126
  as "Mill-Boy," 122–123
  as "self-made man," 132
  early career, 121–122
  phrenology, 142
Clement Falconer, or the Memoirs of a Young Whig (novel), 130–132
Cleveland, Grover, 180

337

INDEX

Clinton, Bill, 232, 246–248, 252, 262
Clinton, Hillary Rodham, 232, 259
Cold War, 226, 233
Colfax, Schuyler, 149
Collinson, Peter, 45–48
colonization, 10, 14, 24, 26, 28
   and Christianity, 28
Colorado Coalfield War, 180
Colton, Calvin, 123
common good, 79
   and ambition, 15–16, 31, 151
   and self-improvement, 18, 35–36, 175
   and self-making, 18, 59, 111, 125
   and taxation, 67–68
   and work, 25
community
   and ambition, 4, 16
   and religion, 36, 59
   and self-improvement, 76, 195
   boundaries of, 29
   denial of, 31, 84, 259
   membership in, 31
   obligation to, 8, 31, 37, 80, 97, 101, 185, 210, 227, 229, 248, 257, 262
Connolly, Margaret, 202
Conservative Political Action Conference (CPAC), 250, 259
Conwell, Russell H., 201
Coolidge, Calvin, 206
Cooper, James Fenimore
   Leatherstocking Tales, 90
Cotton, John, 16–17, 20, 28
Couzens, James, 204
Crawford, William, 96
Crockett, David, 89–93, 101
   and Andrew Jackson, 92
   as "self-made man," 93, 119
   Davy Crockett's Own Story, 93
   Lion of the West, The (play), 91
Cromwell, Oliver, 1, 4–5, 11, 25, 29, 36, 149

Dawes Severalty Act, 183, 191–193
Dawes, Henry L., 191
deaths of despair, 266
Declaration of Independence, 80, 274
DeMille, Cecil B., 205

Dickens, Charles, 179
dime novels, 90, 146, 205, 210–211
Dirksen, Everett, 222
Dix, Dorothea Lynde, 103, 112, 117–118, 126, 274
Douglass, Frederick, 149–150, 181–186, 194
   and photography, 183–184
   as "self-made man," 183, 196
   on collective self-help, 181, 274
DuBois, W. E. B., 194
Duncan, William Cary, 117

Ecker, Frederick H., 212
Eddy, Mary Baker, 201
Edgar Thomson Steel Works, 188
Edwards, B. B., 100
Edwards, Jonathan, 51–52
Ehrenreich, Barbara, 267
Eisenhower, Dwight D., 233
Elliott, Richard Smith, 120
Ellis, Abraham, 239
Emerson, Ralph Waldo, 110–112, 163, 181
enclosure, 24
Enlightenment, 34–37, 45, 49, 55, 57, 69–70, 269
Enron, 261
enslavement, 29, 32, 53, 66–68, 118, 125
Evans, Walker, 213
exceptionalism, American, 42, 61, 105, 110

failure, *see* self-made failure
Faris, John T., 175
Federalism, 62
Fields, Gary, 255
Filson, John, 89
Finney, Charles Grandison, 107–109
Finney, Lydia Andrews, 109
Ford, Gerald, 233
Ford, Henry, 217, 244
Fower, Orson, 137–139
Fowler, Lorenzo, 137, 142
Francis of Assisi, 25
Franklin, Benjamin, 7, 44, 46, 59, 158, 179, 211, 257, 274
   and taxation, 79–80
   as Mrs. Silence Dogood, 43–44

INDEX

as "self-made man," 59, 72, 76, 79, 101, 134, 202
Autobiography, 72–73, 157–159
biographies of, 85
electrical experiments, 45–49, 77, 289
Junto, 36, 44–45
Poor Richard improved, 48
Poor Richard's Almanack, 78, 79
ran away from apprenticeship, 172
social networking, 74
"Way to Wealth," 79
Weems's biography of, 85
Franklin, William Temple, 7, 48, 73, 79
free enterprise, 229, 239
Frick, Henry Clay, 161, 167, 189, 270
as mutually made man, 166–168, 182
as "self-made man," 166, 171–172, 187
growth of empire, 165–166
Homestead Steel Works strike, 188–190
Mellon bank loan, 165
public views of, 165–167, 270
Friedman, Milton, 229, 233, 262, 271
Friedman, Rose, 233, 271
frontiers, 35, 52, 82, 88–94, 108, 111, 113, 119, 121
Frost, John, 133–134
Fuller, Alfred, 201
Fuller, Andrew, 87

Garbo, Greta, 204
Garrison, William Lloyd, 195
Garvey, Marcus, 194
Gates, Bill, 273
Gates, Melinda French, 273
Gekko, Gordon, fictional character, 261
George, James Z., 186
Georgia, enslavement in, 67
Gilder, George, 243–244
Gingrich, Newt, 247
Girdler, Tom M., 219
Giving Pledge, 273
Goldwater, Barry, 249–250, 271
Gompers, Samuel, 179–180, 187
Gould, Jay, 156–157, 161, 217, 269
Graham, Billy, 229
Graham, Sylvester, 142
Great Awakening, First, 34–36, 49, 55, 119

Great Awakening, Second, 105–109, 119, 144, 201
Great Depression, 205–207, 214, 229, 232
Great Recession, 252, 263–264
Great Society, 229, 233–235, 244, 247
Greeley, Horace, 134
Greene, Robert, 11
Greene, Selden C., 204

Haddock, Frank Channing, 201–202
Hakluyt, Richard, 24–25
Hale, Sarah Josepha, 132
Hall, Thomas H., 96
Hamilton, Alexander, 76, 88, 114
Hancock, John, 61, 161, 275
Hardy, Quentin, 272
Harris, Abram L., 200–201
Harris, Louis, 250
Harrison, William Henry, 119–121, 132
Harvard University, 44, 177, 210–211, 243
Harvey, George, 166, 188
Hastings, Daniel O., 214
Hawes, Joel, 105–107, 112
Hawkins, Dan, 267
Herjavec, Robert, 264
Herrnstein, Richard, 231
Hewes, George Robert Twelves, 61
Hoffman, Paul Gray, 238
Holmes, Oliver Wendell, 134
Homestead Steel Works strike, 165, 188, 214
Hoover, Herbert, 205
Horatio Alger Association of Distinguished Americans (HAADA), 229, 240–242, 258, 271
Horatio Alger Awards, 221–224, 238, 241, 257–258
Horatio Alger Awards Committee (HAAC), 223–226, 237, 239–240
Hovenden, Thomas, 162
Howe, Julia Ward, 142
Howe, Samuel Gridley, 142
Howells, William Dean, 176
Hoyt, Edwin P., 223
Hubbard, Elbert, 172
Hull House, 271
human agency, 34–35, 37–41, 49–51, 233
Hunt, Thomas P., 129

339

INDEX

Indian Removal Act, 92, *see also* Jackson, Andrew
individualism, 10, 33, 146, 156, 166, 188, 191, 208, 213, 227, 229, 271
   and conservatism, 235–236
   and women, 113
   development of, 50, 52, 55, 83, 85, 161, 250
   in Great Depression, 207
   rugged, 8, 169, 205, 213, 219, 223, 252
inequality, 156

Jackson, Andrew, 89, 91–92, 94, 148
   and David Crockett, 91–93
   as "self-made man," 97–98, 110, 133, 257
   as solitary oak, 7, 81, 97
   early life, 94–95
   myths about, 96, 119
Jamestown, 58
Jay, John, 64
Jefferson, Thomas, 45, 59, 64, 71, 86, 88, 100
Jenner, Bruce, 1, *see* Jenner, Caitlyn
Jenner, Caitlyn, 1
Jenner, Kylie, 1, 3, 259–260
Jesus, 23
Jim Crow, 67–68, 200
Johnson, Lyndon B., 232–233, 250
Johnston, Eric, 220
Jones, Reg, 251
Jumel, Eliza, 103, 112–117, 126
   as art collector, 114
Jumel, Stephen, 113
Juneja, Aditi, 260

Kardashian, Kim, 260
Kardashian, Kris, 1
Keayne, Robert, 10
   and religion, 16–17, 20–21, 36, 228, 253
   and taxation as duty, 18–19, 31
   and wealth, 28
   Apologia, 16–18, 25
   as "self-made man," 228, 257
   early career, 31
   sexism of, 32
Kinnersley, Ebenezer, 47–48
Kirby, John Jr., 190
Knights of Labor, 186
Knox, Philander Chase, 169

labor rights, 186–190, 229, *see also* Homestead Steel Works strike
   child labor, 212
   protests for, 177, 214
   resistance to, 170, 183, 186, 188, 219–220, 270
   support for, 213
laborers as commodities, 69, 72, 171–172
Lafayette, Gilbert du Motier, marquis de, 70
Lane, Thomas J., 227
Lange, Dorothea, 213
Langston, John M., 196
Larremore, William, 176
Lawrence, Edward A., 106
Layton, Robert D., 186, 274
Le Compte, Joseph, 98
Lee, Gideon, 134
Lesher, Richard, 237–239
lightning rod, 47–48
Lincoln, Abraham, 89, 120, 149–150, 175, 179, 183–185
Lodge, Henry Cabot, 175
log cabin campaign, 120–121
Logan, John, 191
Longfellow, Henry Wadsworth, 134
Lorimer, George Horace, 177
Lowell, James Russell, 134
Ludlow Massacre, 180

MacMannen, John A., 7
Madison, James, 64, 71, 100
Malone, Annie Turnbo, 198
manifest destiny, 133
Mann, Horace, 142
Manning, William, 62
Marden, Orson Swett, 202
Marlowe, Christopher, 37
Mary and Martha, biblical figures, 23
masculinity, 175
   and ambition, 111, 162–163
Mather, Cotton, 37–39, 55, 61
   and Salem witch trials, 39
   Bonifacius, or Essays to Do Good, 43
   Magnalia Christi Americana, 42
   Pietas in Patriam, 39–43
   Silentarius, 43

INDEX

Mather, Increase, 39
McCabe, James D. Jr., 150–152
McClure, S. S., 212
McGaw, Judith, 8, 166
McHugh, William D., 204
McLean, Alney, 87
Medicaid, 267, 269
Mellon, Andrew, 168, 174, 249, 309
Mellon, Thomas, 153–156, 161, 165, 174
   admiration for Benjamin Franklin, 153, 157–160, 202
   and H. C. Frick, 165, 168
   and wealth, 158–160
   as "self-made man," 159
meritocracy, 63, 229–232, 248, 265–266
Merriman, Charles Eustace, 177
Mettler, Suzanne, 269
Middle Ages, 10, 23
Milken, Michael, 261
Miller, Samuel, 86–88
mobility, social, 11, 16, 29–30, 37, 43, 131
   and African Americans, 58, 184
   and Horatio Alger Jr., 216
   and women, 32, 58, 112
   and work, 12, 15, 30, 58, 179
   in early republic, 57, 64, 73, 79
Monroe, Elizabeth, 114
Morgan, J. P., 161, 169–170
   as "self-made man," 175
Morris, Robert, 80
Morton, Thomas, 28
Mott, Lucretia, 149
Murray, Charles, 231
muscular Christianity, 175
Musk, Elon, 272
mutually made men, 8, 166–169, 176

National American Women's Suffrage Association, 194
National Association of Colored Women (NACW), 194, 274
National Association of Colored Women's Clubs, 182
National Association of Manufacturers (NAM), 190, 222
National Negro Business League (NNBL), 196

nationalism, 42, 61, 83, 91, 105, 125, 144–145, 151, 222–224, *see also* exceptionalism, American
   and self-improvement, 110
Native Americans, 32, 35–37, 66, 183, 236
   and deaths of despair, 267
   forced assimilation of, 191
   religious revival among, 53
   stereotypes of, 29, 190
   work, 27
networks, *see* social capital
New Deal, 8, 207–209
   resistance to, 208, 214–220, 229, 247, 269
New Orleans general strike, 1892, 187
Nixon, Richard M., 228–229, 233, 249
Noll, Frank K., 238

Obama, Barack, 232
Occupy Wall Street, 263
Oglethorpe, James, 67–68, 125
Omidyar, Peter, 273

Paine, Thomas, 45, 61
Palfrey, John Gorham, 118
Parton, James, 91
Patriotic Millionaires, 274
Peale, Norman Vincent, 224–227, 239, 257
Penn, I. Garland, 196
Perkins, William, 26
Personal Responsibility and Work Opportunity Reconciliation Act (PRWORA), 247–248, 268
Pew, J. Howard, 215, 220
Pew, Joseph N. Jr., 215, 220
philanthropy, 65–66, 146, 166, 252, 262, 269–273, 334
   and cultural authority, 270
   as justification for wealth, 270–272
   as support for community, 198, 273
Phillips, Wendell, 134, 195
Phips, William, 41–43, 134
phrenology, 137–143
   and racism, 143
   and self-improvement, 139–141
   and sexism, 143
Pilgrim's Progress, The, 44, 84, 210

INDEX

Pilgrims, myths about, 235–236
Pinkerton detective agency, 189
Pittsburgh, Pennsylvania, 153, 158–160, 165–166, 168
"pluck and luck" cliché, 209
Pocahontas, 10, 32
Poe, Edgar Allan, 142
political authority, 6
  and cultural authority, 6, 81
Polk, James K., 123, 125
poorhouses, *see* workhouses
"positive thinking," 201, 203, 225–227, 257
Post, Emily, 204
poverty
  and capitalism, 218
  and colonization, 67
  and inequality, 226
  and race, 243, 248
  and self-made myth, 117
  as a sin, 29, 129
  biblical view, 25
  blamed on public programs, 234–235, 244
  Middle Ages, 10, 23
  prejudice against, 24, 29, 63–65, 178, 229, 248
  "undeserving poor," 31, 218, 234, 247
Powell, Lewis F., 236
predestination, 20, 52, 284
Price, William, 130–132
providentialism, 4, 18, 20, 35, 83, 233, 284
Pullman strike of 1894, 187
Puritanism, 5, 21, 27, 39, 44, 54, 59, 86, 235, 257, 282, 284, *see also* Calvinism

Quakers, 37, 65–66

racism, 8, 67, 182–183, 248, 266
  against African Americans, 67–68
  against Native Americans, 27, 66, 190–193
  and gender, 194
  denial of, 244
  phrenology, 143
"rags-to-riches" cliché, 8, 19, 30, 117, 210, 213, 217, 219, 223
Raleigh, Walter, 14, 26, 29
Ratner, Sidney, 248–249
Reagan, Ronald, 229, 239, 241–244, 246, 248, 250, 252, 255, 258, 271

Renaissance, 10, 12, 21, 37
revival, religious, 36, 50, 105
Rockefeller, John D., 155, 161, 180, 243, 269
Rockefeller, John D. Jr., 180
Rodgers, Daniel T., 4
Rogers, Will, 205
Romanticism, 89, 103, 110, 210
Roosevelt, Franklin D., 207, 213, 216
Roosevelt, Theodore, 174–175
Rubloff, Arthur, 239
Rush, Benjamin, 57–58

Sage, Olivia, 269
Sage, Russell, 269
salvation, 20, 49–52
  and poverty, 23, 25, 34, 55
  for marginalized groups, 52–53, 67
Sandel, Michael, 232
Scheer, Robert, 263
Schurz, Charles, 193
Schuyler, Philip, 63
Schwab, Charles M., 206
self-agency, 4–5, 10–11, 17–18, 33–34, 37–39, 51, 53, 56–57, 82, 104–110, 142, 144, 181, 203, 205–206, 224, 250, 268, *see also* human agency
  and enslavement, 65–67
self-fashioning, 10–11, 82, 103, 108–110, 113, 116, 118, 143, 181, 183, 202
self-help, 182–183, 199, 224
  collective, 183–184, 186, 190–201
  individualist, 181, 190, 201–203
self-improvement, 35, 85, 135–136
  and enslavement, 68–71
  and masculinity, 227
  and race, 181, 184–186, 193, 195, 198
  and sexism, 114
  and social mobility, 31, 57, 83, 111, 161, 268
  for the common good, 20, 43–44, 58–59, 64, 80, 86, 98, 134–137, 149, 176, 186, 203, 252
self-made failure, 66, 81, 177, 202, 205, 213, 228, 231–232, 243, 246, 248, 260, 265, 267–268
self-made myth, 5, 123, 281, 298, 313
  and African Americans, 181, 195, 201
  and anti-taxation rhetoric, 249, 259, 262, 272

342

and capitalism, 1, 155–157, 161, 213, 222, 226, 259
and class, 101, 178, 182, 184, 254
and gender, 116, 118, 182
and individualism, 228
and inequality, 8, 58, 146, 212–213, 230–232, 255, 260, 265, 267, 274
and meritocracy, 229, 232
and personal responsibility, 247
and public policy, 229, 252, 267
and racism, 182, 184
and wealth, 128, 146, 149, 151
and work, 152, 178
as blasphemy, 15
as myth, 6–8, 83
as negative, 101
definitions of, 6, 42, 85, 98, 101, 148, 155, 176, 181
impossibility of, 4, 6, 19–20
in the 1920s, 203–204
in the 21st century, 252
obscure origins, 119, 149, 161
self-made nation, myth of, 81, 88, 133, 235
self-reliance, 109, 174
Seligman, Daniel, 231
service
  and women, 117–118
  as religious ideal, 4, 43
  for economic gain, 24, 175–176, 204
  for the common good, 17, 75, 88, 175–176, 182
  to community and faith, 4, 20, 29, 36, 43, 59, 86, 93, 116, 158, 248
Settlement House Movement, 195
sexism, 8, 112–119, 142, 182, 194
  and self-made myth, 127, 266
  and the First Great Awakening, 54
  in business, 168
  phrenology, 143
Seymour, Charles C. B., 148
Shark Tank (television series), 264–265
Sherman Antitrust Act, 187
Sherman, John, 187
Sherman, Roger, 99–100
Sibbes, Richard, 21
Simon, William E., 233–236, 243
Sioux Nation, 191

Sitting Bull, 191
slavery, *see* enslavement
Sloan, Alfred P., 212
Small Business Administration (SBA), 245
smallpox, inoculation for, 43
Smiles, Samuel, 202, 232
Smith, Adam, 57, 232, 269
Smith, John, 10, 13, 36, 58, 236
  and work, 26–27
  early career, 11–12
  self-fashioning, 12–16, 24, 29, 61
  sexism of, 32
Smith, Love, 240
Smith, William, 78
social capital, 6, 73–75, 125, 159, 163–165, 168–169, 230, 260, *see* authority, cultural
Social Security, 218
solitary oak, 7, 81, 97–98, 102, 118, 125, 135, 156, 166, 181
Sparkes, Boyden, 207, 212
Spencer, Archibald, 48
Spencer, Herbert, 155
Stanford, Leland, 161
Stanton, Elizabeth Cady, 142–143
Stockman, David, 245
storytelling as tool, 8, 101, 151, 209, 222–224, 226, 237, 280n9
Stowe, Charles Edward, 150
Stowe, Harriet Beecher, 2, 134, 149–151, 182–183
submerged state, 269, 329n68
Sumner, Charles, 134, 150
sumptuary laws, 30
Superman, 227
supply-side economics, 243
survival of the fittest, 174
Switzer, Maurice, 177

Taft, William Howard, 187
Taft-Hartley Act, 220
taxation, 19, 31, 79–80, 228, 248–249, 270–273
  rhetoric against, 244, 249, 255–257, 330–331n13
Taylor, Linda, 244
Taylor, Thomas, 26
Temperance movement, 6, 84, 129–130, 136–138, 143

INDEX

Ten Nights in a Bar-Room (novel), 137, 138
Terrell, Mary Church, 194–195, 274
Thiel, Peter, 268
Thomson, William A., 215
Thoreau, Henry David, 111
Throgmorton, Louie, 230
Tiffany, Francis, 117
Tirado, Linda, 267
Tompkins, Patrick, 126
trade unions, 183
Tragical History of Doctor Faustus, The (play), 37
trickle-down economics, 243
Tritle, F. A., 192
Trump, Donald J., 226, 257–259
Trump, Fred, 226, 257–258
Truth, Sojourner, 197
Tubman, Harriet, 197
Twain, Mark, 242
Twitter, 260

U.S. Steel, 170
unions, *see* labor rights
United States Chamber of Commerce, 229, 236, 240
Universal Negro Improvement Association (UNIA), 194

Van Buren, Martin, 119–121
Vance, J.D., 268–269
Vanderbilt, Cornelius, 179
  as "self-made man," 146, 150, 161
Vermont Missionary Society, 86
Virginia Company of London, 14
von Hayek, Friedrich, 234

Wagner Act, 219
Waldo, S. Putnam, 94–96
Walker, Madam C. J., 197–200, 318
Walker, Maggie Lena, 197
Wallace, Henry, 218
Walsh, Richard J., 203
War Revenue Act of 1917, 270
Washington, Booker T., 194, 196, 198, 200, 274
Washington, George, 45, 57, 96, 175
  and enslavement, 69–72
  and work ethic, 68–69

cherry tree myth, 85
Farewell Address, 100
philanthropy, 71
self-taught, 86, 135–136
Weems's biography of, 85
Washington, Martha Custis, 69
wealth
  and ambition, 31, 35, 42, 105, 112, 126, 131, 145–146, 149
  and influencers, 3
  and poverty, 243
  and self-made myth, 132–133, 156, 255
  and tycoons, 161
  moral dangers of, 4, 132
Webster, Daniel, 119
Weems, Mason Locke, 85
Weill, Sanford I., 262–263
Welch, Jack, 251–252
welfare queen, 244–246
welfare system, 234, 244–245, 247–249
Wells, Samuel R., 139
Wells-Barnett, Ida B., 197
West Point Academy, 93
Wheatley, Phillis, 53
Whig party, 93, 119–123, 130
Whitefield, George, 53–54
Whitman, Walt, 83, 111, 142
Whittington, Richard, 30
Williams, A. Graves, 216
Wilson, Charles E., 238
Wilson, John, 17
Wilson-Gorman Act, 249
Winfrey, Oprah, 253, 255, 260
Winthrop, John, 16–18, 24, 27–28, 31, 59
Winthrop, John Jr., 37, 45
  and the common good, 37–38
witch trials, 36, 39, 43, 48
Wolfe, Tom, 261
Wollstonecraft, Nancy Kingsbury, 82–83
women
  and evangelism, 109
  and revivalism, 36, 53
  and self-making, 112, 127
  and work, 20, 113, 118
  as dependents, 112, 118
  in business, 116, 197–198, 310
Woodruff, Roy O., 217–218

INDEX

work
- and class, 25–26, 32, 59, 62, 136, 164, 171–172, 174
- and enslavement, 32
- and gender, 20, 113, 118
- and idleness, 12, 14, 21, 28, 65
- and Native Americans, 27
- and racism, 28
- and self-made myth, 157, 185, 203–204
- and social mobility, 30, 58, 184
- definition of, 3, 20, 59
- idealization of, 56, 61, 172
- in Middle Ages, 23
- manual labor, 62
- sacralization of, 25, 30
- social mobility, 12, 15

work ethic, Protestant, 3, 5, 14, 20–21, 32, 59–60
workhouses, 25, 65–66
World War I, 270
World War II, 216

Young American's Magazine of Self-Improvement, The, 134
Young, Michael, 229–232, 235, 266

Zuckerberg, Mark, 272